LOWENSTEIN:
ACTS OF COURAGE
AND
BELIEF

LOWENSTEIN:
ACTS OF COURAGE
AND
BELIEF

EDITED BY GREGORY STONE
AND DOUGLAS LOWENSTEIN

**Foreword by
Arthur Schlesinger, Jr.
Introduction by
James A. Wechsler**

Harcourt Brace Jovanovich, Publishers
San Diego   New York   London

DEC 13 1983

Tallahassee, Florida

The publisher thanks the following for permission to reprint from the sources listed and acknowledges the following holders of copyright materials:

The New Yorker for "Candidate" by Jacob Brackman, copyright © 1966; for "The Kids Against the Grown-ups" by Calvin Trillin, copyright © 1968; for "New Member" by Flora Lewis, copyright © 1970; for "Lame Duck" by Hendrik Hertzberg, copyright © 1970, 1972 by The New Yorker Magazine, Inc.; and for "Notes and Comment," copyright © 1980 by The New Yorker Magazine, Inc. All reprinted by permission.

NBC News' MEET THE PRESS for permission to reprint transcript of "Challenging A President," "Meet The Press," December, 1967.

David Halberstam for permission to reprint "The Man Who Ran Against Lyndon Johnson" from *Harper's*, December, 1968.

Newsweek for "Man To Watch," copyright © 1971 by Newsweek, Inc. All rights reserved. Reprinted by permission.

Ohio University Press/Swallow Press for "For As Long As It Takes" from *Toothing Stones* by Robert E. Meagher, 1972. Reprinted with permission.

New York Post for "Lowenstein versus Rooney" by Judith Michaelson, copyright © 1972 by New York Post Corporation; for "A Lonely Inquest" by James Wechsler, copyright © 1975 by New York Post Corporation; for "A Rare Coalition" by James Wechsler, copyright © 1976 by New York Post Corporation; and for "Why I Quit," copyright © 1978 by News Group Publications, Inc. All reprinted by permission of the *New York Post*.

United Feature Syndicate, Inc. for "Tammany Hall Revisited" by Jack Anderson, copyright © 1972 by United Feature Syndicate, Inc.; and for "Practical Diplomacy in Zimbabwe" by Jack Anderson, copyright © 1980 by United Feature Syndicate, Inc.

Americans for Democratic Action for permission to reprint "The Watershed of Watergate," from *ADA World*, May, 1973.

Saturday Review for "Suppressed Evidence of More Than One Assassin?" by Allard K. Lowenstein, copyright © 1977, all rights reserved, reprinted with permission; and for "Spain Without Franco" by Allard K. Lowenstein, copyright © 1976, all rights reserved, reprinted with permission.

Walter P. Loughlin for permission to reprint the transcript of his January 1973 interview.

Universal Press Syndicate for "Is There Hope for the U.N. After All?" by William F. Buckley, Jr., copyright © 1977 by Universal Press Syndicate, reprinted by permission, all rights reserved; and for "A Liberal Indulgence" by William F. Buckley, Jr., copyright © 1978 by Universal Press Syndicate, reprinted by permission, all rights reserved.

Jimmy Breslin for permission to reprint "Another Night, Another Room . . . and Death" from *New York Daily News*, March, 1980.

The Washington Post for "Remembering A Man Who Mattered Through The Years" by Richard Cohen, copyright © 1980 The Washington Post Company. Reprinted with permission.

National Review for "Allard Lowenstein, R.I.P." by William F. Buckley, Jr., copyright © 1980 National Review, Inc. Reprinted with permission.

Gregory B. Craig for permission to reprint "Recollections from Youth", 1980.

Commonweal for permission to reprint "A Chance Encounter" by Thomas Powers from *Commonweal*, April, 1980.

The publisher also thanks The Estate of Allard K. Lowenstein for permission to reprint material owned by the Estate.

Photos for insert (following page 180) are reprinted with permission.

Book Designer—Mark Likgalter

Library of Congress Cataloging in Publication Data

Lowenstein: acts of courage and belief.

Bibliography: p.
Includes index.
1. Lowenstein, Allard K.—Addresses, essays, lectures.
2. Legislators—United States—Biography—Addresses, essays, lectures. 3. United States. Congress. House—Biography—Addresses, essays, lectures. I. Stone, Gregory, 1949-
II. Lowenstein, Douglas.
E840.8.L68L68   1983   328.73′092′4   82-23327
ISBN 0-15-154742-4
ISBN 0-15-654302-8 (pbk.)

Printed in the United States of America
First Edition

A B C D E

*It is from numberless diverse acts of courage and belief
that human history is shaped. Each time a man stands
up for an ideal, or acts to improve the lot of others, or
strikes out against injustice, he sends forth a tiny ripple
of hope, and crossing each other from a million
different centers of energy and daring those ripples
build a current which can sweep down the mightiest
walls of oppression and resistance.*

—Robert F. Kennedy
Cape Town, South Africa
June 6, 1966

Contents

Contents

Contents

Contents

RETROSPECTIVE

Contents

INDEX

Illustrations

(following page 180)

Allard K. Lowenstein in the early 1950s
Campaigning with Eleanor Roosevelt, 1960
With Norman Thomas, 1966
Note to Lowenstein from Robert F. Kennedy
Campaigning, 1968
Chairing community issues forum on Long Island
In his congressional office
Lowenstein as seen by David Levine, 1970
White House "enemies list," 1971
Conversation with Brooklyn voter
With family on front stoop in Brooklyn
At ADA National Convention, 1972
Campaigning with Herman Badillo
Voting card "irregularities"—Brooklyn, 1972
With William F. Buckley, Jr., on "Firing Line," 1975
Campaigning for Jerry Brown in the presidential primary in Maryland,
1976
With Warren Beatty, Andrew Young, and Coretta King, 1976
In his office as United States ambassador to the United Nations for
Special Political Affairs, 1978
Allard K. Lowenstein

Editors' Note

"Al Lowenstein's unswerving devotion to his fellow man," said Martin Luther King, Jr., "will ensure him an impregnable niche in the annals of contemporary American history." The man he spoke of was on the cutting edge of many of the seminal political and social movements of the last three decades. Our objective in this book has been to present a view of his life through his own words and those of his contemporaries. Such a portrait, we believe, can not only help us to understand a great man and an extraordinary time, but also serve as a continuing call to action to better ourselves and our world.

Some of the speeches and selections have been edited for space and form, but their basic meaning has been left intact. The originals and additional material are available from the Allard K. Lowenstein Fund. The Fund was set up to help support the cataloging and preserving of the Lowenstein papers and to create continuing memorials to his life. The Fund is seeking additional material by or about Lowenstein; information or inquiries should be directed to the Allard K. Lowenstein Fund, c/o Lowenstein, 151 Central Park West, New York, N.Y. 10023.

We would like to pay special thanks to Steve Cohen, whose invaluable aid at several key points helped make this book a reality. We also want to thank Harcourt Brace Jovanovich for its support; our editor, Howard Sandum, for his perceptive and sympathetic guidance; and Larry Lowenstein, Dorothy Lowenstein DiCintio, and Jennifer Littlefield for their warm and pivotal help.

Among the many others to whom we are indebted, we want to thank especially James Dunnigan, Leonard Krauss, Senator Eugene McCarthy, Sylvia Meagher, Mike Pettit, Jeff Robbins, Andrew Tobias, Congressman Doug Walgren, and the writers and photographers who waived their usual fees and allowed us to reproduce their work here.

Finally, one of the editors, with words too inadequate to say what he feels, would like to thank Rochelle and Margot Allison Lowenstein for their extraordinary patience, understanding, and good humor throughout this project.

Foreword

This book illustrates the remarkable impact the life of Allard Lowenstein had on a generation of Americans.

With his gifts of leadership, sympathy, and intellect, Allard Lowenstein would have made a difference in any age. But he came along, one feels, in an age that peculiarly suited his talents and concerns. Born in 1929, he was sixteen years old when Franklin D. Roosevelt died—too young for the New Deal, a cheerful and untidy time he would have greatly relished; yet old enough to find his way to Frank P. Graham and Eleanor Roosevelt and serve an early apprenticeship in the liberal tradition.

As an undergraduate at the University of North Carolina in the 1940s, he observed at first hand the workings of the segregation system. The Yale Law School in the 1950s gave him an understanding of constitutional process and possibility. Thereafter, on university faculties he developed his skills as a teacher of the young. But he was by temperament an activist. He was never content simply to discuss and document the inequities of society. His commitment was always to redress and remedy.

He sensed the currents of discontent and idealism that accumulated under the stagnant surface of American life in the 1950s and that began to break through in the Kennedy years. He responded, a little earlier than the rest of us, to the bitter failures of the society—to racial injustice, to the Vietnam war, to the misery of the poor and powerless, to the plight of a radicalism that had lost its bearings. A man without fear, he toured the fighting fronts from Mississippi to South Africa in the unending battle against oppression. Returning to his recruiting grounds in the universities, he brought eyewitness testimony of suffering and of heroism. With casual, rumpled eloquence he inspired the young to live the next years of their lives on behalf of others. Hundreds hearkened to his words, and enriched and transformed their own lives.

He did all this within a larger philosophy of social change. He was sure that the energy released in the turbulence of the 1960s could be turned from destructive to constructive uses. A man of reason, he abhorred violence; a realist, he understood that violence sundered the bonds of humanity and defeated its own objectives. His mission in the 1960s was to replace violence by persuasion and to incorporate the disordered wrath of the New Left into the constitutional framework of American political action. He never forgot that democracy is the discipline of consent.

Allard Lowenstein was a rare combination of generous passion and acute intelligence. Wholly devoid of meanness and of pomposity, he radiated candor, humor, and sweetness. With his faith in reason, he believed in dialogue across the barricades and commanded the respect and affection of political and intellectual adversaries. He called for action but not for action's sake. He knew that unbridled emotion could not cure the complex ills of modern society, that sentiment, however virtuous, was no substitute for substance.

He was the supreme agitator of his day. Agitator is a noble word that has too often carried a bad connotation in America. Allard Lowenstein was an agitator in the highest sense—a man who touched the consciences of his fellow citizens, educated their sensibilities, and drew forth their capacity for humane action. "Those who profess to favor freedom, and yet deprecate agitation," as Frederick Douglass said long ago, "are men who want crops without plowing up the ground, they want rain without thunder and lightning."

Allard Lowenstein plowed up the ground and sowed seeds that will come to fruition for the rest of the century. The spectacle of man's injustice to man never destroyed his confidence in democracy's capacity for self-correction. He lived in perpetual commotion, but his apparently inexhaustible vitality sprang from a serene optimism about humanity. His exalted vision of democratic potentiality and his imperturbable confidence in human reason left a rich legacy to which this book bears moving testimony.

Arthur Schlesinger, Jr.

Introduction

My friendship with Allard Lowenstein spanned slightly more than twenty years. It began in late 1959 when Eleanor Roosevelt, with her infinite capacity for arranging small as well as large encounters, suggested I meet "a remarkable young man" who had recently returned from a pilgrimage to South-West Africa and had delivered a memorable report to the United Nations. The document was later to be elaborated in Lowenstein's book *Brutal Mandate*.

He was thirty at the time and had just left Hubert Humphrey's Senate staff; I was thirteen years older and editing the *New York Post*. But in the relationship that endured throughout the ensuing years, I never had any sense of seniority, or generational distance. Now, more than two years after his death, I find it hard to concede that I will not see or hear him again. And there is an even keener awareness of how unusual a presence he was.

I hardly presume to have been "best friend" or chief consultant. I doubt that anyone was. For all of his astonishing gregariousness and the void his death created for so many, there were inescapable intimations of loneliness about him. It was almost as if the self-imposed pressures of his existence denied him time to cultivate the luxury of really close private companionship.

This is not to imply impersonality. He bore no resemblance to the stereotype of the world-saver who pledges fidelity to the cause of humanity but has only impatience for human beings. In fact, he was forever reaching out with concern to individuals and identifying with their torments. He loathed the use of "bleeding heart" as a term of derision. He cared no less deeply about the solitary injustice than about the general condition.

To remark on the nature of his multiple friendships is not to demean them. It is, rather, to disclaim any unique proximity. We had innumerable conversations, many of them in my office (his schedule rarely gave him the home-field advantage), some in social settings, and he occasionally sought advice on political decisions. To some his diffidence may have invited the impression of a desire to be "adopted," and there were those who, without ignoble intent, sought to perform that function. But, unlike most public figures, he had no one who could validly claim to be his manager. (In some of the detailed mechanics of campaigning, he might have profited from such an adjunct, but the closest people to approach such a role were his devoted older brother Larry and equally dedicated sister, Dorothy, who stoically and selflessly tried to keep things in a semblance of order and, with him, confronted the unbalanced fiscal books after the last hurrahs.)

All of which is parenthetical prelude to the main proposition that Allard Lowenstein was a man very much on his own whose place in our national history began to receive adequate measurement only after his death. This collection of his words and some of what was written about him offers a glimpse of the range of his activity and the underlying continuity of conscience and conviction.

An attempt to present these fragments may inadvertently reinforce certain hostile myths about him. It was sometimes said disparagingly that he leaped too feverishly from one arena of conflict to another, thereby diluting his influence in each place. A fairer appraisal, in my judgment, was the one spontaneously voiced by Joe Rauh, himself a combatant on many fronts, after Lowenstein came to his side at an explosive moment in the civil rights movement: "Al always seems to turn up just when he is needed most."

He was indeed a man who seemed constantly in motion, sometimes to the consternation of those who felt they had a moral or strategic claim on his undivided attention. Actually he had an inordinate talent for concentration on a diversity of things. A series of simultaneous involvements is not unusual among public men and women; Lowenstein's intensity level far surpassed the usual performance.

One might even observe that the special aspect in Lowenstein's case was not the number of things he was up to but the importance of most of them, the geographical breadth of his interests and the internal chemistry that enabled him to sustain both intellect and fervor while engaged in his unceasing shuttle diplomacy.

As a young man his favorite personal sport was wrestling, which requires vast exertion in relatively brief encounters. In the public domain he appeared to merge the strengths demanded by that exercise with the endurance of a long-distance runner.

His resistance to combat fatigue often defied plausibility. Even when his wiry, drained face revealed some mortal weariness, he might matter-of-factly announce that he was leaving shortly for Spain, Los Angeles, or Bangladesh. There were moments when I was tempted to urge him to take a time-out. I do not recall that I ever did, possibly because I knew the admonition would be futile.

No doubt the word "compulsive" will be clinically applied to the condition that led him to log so many thousands of miles of air travel, languish so impatiently for many hours in airports, ride so many ill-lit roads, fortifying himself with peanut-butter sandwiches and Cokes or the local equivalents thereof.

Exploring mysteries of motivation is an ancient spectator sport. Those who drift and muddle through much of their time on earth may be most prone to view Lowenstein's journey as aberrational. He may have seemed to them almost obsessively mindful of Mr. Justice Holmes's warning that those who remain aloof from "the actions and passions of their times" do so at the risk of being judged not to have lived. Lowenstein was alternately fascinated and depressed by the vague discontent he found among many of his contemporaries who had kept their eyes on the big deal and achieved (or inherited) a solid share of worldly goods.

It was they, he might have argued—and sometimes did—who had a far more acute problem than he. Much of his message was addressed to those who were squandering their brief mortal tenure in acquisitive pursuits. He was not concerned by their lack of saintliness, but, rather, their conspicuous waste of talent. In the late 1970s, when he was contemplating another race for Congress and being urged not to seek anything short of a "safe" seat, he exclaimed to me: "I just can't sit around becoming fiftyish, fat, and bald when everything's falling apart." At fifty-one he was dead.

He seemed never free of a sense of urgency, as if the lyrics "so little time . . . so many things to do" were insistently running through his head. The assassinations of John and Robert Kennedy and Martin Luther King were shattering shocks for millions; to Lowenstein, who had especially close ties with the younger Kennedy and King, they were baleful, one might almost say a premonitory reminder of how short the interval might be. He had himself been exposed to danger far more than once in tense, polarized scenes.

His chaotic timetable of inexact arrivals and departures invites the canard not only of ineffectuality but also of affinity for defeat. This was the monumental misconception. It is true that he dismissed the nervous counsel of those who styled themselves "realists." Too often he found that smug self-description sometimes a mask for timidity and cowardice. He scorned any narrow definition of "the art of the possible." For Lowenstein history was full of evidence that no infallible form-chart fixed reliable odds on human affairs, and the notion of inevitability belonged to uncreative doctrinaires.

He was equally exasperated, however, by ideological perfectionism and its purist disciples, and by infatuation with the delusions of "the worse, the better." It was almost an uncanny ability to differentiate the hopelessly quixotic from the attainable that so often differentiated him from both the chronic "practical" compromisers and some futilitarians on the Far Left. To maintain a hard, indestructible core of idealism without being divorced from reality was the lesson he sought to master and teach.

Virtually everything he did was rooted in a pervasive belief in the uses of reason. It was not to be confused with innocence. He rarely underestimated the strength of the legions of oppression and intolerance—from Mississippi to South Africa, from Moscow to Madrid. He recognized the resources of entrenched power structures, whether in a presidential establishment or in a machine-ruled congressional district. He had a Niebuhrian vision of the competing potentials for decency and destructiveness that lurked within most human psyches. Even in periods of acute disappointment, however, he refused to yield the field to irrationality.

Allied with his firm faith in persuasion was unceasing affirmation of the individual's capacity to affect events—the "one man can make a difference" note that was to recur throughout Robert Kennedy's later, best, days. This was what his own life was to signify.

Lowenstein was born in 1929, the year of the nation's most devastating economic collapse. In childhood he manifested an advanced interest in the political universe, identifying, for example, with the cause of the Spanish Loyalists as other nine-year-olds did with Brooklyn's Dodgers—perhaps a reflection of the comfortable but socially sensitive middle-class home in which he was reared. After attending the University of North Carolina (where he was to begin his warm association with then university president and later senator Frank Graham), he received a law degree at Yale and served two years in the U.S. Army.

He was first visible on the political landscape in 1952 when he took time off from law school to lead the Students for Stevenson organization.

His last involvement was his free-lance support of Ted Kennedy's thwarted bid for the 1980 Democratic presidential nomination; he was gunned down several months before the decisive convention battle.

This chronology may offer some clues to his voyage. While earliest memories may have been tinged by the Roosevelt resurgence, it was from Eleanor Roosevelt that he was to derive his real sense of the Roosevelt legacy. The Stevenson commitment embodied esteem for the style of civility, wit, and independence that were to characterize much of Lowenstein's own public life. The final Kennedy alliance was a sequel to what he cherished as Robert Kennedy's evolution from hard-nosed operative to champion of the lower depths, and what he believed to be Ted Kennedy's perpetuation of the role.

For Lowenstein, Eleanor Roosevelt personified the caring spirit who acquired (behind an exterior of unworldliness) a shrewd instinct for fusing principle with pragmatism. To him the best of Stevenson was his dedication to the Bill of Rights, unforgettably exemplified in his 1952 address condemning loyalty oaths before an American Legion convention audience and his often lonely resistance to Joe McCarthy's inquisitions. Robert Kennedy's finest hours, in Lowenstein's view, were his enlistments on the side of Cesar Chavez's migrant workers and of other ragged battalions of the nation's have-nots. Stevenson epitomized reason in public discourse; Kennedy was the undisciplined feuder transformed into a rebel with a cause.

Outside the traditional political boundaries, Lowenstein held fast to his friendships with Martin Luther King and Norman Thomas. In some ways it was an oddly ecumenical gallery; despite his many exercises in conciliation, Lowenstein could never dissolve the tensions between the Stevenson and Kennedy camps. Thomas remained "Mr. Outside" to the end, and the Kennedy-King estrangement was a source of deep disquiet. Yet Lowenstein moved easily between the adversary lines. He was perceived to be above suspicion, and an invaluable consultant and confidant.

For his part Lowenstein saw all these celebrities as persons who would matter far beyond their time—not only for the works they had done or stimulated but also for the lives they had touched and set in motion that would perpetuate something of their spirit.

In Washington, two years after his death, an extraordinary gathering assembled to mark the anniversary at a "congressional symposium." As the *Washington Post* noted, "those in attendance could be classified as

'Al people,' " a term initially devised by Larry Lowenstein to identify the diverse troops he had led into so many battles. They were officeholders, civil rights activists, community figures, and unaffiliated doers of good. Beyond participating in seminars devoted to issues of the Reagan era, many used the occasion to recall Lowenstein's impact on their lives.

Impressive as the turnout was, it was only a fragment of a constituency dispersed across the country (and not confined to it), comprising the young and the once-young to whom Lowenstein had been educator, agitator, conscience, consoler, organizer, a voice that remains as unforgotten as it was inspiring.

Some of the "Al people" have won political posts, others are teaching, still others hold civic or union positions. They may now be full-time or intermittent advocates, like many who met in the capital. Their shared remembrance is of Lowenstein's large place in their autobiographies. No computer can register their presence in countless American communities. But how many depart the public stage leaving so large and devoted a company behind? Of how many others is it said subsequently: "If only he were around . . ."

In the years that I knew Lowenstein, I met many of the volunteers drawn to him, not only in political seasons but also when he was engaged in special public-issue projects. They were unpaid, overworked, frequently subject to the disruptions created by sudden changes of plans or unscheduled improvisations. They contributed unrecorded time and energy; yet almost invariably their patience seemed limitless, as if they were sure they were absorbing far more from their service than they were giving.

That was partly because he had a rare gift for imparting to others a feeling of full participation in the excitement of his life. And for nearly all, the experience is still recalled as the time of their lives.

"It is beyond dispute," David Broder wrote, "that he brought more young people into American politics than any other individual of our times."

No one has contested that estimate. But "Al people" can also be found on other continents. A visitor to Spain will discover them among alumni of the anti-Franco underground, to whom he brought personal reassurance in the long years when they desperately needed to know there were Americans responsive to their struggle. He was in Prague in 1969 on the first anniversary of the Soviet invasion, extending his hand to those resisting the new despotism. He was no stranger in Biafra. To paraphrase the World War II Kilroy saga, you could name the troubled place and learn that Lowenstein had been there.

Again one invites the question: in trying to do so much did he accomplish too little? If he had concentrated on the nurturing of his own political fortunes, might he have had a Senate seat and the Senate stage on which to perform? It is hard to suppress such wistful conjecture. Yet it is even more difficult to visualize him formulating a long-range battle plan essentially dedicated to his own aggrandizement.

The more fitting and relevant question is how a man who served only one term in Congress and less than a year as ambassador to the United Nations was able to mold so many lives and shape so much history. Apart from his early presidency of the National Student Association and his two-term chairmanship of Americans for Democratic Action (1971), he was generally obliged to function without any organizational base or through ad-hoc committees. Much of the time he had to rely on lecture fees, a variety of teaching posts—Stanford, North Carolina State, and CCNY were some of the untenured stops—and, from time to time, a desk in a law office to sustain his modest life style and, for some of those years, that of his wife and three children. His own habits were felicitously ascetic; he didn't drink, smoked a rare cigarette (in the manner of a novice), and appeared as often as not in a Windbreaker and rumpled slacks. There was no affectation about his informality; it was simply consistent with a social calendar in which "dressing for dinner" was an expendable diversion.

Somehow, amid what may have often appeared to be disarray, this man was to emerge as an initiator and driving force in two of the most fateful popular rebellions in the nation's annals—the upsurge that led to Lyndon Johnson's abdication and the closely related crystallization of opposition to the Vietnam war. He would have called it preposterous to depict these as one-man miracles. But certainly the record sustains the claim that no other American was a more important catalyst in translating revulsion against the war into a successful revolt against the incumbent president.

What is too little appreciated in retrospect on that tumultuous period is that Lowenstein undertook these missions in the face of a prevailing judgment that he was promoting a lost cause. That view was ceaselessly reiterated by the political professionals and echoed by illustrious commentators. Elder statesmen reminded Lowenstein of the abortive "Dump Truman" drive that erupted and fizzled in the months preceding his renomination in 1948. (He preferred to recall how Truman bowed out four years later after his defeat by Estes Kefauver in New Hampshire's primary.) They intoned that linkage of the anti-Johnson uprising to the antiwar crusade could only trigger a jingoist backlash in Johnson's favor.

Lowenstein was unintimidated. Many chapters of the ensuing story are told in the pages that follow (especially in David Halberstam's "The Man Who Ran Against Lyndon Johnson"). Plainly he detected Johnson's vulnerability long before the idea became respectable or plausible in most Democratic and liberal circles. The problem was to transform sporadic protest and spreading disenchantment into an authentic national manifestation. This could not happen if nihilists or assorted Communist sects, who increasingly dominated the New Left, were perceived as managers or even leading spirits of the insurgence. Devout in his defense of civil liberties, Lowenstein would protest their right to be heard. But he would not let them usurp the show, or impose their tactics of polarization on the broad movement he envisaged.

That the campuses would be a major—but hardly exclusive—theater of operations reflected more than his special appeal to young men and women, dating back to his National Student Association presidency and his subsequent teaching assignments. He saw college students as emissaries to a large section of middle-class America where the political balance could be tilted one way or another in the fight for the country's allegiance. Thus he helped create notably representative committees of student-body presidents and college editors to speak out against the war.

Such respectable groupings enormously helped to impart a mainstream quality to the protest. They also widened the gap between Lowenstein and the befuddled "revolutionaries" with their apocalyptic fantasies of America at the barricades.

For Lowenstein this was not a new challenge. It was at the root of his disagreements with some of his cohorts in the civil rights upsurge that had been his focus in the preceding years. Beyond all the tortuous strategic debates there had been an underlying break between those, like Lowenstein, who glimpsed a vast resource of public sympathy for the equalitarian vision and those attracted by the incongruous gospel of black separatism. This course, he was convinced, was not only a perversion of the spirit of the quest for justice; it could only fortify the resistance of those striving to perpetuate the institutions of "two societies," and alienate the prospective support of decent opinion.

The cleavages within the civil rights ranks, poignantly recalled here in Thomas Powers's "A Chance Encounter," never ceased to trouble Lowenstein. Strongly as he rejected any revival of separatism, he was sympathetic to those who resented the slow pace of progress toward seemingly elementary goals. But some of the frenetic factionalism appeared an unconscionable dissipation of energy and good will. Lowenstein was not an isolated target; such men as Martin Luther King and Andrew Young were also to be vilified behind their own lines in the clamor of battle. In the long run Lowenstein was to be hailed by King, and during his congressional tenure Aaron Henry was to describe him as "the one man in Washington who has a desk in his office and a secretary for Mississippi black people."

Angry sectarianism faded; most of its leaders disappeared from positions of leadership long before Lowenstein's death. It was his own disposition to celebrate the gains that had been won rather than the discords that had marred the crusade.

His resolve to keep open the lines of communication to the widest sectors of the American community increasingly provoked the taunts of the thunderers of the Far Left as the Vietnam war took precedence. He was damned for a major article of his faith—that "the system" could be made responsive if enough people tried hard enough. In the circumstances of 1968 that meant the replacement of Lyndon Johnson and the termination of the Vietnam agony. The snipers seemed to be saying (simultaneously) that the aims were illusory unless "the system" were overthrown and that, even if realized, they would not matter much.

In their terms Lowenstein was derisively portrayed as a sinister "compromiser" and a mischievous agent of the status quo. On the lips of Weathermen and other self-proclaimed revolutionaries, the charges had a certain coherence; Lowenstein was indeed their enemy. The charges were harder to take when they began to permeate the conversation of some who called themselves "progressives" and "independents."

Those who harbored the dream of a nation first convulsed by violence and somehow then propelled toward some variation of a "workers' state" could properly regard Lowenstein as a menacing counterrevolutionary. He was committed to proving democratic society still capable of "revolution by consent." He outspokenly condemned the use of violence and provocation as both wrong and counterproductive. It was not always easy to reassert that stand, especially after the ghastly killings at Kent State and Jackson State, and when Richard Nixon shrilly described student peace marchers as "bums." There were moments when Lowenstein confided his dismay about the inflammatory insensitivity of allegedly responsible men. "Don't they know what they're doing?" he would murmur.

The way was open, he saw before most others did, for a victorious challenge to Johnson. But was anyone of sufficient stature prepared to carry the banner? Lowenstein in effect was the leader of a search committee.

Much of that effort is described here by Halberstam. Robert Kennedy's initial decision to stay out of the contest was a sharp letdown, but Lowenstein was not disposed to turn back. Although he had invested many words and much emotion in seeking to persuade Kennedy to enlist, he was elated when Eugene McCarthy announced his candidacy.

For Lowenstein the excitement of McCarthy's triumph in New Hampshire was shadowed by Kennedy's reversal of his stance and his formal entry into the race. He foresaw the strife that would intensify and the pressures to switch his own allegiance to which he would be subject. Some McCarthy enthusiasts began to whisper that he was a Kennedy "agent" lurking in the McCarthy tent. Such a defection would have been wholly incompatible with his character. Despite his unconcealed prior preference for a Kennedy candidacy, he respected McCarthy's willingness to stand up, and he felt deep commitment to the man who had responded first. He did try—without notable success—to erect bridges between the rival blocs, because he knew, even after Johnson had bowed to the New Hampshire blow and other ominous portents, that the Johnson forces would rally behind Humphrey. And he saw only disaster—despite his own past associations with Humphrey—in a ticket headed by the Vice-President, whose career had been cruelly crippled by his service to the Johnson regime.

The bullets that destroyed Kennedy brutally rendered academic any reassessment that might have been forced by the outcome of the California primary. Lowenstein was high on the list of those to whom Kennedy planned a renewed appeal if he scored as well as he did in that test. But time ran out.

After the assassination, most things had the aspect of melancholy anticlimax. McCarthy seemed stunned and remote as he pondered the bloodbath. The Democratic establishment pulled itself together long enough to engineer Humphrey's nomination. But Mayor Richard Daley's ruthless street warfare during the Chicago convention played into the hands of the confrontationists who had been briefly muffled by Johnson's abdication. Chicago's dreadful street scenes provide a dreary prelude to Humphrey's already ill-fated campaign, and Nixon was to snatch the presidency from the beleaguered Minnesotan who had been one of the war's foremost casualties.

In that morose November, and for long afterward, there would be those who bitterly asserted that the only fruit of Lowenstein's whole anti-Johnson labor had been the Nixon ascendancy. Such musings became especially fashionable as the nation wallowed in Watergate.

History's verdict may be far more generous. The meaning of the upheaval Lowenstein had done so much to generate would steadily penetrate the American consciousness.

In immediate terms it rendered far more difficult any further escalation of a war that had extorted an exorbitant toll in blood and treasure and national morale. Far beyond that, it would inhibit and instruct any future president tempted to start down a comparable road. What had been proven beyond dispute was that the political process could be successfully utilized to force a retreat from adventurism. It was a lesson not to be lost or disparaged. That has been most recently demonstrated in El Salvador, where any sign of a first-installment military involvement stirred instant unease and opposition in Congress and the country.

Saddened and troubled by the Nixon election, Lowenstein exhibited his familiar resilience. If expansion of the war had been almost surely impeded with Johnson's retreat, peace was still far from "at hand." The problem was to keep up the pressure amid the demoralization created by Nixon's advent.

Lowenstein's special role in sustaining the resistance was curiously acknowledged in an encounter he had with Henry Kissinger during Nixon's presidency. For Kissinger, the object of the meeting (held at his request) was to arrange a truce with the antiwar movement.

The proposition was simple. If Lowenstein would pledge to suspend hostilities for six months, Kissinger said, he could be assured that peace would be arranged within that time. The unpleasant corollary seemed evident; if this plea were rejected, Lowenstein and his followers would have to bear responsibility for prolongation of the bloodshed.

I saw Lowenstein soon after that session, and he described it in tones of incredulity and despair. How, he exclaimed (I write from memory, not diary), could Kissinger possibly regard his proposal as serious? Did he really credit Lowenstein with the power to turn off the antiwar protest on the basis of a private conversation with Kissinger that he was not even authorized to discuss in public? Or was Kissinger, for the sake of some future record, cynically making an offer he knew Lowenstein would be obliged to refuse?

Lowenstein's reaction had several facets. For one thing, he was constantly finding wry diversion as well as astonishment in such appraisals of his influence. (That was to be confirmed by the high rating—number 7— he eventually received on Nixon's "enemies list.") Since he was hardly free of introspective self-doubt, there must have been some pleasure in being so solemnly treated as a political magician who could make multitudes vanish until further notice. If at first inclined to offer the whimsical response "Who, me?," he could not wholly fail to appreciate the tribute.

In a more somber sense, the exchange intensified his pessimism about the state of American leadership.

His own view of the war, as suggested earlier, was as distasteful to the Communists and nihilists as it was to the authors of fake enemy body counts. Unpersuaded of the case for our presence, he nevertheless saw an obligation to those Vietnamese whom we had encouraged to fight. The goal was to achieve a negotiated peace—but he had little hope that our autocratic clients in Saigon could wage peace any more adeptly than war. He knew, however, there were courageous democrats being systematically excluded from the Vietnamese government and he tried to speak for them in the American debate. The coalition he and they sought to promote was repeatedly obstructed by Washington and its Saigon front men; Hubert Humphrey's contemptuous analogy of the "fox in the chicken coop" expressed the pervasive sterility that made us captive of the Thieu cabal. (See "Vietnam: In or Out?")

Despite the incontestable evidence of his achievements in the anti-Johnson revolt and the turn toward peace, the label of "loser" was to be recurrently applied to Lowenstein during the 1970s. The win-loss column gave it surface credibility in shallow political diagnoses. He was elected to Congress once and was thwarted in several subsequent contests. But the arithmetic tells little of the real story.

What is surely far more meaningful is the degree to which, after one term of distinguished service, his exclusion became the objective of bipartisan concern. The first time was in 1970, when he was standing for reelection. By joint agreement of Governor Rockefeller and the state legislature, the Long Island district he represented was artfully gerrymandered to make it a hospitable playground for his conservative Republican opponent. The move required at least the tacit acquiescence of some Democratic dignitaries.

Two years later, while most metropolitan liberal Democrats were running in comfortable terrain, he audaciously undertook a primary fight against the venerable John Rooney in Brooklyn's 14th Congressional District.

His "defeat" there was a well-documented scandal. Following a ruthless campaign that preceded the massive corruption of primary night, Meade Esposito, long-time ruler of the Brooklyn Democratic machine, paused to offer his professional respects to Lowenstein. "Al is a great piece of political property and with a little guidance he would have a great future. But not in Brooklyn."

Rooney was an ancient museum piece of the Brooklyn organization. Accustomed to easy reelection every two years against phantom Republican opponents, he had long served as chairman of the Appropriations subcommittee that provided for the extravagant care and feeding of the FBI. He was an uninspired man of the Democratic Right who acquired intermittent notice as a House apologist for the Franco regime.

When Lowenstein's animated campaign, supported by his familiar band of young, dedicated volunteers, began to create the potential of a large upset, Esposito and his henchmen abandoned their initial tactic of aloof ridicule. While wisely protecting Rooney from exposure to debate with Lowenstein, they made the waterfront unsafe for Lowenstein message-bearers. Vile anti-Lowenstein slurs were circulated in the populous Hasidic community where Rooney busily cashed in old chips based on immigration favors and other services rendered. Like many other Democratic machines, Esposito's had long shown symptoms of disintegration. Now it appeared to be literally fighting for its life.

On primary night the Lowenstein coalition, an admixture of the white middle class, emerging black and Hispanic voters, and the usual Lowenstein legion of the young, had good reason to scent victory.

Some of the multiple frauds that made Rooney the "winner" were substantiated in extensive court proceedings. (See "Tammany Hall Revisited" and "Elections and Change in America.") They were sufficiently flagrant and odious to provoke a court-ordered rerun of the contest. An insurgence of this kind is not easily reenacted, especially when limited funds have been exhausted, the mood of "you can't beat the machine" has been revived, and volunteers are dispersed. Lowenstein's vote remained largely intact, but Rooney, with many of the "irregularities" repeated, increased his own. The machine was taking no chances.

So Lowenstein "lost" again. In the grief enveloping his headquarters as the second effort ended, I found him more philosophical than most of those in the crowded room. In such setbacks he always seemed more genuinely concerned about the injury suffered by his followers than by any personal wounds. If he indicated any emotion, it was usually a certain mortification about his inability to have overcome the odds (or the frauds). This may have partly stemmed from the absence of finality. For many political candidates, negative election returns produce a feeling of emptiness on the morning after, as if they find it hard to imagine what they will be doing in the weeks and months ahead. Lowenstein never faced the prospect of a barren agenda.

In short, he was not a professional who dreaded reassignment to the minor leagues or retirement if he could not sustain a creditable batting average. There would always be a new ball game, and no bad day was to be equated with doomsday. That he was successively the target of the Rockefeller-Margiotta combine, the Esposito machine, and the drafters of the Nixon hit list was the meaningful index of his political impact. So, too, was the extent to which his support and counsel were solicited by a variety of presidential aspirants.

In the light of such testimonials, it might have been thought that New York's diverse liberal and reform factions would have been able to unite behind his 1974 bid for the Democratic Senate designation. Their failure to do so was one of his roughest passages.

His credentials for the Senate had been strongly buttressed by his two years of service in the House. Rarely has a freshman congressman so quickly demonstrated a special identity in that sprawling body and won so much respect from so many on both sides of the aisle. ("I suspect that no freshman member of the House since Henry Clay—and not excluding Abraham Lincoln or John F. Kennedy—has made more of an impression on this body than has Allard Lowenstein," the usually low-key Jonathan Bingham observed.) Those who had complained that he would be unwilling or unable to "sit still" long enough to attain any notice or to rise above congressional rules of disorder were soon confounded.

He would be no quiescent member of the club. Neither was he to be a star of any Washington social set; hostesses probably learned swiftly that he could not be relied on to appear with even approximate punctuality at the cocktail or dinner hour.

But he was very much around for congressional business. He formed and solidified many friendships. In his ensuing congressional races and his attempt to win a Senate nomination, some of the warmest endorsements came from members of the House—of both parties—with whom he had served.

In those two years he found himself absorbed by the frustrating machinery as well as the substance of congressional action. As in so many other areas, he refused to view old customs as sacred or irreversible. What he saw and heard led him to compose the thoughtful, incisive dissection of the congressional structure contained in "New Member."

Throughout that term he once again displayed his skill for conducting civil dialogue with those who differed with him—to "disagree without being disagreeable." At the same time he conveyed a quality of inner strength and integrity that set him very much apart from the conventional congressional portrait. The impression he left was spelled out by Representative Ken Hechler in a reminiscence he delivered to the House after Lowenstein had been beaten in his gerrymandered Long Island district in 1970 (a race, incidentally, in which, despite all the rigging, he ran well ahead of the state ticket).

Hechler recalled an interval during that "very rough, bitter and dirty campaign" in which "a very tough issue," involving a simplistic preventive detention bill, came up for a roll-call vote.

"I sensed, without talking with Al, how he was going to vote," Hechler said. "I stopped Al in the corridor before the vote and pleaded with him, for the sake of his reelection, for the sake of his return to perform more effective service in the House . . . to try and be a real politician for once.

"He looked at me rather quizzically and did not moralize the issue but simply asked a few substantive questions about the pending bill. . . . I became impatient and told Al he had no business coming down to Washington, leaving his campaign, and then casting a vote which could lose him the election.

"He again looked at me as though to say: 'Do you really think so?' He waited for the second roll call. I watched him as he studied the bill, the committee report, and asked fellow members not the usual 'how are you voting on this?' type of questions but clear and probing attempts to find out the significance and implications of the bill. Then, at the last minute, he stepped to the well of the House and voted, along with about half a dozen of his colleagues, on the distinctly unpopular side of the bill.

"Cynics will say that by hurting himself politically, Al Lowenstein hurt his influence on the nation. I take a different view. His influence and prestige will grow outside of the Congress. . . ."

His "influence and prestige . . . outside of the Congress" were to increase as Hechler had forecast. But neither the integrity nor the insights he had brought to his time in Congress were to afford him protection in the Byzantine Democratic politics of New York. Back in 1966, when he first sought a congressional nomination in a predominantly liberal West Side district, it was understandable that other liberals chose to compete against him and deny him the nomination. But such fragmentation was far less explicable in the following decade, when he had become so incontestably large and unique a figure in the politics of our time.

I detected a hint of the trouble to come when his name was proposed for the chairmanship of Americans for Democratic Action the year after he had been exiled from the House.

Many of us who had been active in ADA from its inception more than two decades earlier had been urging him for many weeks to accept the post. At that point he occupied no official position anywhere and as head of ADA he would have access to a continuous public platform. For ADA, which had come to be too widely regarded as an alumni association of aging liberals and ex-radicals, his leadership offered the promise of an infusion of the kind of spirited young Americans whom he so universally attracted.

Lowenstein, while initially hesitant to become an "organization man"—even if the organization were one that imposed no rigorous "party discipline" on its leaders or members—finally agreed on condition that there be no bitter contest for the office. He had no diminished instincts for combat with political adversaries but he had no zest for struggle with those whom he regarded as his allies.

We offered him premature assurance that there would be no such discord. Soon, however, we began to hear the sound of a few ADA functionaries querulously asking whether Lowenstein would devote enough time to the job or be otherwise engaged. They seemed oblivious to the fact that the organization in which they retained so proprietary an interest badly needed the stimulus of a chairman who could reach out to a fresh constituency, win or retrieve recognition for ADA in the larger, less sectarian world in which Lowenstein moved, and refurbish its reputation among a younger generation to whom it had little sentimental appeal. To put it bluntly, ADA needed Lowenstein far more than he needed the travail of presiding over it.

In the end the transition was accomplished; the opposition, which had tried to promote an unprecedented third term for the incumbent president as a last-gasp block-Lowenstein move, was overcome without a bruising struggle. But the interlude of uncertainty illustrated Lowenstein's vulnerability to the sometimes stultifying atmosphere of orthodox liberalism.

In 1978, when he embarked on what proved to be his last effort to return to Congress, New York's liberal Democrats could not unite to give him even the belated acknowledgment of an uncontested nomination. The scene was Manhattan's "silk-stocking district," represented in the past by John Lindsay and Ed Koch. The pallor of the Carter reign was already evident, and many of his former House associates had repeatedly pressed on Lowenstein the contention that he could most significantly help to fill the vacuum by renewing his role on Capitol Hill.

To many of us, what happened after his declaration of his candidacy seemed the worst rebuff he had ever suffered—and it came at the hands of many who had often voiced lip service to him. His chief and eventually victorious rival in the Democratic primary turned out to be a wealthy young man who had generously contributed to many wholly worthy enterprises. (See "A Liberal Indulgence.")

Now Lowenstein was to hear some of the liberal luminaries whose support he might have expected apologetically explaining that they had an eternal debt to his opponent for his past fiscal generosity toward their works.

Lowenstein might well have preferred that I not linger on this episode. He never manifested the rancor that I and other partisans felt about that campaign. Perhaps neither was he able to achieve the enthusiasm for battle that he showed in earlier races against reactionary adversaries—whether Republicans or right-wing Democrat Rooney. In this instance there were no large issues at stake; the true question was one of credentials.

What was hard to accept is the indignity of this setback. Yet on a smaller scale it duplicated the narrow self-protectiveness shown by those who had undercut him in his more important quest for a Senate nomination. Lowenstein was viewed as a "threat" not only by the embattled machine-men who had been witnessing the steady slippage of their power but also by some practitioners of the progressive "new politics."

One may assign different reasons to different circumstances. The unmistakable paradox that endured until his death was that he could stir the admiration—if not the assent—of such conservative eminences as William Buckley while facing snipers in his own camp. Buckley, being a star in his own right (as well on the Right), enjoyed dueling with an opponent who tested his virtuosity. He and other conservatives such as Ernest Van Den Haag, Rita Hauser and others were also moved by Lowenstein's grace and tolerance, and by what Schlesinger has identified as "the sweetness" of his demeanor. They did not mistake these traits for lack of conviction; rather, they came to respect the process by which he arrived at them and the undogmatic tones in which he affirmed them. They recognized, too, his genius for discerning areas of agreement behind stridently clashing slogans.

But ecumenical endorsements could not help him prevail in that desultory final primary.

By now that campaign, painful as it was, can be seen as a footnote, or perhaps as a theme for an essay on what might have been if he had gone back to Congress. Lowenstein did not require any protracted convalescence after the defeat. By early 1979, at the Carter Administration's request, he was again in South Africa, where he was to make a major contribution toward breaking the "insoluble" Rhodesian deadlock. (See "Toward Majority Rule and Peace in Zimbabwe.") Again what was outstanding about his performance was his ability to traverse between hostile lines and induce serious communication where there had heretofore been only a dialogue of the deaf.

Much of what he did in that mission and its follow-through in Congress received minimal public notice. A glimpse of his accomplishment during a journey as special ambassador under the aegis of UN Ambassador Andrew Young was to be found in a U.S. State Department cable:

"In a less than three-day visit, Ambassador Lowenstein was able to achieve an unprecedented degree of success in effectively communicating with the highest level of the post's priority audience. . . . A senior Foreign Ministry officer commented, despite the Ambassador's highly critical remarks, that no other foreigner had as full an understanding of the South African scene as the Ambassador."

Introduction

After Lowenstein's death, Young said, "Al exemplified what the prophets of the Old Testament might have done had they been allowed to live and work among such circumstances as ours."

There was nothing messianic in his manner, however, nor did he lay any claims to infallibility. As Schlesinger notes, he was "the supreme agitator" in the noblest tradition, but as often as not the objective of his agitation was a just reconciliation, whether in South Africa or in Mississippi. While he did not consider himself a pacifist, he saw the nuclear arms race as the ultimate madness. Unlike some modern converts to conservatism, he was never beguiled by the Soviet mystique or disposed to rationalize Communist oppression as a "necessary" step toward salvation. Neither did he believe, however, that free people could advance human hope by the attainment of some illusory goal of "nuclear supremacy."

If one thinks about the values and aspirations he was continuously reaffirming—compassion, equity, the reduction of human misery, rational discourse between even adversary nations, the quiet nourishment of the universal impulse for freedom—the nation and world he left behind him were hardly approaching any fulfillment of his vision. Within months of his death, the United States was to elect a national administration that quickly savaged the values he cared about.

This is not to say that he attached any sanctity to programatic liberal reforms. He was always groping for genuinely fresh initiatives and reappraisal of existing institutions. But a proper skepticism about inherited bureaucracies would have been seen as a vastly different matter from repudiation of the underlying dream of a "gentler, crisper world."

The Reagan victory was widely heralded as evidence that the ideas and ideals long identified with Lowenstein had fallen into permanent national disfavor. It is unlikely that he would have conceded that any final word had been spoken or succumbed to the initial loss of Democratic nerve.

As much as any man of his time, he resisted panic in adversity. He was never inclined to see a momentarily negative tide as the irresistible wave of the future. He had, after all, seen Richard Nixon's landslide of 1972 transformed into the wasteland of Watergate.

He did not underestimate the darker side of American politics; he had seen it firsthand too often, and had often been its selected target. You will find in the pages ahead little reckless optimism about the long-run outcome. But I remember time and again his delight in reporting a new discovery that even the most seemingly frozen mind could be thawed by appeals of decency and sanity.

Michael Harrington observed in a Lowenstein reminiscence that there is a politics of change "based on solidarity and love" and another "based on hatred alone." Lowenstein was a perpetual reminder of the distinction.

Was Lowenstein "a success"? Obviously his life was a mixture of triumph and tragedy, and no one can review it without an aching awareness of what his presence might mean in the current national predicament.

To proclaim Lowenstein a "success" in any analogous sense would demean his pilgrimage. He knew that he and those who walked with him still had "a thousand miles to go" in their quest for a just, humane society.

There were those who understandably saw the circumstances of his death as squalid caricature of his lifelong gentleness, his dedication to reason, and his loathing of violence. He had faced and at least sometimes cooled hot-blooded mobs in remote places. Now he confronted a mysterious malignancy of the mind that would defy any ingenuity of communication. In such a rendezvous he was defenseless.

No one will know whether he pondered the ghastly irony of his entrapment or whether there was opportunity only for desperate, futile thoughts of escape. If he had been able to gain time, he would have tried to break through the thick barrier of homicidal schizophrenia. The gunfire came too soon. His last battle was to be on a hospital operating table, where, by all medical accounts, he did not yield without an epic struggle.

But Lowenstein knew well that too many Dennis Sweeneys were stalking the world. His absorption in the assassinations of John and Robert Kennedy was more than a sentimental trip in behalf of cherished friends and valued leaders. He felt it was crucially important to determine whether their deaths could really be traced to isolated aberration or whether the hand of political conspiracy remained hidden.

Often scornful of those addicted to conspiracy theories of human events, he sought assurance that he was not being too gullible about acceptance of official versions. As he wrote in his unfinished essay on Robert Kennedy (see "Robert F. Kennedy and Power in America"): "What is odd is not that so many people thought it [the assassination] was all random but that so many intelligent people refused to believe it might be anything else."

Introduction

To the end he remained unsatisfied with the solitary Sirhan "solution." But no such speculation attended his own slaying.

Lowenstein's interest in the origins of human behavior was emphatically not restricted, however, to a political context. In the public arena he was often seen as an around-the-clock issue-oriented political animal who thought there were societal answers to all our discontents. He had no such simplistic concept of the nature and destiny of the human species, nor did he prescribe any patent medicine for personal serenity. What he sought was the framework for a social order in which there would be infinitely wider opportunity to live more gratifying lives. For him it often seemed that the search for that condition was what gave immediate purpose and coherence to existence. Beyond the search lay vast questions eluding any schematic answers.

He knew he was missing things because so many hours were allocated to so many endeavors that could not be renounced and that remained related in his own mind. At the time of the breakup of his marriage, he talked sadly and softly about it—one of the very few occasions when he let private problems assume a priority in our conversations. He lamented his long absences from home and his frequently unpredictable entrances and exits. He thought "things could have been different" if his pace had been less hectic. He did not—perhaps could not—bring himself to say that he wished he had run any different course. But separation from Jenny and the children he loved was plainly a defeat utterly different in dimension than those he had survived with so much dignity in public life.

In those hours and for a long time thereafter he seemed to be asking himself more insistently the question he had often addressed in a different context to public audiences: "What on earth are we on earth for?"

What he could not know was that at least part of the answer would come in the outpouring of love and grief and durable remembrance stirred by his death, and the pride his children would carry through their lives.

"If you seek his epitaph, as they say, look around," Charles Kuralt said after his death. It is not fanciful to suggest that the spontaneity and confidence apparent in the popular movement for a nuclear freeze owes some of its inspiration—and personnel—to the heritage of the "impossible" insurgences he led.

Too much of what he said and did is not engraved in any official record or document. Missing, too, is much of what many felt about him. For myself, I will long recall the voice of a middle-aged, mournful black woman, talking about him at his campaign headquarters on the night in 1972 when he was being counted out by the Brooklyn machine. After Lowenstein had spoken softly and gracefully to his tearful, bitter troops, I heard her say quietly:

"He is someone who is somebody who can cope with that fact."

That he surely was.

James A. Wechsler

MAN IN
MOTION

YOUTH AND THE TIDE
OF HISTORY

Ninth National Student Congress,
August 29, 1956

Once described as "a protean man of virtuoso talents," Allard K. Lowenstein devoted much of his public life to advocacy of social justice, civil rights, and political reform. He addressed an extraordinary range of issues, often with a fresh approach and distinctive voice.

As a petitioner, he urged the United Nations to take up the long-neglected question of oppression of black people in South-West Africa, now Namibia. As an organizer, he recruited students to work for civil rights in the South and showed skeptics how Lyndon Johnson could be defeated in his own party. As a congressman, he advocated creative policies and criticized institutional inertia.

As a diplomat and international specialist, he outlined foreign-policy opportunities. As an investigator and critic, he raised fundamental questions about the facts of Robert Kennedy's and other assassinations. As an essayist and speaker, he laid out political possibilities and probed the dangers of apathy and violence. In other arenas, he pressed an assortment of allied concerns.

While Lowenstein's roles and activities were varied, they shared common themes. Though he was concerned with action as well as theory, he relied on reasoned persuasion and debate to gather support. He pursued his principles and commitments with an independence, tenacity, and

3

resilience that variously astonished, chagrined, or enthralled friends and observers.

Impatient with conventional orthodoxies and ideologies, he frequently broke through stereotypes in defining and addressing issues. His habit of approaching political questions from different angles led him to challenge the boundaries of public thinking and of citizen initiative. But it also led him to viewpoints which were sometimes misunderstood.

Of the qualities that help explain Lowenstein's special influence on students and others impatient with the present, one of the most unusual was his ability to draw connections between an individual's personal concerns and the pressing social and political questions of the day. He might treat a single subject with philosophical reflectiveness, light satire, cold logic, or passionate appeal. Whatever the puzzle or challenge, however, the assessment that emerged reflected a special stance, a special way of approaching political thought and action.

During the 1950s, Lowenstein was already pursuing many of the causes that emerged with explosive force in the 1960s. In 1950–51, he served as president of the National Student Association, and in 1956, in the middle of the "silent generation" era, he addressed one of its annual conventions. A portion of his speech is reprinted here.

We are the privileged and antiseptic generation. We move in the backwater of great events, well clothed, well housed, and well fed. Struggle is not our hallmark and greatness is not our necessity. We are becoming lazy on the victorious sacrifices of our older brothers and on the nonfulfillment of gloomy prophecies.

Somewhere where we are not, destinies are upended and centuries disturbed, but in our pleasant world opportunity knocks again and again, and it is the merest shadows that somehow the great things are no longer ours to do something about. When immensity spawns futility, the petty and the fleeting become the ultimate, and the rest recedes into mystery and irrelevancy. We are a people whose national energies and imagination flourish in crisis, and we rejoice now that crises are past and life demands less national virtue than it used to.

Of course there are still those who forebode about disaster, but vacations are longer, diseases fewer, and suburbs multiply. And how to warn of dragons and not speak negatively, in a time when everyone knows the need for positive thinking? So a few warners and mourners prattle about Asians and atoms from their convertibles, but their timing is out of joint.

And most of them come to relax too, because the prettier wives who are, with less effort, producing healthier children and more nutritious meals, marry unaware of or undaunted by epic premonitions. If destiny wishes to rendezvous with this generation, she will first have to find us.

And how soon we may know the folly of playing hide-and-seek with the fates. How short-lived this luxury of indolent unconcern may be, and how grim its cost, if one generation's evasions are to be its children's doom.

For moderation warped into negation today is patience exhausted into violence tomorrow. Opportunity frittered into languor in youth is usefulness mired into mediocrity later on. Courage watered into convenience in school is conscience undecipherable under expediency afterward. Prosperity lapsed into arrogance abroad is admiration glided into envy and then embittered into resentment everywhere. And thought smothered by comfort collectively is opportunity frittered, courage watered, moderation warped, and souls unstirred. Thus greatness flabs into fatness and vision fades into hindsight. Even if God spares civilizations after such undoing, He does not restore to individuals the years when challenge and nobility grizzled into stupor and waddled toward waste.

The undemanding bravery of war generations and the stoic unrest of depression generations came of people like ourselves. But new occasions teach new virtues. And now less strikingly, more patiently, and more urgently, we shall have to energize and discipline ourselves that these times of national calm become funds of growing individual strength, and the quietudes of transient respites are not invitations to final calamity.

It is time long since that helpfulness galvanized and kindness liberated became symbols of our unparalleled and unearned great national luck; that energies more than ever were turned to the intangibles of building worth in the vast, if illusory, security so gratuitously provided by our abundance; that generous impulses and high instinct were nourished by a society arrived at unimaginable technological achievement.

Wise and good men have long thought that if humanity ever came to be as well off as humanity has come to be in our here and now, the human grandness which privation can prevent would assert itself triumphant as the golden rule in the golden age. The dreams and hopes which sustained our harried ancestors through centuries of misery, now at last at hand, in anguish ask honor to the great ideas revealed or evolved during the upward struggle of man from the trees and caves.

The irony of God's wisdom has made present imperatives of ancient ethics. For in the quality of our brotherhood and in the scope and depth

5

of our willingness to give and to learn from giving lie the key to the nature of the future. Can we deserve to survive if indifference palsies grandness into pettiness and national success, measured materially, blinds us to troublous fact outside our borders and inures us to bypassed humanity outside our circles? In the strange new war for men's allegiances, limited violence threatens an aggressor with wider damage elsewhere, however his armies do. And unleashed violence threatens aggressor and victim alike with obliteration.

So new weapons take priority, and the Lord in His goodness has given us the material to win, if we but grasp the stakes and rouse the will. In our wealth we have the wherewithal to be more nearly generous; in our content we have the incentive to awake in ourselves our finest; in our democratic concept we have the vehicle best suited to carry men's chiefest hopes. It is almost as if we are dared to selfishness in our well-being, so we may know finally that all the vast material gifts cannot by themselves preserve themselves or their masters.

Survival may ever be in balance and survival of freedom will long be in doubt. But we cannot but have the faith of men who know the love of the Lord for His creatures that if we seek to do right contagiously He will help us to see realized the gentler crisper world men could inherit.

REPORT ON A "SACRED TRUST"

Address to the United Nations Fourth Committee, October 17, 1959

As a student and activist in the 1940s and early 1950s, Lowenstein had been primarily involved in domestic politics and civil rights struggles. In the late fifties, however, he became increasingly active in international issues. In 1957, he worked with Eleanor Roosevelt at the American Association for the United Nations and soon thereafter became a foreign-policy adviser to Senator Hubert Humphrey. In that period, he traveled to the Soviet Union, the Middle East, and, for the first time, South Africa.

In South Africa, he established contact with African and white opposition leaders and became more aware of the extent of racial oppression. While speaking at a nonwhite university, he also heard for the first time about the even greater plight of Africans in the territory of South-West Africa (now Namibia). He listened to a firsthand description of conditions in that territory, which had been entrusted to South Africa under a League of Nations mandate, but which was now regarded as an exclusive possession.

After returning to New York in the fall of 1958, Lowenstein met with the Reverend Michael Scott, a former Anglican missionary who had been expelled from South-West Africa years earlier and had since served as the United Nations spokesman for several South-West African tribes. "Nothing I had heard about Father Scott had prepared me for the remarkable impact of the man," Lowenstein later wrote. "He was somehow both blunt and gentle . . . full of restraining patience and an urgent impatience, as if the two go hand in hand: the patience of a man certain that time would produce victory, an impatience that men do not prod time as much as they could."

For years, Scott and a handful of others had pressed the UN to help end South African domination of the nonwhite population of South-West Africa. His efforts were hampered because the Cape Town government prohibited visits by unauthorized persons to nonwhite locations and denied native representatives the right to communicate with the outside world about the conditions in which they lived. Without facts and documentation, Scott was fighting a war without ammunition.

Learning of Lowenstein's commitment to fighting apartheid, Scott asked him if he would travel to South-West Africa to gather information to help spur UN action on the issue. Lowenstein eventually agreed and recruited two other volunteers, Sherman Bull, a medical student, and Emory Bundy, a teacher and former student-body president, to aid in the undertaking. Native leaders were secretly notified of their impending arrival.

The trip began in South Africa in mid-June of 1959. After making contact with African and other opposition leaders, Lowenstein spoke at the annual meeting of the National Union of South African Students and voiced the support of students in other countries for the group's antiapartheid stand.

During the meeting, he was approached by Hans Beukes, a student from South-West Africa who had been denied a passport for study in Norway. After listening to Beukes describe his troubles, Lowenstein, Bundy, and Bull made plans to help him leave the country. Several days later, Beukes was smuggled across the border, in the back of a Volkswagen, to Bechuanaland and freedom.

In Johannesburg, as the Americans prepared to depart for South-West Africa with cameras, recording equipment, and letters of introduction, their car was ransacked. Documents from their stolen luggage were later quoted at the UN as "private papers which have come into the possession of the South African government."

The three men were limited to two weeks in South-West Africa. From the moment they stepped, illegally, into the native areas, their journey *took on the attributes of a spy adventure. Relying on furtive native planning and communications, including secret recognition codes, and usually operating under cover of darkness, they met with tribal leaders and spokesmen. They took careful notes of conditions and recorded as many statements as possible.*

Despite the dangers the trip had its lighter moments. In one meeting, native spokesmen expressed doubt that the American recording "machine" thrust in front of them could "understand" their language. A playback of their voices caused surprise and delight while resolving their doubt.

At a final and critical encounter with Chief Hosea Kutako of the Herero tribe authorities were reported to be approaching the area. Driven hurriedly into the desert, the three men were pursued at one point by another car and hid alone in the darkness for several hours. Finally, a tribal emissary appeared out of the night and transported them to a key rendezvous with an undercover white contact in the territory's capital city, Windhoek. Within hours, the contact had smuggled most of the vital materials collected by the three Americans out of the territory.

That fall, Lowenstein, Bull, and Bundy were authorized by tribal leaders to serve as their spokesmen before the Fourth Committee of the United Nations.

I do not think I can adequately express my gratitude to the Fourth Committee for allowing us to appear before it.

One of the most unforgettable aspects of our trip through South-West Africa was the reaction of the non-European peoples with whom we met. To them, our arrival and concern over their plight were a source of such great encouragement and hope that—glad as we were to bring encouragement and hope to suffering and patient human beings—we were concerned lest too much be expected from our visit.

Often we were told that we were the first "Europeans" with whom the African people had even been able to meet as equals—let alone as friends—since the departure of the Reverend Michael Scott many years before. Sometimes we were received as the first response to years of petitions to the United Nations, and even of years of prayers to the Almighty—the first harbingers of help on the way. And, as you can imagine, these were no easy hopes to dash.

Indeed, there were many times when we had to try to draw a fine line between bringing encouragement and hope without creating false hopes or premature expectations. And the promise we always made, the promise we intend to do everything we possibly can to keep, was that we would do our best to take the story and the message of the non-European peoples of South-West Africa to this forum, and to the people of the world beyond the deserts and the seas.

It was to be expected that the Union of South Africa would not be enthusiastic about our telling our observations or conveying the messages sent by us to the United Nations. These are, after all, messages sent in many cases by the same people, or by representatives of the same people, to whom the Union government has for many years refused passports when they sought to come here to speak for themselves. And it was no doubt unlikely that the Union government—having done its best to keep these representatives bottled up in South-West Africa—would welcome a successful evasion of the intent of a ban—even though the ban be an unlawful one—imposed by the same government.

We are not in any way experts on South-West Africa. We are at best inadequate substitutes for the people who are experts, and who should be here speaking for themselves with a knowledge and eloquence we cannot approach. It is, it seems to us, a most serious indictment indeed of the whole attitude and policy of the Union government that we have to appear here at all. Clearly there would be no need to impugn the motives or besmirch the good names of any of the present petitioners if the Union government were only willing to allow the people who should be here to come.

Everywhere we went in the territory we found that the non-European population lives in an atmosphere devoid of the simplest, most fundamental human rights, and bereft of any hope of obtaining these rights from the present government at any future time. Furthermore, we found that this police-state atmosphere is insinuating itself into the lives of the European population as well. It grows increasingly difficult, for example, even for Europeans to voice publicly fundamental disagreements with present racial policies. It will be said that few Europeans disagree fundamentally with present racial policies; we would observe only that we encountered such Europeans, and that their hesitancy to speak out, and their fear of being quoted, betray an unhappy erosion of traditional freedoms, even within the limited European community.

There are surely many matters about which our relatively brief visit in South-West Africa does not qualify us to speak. But the presence of fear

10

is not one of these, and fear, we must report, is the lowest common denominator of South-West Africa.

We will not soon forget the stories of arbitrary arrest and police brutality which are the daily bread of the African people; nor the prisoners in their red-striped clothes working in a private home in Keetmanshoop; nor the grim determination of the African leaders—both those elected and those appointed by the South-West Africa Administration—in the Windhoek Location not to let their people be forced many miles from their jobs into a new location, whose regulations sound more appropriate to jails than for homes.

This is perhaps not the appropriate time to parade before you the long list of specific violations of the letter and spirit of the Mandate which afflicted our eyes and ears during our sojourn in South-West Africa. But we would be remiss if we did not call your special attention to three particular situations of immediate concern. One of these is the increasing imposition of Afrikaans and of the tribal languages to the exclusion of English in the educational system. This imposition proceeds vigorously in the face of the theoretically bilingual nature of the Mandatory Power and is not slowed down in the least by the earnest wish of many Africans to learn English as a *lingua franca* and as a vehicle for communication with the outside world. It is needless to point out that for any non-Europeans in South-West Africa the pursuit of studies beyond Standard 8 is greatly inhibited, to say the least, by the enforced downgrading of English.

A second urgent problem is presented by the continuing forced evictions and threats of eviction of unconsulted and unwilling non-Europeans from ancestral and often relatively superior lands. Quite apart from the human misery such evictions entail, they serve to underscore the hapless status of these "wards of civilization." One of the most flagrant and pressing of the eviction problems is of course the one which has arisen concerning the Rooie Nasie Nama reserve at Hoachanas.

And a third such urgent situation has developed from the increasing use by the Union government of the ban as a weapon against African leaders whom it does not like. The world has long been familiar of course with the manner in which the present Union government arbitrarily, without trial, and customarily without stated reason, orders Africans or other opponents of their government to go to a particular spot and stay within a small radius of that spot for a number of years. As outrageous as this procedure may be, it becomes the concern of this committee only when it is applied in South-West Africa; and it is now being so applied.

It does not seem unreasonable to wonder if the Union government is not inclined to suppress and repress the development of leadership and of opportunities for growth toward self-government among the indigenous population of South-West Africa, instead of encouraging and helping such development.

For these and many more reasons, we have concluded that the government of South Africa is unfit to continue as the trustee for the conscience of the world and should be stripped of its rights as a mandatory power. It is hard to find any evidence that, despite the clear injunctions of the Mandate, the Mandatory Power in thirty-nine years has done anything significant to help the indigenous population of South-West Africa to develop toward self-government or to improve its living conditions.

I know as do you that suffering is still the rule for the human race. We know that injustice, inequity, disease, frustration, hunger, and oppression still tell the story of most of our brothers on most of this planet. And we all well know that the miseries of centuries are not eradicated in minutes.

But that not everything can be done at once gives no sanction to doing nothing at all, or indeed to doing anything less than everything that can possibly be done. And surely there are some situations which cry out to our consciences more cogently and with greater urgency than others.

May I ask that you suppose for a moment that this organization—founded in continuing refutation of racism—were to receive appeals for help from people who claimed to be denied the most elementary of rights because of their race; who claimed to be living in abject and enforced poverty while neighbors of another race lived in almost unequaled prosperity; who claimed that their ancestral properties were being taken from them, and that their right to move about in their own land and abroad was restricted almost to the point of nonexistence. Suppose it were further alleged that by law the government over these people were selected by 10 percent of the population, determined by race; that no voice in the determination of public policies were accorded to the remaining 90 percent solely because of their race. Now imagine if you can that the ruling authority admitted—perhaps "boasted of" would be more accurate—the existence of the laws upon which these conditions were based, and vowed that they would never be changed.

Finally, conceive for a moment, if you can, that the territory ruled by this racially "pure" 10-percent government were an international ward, a "sacred trust of civilization," an area not by the most generous of definitions belonging to anyone's "interior."

Here surely would seem one instance where all mankind would work together to demonstrate that, whatever disagreements may mar brotherhood or even jeopardize survival elsewhere, organized, governmentally instituted racism has no place on this planet in our time. And surely it would be intolerable that legalized racial oppression should be the avowed policy of a government holding sway over other human beings as the trustee of mankind.

Yet these are precisely the facts of the South-West African situation, and to date the great world outside this unhappy international territory has done almost nothing about it. The existence of the racially oppressive policies in South-West Africa is not, in the main, even in dispute. Does anyone dispute that no non-European can vote, or that this decitizenizing is racial in origin? Does anyone pretend that equal educational or medical facilities—even if separated—are available to non-Europeans? Will someone tell us that the "pass laws" are the fabrication of some public-relations genius seeking to discredit the South African government by inventing diabolical rumors about regulations which simply do not exist? Or does the government in power at least seek to offer hope of something better to come?

In the face of talk, where diplomats assemble, of possible "compromises" of differences between trustee and world there is on the scene actually continuing enactment by the 10-percent government of further legislation to force human beings apart because of the color of their skin.

The apparatus of growing oppression is there for all to see, is in fact vaunted as a "solution" to the "native problem," is defined and proclaimed as "good" for the hapless folk who have nothing to say about its construction or implementation but who cannot, even by brilliance or saintliness, escape its consequences.

It is these facts and these hopes that suggest to me that the appeals of the people of South-West Africa must touch our consciences with unique urgency, even in a world torn by injustices and still largely ruled by suffering. Surely mankind must expect and pray that in so flagrant a case of international injustice, all civilized nations which suffered through the war against Nazism or which are adherents of the Universal Declaration of Human Rights will soon cooperate to ease the plight of the suffering peoples of this "sacred trust."

The simple, unavoidable fact is that a sacred trust of all of us now rests in the hands of the only government on earth that dares to exalt the same types of laws that united humanity against Hitler, and that have been repudiated alike by science and by all religions, by the spokesmen of democracy, of communism, and of all gradations and styles of government between.

It is perhaps an ironic challenge and opportunity that the one government in the world based on racial discrimination should also be the one government in defiance of the United Nations, and of opinions of the International Court, about its responsibilities in an international territory. And, as recent witnesses in this troubled land, we implore the statesmen of the world, for the sake of all of us, as well as that of the people of South-West Africa, to work together here to end oppression there.

In the troubled scales of the human travail few situations have called more poignantly for action, and few situations have required less action to produce hope for results. For ourselves, we have come to feel that we all may well find the response to our own quests for eternal assistance weighted heavily by how we respond to the prayers of those unimportant but very human beings, who because of superior force but in the name of a "sacred trust of civilization" live such anguished existences in their own land.

The testimony, documents, and tapes provided to the United Nations by Lowenstein, Bull, and Bundy helped spur action in that world body on South-West Africa. Seven resolutions aimed at reducing oppression there were adopted by the General Assembly, and plans took shape to press the mandate question before the World Court.

Although the U.S. government had not supported the resolution that enabled the three men to speak, it eventually voted for the 1959 resolutions. The following year, however, it again abstained on several resolutions supporting change in South-West Africa.

14

BRUTAL MANDATE
1962

After his UN work, Lowenstein was increasingly active in the grow-
ing civil rights movement and frequently noted the connections between
the fight for racial justice at home and overseas. He traveled to the
South several times, worked for antisegregation boycotts, and helped or-
ganize support for the sit-ins.

In 1960, he was chairman of William Fitts Ryan's successful campaign
for Congress from Manhattan's West Side, the first congressional break-
through of the Democratic reform movement in New York. Later that
year, he served as an alternate delegate to the Democratic National
Convention and spoke against apartheid in places ranging from New
York, to Minnesota, to Berkeley.

In 1961, he was appointed assistant dean of men and lecturer in po-
litical science at Stanford University. The following year he completed
Brutal Mandate: A Journey to South West Africa. *Portions of the book*
are reprinted here.

Wherever we went the story for the black man was the same: terror,
poverty, isolation, oppression . . .

And here, unlike the Union, there are no resident foreign correspon-
dents and few travelers to focus world attention. There are virtually no
sympathetic Europeans, and there is not a single African doctor, lawyer,
engineer, or college graduate of any kind to buffer the simplicities of
unchallenged white domination.

15

If you are black you are poor, and if you are black you can do nothing to change either your blackness or your being poor. So having nothing and doing nothing fuse like chewing and swallowing, and only the occasional exception reminds you that these are separable functions.

You are ill, too ill to work, and you stay home after years without a day missed. The police raid house to house in the Location and find you in your bed. You explain that you are ill, and are beaten until the police grow tired of the sport. Then you are arrested, for no one is allowed to stay away from work without first securing the permission of the white employer. But if you are particularly useful to the white employer, or if he is a kind man and you have not before been absent for many months, he may fetch you from the prison and pay your fine, subtracting it from your wages; and you will bow the head and smile and say, "Thank you, Baas." You scrimp four months to buy a ticket for the train to visit the family of your wife ninety miles away. You get the necessary permits, buy the necessary ticket, and then the white man will not let you on the train. There are no reasons given, but you bow the head and smile and say, "Thank you, Baas."

The stomachs and spirits of those who endure such permanent tactical quiescence pay a frightful price for repressing so much that is natural. But the price of behaving otherwise is incalculably worse.

Even people suspected of no infringement of any regulation are not free from the attentions of the police, who reach everywhere and terrify all nonwhites; which is, after all, one of their functions.

One morning, while wandering through the part of Windhoek where the European business area frays off into African slums, I noticed on a side street a stately Herero lady playing with a dog. She was dressed in the elegant robes and headdress of the Herero women that so mock European efforts to picture the African as a hopeless sloven. Balanced impossibly on her head were a pail and some packages. The dog was barking and wagging its tail; the lady was petting it; and visible in the background were the shacks and dust that mark the beginning of the African Location.

I hurried toward the lady, smiled, pointed to my camera, and asked if she would mind petting the dog a moment longer while I took a picture. There was some difficulty communicating precisely what it was I wanted, for white men do not often approach African women on the streets of Windhoek with such purposes in mind, but at last everything was set.

Even the dog seemed to be cooperating. Then suddenly, out of nowhere, descended an Afrikaner policeman who had apparently been gazing at our little scenario for some time.

I wondered what we had done that had offended any tentacle of apartheid, and worried about petitions to the U.N. and exposed film that were on my person, but at first the policeman hardly seemed to notice me. He battered the woman with a torrent of noisy Afrikaans. She clutched the dog and looked around terrified, first toward the haven of the Location and then at me.

A few minutes of this crumbled my resolve to say nothing; the least I could do was to offer an apologetic explanation. This I did, to the general effect that the whole affair was my fault, not the lady's, and that I was terribly sorry if we had committed some sort of offense.

The only effect of this intervention was to confirm whatever suspicions the policeman may already have had that I was a foreigner, and to turn his attention to me. "That's the trouble with you people," he growled in guttural English. (It wasn't clear to me *what* people.) "Always pampering the natives."

He seemed uncertain how to proceed. Perhaps he was wondering if this were sufficient explanation to a foreigner for his treatment of the woman. "And her mistreating that little animal. They have no human feelings, none at all," he said, meaning the woman. Then, waving his club in her direction and barking in English, he ordered her to turn the dog loose, which she did.

The dog stayed where he was, licking her shoes, and we stood around in awkward silence. . . . I remained speechless, ashamed of my caution and afraid that I might not be able to sustain it.

But I shall not soon forget the terror and hate in the eyes of the African woman as she stood upright and dignified, still balancing her pail and her packages, a civilized human being at the mercy of a barbarian, while a cipher stood silently by. . . .

The incident really ended there, insofar as it ended anywhere. The dog released, the policeman moved toward me, but just as I started to fear the worst he said in confidential, almost paternal tones that I must beware of the criminal Kaffirs—the club began to wave toward the woman again—who otherwise would steal the clothes off my back and ruin my holiday. I tried to smile (this seemed to confirm that I was indeed a stranger on holiday), mumbled something polite, apologized to the lady for having delayed her, and left as calmly as I could. The club was still waving and the policeman was again shouting as I passed beyond earshot.

I relived the whole affair many times afterward—the shame at my cowardice, the concern about the ultimate fate of my partner in crime and a fleeting satisfaction that I had at least managed to communicate an apology to her in leaving, the curiosity about whether I would have behaved better if I had not been laden with incriminating matter; above all, the sickness of humiliation and impotence lingering in the stomach.

These are not things to forget, not even if you are white and hence not a direct victim of such things personally, not even when the perpetrators of such things spread hospitality and kindness around you like some pleasant-smelling salve applied to the wrong wounds. . . .

There are places where time soothes—where the passing of time is in fact the only real hope for peace. But this is not so in South Africa, where the African has less voice than he had a century ago and where the white man has less inclination to listen to what the African wants to say.

In South Africa time is now an abrasive, a countdown, a dead end. However her problems may finally be resolved, South Africa will need generations for soothing and healing; but before this process can start, time must become the ally of goodwill and rational behavior. There are no quick solutions for South Africa. There are only things that might make slow solutions possible.

The General Assembly of the United Nations has now formally called on its member nations—by a vote of 97 to 2 with 1 abstention—to take "separate and collective action" to bring about the abandonment of South Africa's race policies. It should be clear that such action cannot come too soon.

But it is odd how great the gap between words and deeds seems to be when it comes to acting on the basis of one's own prognoses. Or perhaps the gap is between the saying of something and the believing of it; so that men can issue the direst of predictions and undertake only the most piddling of preventives, as if they did not believe their own prophecies and only wish to be numbered among those who will be able to say "I told you so" if the worst should come to pass. Thus foresight is wasted and unnecessary calamities take place as predicted.

It is a commonplace in South Africa and among those who follow her affairs elsewhere to say that time is running out, to warn against the carnage just ahead, and then to pass on to other matters. In this way even now the urgency is being sapped from the desperate appeals that are reaching the outside world; and farsighted men find their determination to act against South Africa before it is too late diluted by secret hopes that their own predictions will turn out to be wrong.

But if time is running out for South Africa, so is it also running out for America in South Africa. For the machine guns and horsewhips of Sharpeville and Cape Town are no farther from America's jugular than are the jungles of Laos, the firing squads of Havana, or the bridge at Andau.

There was a time not very long ago when the word "America" sang out hope and generosity and compassion, as indeed it still does where the contrast is at hand between American drift and Soviet despotism. But to much of the globe Soviet despotism is still only an American accusation, to be weighed against observed American performance and untested Soviet promises, and against the immediate impact of each on pressing local miseries.

How are men to judge this performance if we go on, in Michael Scott's memorable phrase, "condemning tyranny in one part of the world and condoning it on specious procedural grounds in another"? Or if, in swift succession, we find occasion to lecture Angolans against the use of violence; to oppose U.N. resolutions calling for "consideration" of sanctions (i.e., the only nonviolence that might work) against South Africa; and to organize and underwrite an invasion of Cuba? And if Castro in two years had provoked us sufficiently to warrant an announcement after the invasion that our "patience" is not "inexhaustible," is it unreasonable for many to find a suggestive contrast between this announcement and the fact that several centuries of oppression in southern Africa appear to have fatigued this "patience" hardly at all?

It is tragic, and may yet be tragedy triplicated, that so often this kind of American performance leaves an open field to communist promises. Tragedy first for the people whose agony is extended by our confusion and myopia. Tragedy next for Americans who are inviting a debacle that will not spare them because they were ignorant of its causes and unaware of its dimensions. Tragedy, finally, for the whole human race, including those who turned against us when we left them nowhere else to turn, if our failures enable the Communists to capture the world. For then no men, not those who suffered in southern African nor those who caused the suffering nor any others, will know either peace or freedom.

19

So it may be said that the fate of continents and coalitions, and perhaps of generations, hangs in the balance in southern Africa; and the consciences of great nations sleep now at their own peril.

I have puzzled over it and am not sure I can explain, even to myself, the deep and unsettling affection I have come to have for South Africa. Someone from Mississippi might understand this sort of affection—someone from Mississippi who deplores the social system that produced him but who loves Mississippi for all his disapproval of her habits of life. But then that would be loving one's home, as one so often loves members of one's family whose behavior one does not condone.

Something of my feeling for South Africa surely comes of her natural charms, but I have been to other places with climate and scenery as admirable and have escaped uncaptured. One loves places too for people with whom they have been shared, and what an extraordinary assortment of humanity shares southern Africa. This is the land where the traveler from Umtata to Vryheid passes through Port Shepstone and Amanzimtoti and Pietermaritzburg and Ladysmith on his way, and magic seems to inhabit even the names of the most wayward, lusterless places.

But when all these things have been added together there is yet something more that enchants the whole far beyond the sum of its parts. I suspect that what is unique about this country, what grips the emotions beyond landscapes and breezes and friendships, is the enormity of her misery.

There is much to be said of the grandeur of this wounded, crying place, of her game parks and her history, of such great opportunity buried in such great opulence; and it is right that these things should be said. But there is much that must be said too about the central, overwhelming fact of her present condition, and on balance these are the more important things to say at this time. For this is a place gnashing her teeth and weeping and bleeding and destroying herself as no other place in the world, a place of ordinary men turned heroes and of ordinary men going mad. Nowhere else on earth is the lunacy of man's abuse of himself so grotesquely underlined by visible evidence of what might otherwise be. And this tragic success in perverting so much that is so lovely and so promising into a sleepless nightmare for most of her people commands a compassion, where otherwise might abide simply admiration or envy.

Many are the visitors whom South Africa has afflicted in this same, strange way. But these are usually not the visitors who skim her surface and praise her business climate and her rose gardens. For the more you love this land, the more you understand and are held by her, the more you know how harmful is this kind of praise; and those who love her best know all the worst about her, and will speak out not to praise but to protest and to sound alarms. And those who hold the power in this place, who love not South Africa but some mad dream that never was and can never be, will brand them traitors and enemies for sounding such alarms, and jail or deport or ban them. Indeed one wonders what there will be to say in time to come for these people who, when all power was theirs, used it to degrade and torment, and could find not wisdom nor love to soften arrogance.

There is so much of South Africa that I have never seen and that I yearn to see. I have been there only by winter, and then too often in haste or flight. I have missed the sea from the top of Table Mountain, and Pretoria banked in jacarandas for the spring, and the Garden Route in flower. But most of all I have missed seeing this crisp and bountiful child of Nature blessed with the concord that can be the order of human existence where so much is available to all if no one takes what should belong to others.

That is the greatest beauty of all, and that no one has yet seen in South Africa. But those who love her most will work and fight and pray that somehow this will come to pass while they are still around to glory in the wonder of it.

MISSISSIPPI: A FOREIGN COUNTRY IN OUR MIDST?

Address, Stanford University,

October 2, 1963

The telephone call came in midsummer, 1963, while Lowenstein was in North Carolina. At the time, he was at the vortex of the drive to integrate the city of Raleigh, where he was teaching at North Carolina State.

The caller told Lowenstein that lawyers were desperately needed in Mississippi, where civil rights workers were subject to every kind of harassment with little or no legal check. With the campaign in North Carolina substantially won, Lowenstein left for Mississippi.

For several years, the Student Nonviolent Coordinating Committee (SNCC), the Congress of Racial Equality (CORE), the National Association for the Advancement of Colored People (NAACP), and other groups had mounted in that state an unheralded struggle against police terror and rigidly entrenched opposition. These groups were loosely linked in a statewide Conference of Federated Organizations (COFO). Since 1960, Robert Moses, a legendary black organizer from New York, had worked unremittingly across Mississippi for the civil rights cause. Other figures had included David Dennis of CORE, Dr. Aaron Henry of the NAACP, Fannie Lou Hamer and the Reverend Edwin King. In June

Mississippi: A Foreign Country in Our Midst?

1963, NAACP leader Medgar Evers had been murdered, and his brother, Charles, took up a key civil rights role.

Lowenstein arrived in Mississippi on July 4. He was shaken by the extent and ferocity of state-sanctioned oppression of black citizens. One of his first stops was a SNCC rally in Greenwood.

"I had never seen anything like it in the United States," he later recalled. "That day was ineffable: you can't put into words what it was all about. People trying to sing freedom songs and trying to eat food in pleasant places were in danger of being arrested, beaten, and killed."

Soon after he arrived, Lowenstein began working with local leaders to create new and more effective tactics.

"It occurred to me that whenever there was an election in South Africa, the Africans would hold a national day of mourning," Lowenstein later said. "It struck me that in Mississippi the law was that Negroes could vote so why should you have a day of mourning? You should have a day of voting."

As discussions with Moses, Evers, and others proceeded, they focused on the coming gubernatorial elections, from which nearly all blacks would be excluded. Gradually, the idea of a Mississippi Freedom Vote to dramatize black disenfranchisement and focus a national spotlight on the state took shape.

COFO leaders approved the idea and concluded that outside student assistance would add valuable manpower and national publicity to the Freedom Vote campaign. Lowenstein was asked to recruit volunteers. As part of that effort, he made this speech at Stanford University.

I have a feeling when I come back to Stanford which is always overwhelming. It's a privilege to be back at Stanford, and I feel that as long as I live there will always be a part of me that will feel at home here.

One reason I love to come back is I always get the most fascinating tales about myself, even more fascinating than the ones in Mississippi. In Mississippi, I'm just sort of a Communist agitator who comes in and has to be gotten rid of. But here it's always more sophisticated.

So far since I've been back, I've discovered that I'm banned from coast to coast from thirty campuses, at least two of which have offered me jobs, and I thought I'd better phone and tell them that. [Laughter]

But I think my favorite rumor of the day, which I'm told is the imaginative contribution of one of my greatest admirers in the political sci-

23

ence department, is that my present ambition is to become the first Jewish President of the United States. [Laughter] I want to deny the charge simply because of what Harry Golden said in connection with the present campaign, which I agree with, and that is that I've always known that the first Jewish President of the United States would be an Episcopalian. [Laughter]

The topic listed tonight is "Mississippi: A Foreign Country in Our Midst?"

I hasten to say that I've never before heard the suggestion that Mississippi is a foreign country in our midst. The nearest I've seen was the *Chronicle* editorial some time ago which said that Mississippi should be proclaimed a National Wilderness Area. It said, "Warned by the near extinction of the whooping crane, should we not safeguard the remaining specimens of the whooping Southern Governor?" [Laughter]

I don't think that Mississippi is a foreign country in our midst—and I think one reason it's important to talk about Mississippi is it is very much *ourselves* in our midst. Mississippi is a place where America is at its worst, but it is also a place where anyone who is an American can see himself at his worst.

Try it on yourselves: How many of you, even when you sympathize with the civil rights movement, have thought to yourselves, "Well, of course, it's impossible to give the Negroes the vote in the Delta because, after all, they outnumber the whites"?

How many of you haven't said to yourselves, "Obviously, it's really asking too much to expect the white people in the Delta to allow the Negroes to vote overnight because, after all, they might elect Negro mayors, they might even elect Negro sheriffs"?

How many of us haven't in our own hearts accepted the implications in the fact that because Mississippi is 42 percent Negro—and parts of it 70 percent Negro—that therefore Mississippi does have special problems which excuse the white behavior, not because we like brutality or because we agree with white supremacy, but because, after all, we have to expect that the white race is always really going to rule things? I think most of us are guilty of this kind of thinking.

I think Mississippi is a sick place; it's so sick that to go to Mississippi is to leave America in the way that we think of America and to see America in a grotesque mirror in which all our warts are magnified. But they are our warts. It is us. It is our racial sickness, not some foreign breed, although you do feel occasionally surprised when you go into a store and

24

discover that you don't have to change currency to buy something.

But you do feel as you stay in Mississippi more and more that this could be anybody, that this group of students at Ole Miss, whose behavior astonished the conscience of the country, is the students at most places, given the kind of atmosphere in which they live, the kind of training they've been raised on, and the kind of fear that all of us as white people are subject to when we're raised in a culture in which inherent is the notion that somehow we are superior.

I've thought very hard about what is the most useful thing I could do in, say, half an hour, to tell about Mississippi, and what I did was to jot down little episodes. I've brought with me a number of documents that I had thought at one point I'd read you about the socioeconomic situation in Mississippi, but I think that's gilding the lily at Stanford.

I don't think anybody here needs to be reminded that the Negro income in Mississippi averages about 35 percent of the white, or that the Negro illiteracy rate in some parts of Mississippi, because their schools are simply unable to teach reading and writing and the people are unable to afford going even to free schools—when they exist—still runs as high as four out of five adults.

These things are blots on our escutcheon that are statistical and that we know about and we hear over and over again. And I felt that the most useful contribution a person can make who has been in Mississippi to people who have not been in Mississippi, perhaps, is to go into the specifics of what is now going on and hope that out of this will come more than a statistic, will come in your hearts a feeling that you are involved in Mississippi, not only for the residual reasons of world prestige and not only because your conscience bothers you to know that there's injustice, but because this is the most egregious part of America, the most egregious travesty of the things we say we believe in, and because you are of the most privileged part of America and are the most privileged products of the greatness of our society, and that therefore you have particular involvement in the situation, and that perhaps in telling personal things about it, it will evoke from you a wish to be involved in any way that you can.

My involvement in Mississippi, let me say, is minor, because I can leave. I can go over the border into Louisiana and go back into a society in which the state police, the state government are moderated by the presence of New Orleans, by the existence of a tradition of discussion across racial barriers.

But, in Mississippi, and this is the point of departure in any discussion of that state, progress does not come in any visible way to the people living in it, because the sense that resistance is going to be successful dominates the white community, and those who don't agree are intimidated into shutting up or leaving.

The Episcopal bishop of Mississippi, in his home in Jackson, soon after he'd had a stroke, having said that he deplored the violence in Oxford or some other radical pronouncement, was beaten up. Officially, he was beaten up by people who were deranged. I think this is probably accurate. The trouble is that if that is what being deranged is, then a substantial percentage of the white population in Mississippi is in a stage right now that borders on derangement.

When Mr. Beckwith shot Medgar Evers there was a revulsion against the assassination, I'm told, even in the white community.

But by the time I got to Mississippi four weeks later, the citizens of Leflore County in one day had collected $1,500 in a fund for Mr. Beckwith. And this does not indicate to me a continuing guilty conscience over the assassination of Medgar Evers by someone whom he had never met.

Now, Medgar Evers was assassinated. But Medgar Evers's assassination was not an exception, and it's for that reason that his assassination, I think, needs to be understood.

In Mississippi this summer, during three weeks that I was there, there were four Negroes killed—three of them by officers of the law. In one instance, in a town called Tchula, a voter drive was being conducted for Holmes County. In Mississippi the law requires that anybody who goes down to try to register has his name published in the public press for two weeks prior to his registration being consummated. Thus, any Negro who goes down to register is immediately known about.

And in Tchula, of the twelve Negroes who tried to register to vote, one of them was a man called Turnbow, who was a tenant farmer in his sixties, a quiet, gentle person. He'd never marched or done anything very militant. He just simply went down to register. And the next day his home was bombed and his house shot into, his plot of land disrupted, the work he'd put into painting his stairs and his lifetime of effort to have a little better place to live than most tenant farmers in Mississippi destroyed.

But what was extraordinary again was not that Mr. Turnbow's home was bombed, but that the following day the sheriff of Holmes County arrested Mr. Turnbow. And he was taken to the county courthouse along with four people who were in his house when the sheriff came. The four people were photographing the destruction and they were accused of impeding an investigation.

And when the local newspaper in Lexington, the nearest town with a newspaper, published the news—"Negro Home Hit With Firebomb; Three White Men Fire Shots," and so forth—I might say that this newspaper is published by the only person in the state of Mississippi who publishes this sort of information, an extraordinary woman named Hazel Brannon Smith, who is now being sued for libel for $100,000, who has now lost all of her advertising, and therefore probably will not be publishing her newspaper even within the month.

But the gentleman arrested in Tchula, Mississippi, along with the people found photographing his house after the bombing, is again important for the same reason that Medgar Evers is—that it is not an exception, that in town after town in Mississippi when someone attempts to register to vote, the most fundamental of the rights that we start out with in all other parts of the United States, their homes are not safe.

In Jackson, during the time that I was there this summer, the number of people arrested, or beaten and then arrested, or arrested and then beaten, exceeded 1,200. One day in Jackson, as the voter drive was picking up steam and Negroes were going down in numbers to register to vote, they closed the registration books, suddenly, despite the Constitution of Mississippi, which provides that they shall always be open. The books were simply closed until such time as the intimidation began to take its effect.

Negroes who were fired from their jobs for trying to register to vote are countless in Mississippi. Negroes whose children have been picked up (in Jackson usually the time is close to midnight, in the traditions of a police state) and taken off to what's euphemistically called the "State Fairgrounds Motel" runs into the hundreds. So that the parent knows that he may be struck at through his job, through his home, through his children, and that in the end the likelihood of his being successfully registered is remote anyway because the way in which registration is conducted in Mississippi makes it almost impossible for anybody to register whom the registrar does not wish to have registered.

This is the Mississippi State Constitution, on which the quiz is given. The Constitution runs two pages back to back, single spaced, for thirty-four pages. Naturally, the state of Mississippi doesn't provide you with

27

the Constitution. This is the work of the civil rights movement in Jackson, mimeographing these, so that people who will do so can spend the time attempting to go through the Constitution, article by article, absorb enough of it to give the Negro, or potential registrant who is willing to risk the retribution to himself, or his family, enough information so that he has some chance of answering questions when he's asked them when he tries to register. In Ruleville, Mississippi, Negroes who tried to register discovered suddenly that the water had been cut off not only from some of their homes, but also from the church in which they had met to plan the effort to register. There isn't any protection against this sort of thing in Mississippi because the state courts are all controlled by the same people who are doing the arresting.

And it is no secret, I think, that the way Mississippi juries behave is an extraordinary indication of the fallibility of the Anglo-Saxon system of justice.

I sat in a trial in Oxford where witness after witness testified about the fact that the man being tried threw Molotov cocktails at the U.S. marshals during the Meredith episode. There wasn't even any contradictory evidence that I could hear, except that the man himself denied that he threw the cocktails. But he was never put on the witness stand because they didn't want him cross-examined—and because they didn't need to put him on the witness stand. They knew their jury and he was acquitted. If a man can be acquitted after witness after witness has testified to seeing him throw Molotov cocktails at U.S. marshals, you don't have to worry about what's going to happen to you even if you are arrested in Mississippi for violating someone else's rights.

And the federal courts in Mississippi aren't any better—at least not much better—because one of the two judges that one has to deal with, Judge Cox, was Senator James Eastland's law partner and was appointed district court judge because it was necessary at the time—or so the attorney general thought—to appoint somebody that was acceptable to Eastland in order to get other judges in the rest of the country cleared through the Judiciary Committee, of which Eastland was chairman.

Right or wrong, Judge Cox now sits in Jackson. And if you want to know what that means, I think you might want to hear about the extraordinary case which occurred not very long ago in Rankin County.

A Negro got registered and went back with two others to try to register them. And when they got to the office of the sheriff, where the registration was to occur, they were manhandled and ultimately physically

28

evicted from the place of registration, with sufficient injury so that it was necessary for them to receive extensive medical treatment.

This matter was taken into federal court because it is a violation of the federal law to beat people up who are trying to register. And in the federal court, the deputy sheriff of Rankin County performed the astonishing feat of denying under oath that he'd been present when the beatings occurred. Well, sufficient evidence was brought in, witness after witness, to show that the deputy sheriff had indeed been present and that he had indeed participated in the beatings.

And Judge Cox, having heard all the evidence—a federal district court judge—not only dismissed the suit against the sheriff and the deputy sheriff on the grounds that there was no proof that the beatings were connected with their effort to register—although nobody ever adduced any evidence that they were connected to anything else—but he also dismissed the perjury of the deputy sheriff on grounds that, after all, the evidence had been improperly received in the courtroom and therefore it was improper to consider whether perjury had been committed in improperly produced evidence.

Now if this doesn't invite the sheriffs and deputy sheriffs of any county to do what they can in a federal court, I don't know what it does do. And if this isn't impeachable proceedings on the part of the judge, I don't know what is. But he is the federal judge.

And so to get justice in Mississippi you have to go not to state court, not to a jury, but you have to go to the federal court in New Orleans. And to do that normally requires at least, even in an emergency situation, four to eight months.

In Clarksdale, Mississippi, as well as in other towns, there is an injunction in effect today that's so sweeping that it almost makes it illegal to breathe if you happen to be a Negro. The injunction makes it very plain that anybody who does anything, advocates a boycott, pickets, advocates any kind of demonstration, takes part in any public manifestation of displeasure with the current social situation, or conspires to do any of these things—meaning discusses this with anybody—is violating an injunction served by the court of Coahoma County.

And if you violate this injunction, what happens to you? You're hauled off and arrested. And then what's your recourse? Your recourse is to the federal court: you have to get through Judge Cox first, who takes these appeals under advisement and they're never heard from again. So then you've got to get them out from him to the federal court in New Orleans.

And it may be six months, it may be eight, before you're out of jail again for having gone downtown in Coahoma County and violated an illegal injunction which tramples on the most fundamental safeguards of the American people.

So that you have a situation in which not only is the registration to vote, the most minimal kind of political right, dependent on the courage of people to take unbelievable risks with their lives, their jobs, their families, though in the end they probably won't get registered anyway, but also any other forms of protests are almost equally foreclosed.

Picketing is foreclosed by the fact that you end up almost inevitably spending a lengthy period of time in jail. Do you know how much bond money is now up in Jackson for people who have been arrested for things as shocking as carrying the American flag on Flag Day? They arrested fifty-seven people for carrying the American flag on Flag Day, and to get them out of jail the NAACP had to put up bond money, not just for the fifty-seven but for all those arrested in Jackson so far, $450,000, with nothing to show for it except that these people are not now rotting in jail waiting for their cases to be tried. And when they're convicted, there'll be the expense of appeal until finally they get to the circuit court in New Orleans where eventually all these convictions will be reversed.

But in the meantime, harassment, the financial debilitation, are something which you can't believe until you try to figure out what to do about it. What do you try to do about it? What is there to do?

In Jackson, the other day, kids got impatient. Nothing had happened in Jackson for a long time since Medgar was shot and the books were closed on registration. So they tried a mass demonstration. They came out of a Negro church and started parading downtown. Now in Jackson, the Negro headquarters are on Lynch Street [laughter], which merges with Terry Road, which goes into the white business community. At the place where they merge, when the kids got there, they found the police. But they weren't standing there with dogs or hoses; there wasn't anything like that.

There were rifles. And the rifles were pointed at the kids. And the police lieutenant said, "Another step and we shoot." And if you want to know what Mississippi can mean to people, you should have heard the kids standing there yelling, "Shoot us. Shoot us," until the older Negroes turned them back around. So they don't march in the streets of Jackson anymore.

One day in Clarksdale—I think my most valuable contribution to civil

30

rights occurred this particular day in Clarksdale—I appeared in this suit, which is black, and is not my normal attire, as some of you may recall. I had with me a briefcase. I'd been called to come quickly the day after this injunction was served.

I got there wearing my black suit—it was a very hot day—and I had on dark sunglasses, and we were standing on the steps of the church where Martin Luther King was supposed to appear to make a speech. And with this briefcase and the sunglasses and the black suit I was visible.

I'm not given to melodrama in these things—after South Africa and whatnot, you expect that something may go wrong somewhere—but that day I had said to someone, who was in Oxford, that if I didn't get back that night it would be good if he would be so kind as to telephone to find out if I were in jail or a hospital and, whichever it was, to find out whether I could be brought someplace else. [Laughter]

So I drove into Clarksdale with melodramatic premonitions that I might not get out that night, the last white person who had gone to Clarksdale in such a situation not having gotten out for three weeks. I went up to the church steps and there I was, standing in this attire in the hot sun, with the police driving around in their helmets and Confederate flags and whatnot.

And I was really astonished to discover that as the day wore on and the heat got worse, they got more and more polite. And this whole thing mystified me until finally a photographer came over to me and said, "Is it true that you're in the FBI?" [Laughter]

The local gendarmes had told him this. They had said, "Those goddamn feds've even got an FBI agent standing up there with all them niggers." [Laughter]

Well, there were 300 people besides me and none of them looked like they were in the FBI, so I suppose that this was my most useful contribution to civil rights, because it kept anybody from being beaten up that day. Not even the Negroes were mistreated, let alone the whites. And we got through that day.

But the next day, I was standing just inside the church and there was a woman—I later found out she was eighty-four—looking out while people were being hauled off in paddy wagons.

And I heard this old woman saying—I don't guess that I can ever re-create it right, but I'll do the best I can—"What did we did, what did we did that made 'em hate us so?"

And she was talking to herself. Then she said, "I gave them my two

31

boys; one of them they took off into a war and killed, and now I can't even go on the streets of my own city."

And I reached over and just took her hand and she, I think for the first time, saw there was a white person present. And she broke up, and I did. And we went in and sat down in the church.

And then she told—one wishes one could have the gift of poetry that comes naturally to some people—the story of her life in Clarksdale. And I suppose if there's anything that's permanently with me from Mississippi it was this woman, who had been cleaning white people's houses through the rear doors for all these years, whose children, one of them now dead, had been good enough for her country to take, but who was unable to walk in the streets of her own town, saying, "What did we did that made 'em hate us so?"

She had been, incidentally, arrested and was not bailed out.

In Clarksdale, they started the policy of "jail without bail." The idea behind "jail without bail" is that it will hit the conscience of the white community in due course. And if enough people are arrested ultimately it will hit the pocketbook—as Martin Luther King once remarked, "The only book Americans can read is the pocketbook."

In Clarksdale, they tried this until it was discovered that everybody who was arrested was put into the same cell. Now the consequences were that in a cell designed for six or eight people they ended up with sixty people. And with the Mississippi heat and the prison ventilation and sanitation facilities, it produced very close to an epidemic among the prisons. Finally, they sent out an urgent message with the first one who got out: "For Heaven's sake, stop flooding the jails, because you're only flooding one cell." It is, of course, a very effective way to prevent an appeal to the conscience, even assuming that there remains a conscience in the white community to appeal to. And I'm not too sure, in Mississippi, that that conscience can be appealed to.

It's important to understand that while there are marvelous white people standing up against this, the atmosphere is so totally hysterical, the newspapers are so unbelievably unreal in what they report, that the atmosphere is "We can win if we hold out." There's no sense in Mississippi that integration is coming and let's gradually accommodate to it.

There is a sense that there's a sinister Communist plot, headed by the Kennedys, who are the most nefarious influence in history. The President of the United States is considered to be an indisputable agent of the

Communist conspiracy. In fact, not only of the Communist conspiracy, but simultaneously an agent of the Pope. [Laughter] It's great if you get all of your evils in one bag. The weekly newspaper in Oxford, home of the University of Mississippi, had a column which seriously discussed whether the President would next send in troops to close down Protestant churches after he'd closed down white schools in Mississippi.

Now, the thing about all of this is that when you understand an atmosphere in which this is the milieu of opinion-forming, in which everybody thinks that if you just hold out long enough all these terrible things are going to stop happening, and the President, next time around, won't be a Communist, and we'll have the troops withdrawn and this will all go away, then you begin to understand, I think, why what's being done in Mississippi today is so unique.

We've had troubles in Raleigh, North Carolina, we've had troubles all over the South, we've had troubles all over the North. But it is in a different context, a context where there is still the rule of law. Even in Gadsden, Alabama, which is a nightmare, and Selma, Alabama, where hundreds are arrested and where cattle-prodders are used on the bare feet of people who have been running over glass and where other attractive instruments of police action recur, there is still the sense of victory coming, there is still the sense of progress and change. And it is in this sense that Mississippi appeals particularly to our consciences today.

When you list all the possible ways of trying to break through this nightmare in Mississippi, when you consider the fact that you cannot picket, that even boycotts produce tremendous retribution and are conducted with tremendous difficulty, that you can't vote, that you can't mass-demonstrate, that there isn't any way you have of expressing protest, it leads to the necessity of figuring out something else that can be done. And we've come up with two ideas, however tentatively.

One is this mock vote. The idea of the mock vote is that since Negroes cannot vote in Mississippi, the elections are not valid, because 42 percent of the population is disenfranchised. And so in the mock election, held at the same time as these alleged elections, there will be an opportunity to demonstrate the intensity of desire of the population, of the people of Mississippi who are disenfranchised, to have the right that all Americans are supposed to have.

Now, this has several virtues. The ones of demonstrating that Eastland isn't Mississippi and so forth are important. But it also has the value of giving the Negro protest movement some form of unity and some way to stick together on something that there is almost nothing that can be done to stop.

Presumably, some white sheriff, in keeping with the patterns in Mississippi, will break into a Negro church during the voting and arrest somebody. And someone else will probably shoot somebody, or whatever strikes his whim at the moment. And these are the risk that any movement in Mississippi faces.

But these are minimal risks compared to the risks involved in walking down Lynch Street, to have police rifles pointed at you, or spending six months in Coahoma County jail with no way out because you tried to picket. So the protest vote is an effort to unify and speak up in the only way that seems possible at this moment in Mississippi.

The other project that's still being toyed with is the idea of a mass assistance campaign from outside Mississippi next summer. As Dr. Pitts said the other day in Alabama when the mayor of Birmingham said that they want to settle these things themselves, "You've had several centuries to settle these things without outside help and you've failed. And now we're going to get all the outside help we can."

So next summer in Mississippi we're hoping to be able to arrange sufficient assistance from outside Mississippi so that even if white people in Mississippi want to pretend that they're ultimately going to win, they'll know that they're not; they'll know that ultimately this country will not tolerate Mississippi going on as it has.

I think that the conscience of Mississippi will not be reached until people there begin to get the facts, until they begin to understand that the *New York Times* and *Time* Magazine and *Life* Magazine are not Communist plots, that the Kennedys are not tools of Moscow, that the Pope isn't running around as the chief agent of miscegenation and the Catholic Church hasn't been turned over to sinister forces that are trying to destroy the sacred way of life of Mississippi white people, but that this is the pattern of the world and that they must get back into it. And no more do we want to destroy white people in Mississippi than in South Africa or anyplace else, and that, in a sense, we're trying to help them.

But, whatever happens, it seems to me that it's time that there was a response to Mississippi commensurate with the degree of oppression and bitterness that the people there live under. And so next summer we're hoping to be able to get agreement among the Negro civil rights organizations to have a large number of people from outside Mississippi come in and help and bring enough people into the state so that there will be an awareness among whites that you can't beat up everybody in the United States, and that every time you beat up one person who's committed to the terribly radical thing of getting people to vote, and this is all that our project is aimed at, ten more will come, and that Mississippi is a part of the United States and is on our conscience as Americans, and that whatever our compassion may be for the difficulty of social change, the time has come when people who are fighting against social change have got to accept the fact that they're going to make the social change harder by fighting against it.

So this is what our hopes are in Mississippi. It's not an optimistic forecast of the situation. I couldn't honestly be optimistic now about Mississippi except that I think you know, and I know, that we are going to win in Mississippi, that the feeling that somehow there is no progress is wrong. And that from the perspective of the United States and of the world, this little island of embittered people, shooting and beating and turning to brute force to terrify, are in the backwater of civilization and are going to be lost. Mississippi is not a foreign country in our midst—it's the foreign part of all of us in our midst. And we help ourselves, I think, as we help Mississippi.

Thank you very much.

Lowenstein's efforts drew about 100 students, mostly from Stanford and Yale, to Mississippi during the final two weeks of the Freedom Vote campaign. Aaron Henry and the Reverend Edwin King, a white minister, were nominated to head the ticket and in November they received more than 80,000 votes from disenfranchised blacks.

On election night, Moses said of Lowenstein, "While he wasn't sufficient to bring it off, he was certainly necessary and without him we would never have brought it off the way it came off." Lowenstein told the crowd that the nation's leaders "can't stand up in the UN, they can't send their ambassadors to countries in Africa or Asia . . . and say they stand for the free world against the slave world unless they are prepared to stand for the free world in Mississippi."

After the success of the Freedom Vote, plans to bring in even larger numbers of students for a Freedom Summer in 1964 were made. Efforts were also proceeding to form a Mississippi Freedom Democratic Party to challenge the segregationist regular party at the Democratic National Convention the following year.

In August 1964, the convention met in Atlantic City. The MFDP pressed its case before the party's credentials committee and a national television audience. Eventually, an offer was made by the Johnson Administration to seat the white party delegates provided they supported the party's ticket and also to seat two members of the MFDP. A rule would also be adopted barring the seating of any future delegation selected through discriminatory practices.

The white delegation rejected the offer and walked out of the convention. The civil rights movement was badly split over how to react to the offer. In the end, the MFDP rejected it. Lowenstein had felt the seating offer was inadequate, but he also believed that the bitter arguments it triggered threatened to obscure the broader accomplishments of the Mississippi movement. The disputes and tensions that surfaced in Atlantic City were to divide the civil rights movement for years to come.

CANDIDATE

Jacob Brackman

The New Yorker, March 12, 1966

The New York Democratic Party reform movement was founded in the 1950s by party dissidents, including Eleanor Roosevelt and Herbert Lehman. From its earliest days, Lowenstein was involved in the movement's effort to topple the old-line, patronage-laden Tammany Hall machine. These activities continued through the sixties.

In 1965, after playing a key role in the unsuccessful mayoral bid of his old friend reform Democrat William Fitts Ryan, Lowenstein was named director of the Encampment for Citizenship, an annual six-week assembly promoting youth activism. He recruited youths who had been involved in such political and social efforts as the civil rights movement and the Berkeley Free Speech movement. Among the guest speakers invited that summer were Paul Goodman, William F. Buckley, Jr., philosophers Paul Weiss and Richard Bernstein, John Lindsay, Abraham Beame, and Robert Moses.

The following year, he became a candidate from Manhattan's West Side in a reform procedure designed to select an opponent for veteran congressman Leonard Farbstein. The three other candidates were also young liberals, who shared similar stands on the issues. Noting the international focus of some of Lowenstein's concerns, one of his reform movement friends jokingly suggested the slogan "Yesterday the World, Today the 19th Congressional District." The following article examined the candidate and his outlook.

One morning this week, we may pick up our breakfast newspaper and read that the New York Reform Democratic Movement has chosen Allard K. Lowenstein as its candidate for Congress from the Nineteenth District, a saxophone-shaped territory that hooks around lower Manhattan and runs up the West Side to Eighty-sixth Street. Then, again, we may not.

Mr. Lowenstein is a thirty-seven-year-old attorney—a rugged-looking man, easy, humorous, and earnest, who can be found in a state of repose only after sensible people have been in bed for hours. By day, he races through appointed rounds of conferences, kaffeeklatsches, and rallies. At night, he takes off his shoes, squats, Indian-style on the floor of a friend's apartment, and explains, in an uncannily lucid manner, what must be done about Rhodesia or Vietnam or Mississippi or Harlem. His friends tell us that he has been pursuing this regime for years, but that they have become less tolerant of his informality now that he may be running for Congress. (A candidate, it seems, must not discuss "the issues" in his stocking feet.) Any way you look at it, Lowenstein is not at all like the usual office seeker, even though for the last three months he has been, in a sense, seeking office, as one of four candidates being considered by the Reform Democrats. The truth of the matter is that he has spent the past twenty years dashing about the globe toiling in the service of Causes: in Spain, helping the organized opposition to Franco; in southwest Africa, investigating conditions, smuggling out anti-apartheid tape recordings, gathering evidence of oppression to present to the United Nations, and writing "Brutal Mandate," a widely admired book about the South African situation; in Mississippi, working for "the movement" before that became modish; in Manhattan, campaigning for William Fitts Ryan in the early days of Reform Democratic insurgency; in Washington, serving as legislative assistant to Senator Frank Graham and, later, as foreign-policy adviser to Senator Hubert Humphrey; at Stanford, teaching international law; at North Carolina State, teaching political science; in Los Angeles, serving as a delegate to the Democratic National Convention; in Atlantic City, counseling the Freedom Democratic Party; and, from Oregon to Massachusetts, helping to found a national group called Americans for Reappraisal of Far Eastern Policy.

By the time we had finished splicing this roster of credentials together, we were beginning to suspect that Lowenstein must have doubles planted in trouble spots around the world, poised for action whenever the need arose. We expressed some wonderment over his activities late the other night, when we happened to catch him alone in his makeshift headquarters on West Eighty-first Street. He laughed. "Very often, young people in our society don't take advantage of the fluidity and freedom they have," he began, untying his shoelaces. "So many people act as if they were in seventeenth-century England, had got themselves apprenticed as carpenters at fourteen, and couldn't change it. Then they go on through some ladder-climbing course. I suppose that's all right if you're psychologically so set up that not leading that kind of life leaves you feeling insecure and unhappy. But I'd say that the wisest accident of my post-college life is that I've never really tried to plan ahead. I've tried to do what seemed useful and interesting as the time came. I know that occasionally people who love me have wished they knew what I was going to do, and thought it would be better for me if I settled into being a lawyer, but when I was supposedly practicing on a full-time basis I got so deeply involved in other things that I wasn't much of a breadwinner at it. You see, the priority of your goals gets complicated if you're trying to build up a law practice and are always being tangentially pulled into struggles you believe in."

We said we imagined that many a young man would choose the foot-loose, heroic manner of existence if it were not for the dreary prospect of starvation.

Lowenstein dismissed any such concern. "Now, I have a very uneducated palate—I eat hamburgers and hot dogs a great deal," he said. "I don't smoke or drink, and my clothes are hardly stylish. So although I've always wished there were greater sums available for the things I care about, and although I've been improvident about saving, I've been able to earn enough by teaching and occasional writing and legal work to get by."

We asked Lowenstein if he ever found himself craving the security of job and family.

He smiled, and scratched one side of his neck. "I came very close to getting married once," he said. "But marriage, of course, can get in the way of your doing the things you are moved to do. It depends on whether you marry a person who shares your feelings of wanting to live a life of some service. I guess that goes back to your question about security. Security is something internal. And for some people to feel right inside they must know they have a lot of money or a job they aren't going to lose. But that's a matter of what they've learned to want. I couldn't separate my life into a career part and a private part, the way many men do. I feel curious about ways of living I haven't seen and kinds of experience I haven't had. We live a very short time. Aren't we foolish to restrict ourselves arbitrarily even more than time itself restricts us?"

We inquired whether Lowenstein recommended a career of global gallivanting.

He appeared nonplussed at the very thought. "If you simply wish to enrich and deepen what you understand and what you've done, without real involvement, you risk becoming a dilettante and a tamperer," he said. "What life is all about is how you spend the day, and each day becomes part of this totality of involvement. So you build, as you go along, a life in which you may do many different kinds of things, in different situations, with different kinds of people. But it all has a common denominator that gives it some sense, some direction—the sense that your total activity is going to make a better situation for people to live in."

We knew that for years friends of Lowenstein's had been asking him "Why don't you run for Congress?" in precisely the tone of exasperated benevolence in which they had been asking him "Why don't you get married?" or "Why don't you stick to one job?" Now we asked him why he had waited so long to seek public office.

"Isn't the notion that you have to achieve some titular power to have influence and help bring about social change pretty dubious?" he replied. "You know, I don't suppose there are many people who have had as great an impact on as many other people as Norman Thomas has in this country. Because here's a man who clearly never had the remotest possibility of holding office once he'd chosen the path he chose—the path of saying what he felt was right and sticking by it. One can disagree with his position on specific issues—in fact, anyone who doesn't disagree with Norman Thomas on something must not be thinking. But his whole life has been dedicated to the idea that there is value in humanity. He's been willing to sacrifice his own power to worthwhile principles, to lost individuals. That kind of life lights up the sky, and there are dozens and dozens of state senators and United States senators who have never achieved anything like it. One of the great calamities in American politics is that politicians so often don't say what they think, because they believe that people wouldn't sustain them if they did. There's always a kind of blind-man's buff going on, with political leaders not providing leadership for fear of the consequences, and the electorate not being able to express itself because the leaders aren't giving it a voice. Something terribly important to democracy is lost here. You have to realize you're going to run on the things that matter most, you're going to try to make as honest a stand as you can and as effective a campaign as you can, but if you don't win the office, that's not the only thing that matters."

We asked Lowenstein if he could define exactly where he stands politically.

"I think of myself as a liberal," he replied. "That's a vague word. It doesn't define how you stand on a specific issue, because one aspect of being a liberal is that you're not told by any one line how to stand on issues. You find your own truths, if you can. But I think liberalism in the United States must face some of the failings and shortcomings of its shibboleths."

We asked Lowenstein if he was thinking of his early involvement with civil rights.

He smiled, and admitted he was. "We had a very basic notion back in those days that the processes of democracy this country had already evolved would solve external injustices," he said. "Those processes were the ballot and the courts, and that was it. You educated public opinion, you voted, you went to court when you were being denied basic rights, and so forth. Well, those things *weren't* removing injustice, and probably would never have done so. And so what happened was that there began a breaking down of proper procedures by people determined to get what the Constitution said was theirs. The restaurant sit-ins began it. But they didn't do the job, so we ended up marching. If someone had told me five years or eight years beforehand that I would ever march in a column of a thousand people—as I did in a march against segregation in Raleigh—I would have thought he was quite mad, because it would not have occurred to me that this would be either proper or necessary. But it was necessary and it was proper. Then, when even demonstrations didn't produce the needed results, we had to go further. In Mississippi, for instance, you couldn't picket, you couldn't march, you couldn't vote— you couldn't do any of these things. Proper procedures were so thoroughly blocked off that if you waited for them to work, you'd wait a millennium. We had to conceive of a whole *new* series of tactics. We came up, in Mississippi, with the idea of the first 'Freedom Vote.' And, again, if someone had said a few years before that there would come a time when we would organize a supplementary election outside the established local voting system, I would have thought he was mad. Yet it was necessary in Mississippi. And even our Freedom Vote wasn't enough, because the reign of terror was so great that our workers couldn't walk on the streets. We had to let people know what was happening to us. There was no press coverage, no way we could get out of the morass. It was almost like being absorbed by quicksand, with nobody even knowing about it. You could be beaten and arrested, they could do what they wanted with you, and there was nowhere to turn. Every American who hasn't experienced that might be wiser if he had. It gives you some idea of what freedom is all about, to go through a situation where you're completely at the mercy of brutality—where there's no appeal. That was Mississippi in 1963. The real radicals always said that the country didn't care, that the country was basically indifferent to the oppression of Negroes, but I always felt that if we could let people know what was going on, they wouldn't stand for it. 'Well,' we said, 'all right, bring people into Mississippi.' And so there began this sort of series of new procedures that are finally starting to make the old procedures work, even in Mississippi—where more Negroes have been registered to vote in one year than were registered in the previous century. Rednecks who'd worn buttons reading 'Never!' are now saying that we've got to accept the change. Very soon you'll have congressmen from the South who will be more liberal than congressmen from New York. Because they'll be an accurate reflection of the needs of that area."

"Then the old liberalism still works after all?" we asked.

Lowenstein sat silent for a moment, running one hand back and forth over his hair, which he wears close-cropped. "I'm not sure it's that simple," he said, at last. "When I was in college, I think we all felt that if we could produce a society in which we'd removed the scourges of war and dictatorship and racism and poverty, we'd have a happy society. That was the liberal creed. Yet it's a fact that now, for the vast majority of our people, we've removed many of the external forms of misery, we've attained our goals, and there's still the hollowness. Our personal lives, in many cases, have been successful without being fulfilled or happy, the way we thought they would be. We live in a society today that may be even more fundamentally unhappy than the old one. We have to figure out what's missing at the center of the person now."

"You mean you're becoming a Hobbesian?" we asked.

"Earlier generations had to overcome the Depression or win a war,"

42

Lowenstein replied. "My generation had none of that. We came out of college with everything green before us, and we used to think that by this time our problems would really have evaporated. There's a sense of internal loss now, and it cannot be blamed on democracy, because democracy has given us opportunities and freedom and great material wealth. People in my generation have developed a fatigue, a sort of premature old age, that's exceedingly difficult to combat. Many of them perhaps feel now that they can live only for their children, because maybe their children will find some other way to solve problems. We've discovered that time goes awfully fast and that what was once going to be forever is now half gone, and a little bit empty. So we go on living in some fraternity memory or some football-weekend memory when things seemed very much more roseate. Why haven't things turned out the way we'd hoped they would, now that we've got the house and we've got the car and we've got air-conditioning when it's hot and heating when it's cold? We've got all the opportunities that freedom can give, but, still, what good is it all accomplishing? It's in this kind of poignant struggle for meaning that I think disappointment has come, because nobody ever before in history, as far as I know, has had a generation in which all the external things were there and in which the internal lack had to be so clearly an internal lack. That's why I feel so relatively lucky in not having expected to find that material or political or titular goals represented the end of a quest. You don't just set goals and, when you reach them, find that they equal happiness. I understand that these struggles will go on as long as I live, that within the quest itself much of the fullness of life exists."

Lowenstein narrowly lost the reform designation, and the winner, Councilman Theodore Weiss, lost a disputed election. (Ten years later, Weiss was elected to Congress from the same district.) Meanwhile, Lowenstein backed a major New York anti-Vietnam war demonstration in April and remained active in local and national causes.

VIETNAM—IN OR OUT?

Address, University of North Carolina, May 17, 1966

Though a supporter of Lyndon Johnson in 1964, Lowenstein had reservations about the President's public record; he had, in fact, opposed Johnson's nomination as vice-president in 1960. U.S. intervention in the Dominican Republic in 1965 further reduced his confidence in the Administration's foreign policy.

As Johnson stepped up American involvement in Vietnam, and as casualties grew, Lowenstein devoted a growing amount of time to organizing opposition to the war, and to U.S. policy toward China as well. His speeches increasingly harped on the war as a moral and political disaster. In 1965, he helped organize an early antiwar teach-in. Working with the Reverend William Sloane Coffin, Harvard University instructor Barney Frank, and others, he sought to focus national attention on U.S. Far Eastern policy and increase public awareness of where it was leading. With public sentiment on the war inchoate, however, and without major congressional support, the antiwar movement initially generated little political steam.

By 1966, an acid reappraisal of the rationale for Administration policy seemed increasingly necessary. Lowenstein's criticisms of the war had been applauded in Manhattan liberal forums, but he believed the potential for antiwar action extended far beyond New York's West Side reform circles. Mobilizing this sentiment as an effective political force became, increasingly, a paramount goal for him.

Vietnam—In or Out?

In May of that year, he was invited to participate in a panel debate on Vietnam at his alma mater, the University of North Carolina at Chapel Hill. The other participants were George Cabot Lodge, a former government official, Professor Arthur Larson, a critic of the war, and Dr. Henry Kissinger, of Harvard. Part of Lowenstein's remarks follow.

This discussion presents certain dilemmas, because there are wide areas of agreement among all of us on the panel. That perhaps is one of the problems in the American debate on Vietnam, that there is a tendency on all sides, except people who are far removed from the discussion's center, to seek consensus.

I would like to start out by saying that I am in almost total agreement with Mr. Larson's proposals as far as they went. I would add to those two or three additional proposals which seem to me to be essential to carrying out the ones that he has listed.

The first of these is that if we really are serious about seeking a solution in Vietnam that will stick, we must simultaneously pursue a reappraisal of our attitudes toward China. It seems quite clear to me that unless we are able to seek a detente with China on the whole problem of Southeast Asia, and the problem of Taiwan and Chinese membership in the UN, and other areas of exacerbated hostility between us that China is in a position to keep negotiations from ever succeeding in Vietnam. And it has very little reason not to do so, since at the moment China seems to profit a great deal from the fighting going on between ourselves and the Vietnamese.

Second, I think that if we're serious about seeking a way in which to demonstrate our sincerity about negotiating, we must cease the bombing permanently, not as if it's an act of grace but because we are wrong legally, in fact, to be bombing North Vietnam, we're wrong militarily, and a continuation of the bombing indicates to the North Vietnamese at least that all the talk that we make of our desire to arrive at a negotiated settlement is insincere.

The original excuse for the bombing was that it would persuade the other side to come to the conference table. No one even uses that excuse any longer. Our military people concede that will not happen; they now say it's to interdict supplies coming from the North to the South. Interdicting the supplies hasn't occurred in anything like the measure to which we were promised it would and we are now told that we have to continue the bombing as a morale factor for the South Vietnamese.

45

But it's very difficult to know what we now think we are achieving by the bombing except to risk the likelihood of pursuing other planes across the Chinese border, which we now seem to be heading toward, certainly to risk ultimately the bombing of the bases in Thailand from which we are now attacking North Vietnam and risk generally a lateral escalation across the whole of Southeast Asia that would make the entrapment that confronts us now even more difficult to escape from.

Ultimately we have to face the basic question of why we are in South Vietnam with a great deal more honesty and candor than we're doing it.

You can argue that we're there in order to guarantee self-determination for the Vietnamese people or you can argue that we're there to defend America's vital interests and that we can't consider leaving until a non-Communist government is safely installed. Secretary Rusk has said both at times. I don't think you can argue both.

You can argue either that we were right in 1956 not to allow elections because the Communists would win and we couldn't have that happen, or you can argue that we favored free elections then and do now. But you can't argue both, which we try to do.

You can argue that China is the enemy and is conducting a series of wars of national liberation and must be stopped in Vietnam or else we face a kind of accumulation of Munichs or you can argue that China is irrelevant to the whole problem of the war in Vietnam and that we must not confuse an overall review of our attitude toward China with the problem of Vietnam, but you can't argue both.

You can argue that we are only there for the self-determination of the South Vietnamese people and that therefore we can't meddle in what's going on there, or you can argue that our life line is at stake and that we must stay there because it's not clear what the South Vietnamese people want, in which case I don't see how you can say that we can tolerate the present situation degenerating further because we can't meddle. I don't think we can go on arguing simultaneously both sides of the coin of what our presence means to South Vietnam.

I can go on listing the kinds of contradictions in our general rhetoric that I've been listing, but I cite these few only because I think that they illustrate what seems to me to be the saddest consequence of the war in Vietnam in the United States, which is that we have been crying wolf in a situation in which in fact it's very difficult to establish what wolves we think are at the door or why. That doesn't mean I like the Viet Cong. It doesn't mean I like the idea of the Communists, or quasi-Communists,

46

winning control of an area. But it does mean that in asserting that this is another war of national liberation, of the Communists' trying to subvert the free world, we're using rhetoric in a way which can't help, in my judgment, but prejudice and poison the possibility that when wolves really are at the door, when indisputable aggression has in fact occurred, that the American people will not respond to it in the way they need to if we're to stop expansionism when it occurs in other places. But the facts in South Vietnam have not borne out the rhetoric—we've cheapened it.

And what I would suggest to you tonight is that if we think we're there defending democracy—if that part of our rhetoric means anything—then the way to defend democracy begins immediately with the bringing in of vast numbers of observers through the United Nations and other parts of the international agencies—a sort of combination, maybe, of the Mississippi Summer Project with the Honest Ballot Association done on a world scale, where we hold free elections open to *everybody* to participate in South Vietnam.

But if we're there not to defend democracy—if that line is now out, as Dr. Kissinger suggests—if we're in part fighting for ourselves now, then, of course, one has to weigh that also very coldly. Are we helping ourselves in what we are doing in South Vietnam right now? And my contention is that we are immeasurably hurting ourselves with each step in the direction of an escalated war.

What conceivable gain do we have to make up for the incredible loss that we're suffering in terms of people's respect for our pretenses of believing in self-determination and in believing in peace? So I would suggest that we're not stopping Communism, we're helping Communism.

We cannot win a war in South Vietnam—isn't it possible to accept that as fact now? We've had years of the military people and very distinguished civilians going to South Vietnam and coming back and telling us that we're about to win, and I have in front of me the quotations dating back as far as when Lyndon Johnson was vice-president and went in 1961 and then following through. But it doesn't happen. Why doesn't it happen? Because it is a militarily unwinnable war. Can't we understand that?

The only way you can win a war on the mainland of Asia, with China getting more and more upset about what we're doing, is to be prepared for a nuclear war. Do you win a nuclear war? Does anyone really think that that's winning a war? So let's start with the basic fact and not go playing games with rhetoric. The more that we continue to pour people in, the more they pour people in—and they have more people there.

So let's face what the military situation is. We are not going to win. We are going to have more and more people committed there. We are going to have 400,000. We are going to be doubling the bombing strikes. We are going to make ourselves more and more committed to a situation from which we cannot extricate ourselves honorably, and then all of us who feel that the initial commitment was very possibly well intentioned face a much more serious question, which is what justification is there now for what we are doing there?

I've just come back, as the moderator said, from the Dominican Republic. We went into the Dominican Republic because we said that we were protecting American lives. That was when there were about 2,500 Americans. When all but fifty had been pulled out, we sent in another 20,000 Marines. We then explained that we were there to stop the Communists from taking it over. Everybody now knows that that was not going on in the Dominican Republic a year ago. I wish we could discuss that, because we made a tragic blunder in the Dominican Republic. Fortunately, there is some hope that we can reverse course there now. The tragedy of that mistake is being repeated on an irreversible scale now in South Vietnam, where in fact we are creating a situation that we can't get out of without an endless land war in Asia—for what?

The solution in Vietnam must be a political solution, and if that's the case, then the price we pay politically for what we're doing is one of the great considerations in what we should be doing. I would say, unlike Dr. Kissinger, that our greatest problem in the world today is that we are not identified with the forces that are seeking basic social change, and the reasons we're not are episodes like the Dominican Republic and Vietnam. And these forces seeking social change are, in fact, going to cause turbulence in the world in the next decades. We would be much more faithful to our heritage and to our interests were we to align ourselves with these forces everywhere possible, rather than to make ourselves roadblocks as we have too often.

Now in Vietnam, because of the peculiar situation that we've adverted to, that's not easy to do now. But there was never a commitment made by anybody in Vietnam to send in an American army of 400,000 people to Vietnam. President Kennedy was clearly on record against it. President Eisenhower refused to do it at Dienbienphu, when the French asked him to. The commitment in Vietnam was to assist the South Vietnamese in ways that began to be originally technical and economic, then to be military advisers. There's been no vote of the United States

Congress, no resolution of the United Nations General Assembly, there's been no action of SEATO asking this. The commitment is a self-ordained commitment for governments which we, in fact, do manipulate, whether we like to say it or not. We manipulated Diem into power, we manipulated the situation that arose later, and we've manipulated the situation that's led us into this impasse.

Now, I know it's not a simple situation. You can't wave a wand and say "Peace tomorrow." But you can say that the direction of what we are doing is wrong, and that while we're all using rhetoric about how we want to get free elections and a discussion that will lead to some sort of solution, we're not taking the steps that would make that possible when the other side gets around to it.

If free elections are not in fact possible, the people of South Vietnam could not demonstrate more desperately what they feel about the Ky government which we created than they've been doing. And if we're blind enough not to face the facts of what it means when whole provinces defect and when thousands and thousands of people riot and demonstrate in the capital city, which we've inundated with money for years, then we don't understand what language is being spoken by people who, not having free elections, have chosen the only other means at their disposal to indicate their disapproval of their present government.

So I implore people, once and for all, to get past the notion that if we say we're for free elections and they can't be held because there's no tradition of it, or there's terror, that therefore when people demonstrate in other ways their feelings, that we can also ignore that. We do that at our peril, to the peril of our national security. And it's that question that ought to be primary for all Americans now. Figure out a way that we can reverse course before this leads us into a collision that's desperately useless for us and that can mean the end of the whole concept of a peaceful world looking toward a decent life for people in it.

CHALLENGING A PRESIDENT
"Meet the Press," December 3, 1967

Throughout 1966, as the Johnson Administration drifted toward deeper entanglement in Vietnam, paying little attention to the fledgling antiwar movement, Lowenstein busied himself with his usual array of activities, ranging from organizing opposition to U.S. policy in the Dominican Republic to advising Robert Kennedy on the latter's trip to South Africa. It was Lowenstein's first serious contact with Kennedy.

The highlight of the year was his marriage to Jennifer Lyman, whom he had met a year earlier in New York.

By the end of the year, Vietnam was occupying more and more of his time. In the fall, he helped organize 100 student leaders to send a letter of protest to the President. The letter received national attention and helped demonstrate that the student antiwar movement was not limited to an unrepresentative fringe.

"A great many of those faced with the prospect of military duty," the letter said, "find it hard to square performance of that duty with concepts of personal integrity and conscience. Unless this conflict can be eased, the United States will find some of her most loyal and courageous young people choosing to go to jail rather than to bear their country's arms."

The student letter was followed by a series of meetings with Administration officials in which the concerns of the student leaders and other war critics were casually dismissed. Incredulous at the Administration's intransigence and refusal to contemplate a reversal of course, Lowenstein reluctantly concluded that the only way to change the Vietnam policy was to change the president.

"If a president is wrong, but popular, political realities make opposing him difficult, however right," he wrote at the time. "If a president is right, but unpopular, supporting him may be a duty, however difficult. But when a president is both wrong and unpopular, to refuse to oppose him is a moral abdication and a political stupidity."

With that as a guiding philosophy, Lowenstein and Curtis Gans, a recent staff member of Americans for Democratic Action, began organizing the "Dump Johnson" movement. Few took it seriously.

Lowenstein and Gans did not have a candidate, but they reasoned that a standard-bearer would emerge as the drive gained momentum. Over the next few months, they met with several leading antiwar Democrats, informing them that a large and growing army was ready to rally to an antiwar candidate. There were no takers, but the campaign continued to grow.

"By mid-October," Theodore White wrote in The Making of the President—1968, "it was obvious that a nationwide base was there, yet still formless and unnamed, consisting of individuals working as individuals, or groups working as isolated groups, lonesome socially and regionally, needing a capping event, a public climax, to draw national attention and, above all, a candidate."

On October 18, 1967, a national group, the Conference of Concerned Democrats, was formally unveiled, headed by Donald Peterson of Wisconsin, Gerald Hill of California, and Allard Lowenstein of New York. In November, Senator Eugene McCarthy of Minnesota privately informed the CCD leaders that they need search no further for a candidate. On November 30, he announced his candidacy in Washington and shortly thereafter flew to Chicago, where he addressed the national meeting of the CCD. The following day, Lowenstein was questioned about the race on "Meet the Press."

MR LAWRENCE SPIVAK: Mr. Lowenstein, as you know, it has been widely reported that you and your organization of Concerned Democrats tried to get Senator Robert Kennedy to do what Senator McCarthy is now doing. Is it true that you did try to get him to make a stab for the Democratic nomination in '68?

MR. LOWENSTEIN: I think all of us that feel that the present policies are disastrous were looking for a candidate who would challenge President Johnson in the Democratic primaries, and we certainly entertained hopes at one point that Senator Kennedy would do that, but he made clear from the beginning that he wouldn't, and we made clear from the beginning that if he wouldn't, we were determined that we would challenge President Johnson anyway. . . .

MR. SPIVAK: You were recently described as being "a loyal and experienced operative of Senator Robert Kennedy."

What is your answer to those who say that you and Concerned Democrats are using Senator McCarthy as a stalking horse for Senator Robert Kennedy?

MR. LOWENSTEIN: I think it is flattering to be called the loyal and experienced operative, whatever an operative is, and Senator Kennedy wouldn't be a bad person to be loyal and experienced on the behalf of. I think he is one of the great men around, but the fact is, I don't work for Senator Kennedy or for Senator McCarthy. I would like to see all the Democrats in the country who feel discontented with the direction of the party and the country rally behind an alternative who can win, and I think that alternative is Senator McCarthy.

Senator Kennedy hasn't in any way put me up to this or put anyone else up to it. He is very clear; he speaks very well for himself. In fact, I like what he says, but I don't tell him what to say, and he doesn't tell me what to say.

MR. SPIVAK: Regardless of anybody's present intentions, yours and Senator Kennedy's, do you believe that a strong showing in the primaries by Senator McCarthy could lead to the nomination of Senator Kennedy?

MR. LOWENSTEIN: Yes, I think a strong showing by Senator McCarthy will produce an open convention, and I think that could lead to the nomination of a great many people, almost all of whom would represent a distinct improvement over the prospects of the Democratic Party if the incumbent is renominated. Senator Kennedy, like most of us, would, I believe, profit from an open convention, but I don't think that guarantees that Senator Kennedy would emerge as a candidate at all. If Senator McCarthy does as well as he is going to do, I think what will happen is that he will become a major figure on his own with momentum rising in his behalf, and there is no telling at that point what the convention will do.

MR. SPIVAK: The *Washington Post* quoted you as saying this morning that the Conference of Concerned Democrats would make no formal endorsement of Senator McCarthy. Why has there been—I don't know whether they are or are not going to endorse him, but why has there been any hesitation in endorsing him?

MR. LOWENSTEIN: I think the feeling in the Conference, as with any large group of independent-minded people, is influenced by events, and yesterday the general sense of that Conference was that there would be opportunities to decide on specific candidates in each state. Last night, after Senator McCarthy's appearance, his speech and his visit with the Democratic politicians who were gathered there from all the primary states where he plans to enter or is thinking of entering, I think there was a marked change in the feeling of the Conference. There was a sense that Senator McCarthy was fighting to win the nomination and that as practical, Democratic political people, it made no sense for us not to say what we really feel, which is, if he is in it to fight to win it, we are for him. Since he came through clearly yesterday in that vein, I believe the Conference is very likely now to come through clearly in support of that attempt. . . .

MR. ALLAN OTTEN: If you and your organization fail in your efforts in the primaries and at the convention and President Johnson is renominated, are you prepared to pledge your support to him then against the Republicans?

MR. LOWENSTEIN: As Adlai Stevenson once said about a much less difficult prospect, we will jump off that bridge if we come to it.

MR. OTTEN: Can you conceive of your organization becoming active in a third, peace, party?

MR. LOWENSTEIN: Our organization certainly wouldn't because we are Democrats. There might be people in the organization who would support a Republican or support a fourth candidate—or whatever you are if you have three already.

MR. OTTEN: Would you assume that is a fairly large number of the people involved?

MR. LOWENSTEIN: No, I think that most of the people involved have made their commitment to be Democrats and to fight in the Democratic primaries, and since almost all of us are convinced that our efforts are going to be rewarded with an alternative nominee, we don't really speculate very much on what will happen if that does not occur. . . .

MR. SPIVAK: Mr. Lowenstein, Senator McCarthy indicated that he is a regular Democrat and that he won't bolt the Democratic Party if he

53

doesn't win the nomination, that he will support President Johnson if he gets the nomination. Why won't you say so, why are you evasive on that?

MR. LOWENSTEIN: I was asked, I thought, what Democrats supporting McCarthy would do, which is 22 million people.

MR. SPIVAK: What will you do? Will you support President Johnson if he gets the Democratic nomination or will you bolt the party?

MR. LOWENSTEIN: If the President were renominated on his present program and the Republican Party offered a candidate who was giving an alternative to what is happening in the war and at home as a result of the war, I would feel that my obligation as an American was to support that candidate who gave the best hope of reversing what I consider a policy leading the country toward disaster.

May I say at this point that one of the reasons that the press seems mystified as to what is happening, or regarded as unlikely that this sort of effort would develop, was that it does not yet understand in general the depth of feeling among a great many of us that the country which we love very deeply is headed toward a very serious disaster and that under these extraordinary circumstances our obligation is to find ways of reversing that disaster.

If you foreclose the options in politics by saying you can't oppose a sitting President and you can't do this and you can't do that, then the frustration has to spill over into nonpolitical or nonelectoral protests. I don't want that to happen to this country. I don't want to see it torn apart internally with increasing recourse to tactics which are not consistent with democratic tradition, but I can fully understand why, if, as the political people in the media say, you can't reverse the policies through politics, people, in frustration, may turn to other means and have begun to do so.

So what we are trying to do is out of a very deep conviction that this country that we love very deeply and which many of us have served in its armed forces and other places has an obligation to respond to electoral pressures to get back on the road which it was on for so long, a road on which there will be a decent peace achieved and possibility for justice for all Americans.

MR. SPIVAK: You supported President Johnson in 1964. Are you opposed to him now solely because of Vietnam?

MR. LOWENSTEIN: No, I think that our support for him in '64, though, is important to note, because it does illustrate that contrary to the sort of gossip that one hears in the sniper fire from one place or another, we are not opposed to him because of his style or his personality or the fact that he is from Texas. We worked for him in the face of that style and his being from Texas, and all the rest of it, very hard in '64, but he ran in '64 on a platform, and that platform in our view has not been implemented. And he ran against a candidate that we opposed because that candidate said he would do the things which in fact the President has done. So we are consistent now in saying that the very reasons that led us to support him four years ago are the reasons which lead us now to oppose him. . . .

MR. E.W. KENWORTHY: Unless Senator McCarthy later decides also to go into New Hampshire, the first primary he will enter is Wisconsin on April 2nd. How do you propose to keep him before the public eye for the next three months?

MR. LOWENSTEIN: I don't know. He will be in the public eye. I am not sure that is the problem. It may be more difficult to keep the momentum going that is already developing, of people feeling that they have this electoral process to participate in, if there is no primary until April. But his position, his courage, and his attractiveness are going to, I think, make him a major figure in the next few months.

My goodness, he is twice as intelligent as Romney and twice as handsome as Reagan, and they seem to stay in the news all the time without running. I don't see that that is a great problem.

MR. KENWORTHY: Mr. Lowenstein, he can't win in Wisconsin just by taking the Madison District. How do you propose to organize, say, in Wisconsin? How do you propose to bring out this vote?

MR. LOWENSTEIN: Our committee in Wisconsin, the Concerned Democrats, has found that support for Senator McCarthy in Wisconsin is extensive throughout the state. We will have the support of very significant party-structure people all over Wisconsin, and I don't think that Senator McCarthy is going to be limited in his appeal at all to the university communities. And in most communities disaffection from President Johnson is as intense—that is one of the peculiarities. People may disagree with the precise definition of why they don't want Johnson renominated, but he has achieved a rather remarkable consensus in the country that most people don't want him renominated that we find, and I think our job now is to make them see that it is a possibility, despite the sort of strictures you get out of political science books, to defeat for renomination a sitting president. When that reality is made clear, I don't think we are going to do any better in academic communities than elsewhere. . . .

MR. OTTEN: If President Johnson is renominated despite all your efforts, might not the result of your activity merely be to weaken him and help elect a Republican who from your point of view is no different or even worse on the Vietnam war and also opposes many of the domestic welfare programs that you espouse? What will you have accomplished for your beliefs by doing that?

MR. LOWENSTEIN: I think you credit us with almost occult powers if you think anything we do can further weaken President Johnson. That would be an achievement beyond our capacity. President Johnson has managed to so weaken himself that there is very little we can contribute to that process.

What we have to do and what we are trying to do is to make clear to the country that alternatives to President Johnson are not limited to right-wing Republicans who will make promises to end the war, which they can't do; that you can oppose President Johnson from a liberal, rational approach to the war and to America's domestic crisis; and that by offering that option to the country we will make possible that the anti-Johnson feeling will not be translated into a sort of superhawk position.

Most people who are opposed to Johnson may not be very clear in their minds about what they prefer as an alternative. What we are saying is, if you give them a coherent, competent program with an attractive candidate that they are likely to feel that this is an improvement over what they have got, and if we don't do that and the right-wing Republicans do, then I am afraid we end up with what the press will then call a swing to the right. I don't see the swing to the right. I see a swing against Johnson, and if we make liberalism coequivalent with Johnson, then there will be a swing against liberalism.

MR. OTTEN: You don't think your activities might spill over further and by putting a number of liberal Democratic Senators and Congressmen on the spot and by siphoning off campaign funds from them that you would elect a good number of Republican Senators and Congressmen who might not otherwise be elected and make a very conservative Congress?

MR. LOWENSTEIN: I think President Johnson did very well toward electing Republicans in 1966, and he was considerably more popular then than he is now, so part of the reason I would like to get a Democratic candidate who can win is that I want to save Senator [George] McGovern and Senator [Gaylord] Nelson and Congressman [Donald] Fraser and other very fine Democrats from the burden of having to run on a ticket

56

headed by a president who is going to be repudiated if the policies continue. . . .

MR. SPIVAK: Mr. Lowenstein, you have been reported as saying that the response you have had around the country to your "Dump Johnson" movement has been—I think the word was "overwhelming." Do you believe it is overwhelming enough to nominate—

MR. LOWENSTEIN: To overwhelm Johnson?

MR. SPIVAK: To overwhelm Johnson and to nominate Senator McCarthy? Do you really believe that?

MR. LOWENSTEIN: I believe it is overwhelming enough to win primaries and then we have to see the next event. Of course, you can't elect enough delegates in primaries to carry the convention, but you can elect enough delegates in primaries to influence the Democratic political organizations to reexamine whether they want the President renominated.

MR. SPIVAK: One of your major reasons for supporting Senator McCarthy is the question of Vietnam, and I think you have made that very, very clear. Judging from his own statements it is not quite clear what your candidate stands for on Vietnam.

Do you know what he stands for on Vietnam?

MR. LOWENSTEIN: I think it is much clearer than what the President and Secretary Rusk stand for in Vietnam.

MR. SPIVAK: No, but do you know what Senator McCarthy stands for in Vietnam? Do you know what he wants to do?

MR. LOWENSTEIN: Yes.

MR. SPIVAK: What does he want to do?

MR. LOWENSTEIN: He wants to reverse the course we are now on.

MR. SPIVAK: That is a generalization. How would he do it?

MR. LOWENSTEIN: Do you think it is a generalization to say that instead of going backward we are going to try to go forward?

MR. SPIVAK: How? The important question is how do you do it? What would he do that the President isn't doing?

MR. LOWENSTEIN: You stop the escalation of the war; you make very clear that your purposes are to withdraw through international supervision. You step up the effort to define your objectives in a way which doesn't suggest that we are permanently there. You halt the bombings that have made the casualties of American soldiers increase by one hundred fold since they began. I don't mean the bombings have killed Americans, but they have made counterescalation inevitable and thus have helped to make the casualty rate impossible for—

MR. SPIVAK: You stop your own escalation. How about the enemy's escalation? How do you stop that?

MR. LOWENSTEIN: Each escalation of the enemy has followed an escalation on our part.

MR. KENWORTHY: When you come right down to it, at the end, aren't you still waiting for Bobby? In fact, isn't Senator McCarthy still waiting for Bobby? Didn't he invite a vote for him and say there would really be, if there were enough of them, a vote for Bobby Kennedy?

MR. LOWENSTEIN: I think this is the oddest characterization of what we are doing. If there is one thing we are not doing, it is waiting. We have been moving for three months. We have built an organization in three months. We have gotten it started in states where people said it couldn't be done. We are certainly on the move, not waiting.

THE MAN WHO RAN AGAINST LYNDON JOHNSON

David Halberstam

Harper's, December 1968

Following the Democratic National Convention of 1968, journalist David Halberstam wrote a classic account of the Dump Johnson movement.

April 1967

The organization of it all, defeating Lyndon Johnson, starts as far back as March 1967, though few people realized it at the time. It is a period of national malaise; the country seems to be sucked deeper and deeper into a hopeless war and there seems to be no political alternative to the President in the coming campaign. It is a time of mounting frustration for most Americans. The peace movement seems to be coming to a decisive point; it is not yet respectable but it is becoming more so all the time. It is not yet a political movement but it just might become one, and now some moderate critics of the war are hoping to keep the peace movement from becoming too radical and thus scaring other more moderate Americans who are uneasy with both the war and with the draft-card burning.

I am doing an article on Martin Luther King, whose role seems vital in the protest, and I go by to see Allard Lowenstein, an adviser and friend of King's. Lowenstein, who is playing an increasingly important role in the politics of dissent on the war, spends the lunch talking about the role of the moderate Left in trying to dominate the opposition to the war; it is going to be people like Norman Thomas; they are trying to broaden the base of the peace movement. The liberals are badly divided and frustrated at this point. They are largely Democrats, their party is in power, and their party made the war. They are under attack now as they have not been for more than thirty years from people on the Left; worse, their critics are younger and have more appeal with other young people. Indeed Lowenstein is one of the few young liberals left in the country with any kind of appeal on the campuses, and that appeal stems more from his personal efforts, his interest in young people, his countless appearances on campuses, than it does from his particular political philosophy. Now at this lunch Norman Thomas' name comes up again and again. "What!" says Lowenstein aghast. "You've never met Norman Thomas? Friday at our house. You've got to come. Norman Thomas is the most beautiful man in America."

Off we go to Lowenstein's apartment in Manhattan on Friday. It is an extraordinary evening. Norman Thomas, almost blind, is there, and so is Frank Graham, former North Carolina Senator who was successfully red-baited years ago. With Thomas and Mrs. Roosevelt, Graham formed the trinity of Lowenstein's political heritage; they are all people he describes as "sweet," a word he uses often. Mrs. Lowenstein, young, quite pretty, quite confused, quite pregnant, is there, as well as about twenty students, none of whom know each other. It is the mark of a Lowenstein gathering that no one knows anyone else, but everyone knows Lowenstein; they all get together to share the common goal, which is whatever Lowenstein dictates.

But Lowenstein is not there. Lowenstein is flying in from someplace where he has just made a rousing speech or two, and he is circling overhead unable to make the introductions. The students are angry about American life and the war, and they are giving Norman Thomas a very hard time. One of them—a young girl with Radcliffe-length hair—is describing the war. Someone points to me and says that what she is saying isn't true and that I was once there. She turns and says, "We don't give a damn whether you were there or not." She continues with the argument, pouring it on Mr. Thomas: the war is racial and genocidal, it is the white man deliberately killing yellow men. Why doesn't the Pentagon just use the H-bomb and do it a little more quickly? Mr. Thomas, frail in all but voice, argues that Vietnam was a mistake, it was too much vanity, it was a nation more proud than wise; but it was not genocide. The girl continues, getting angrier and angrier: Vietnam is the logical extension of American life. Vietnam was inevitable, given the moral corruption of this country. Again, Thomas argues back: no, it is a mistake, many of the people in charge of this country feel about Negroes the same way you do. This country made a mistake but it is not a racial mistake. Do those generals, the girl shrieks, do those generals feel anything about Negroes? Yes, says Mr. Thomas.

Eventually, as the evening is breaking up, Lowenstein arrives, rumpled as ever. He introduces everyone to the people they have just spent the evening with, and packs everyone off to a West Side reform-club meeting where he then spends half the night attacking Johnson and the war and promises that the Democratic party, the party of Eleanor Roosevelt, will not permit Johnson to run again. Johnson will be beaten. The politicians are wrong. No one is *for* Johnson. It is in the air. Volunteers are asked for. A few put their hands up. It all seems very vague, and somehow Lowenstein is hard for me to take seriously; I have the same reservations about him that I have about Humphrey, that he is somehow intellectually promiscuous, that he jumps around from cause to cause, that all liberal causes are equal, that he is somehow the perpetual student leader, that there is a lack of toughness and discipline in him.

We had first met ten years ago in Nashville, Tennessee; Lowenstein was an old friend of my roommate Fred Graham (then a law student, now Supreme Court reporter for the New York *Times*). They were friends from Yale, where they used to wrestle; Lowenstein is a physical cultist, and works out wherever he goes in America. Every town with a jet airport has someone who wrestles with Al Lowenstein. At that time Graham introduced him as (a) the oldest student leader in America. (b) someone who knows everyone in America. That image of him has not changed over the years in my mind, though it will start to change now.

May 1967

Martin Luther King is speaking at Berkeley on Vietnam and there are 5,000 cheering people in the audience as well as several people sitting in trees for a better look. One of them is Allard K. Lowenstein. He is just in from some California school to the south, he is passing through to give some focus to the dissent on Vietnam, organizing it, channeling it. All the ads that are appearing in the New York *Times*—Mister President, College Editors Protest Your War; Mister President, Student Council Presidents Reject Your War; Mister President, Peace Corps Returnees Will Not Condone—are the work of Al Lowenstein. Can we have dinner, I ask. Have to fly off to Oregon, he says. Meetings there. "It's tough," he then adds. "These kids. No one really knows how alienated they are. Trying to keep them in the system is very, very hard. They're bitter and they're angry. They really resent this society. Of course there are a lot of things in this society that are very resentable."

August 1967

Sitting on the patio of the Continental Hotel in Saigon with John Chancellor, I match his depressing stories about official Washington with my depressing stories about unofficial and official Saigon. A young man, very clean-cut, watches us for about twenty minutes, then comes over, identifies us correctly, and asks, quite surreptitiously, if we have seen Lowenstein. (Thirteen months later at the Democratic convention Chancellor will recall the moment and refer to the young man as "Lowenstein's advance man.") I saw him in New York, I answer. No, says the young man, he's *here* now. Sure enough, several hours later Lowenstein materializes; it is election time in Saigon and he is here as an observer. Lyndon Johnson has sent *his* team of observers, but he has failed to pick Lowenstein. Al has flown over, Air Lowenstein, to judge the elections, since he intends to criticize Vietnamese politics in the year to come and he does not intend to be one-upped by people asking, were you there? He is there, though of course observing a Vietnamese election is almost as futile as participating in one. Nevertheless he seems to be known to everyone in Saigon, particularly underground politicians.

Lowenstein beavers around Saigon, returns to New York to file a minority report on the elections and continue the embryonic organizational work of the Dump Johnson movement. It still looks like a pipe dream. But protest against the war is constantly growing in America; the migration is inevitable, always hawk to dove. I remember what Galbraith said about the conversion process: "It's easier than you think because we believe it and we've thought it out and they haven't." Lowenstein is inevitably optimistic; he is working hard at the grass-roots organization, and traveling around the country forming the early network. At this point the organization is largely Lowenstein and Curtis Gans.

The Dump Johnson movement formally began on August 15 with Lowenstein's speech to the National Student Association, which is his great stomping grounds; he was the last NSA president before it became tied to the CIA and he has continued to nurse his relationship with the organization, keeping up his contacts and, in the last year, channeling the efforts of its leaders against the war. By August all the NSA leaders' letters to the President and to Rusk were still unanswered and the feeling of frustration, of being ineffectual, is massive. Lowenstein moves in to direct it to national purposes. "The feeling at that meeting," says one kid, "was that we had gone just as far as we could go through the normal procedures. They just acted as if we didn't exist, and we weren't serious. And we didn't want to go into the resistance, at least not yet. So we were ready to try what Al wanted. It was the last stop on the way."

Lowenstein has always been a target of the radical Left—a symbol of the liberal anti-Communist in their midst—and their antagonism would intensify in the year to come. Even as he was speaking, the Students for a Democratic Society element of the NSA picketed him with signs reading: "Don't listen to the CIA Agent Downstairs." Lowenstein sees the kids as a vital link in any attempt to beat Johnson. He thinks any movement must come from within the Democratic party, and though there are many nominal Democrats opposed to the President, the party apparatus will support Johnson, and labor, increasingly conservative, will also support him. Thus the place of the apparatus and labor must be taken by someone who can energize the ideas, and do the legwork and the dirty work of the movement. What better answer than the kids? Because of this, the radical Left sees Lowenstein as manipulative, using its contemporaries for his own work, exploiting them on behalf of the system, working, in substance, for Lyndon Johnson. "Hubert Lowenstein," one SDS kid will call him a year later. But the meeting goes well; the kids are ready to try it, to try anything. Lowenstein promises them, somehow, a candidate.

The next day he flies to New York to be with Mrs. Allard Lowenstein who is about to have a baby. At 9:00 A.M., Mrs. Lowenstein starts her labor pains. The doctor assures Lowenstein that the baby will not come until the next day. At 10:00 A.M., a distraught Mrs. Lowenstein looks up to see Curtis Gans dragging Al off to an organizational meeting in Washington. First things first. "Back by 2:00 P.M.," he says. Then he catches the shuttle, attends the meeting, and returns to meet his new son, Frank Graham Lowenstein.

October 1967

Lowenstein is always ebullient. Probably that's one of the reasons the New Left doesn't like him, just as a lot of liberals now dislike Humphrey for the optimism of his tone, in what is to them essentially a dark time. Lowenstein is no Humphrey. He sees all the darkness, and sees it as clearly as they do, but he is resilient, optimistic, and keeps saying that the system can work, which is to them a sign that he does not really mean what he says about darkness, that it is not to him darkness but just a dark issue upon which he can campaign.

We have lunch, swapping notes on Vietnam and the campaign. His early organizational days are difficult, yet he is optimistic as ever. The older liberals are also giving him a hard time. "The Joe Rauh liberals," in Lowenstein's phrase (Rauh does not think anyone can be to the left of him, says one observer of them both, and Lowenstein, who does not think anyone can be to the left of *him*, is to the left of Rauh), are dubious about the attempt to take Johnson on directly; they believe it will only enrage the President and make him more intractable, and that the only answer is a peace plank at the 1968 convention. ("When was the last time you heard of rallying millions of people to a plank?" asks a momentarily amused Robert Kennedy.)

The factional quarrel simply reflects the extraordinary divisions within the liberal ranks both because of the war and because of changing goals and values. Some older liberals such as Galbraith are cooperating; "he was the first major figure in the country who actually encouraged us," says Lowenstein. Though the war is not going well and no one believes the predictions of the President or the Generals, no one believes either that this has been transmitted to the public. Johnson is the sitting President; the mythology still holds: The politicians tell the press that the President is invincible, and the press tells the population that the President is invincible, and the politicians read in the press that the President is invincible. Invincibility by mythology.

Lowenstein is still looking for a candidate and is convinced he will have one. Kennedy is his first choice, but is dubious. Meanwhile, he and Gans have worked out a system. They go into state after state creating their network. Gans compiles the lists of people who might be favorable: ADA lists, names given by friends. Anything for a base in each state. Then Lowenstein appears in a chosen area and holds two meetings, one a private session with the local politicians or political activists who might be favorable and the other a public one. The public one is used to convince the normally nervous politicians. This is, after all, the Democratic party, and at the beginning there is no reason to believe that what Lowenstein and Gans are doing is very much different from the other one thousand quixotic political suicides which are offered to a politician each year. The politicians are nervous at the private meetings, but not opposed. The public meetings, in contrast, usually go much better, with bigger attendance and more enthusiasm than the politicians expect. ("This is a year," Galbraith said in August 1967, "when the people are right and the politicians are wrong.") So the public meetings encourage the politicians.

There were several crucial moments early in the campaign, Lowenstein says. One came in Wisconsin. Lowenstein and Gans considered this a particularly tough state because the anti-Vietnam feeling there was violent and had largely been taken over by the radical Left. So the problem was to induce some moderates to move towards the issue. They had the name of Don Peterson of Eau Claire, an ADA board member. Their notes said that he was a good man, the best kind of citizen-liberal, but it would take "one hell of a selling job." Lowenstein's first appraisal of Peterson was that he was "nervous but sympathetic," which was not unusual in those days; a lot of people were sympathetic but uneasy about a political challenge which might reflect on their patriotism. Lowenstein met with Peterson, taking several hours to explain what he was doing and why. Finally Peterson looked up at him and said very simply, "That sounds like what we should be doing. I'll have to talk to some of my people first." A few days later he called to say he was in.

In Minnesota, they also held an early September meeting; like Wisconsin, Minnesota was crucial because its convention was an early test (which would show unexpected McCarthy strength). Lowenstein had expected about fifty people at a church meeting and instead found several hundred. Still, the nervousness was there; an old friend of Lowenstein's who was a state official told him, "I can't be seen with you. But my wife will work for you. And if you can meet me tomorrow privately we can talk a little and I can give you a few names." After the meeting Alpha Smaby, a member of the Minnesota legislature, signed up; she had a particularly impressive reputation in Minnesota politics and Lowenstein was elated. She was the first elected public official to come out for them. "Her coming over meant that it was more than the out-left and the kids in this thing. It gave us respectability."

Respectable is a key word and helps separate Lowenstein from the radical Left. Lowenstein still believes in the system, and its limits on dissent. Lowenstein believes that by working through the respectable student leadership, through the middle class, you could most effectively spread the word. He was at his best this way, suitably idealistic.

"The Dump Johnson movement was a typical Lowenstein operation," says one friend who has watched him work over the years. "It was Lowenstein working outside the normal apparatus, functioning almost out of his own hip pocket, using his own personal contacts and his own charisma, not responsible to anyone above him, and influencing people to the *right* of him. That's his great strength, talking to these clean-cut young kids, getting them back into the system. He doesn't work nearly as well to the left, and he loses his patience; it's as if he doesn't think people have the right to be to the left of him. Al likes to start things, but when they get out of hand and get revolutionary, he doesn't like it. The trouble is, they're bound to in this country because someone like Lowenstein is trying to work within the system and save it, but of course he doesn't have the support of the system. The system doesn't give a damn about being saved. So he starts these movements, like the Mississippi Freedom Democratic party, but when they get stalled or bounce off the system the kids get discouraged or become more radical, just like the Mississippi Freedom Democratic party did. And they break with Al and he gets hurt, and they become a little cynical. Now this Vietnam thing, he's perfectly type-cast for it. There's no one for outlining moral questions in practical terms and exciting people to the challenge ahead like Lowenstein. But what happens if it fails? Will you have more disillusioned kids, turned off by the process, thinking Lowenstein fooled them?"

November 15, 1967

Lowenstein's candidate will be Gene McCarthy. The first choice was Robert Kennedy (even McCarthy's first choice was Robert Kennedy; when Lowenstein finally asked him, he said Yes it should be done, but Lowenstein should see Kennedy since Kennedy had a much broader base, an indication of how strongly McCarthy, who actively disliked Kennedy, felt about Johnson and the war). Lowenstein, of course, had been in Kennedy's camp for two years; Kennedy was clearly the heir apparent for a generation of young men in their thirties and forties who still harbored liberal instincts but who felt that the goals and values of American life had changed. He saw the same darkness that many of these young social critics saw, and his language and his attitude seemed to fit the times: a tough-minded view of the reality of the country, a hope that nevertheless it could still be turned around.

Kennedy had sought deliberately that position of leadership, but now in 1967 he was in a particularly difficult position. He was young, he seemed to have a very good chance for a future race, and he was tied to the past and the party professionals and hesitant to make a challenge in his own party. If anything, he dominated the party and the area of dissent too strongly at this point. The liberals all waited; if Robert Kennedy made a move, they would make a move. If he didn't make a move, there would be no move. The Kennedy organization functioned well at the top, many of the brightest and most talented young men in the country were ready to go to work, but there was no grass-roots coalition on issues. One man made it all or broke it all.

Here Lowenstein differed; he was determined to go ahead whether or not Kennedy made the race. They were friends now, though originally very different in their politics. Lowenstein had supported Kennedy for the Senate in 1964 and afterwards had become an informal adviser, a valuable connection to New York reform circles for Kennedy and a valuable reporter for him on what was happening among young people. But in September Lowenstein, who had been urging the race all year, went to Kennedy and said that the moment of truth had come; it was past the time of writing magazine articles on the ghetto and making speeches in the Senate on Vietnam; the army was ready, it would march, the President was ripe to be beaten, it could all be done. The enemies Kennedy would make by running were enemies he already had. The friends he would win were more important, for they would be dominant in American life in the decade to come. By the time of the convention, the party, which was obviously badly shattered, would be very glad he was making the race, but most of all he had to run this year, the issue went far beyond normal party loyalty; it was a question of moral imperative.

Lowenstein, of course, was not the first person to offer Kennedy advice on a 1968 race. In late 1967 almost everyone he met offered him advice, half of them telling him to go, half telling him not to go, and he was caught in the middle. Though he was getting encouragement from people whose advice he valued on *social* issues, he was getting just the opposite advice from people whose judgment he trusted on *political* matters, the professionals who were telling him, no it couldn't be done, he would destroy himself in the party if he tried.

At any rate Kennedy heard Lowenstein out and admired his sincerity and idealism and intensity and then finally, reluctantly, said No, he could not go, he had just talked with Mayor Daley and Chairman X and Governor Y, and they had all said the same thing, you can't do it, it's not your year, you must wait; we like you, we loved your brother, and we think very favorably of you for 1972. And so Robert Kennedy reluctantly passed this on to Lowenstein, saying simply, I'm sorry, I can't do it. Lowenstein had looked at him for a long time and then answered, "The people who think that the honor and the future of this country are at stake don't give a shit what Mayor Daley and Chairman X and Governor Y think. We're going to do it and we're going to win, and it's a shame you're not with us because you could have been President." Then as he left, he said that he was going ahead with the plan and that if Kennedy changed his mind it would be too late, he would not be able to come over.

After he lost Kennedy, Lowenstein went to George McGovern, long a leading and articulate dove in the Senate ("If George McGovern had made the race I never would have entered," Kennedy once told friends), a man not well-known nationally because the Kennedys had so dominated the liberal wing of the party. But McGovern had a difficult race coming up in South Dakota; he did not want to turn Lowenstein down, so he suggested Lowenstein go out to South Dakota for a couple of days and sample the water and see whether it would be possible to make both races and just what the mood at home was. Lowenstein spent several days in the state, and reluctantly concluded that while the opposition did not seem strong enough to defeat McGovern, it would make things difficult for him if he were a Presidential candidate as well. He would have to run two campaigns very different in tone and it would eventually be at the least embarrassing and possibly even disastrous. McGovern did not close the door on the race; indeed he hinted that if no one else would do it, they should come back to him. Then he suggested Lowenstein talk to Gene McCarthy. Lowenstein did, and McCarthy was ready. He had already thought about the necessity of the race, he sensed some of the changes in American politics, including the fact that, while he lacked national exposure, the exposure would have to come to anyone challenging the sitting President, that you can now make a candidate in about two or three months. He accepted.

Gradually there is a change in one's view of Lowenstein; he no longer seems the college debater and college student council president emeritus, a person that you never disagreed with politically but that somehow you never took that seriously. "I always thought of him," said one friend of his earlier days, "sitting there in the back of his parents' restaurant running his various campaigns and organizations." Rather there is a new toughness and fiber to him; it is as if the challenge of this particular campaign is worthy of all that energy which up to now was diffused in so many different directions. Now he seems consumed by his task and somehow toughened by it.

The Dream

Lowenstein's political origins were not that different from many others of his generation. He is thirty-nine, son of good upper-middle-class Jews; he saw the American dream work in his own family—a family that went from poverty to a decent life while Europe burned—saw the New Deal transform the sons of immigrant parents, give them respectability; he believed in the American dream, which worked with sufficient coaxing. That generation believed in certain assumptions of American life, that it could work. It had gained a certain amount of material success, yet it had not lost its sense of cause and issue (which would primarily focus on the question of race in the late Fifties and Sixties).

In the late Sixties, Lowenstein was, in a sense, a refugee from the New Deal, hoping to make the dream work again. "The spirit of Eleanor Roosevelt hovers over this meeting," he told one group trying to put together an anti-Humphrey coalition in June 1968. "We want to regain the country which our civics teachers taught us about, the country that inspired our parents to tell us democracy is the best way to bring about social revolutions." As a young boy Lowenstein kept a map of Spain on his wall, and he always retained Spanish relief work among his many causes; indeed, one of the Lowenstein legends among his college friends goes like this: someone calls his house and asks for Al. "Al's not here," answers his mother. "He just left for Spain . . . you know, he never did like that General Franco."

For a long time Lowenstein flitted in and out of liberal causes, sampling reform work in New York, a trip to South Africa, then to Europe to work for Spanish political refugees, integration work in the South, even working for a time for Senator Hubert Humphrey. ("Al never was too good on Hubert's staff," says one friend. "He was always saying yes to every request, putting Hubert's name on everything, when his job really was to keep Hubert's name *off* everything.") There was one serious romance during this time with Barbara Boggs (predictably he refused to give her an engagement ring because he would not support South African mines), the daughter of Congressman Hale Boggs, a romance and engagement jeopardized by Lowenstein's almost spastic travels, and the conservative Catholic Boggs family's deep-seated opposition; finally the family broke it up. (The Boggs' other daughter later married a young reporter for the New York *Times* named Steve Roberts. Roberts, like Lowenstein, is Jewish and for a time he could not understand why Boggs was so nice to him. "Then one day I realized—it was because I wasn't Lowenstein.")

During all this time Lowenstein seemed to specialize in causes rather than jobs. In 1961 he taught and served as assistant dean at Stanford; he left after taking the student side in a student power question. He went from Stanford to North Carolina State, where he taught political science for two years and eventually clashed with state authorities over his support of local Negro demonstrations. The head of the state senate told reporters it was disgraceful, North Carolina paying this man $7,500 a year and he's messing around with blacks. Reporters called up Lowenstein and he said, yes, it is disgraceful, $7,500 a year is much too little. There was a furor over whether he would be reappointed. Finally he was; the moment he won the academic freedom point, Lowenstein resigned. "Al was always the moralist," said someone who knew him well in those days. "He always wanted to look at every question and every issue from the moral point of view. But finally there was some doubt. Was he forcing the moral issue? Did he always have to see himself in a moral light? Is there a moral issue in everything? Or do you create a moral issue in order to keep being fluid, to avoid responsibility and settling down and growing up?" But another friend from the same era believes the Dump Johnson movement and Lowenstein's chance to have a Congressional seat will give what he has always needed in American life, a base and a platform. "Most of the doubts about Al came not so much because of his causes, but because with his causes he had no normal job. He was going against the puritan ethic of American society: A man is talented? Therefore he should have a job, write a thesis, help his career, work for some Senator, teach, do something from nine to five, and then have his ideals. So people looked at Al and there he was without a job and just running around with causes from nine to five and they had their doubts. But the Dump Johnson thing has given him a national platform already and if he wins the Congressional seat it will be even better. People will be more sympathetic because he'll have a title and a position, and they'll be reassured."

December 1967

Lowenstein goes on "Meet the Press," a rare appearance for someone who is a non-Establishment figure. The interview reflects the general disbelief that he is serious or that the movement can affect anything.

Spivak: "Will you support President Johnson if he gets the nomination, or will you bolt the party?"

Lowenstein: "If the President were renominated on his present program and the Republican party offered a candidate who was giving an alternative to what is happening in the war and at home as a result of the war, I would feel my obligation as an American was to support that candidate who gave the best hope of reversing what I consider a policy leading the country toward disaster. May I say at this point that one of the reasons that the press seems mystified as to what is happening, or regards it as unlikely that this sort of effort would develop, is that it does not yet understand in general the depth of feeling among a great many of us that the country which we love very deeply is heading toward a very serious disaster and that under these extraordinary circumstances our obligation is to find ways of reversing that disaster. If you foreclose the options in politics by saying you cannot oppose a sitting President, you cannot do this, you cannot do that, then the frustration has to spill over into a nonpolitical or nonelectoral protest. . . . I can fully understand why if the political people and the media say you cannot reverse the policies through politics, people in frustration may turn to other means and have begun to do so. . . ."

Otten: "If President Johnson is renominated, despite all your efforts, might not the result of your activity merely be to weaken him and help a Republican who from your point of view is no different or even worse on the Vietnam war, and also opposes some of the domestic welfare programs that you espouse . . . ?"

Lowenstein: ". . . What we have to do and what we are trying to do is to make clear to the country that alternatives to President Johnson are not limited to right-wing Republicans who will make promises to end the war, which they cannot do, that you can oppose President Johnson from a liberal rational approach to the war and to America's domestic crisis, and that by offering that option to the country we will make possible that the anti-Johnson feeling will not be translated into a sort of super-hawk position. Most people who are opposed to Johnson may not be very clear in their minds what they prefer as an alternative. What we are saying is that if you give them a coherent competent program with an attractive candidate that they are likely to feel that this is an improvement over what they have got. And if we do not do that and the right-wing Republicans do, then I am afraid we end up with what the press will then call a swing to the right. I do not see the swing to the right. I see a swing against Johnson, and if we make liberalism co-equivalent with Johnson, then there will be a swing against liberalism."

January 1968

Al Lowenstein's life and position are forever complicated. Though the McCarthy campaign is getting minimal attention in most of the press, his backers are beginning to be optimistic; they are trying to convince McCarthy that the pace is somewhat different from that of a Senate race and they think they are breaking through. But Lowenstein's position in the campaign is vague. He is still working for the Dump Johnson movement, and the Dump Johnson people have taken over the McCarthy campaign; people like Gans and Sam Brown who emerged from the early meetings are the key people and so are the kids that Lowenstein helped recruit for the drive, and they will all go into New Hampshire. (The Kennedys have always wanted McCarthy to enter New Hampshire and stay out of Massachusetts, and so McCarthy's immediate instinct was to go into Massachusetts, which he did, and stay out of New Hampshire, which he almost did; then Lowenstein and a few others put enormous pressure on him, arguing he must make every test, that the very fact New Hampshire is considered hawkish and Wisconsin dovish means that he must go into New Hampshire and do well, otherwise a victory in Wisconsin is meaningless.)

But Lowenstein's relationship with McCarthy is curiously ambivalent. Part of it is formed by the suspicion within the McCarthy camp that Lowenstein is an agent for Kennedy (and there is already some very strong anti-Bobby feeling in the McCarthy camp). Much of it is a question of style: Lowenstein and Kennedy get along well because they are both basically evangelical, they believe a man can make a difference, that the country can be turned around. McCarthy is quite different. He is a more intellectual, more cynical, more caustic man: the race has to be made for moral reasons, but it is not a crusade. The very qualities which make Lowenstein so effective with the clean-cut idealistic kids make McCarthy wary of him, wary of him instilling all that much hope and belief, creating images of a world that McCarthy feels does not exist.

In November in Chicago McCarthy had gone before a conveniently convened meeting of Lowenstein's Coalition for a Democratic Alternative. Lowenstein wanted him to announce his candidacy there, but anti-Lowenstein forces had dissuaded him. Lowenstein, sensing that these people wanted some hope and energy poured into them, some fire to keep them going, pulled out all the stops, and gave a rip-roaring speech about what they were going to do to Lyndon Johnson. McCarthy was appalled. He considered Lowenstein demagogic and he did not like the incendiary quality of the speech. He planned to run in a decidedly different manner, believing the protest was already there, the issue was already too explosive, and his only job was to provide an outlet for that protest. Lowenstein in turn was shocked that McCarthy did not even bother to visit the several thousand people in the overflow crowd at the Chicago meeting. From that day on there is something of a difference between them. Lowenstein is in the McCarthy camp, but not *of* it; probably, if anything, he is simply too much of a politician for McCarthy, who wants as few politicians near him as possible. Possibly when Lowenstein is around, McCarthy senses he is listening to a voice of the Kennedys.

Yet Lowenstein is increasingly optimistic. He is convinced that McCarthy has a real chance in every primary ahead and he believes Kennedy will someday have to enter the race. The Tet offensive has hurt Johnson badly. Johnson's credibility has always been at stake on this war, going back to 1964 when he ran as a peace candidate and then almost immediately expanded the war. The real question on Vietnam which neither Johnson nor the party had faced in 1964 was: all the way in or all the way out? Thus, immediately after the election Johnson's credibility began to be doubted by the intellectual judges within his own party, and steadily,

74

month by month and year by year, that doubt had grown. Johnson, it would turn out, was not a particularly good politician; he was always willing to maneuver for short-term popularity without sensing the long-term consequences. Every time Vietnam came up as an issue, Johnson would fend off his critics. He would fly to Hawaii, or to Vietnam, or bring a Congressional Medal of Honor winner to the White House, or fly Westmoreland home to talk to the nation and the Congress, and each time he did this it would work: the doves would retreat, healing their wounds, the polls would show the people still loved the President and the war after all. But the price was a dangerously high one; he was buying time for the war by expending his own personal credibility. When finally the reality of the war, that it was unwinnable, that all the basic American suppositions about Vietnam were fallacious, would surface with a terrible finality, Johnson would be a hollow man. Johnson on his best day is not lovable; he needs to be effective and the war had ravaged his effectiveness at home and abroad. His much-discussed, much-praised consensus, it would turn out, was a convenient consensus of the moment, not an idea or a consensus of what Americans might be, but rather the parceling out of varying parts of the pie to varying interest groups, good interest groups, bad interest groups, in the hope that this would somehow give them what they wanted and prevent their judging him too harshly on other matters! Lyndon Johnson had turned out to be a bad politician. That helped Allard K. Lowenstein a lot.

April 9, 1968

The impossible has happened: Johnson has been dumped. He has withdrawn, sensing further defeats in future primaries, culminating in California, where his strength is minimal. McCarthy is a handsome victor in Wisconsin, Kennedy is in the race, and most people see Kennedy eventually defeating McCarthy in enough primaries and taking over the leadership of the dissenting Democrats. But for the moment Lowenstein is caught in the middle: committed to McCarthy but a Kennedy man at heart, in style, in loyalty. Rumors swirl that he will desert McCarthy for Kennedy. But Lowenstein invited McCarthy into the race and cannot desert him. There are, of course, entreaties. Kennedy is having trouble with the Jews, the liberals, and the kids, and Lowenstein would be an excellent bridge for bringing them back. Kennedy has kids, but as he points out, somewhat sadly, he has the B and C kids and McCarthy has the A kids.

There is some talk of a New York Senate race for Lowenstein if Lowenstein were acceptable to the McCarthy people. "It could be fun," Kennedy says, "we could really shake them up." But the McCarthy people are dubious and the Senate idea is junked. "You running for Congress," Kennedy says, "is like the Pope running for parish priest." Kennedy suggests a possible job in an Administration. Lowenstein rejects the bureaucracy. Except for one job, he adds. "I know what it is," says Kennedy. "Secretary of the Army." Where the action is. Yes, nods Lowenstein. But he cannot go over to Kennedy though his relationship is strained with the McCarthy camp, particularly in New York where the anti-Kennedy feeling is often as strong as the anti-Humphrey or anti-Johnson feeling. But in late March the rumors have persisted that Lowenstein will defect and Kennedy, hearing them, spots Lowenstein on a bus filled with New York Democrats and asks if it is true. Lowenstein says no. Kennedy retreats to the back of the bus and then scribbles a note to Lowenstein: "For Al, who knew the lesson of Emerson and taught it to the rest of us: 'They did not yet see, and thousands of young men as hopeful, now crowding to the barriers of their careers, do not yet see if a single man plant himself on his convictions and then abide, the huge world will come round to him.' From his friend, Bob Kennedy." The loyalty endears Lowenstein more than ever to Kennedy, but does not soften the feeling among many of the McCarthy people. Looking for a way out of this bitter split, he decides to concentrate on his own Congressional race, and failing to get a nomination in the city, is invited to run in Nassau County, Long Island. He still works in the McCarthy campaign but it is loyalty curiously tempered by a basic belief in another man.

July 4. 1968

He is the Democratic Congressional nominee from Nassau County's fifth district, having won a carpet-bagger's victory—14,881 to 10,908—over Albert Vorspan, who is a resident of the district, a candidate with good liberal credentials and the backing of the organization. The Lowenstein victory was put together more on energy than organization. What was notable about it was, first, the rallying of many McCarthy kids, some of whom had become a little disillusioned with McCarthy in recent months, and of Kennedy people who also went to work for him. It was also marked by the appearance of high-school kids. (Lowenstein's young people get younger and younger, which as one critic says, may not necessarily be a good thing.)

Lowenstein also organizes the Coalition for an Open Convention in Chicago, a last-minute attempt to bring together the forces that oppose Humphrey and get some anti-Humphrey momentum. Lowenstein sees Humphrey as much weaker than the delegate counts indicate but propped up by the basic split between the Kennedy and the McCarthy forces. McCarthy is unable to make a real gesture toward the Kennedy people; he did not like Robert Kennedy in life and he will not say about him in death things he refused to say while he was alive. The Kennedy people, shattered, are largely unable to move toward McCarthy. There are too many bruises and there is too great a difference in style; the best of the Kennedy people, who might be attracted because of the issues, find no place in the McCarthy campaign for themselves, and McCarthy does not really want them. Kennedy, like his older brother, always had the ability to make intellectuals feel they were of value in the inner circle, that they were making points and influencing his decisions; but there is a loneliness and an austerity to McCarthy's decision making. He is an intellectual. No other intellectuals need apply.

Lowenstein's coalition is an attempt to go to the second- and third-level people in both camps. It is marginally successful at best. The Mc-Carthy people at the top are dubious, regarding it as an attempt to take McCarthy's campaign and hand the work over to some other candidate (McGovern? Teddy?). Young Mary McCarthy is asked if she's going to the Chicago organizing meeting. No: "Just one thousand friends of Al Lowenstein at the meeting," she says. The meeting itself shows again the deep splits. The good Democrats, the middle-aged and even younger people, with whom Lowenstein has worked all year, are strongly anti-Humphrey, but they are *Democrats* first, and they are leery of a meeting which will offer a resolution calling for a refusal to back Humphrey; that would tie their hands and hurt them back home. They have already taken a stand which is considered radical. If they go too far they may be read out of the party.

For some of the young radicals, however, the Democratic party is at best a passing phase; they gave it a chance, and look what it did. A fourth party beckons and they are anxious to come out of the meeting with a resolution pledging everyone there not to support Humphrey if nominated. It is the kind of split Lowenstein has faced all year. Then he leaves his position as chairman of the meeting and speaks against the radical motion. He wins and saves the meeting for the older, more traditional Democrats.

But one of his toughest critics. Paul Cowan, who broke with Lowenstein over their year in Mississippi, rejecting liberalism for radicalism, writes of the meeting: "The half-conscious assumption of most of the adults there is that liberals like Eugene McCarthy or Al Lowenstein can contain the new rebels more effectively than Hubert Humphrey, Richard Nixon, or George Wallace. They will encourage people like Reverend Jesse Jackson [SCLC man in Chicago, manager of the highly successful Operation Breadbasket] and the members of the student caucus to speak—protect their civil liberties—but discourage them from acting out their ideas—exalt unity to prevent disruption. The McCarthys and the Lowensteins are the most effective champions of the country of the order that the upper-middle-class Americans who support them want to maintain. . . . Al Lowenstein, whom the Establishment press is billing as the founder of the New Politics, is in fact the ideal spokesman for the new politicians. He is bright enough and brave enough to communicate with the dissident groups his contemporaries fear, and enough of a master of manipulation and persuasion to keep many of the dissenters inside the framework of conventional politics. . . . Still, Lowenstein and the new politicians who make up the majority of his coalition will be remembered as sad figures, not as heroic or evil ones. In another year Lowenstein might have been Franklin Roosevelt or Lyndon Johnson, a genius who created a pluralistic consensus and saved the country, or the villain who destroyed democracy by insisting on unity at all costs. But not now. The splits in America are too deep for any healer. No man can play the role for which Lowenstein has cast himself. . . ."

August 1968

A Sunday flight with Lowenstein to Manhattan, Kansas, where he will address the annual meeting of the NSA on the first anniversary of the Dump Johnson movement, at a time when the McCarthy movement, despite its earlier victories, looks like a failure. Inevitably we will fly at the least convenient hour and arrive at the least convenient time; and eating and drinking will be impossible. (Lowenstein does not care about food and drink. He drinks chocolate milkshakes for breakfast—fuel—and has Coke with dinner.) On the way out we talk about the campaign. A few weeks ago he thought Humphrey could be stopped. But McCarthy has been a little lethargic. The Kennedy people have moved to Mc-Govern, but right now Humphrey is far ahead on arithmetic. A stewardess comes over, excited because there are politicians aboard. She is introduced to Lowenstein, who is a genuine Congressional candidate. She is highly pleased and tells him she would like to go to Vietnam to kill some gooks. There are gooks on both sides, he says. That's tough, she says.

We arrive in Kansas City about 1:00 A.M., are met by five young people, Lowensteinites, college graduates, all part of his great apparatus, all enthusiastic. They are young and clean-cut and they regale him with all the inner gossip of NSA; it is like being with a star football player when he returns to the campus after a year's absence. They are among the handful who organized the Dump Johnson movement a year ago. On the way to Manhattan there is a great review of that historic battle, all very good stuff for me, but it is 4:00 A.M., New York time, and oppressively hot, and I fall asleep. We arrive at the motel. Lowenstein apologizes for my discomfort. Impeccable manners. The next morning we are supposed to meet him at 10:A.M. With great effort, I get up and make the appointment. No Lowenstein. Three hours later still no Lowenstein; but his press secretary, Mary Lou Oates, is sighted. She is through with it all, she says. It's all over, everyone in Kansas is freaking out. It's the California kids, the California kids, they're behind it all, they're way out ahead with drugs and Speed and they're bewildering these other kids at the convention and making them freak out. There's no hope. Where is Lowenstein, I ask. I left that job, she says. At 4:00 P.M., Lowenstein shows up, running, spinning, bouncing off people. "Being a friend of Lowenstein's," Jack Newfield once said, "is like being on a hold button on a phone." Everyone comes running to tell him something urgent. Lowenstein deals in nothing that is not urgent.

But the question is, can he still cut it? He is one of the last great hopes of liberalism. Will even the clean-cut kids be disillusioned? He had promised them a year ago that the society could work. Did he lie? Well, everyone is talking about his own personal hang-ups. "A bad sign," says Lowenstein. "They're turning inward. When things are going well, they tell you about the political stuff they're working on. Now it's all personal. They feel so damn ineffectual. They feel activism is meaningless. They're all too tired and too beaten out. A year later all they can see is the collapse. They can't see what they've accomplished. . . ." Someone runs over to him. "Okay, what's your problem?" Lowenstein says. The kid begins by saying, "I hope you haven't come to tell us what we can do and how we can do it because we don't need any more of that crap," and ends by telling him, "The only thing to do this year is go for the Congress."

There are surprisingly few McCarthy buttons around, not that there are Humphrey or Nixon buttons; just fewer McCarthy buttons than you would expect. Lowenstein spends the afternoon as if at a reunion. In the late afternoon, we go to hear Tom Hayden speak. Hayden is young, tough-minded, a member of SDS, a visitor to Hanoi. He is not a particularly good speaker, but he is revered by the New Left. At the workshop he discusses Chicago plans and needles Lowenstein: "The professional CIA-oriented politicians who occupy one part of McCarthy's campaign . . ." The New Left is constantly trying to attack Lowenstein as a CIA member. It has no proof. He was the last head of the NSA before its CIA subsidy, yet the attacks continue. ("I'm not saying he's a CIA agent," said Warren Hinckle in one of the milder radical Left attacks. "But he has to be very naïve or very unlucky. . . ." It all has a familiar ugly ring.) The Yippies say Hayden will nominate a pig for President. The pig will offer to debate Humphrey. The pig will go to Paris for the peace talks. Someone asks Hayden about the possibility of violence in Chicago. "I believe in violence," he says. "I think this country will change only by violence, but I'm against it in Chicago because we're bringing people who don't know each other onto terrain they don't know and the police do know."

That night there is a debate between Robert Scheer, Hayden, and Joe

Duffey, a theologian from Hartford who supports McCarthy. Lowenstein chooses not to participate; he is in a weak position because these kids all want to go to Chicago and McCarthy has come out against demonstrations in Chicago, which binds Lowenstein. Both Scheer and Hayden are annoyed by his copping out. Scheer is an excellent debater, perhaps the best orator of the New Left, dramatic, strong, painting a wide and broad canvas of American evil staining the world. He says, "Without the radical peace movement there would have been no McCarthy campaign. We forced them to find their consciences." Then: "Is Al Lowenstein going to support Hubert Humphrey?" (In the audience Lowenstein whispers, "He makes his living off me. He told the students earlier that he came here only because I told them not to go to Chicago.") "If McCarthy comes out and says Wait until 1972, then nice a man as he is, he sold you out." There are several more attacks upon McCarthy and the campaign. In the audience Lowenstein whispers, "All year the radical Left said, don't go into the McCarthy movement. It's a plot to make the peace movement look weak. Now they want sympathy for how well they did, even if cheated because the system can't work. They want it both ways." Now Hayden is saying that the situation will soon be one "when you will have to decide whether to be a good German or not. No candidate for President will be safe to speak in this country. . . ."

Later Lowenstein speaks. The speech was scheduled for 4:00 P.M. but somehow it ends up being set for midnight. So at midnight, with Scheer and Hayden and a determined delegation of SDS kids in his audience, Lowenstein begins to total up the board on the year to see what they accomplished. They ended the "inevitability of Lyndon Johnson's election and we might have done more except for June 4th. We did it without a major name, money, or the mass media. We showed that the system is not so resistant to change but that it is badly corroded. Now, however, we know more about what we're dealing with. . . . Even the most recalcitrant of leadership has become more responsive on Vietnam. Hubert Humphrey found out that he always agreed with Robert on Vietnam."

Then, as he is speaking, the SDS people put on what is called guerrilla theater. Someone tagged "Big Daddy" (the Left's nickname for Lowenstein) plays a recorder and invites a bunch of kids on to Chicago. The students arrive, do a dance, and are suddenly machine-gunned down by two men in khaki. Lowenstein stops and waits until the pageant is over.

"The kids who went to Chicago were just machine-gunned by someone from SDS," he says. Applause. "But on the basis of past experience, they will recover." The intensity of feeling against Lowenstein among the New Left is really astonishing. It is very deep and very bitter; he is probably their foremost enemy. In a generation where liberalism is weak on the campus and they are so strong, Lowenstein is one of the last effective liberals competing with them, and thus a very real target.

He continues: "The McCarthy people turned around public feeling on the war, made the opposition to it respectable, and only a small minority in the country now believes it can be won. This is the last stand of decaying institutions which have not met the needs of time. So that despite the enormity of your disappointment and my disappointment there are still some positive signs. The exalting fact is that ordinary people in a complex society felt they could affect the honor and future of their country and they did and out of this will come the kind of America we want."

A series of questions follow, mostly about whom he will support. He doesn't think it will be possible to support Humphrey.

"Is there a chance you will support Humphrey?" someone asks.

"Extremely remote," he says.

"So we won't be surprised if you do," says the same student.

The questions continue. Have American values caused Vietnam? Is Vietnam just a moral extension of America? Lowenstein grapples with it. "What we have in this country is the miseries of abundance," he says. "It is here that liberalism has been a failure. We grew up, a generation of us, with the assumptions of liberalism, that when you got rid of poverty and injustice you were happy. But that is not true, people are not more happy." The questions continue to come in, largely from the SDS kids, all of them in a sense calling for a confession of failure, and finally Lowenstein responds: "The problem with radical rhetoric is that it's very good, it's the best rhetoric there is in assessing liberal failures. It's very accurate there. But then with their own programs they give little more. As much as we liberals have failed and I think our failures are obvious now, I don't see any easy alternatives. We did change some things, we learned some things, and the fact that Bob Kennedy was murdered and Gene McCarthy was disorganized doesn't show me that the system won't work." He finishes and as he leaves the podium he is joined in a semi-debate by Hayden and Scheer; they want him to tell the kids to go to

Chicago ("But don't you want to prove that it's a rigged convention?" asks Scheer innocently). They keep pushing him on this, reminding him that he had been in previous demonstrations, and finally Lowenstein, exasperated, says, "I don't have any answers, but you don't have any programs. I can see events where I'll be as much a part of the resistance as you are. I hope it doesn't happen. But I don't think the final evidence is in that we've lost everything we started out to do and that we can't get out of the war. I think with the removal of Johnson they will understand the political crush of the war and they're opportunistic enough to get out." But Hayden and Scheer think that in discussing the success of the Dump Johnson movement Lowenstein has underestimated the role of the Vietcong and the Tet offensive. "You're leaving out the Tet offensive," Hayden says, "the fact that the war was unwinnable."

Lowenstein answers, "That's just it. We didn't have the Tet offensive when we went in last November but we went in anyway."

Friday, August 23, 1968

Lowenstein arrives in Chicago, a city sweltering hot and filled with police. He is probably the only Congressional nominee in America who wears a Biafran pin. "They come and ask you and you can't turn them down. You can't say, "This year I'm busy, come back in a year when my own country is less turbulent.' " He is in Chicago juggling his many roles: McCarthy pioneer, Kennedy scout, Congressional nominee, aging student leader, possible New York delegate, and white liberal with considerable black contacts. (He is a board member of Dr. King's SCLC. Since almost every other board member is a black Baptist minister, he was first listed on their programs as Reverend Allard Lowenstein. He called up a staff member to correct it and point out that he was Jewish. The next time he was listed as Rabbi Allard Lowenstein.) Mostly he is part of a loose coalition which is trying to stop Hubert Humphrey. Nominally that coalition is pro-McCarthy but there is the belief that in the week of the convention McCarthy will behave as he has in the last three weeks, too vague, too proud, unwilling to force his way into the vacuum, and thus that it will not be McCarthy.

Earlier in August McCarthy went to Maine for a five-day vacation with the omnipresent Robert Lowell. Kenneth Curtis, the Democratic Governor of Maine, who was wavering on Humphrey, had been softened up and was waiting for a phone call, perhaps even a meeting. It was a great five days but they never called the Governor. Now a strategy emerges: hold for McCarthy and McGovern as best you can, unite on a peace plank, try and force a split between Humphrey and Johnson on their Vietnam position, hope the alliance shatters, and then start picking up the pieces, holding Humphrey off on a first ballot. Behind all this is the hope that Ted Kennedy can be nominated.

There are some indications from Hyannis Port that under certain conditions it might be done. It would have to be a draft of sorts and it would have to be delicate. The Kennedy people are not particularly enthusiastic, and they do not want to be sucked out in the open for the Presidency, miss it, and then feel the steel trap of the Vice Presidency snap around their man. Lowenstein is committed to McCarthy as long as McCarthy has a chance, but it is quite clear that most of the McCarthy people have given up hope; McCarthy has his part of the convention but it is not likely to grow.

Lowenstein goes off to see some Negro leaders, particularly the Reverend Jesse Jackson. Jackson is perhaps the man in the King organization most likely to fill the leader's place, perhaps even the prototype of a new Negro leader in the North. He is young, handsome, dynamic, a fine fiery speaker, sort of Afro-mod-Baptist. Jackson had been leaning toward Humphrey (as were many older and more traditional Negro leaders), for McCarthy's failure to touch the nerve in the ghetto was a significant failure of his campaign; he simply refused to talk in a different tone, with more passion and more concern to any segment of the population. He may have realized the blacks needed it and perhaps even deserved it, but he believed that there were not twenty-five different kinds of Americans; he felt his record and what he was saying on the ghettos were enough. But they wanted passion and tangible signs of concern; they were not white America; their problems were greater and they would not be addressed in the same low key as white America. But now Rev. Jackson is shifting back toward McCarthy. Part of it is enormous pressure by the Kennedy-McCarthy people on Jackson, plus intense pressure on McCarthy to go and talk with Rev. Jackson's people. He is considered crucial; for though he is not well-known in the white political world, he may well be the most prestigious black still working inside the system. His credibility is great and his endorsement would be of immense value. He has been cool toward McCarthy, feeling the reservations that many Negroes feel; but about a month before the convention McCarthy had met with him and spoken to his church, one of the few times the McCarthy advisers had been successful in prevailing upon the candidate. "Now don't you go out there and condescend to my people. Don't you talk down," Jackson had told him. "You just go out and drop your load." It had gone well and Jackson's estrangement from Humphrey was intensified. Now on Friday night he was telling Lowenstein that he was thinking of endorsing McCarthy. "Hubert Humphrey is a grape of hope that has been turned into a raisin of despair by the sunshine of Lyndon Johnson," he said.

Saturday, August 24, 1968

The question is: will Allard K. Lowenstein be on the New York delegation? At present he is not, thanks to an extraordinary amount of internal shuffling and bickering among the delegates and also to Lowenstein's unique ability to attract the lightning. This does not displease the Humphrey people, since he has been a particular thorn to them all year. But now, under national exposure, it is becoming more difficult to keep Lowenstein off the delegation. He is a national figure within the party and an explosive, articulate speaker, one of the major critics of the war, and his absence would be difficult to explain. So by Saturday morning there is pressure to put him on the delegation.

Lowenstein finds it all very funny. "Even Humphrey is going around saying he wants me on the delegation," he says. "There's a conga line. They're all on it. They all really want to keep me off the delegation. But they also want to make sure that someone else gets the blame." Almost anyone else would be annoyed by all this shuffling around; not Lowenstein. He enjoys it. It means more intrigue, more meetings pro, more meetings con, more wheeling and dealing. He loves the wheeling and dealing as much as he loves the moral issues. "Al is a political nymphomaniac," a friend says.

Sunday, August 25, 1968

Allard Lowenstein the cheerleader: spreading good cheer, optimism, and hints of Teddy Kennedy. The McCarthy people are gloomy and depressed; at caucuses the hint that Kennedy might be willing to run brings a marked change in the atmosphere, a sense of hope. At this point Kennedy represents the only possibility of stopping Humphrey. Lowenstein feels there is an easing of the bitterness between some of the Kennedy and McCarthy people on the peace plank and a growing awareness of the problems the Humphrey people have trying to get out from beneath Johnson's vanity on Vietnam. But there are problems everywhere. "Some of the McCarthy people are going around pleased because they think Unruh is for them. But the opposite is true. If he's for them it's a sign he thinks the game is over and he just wants to make his own separate peace with the California peace people, tidy up his lines for the next Governor's race. If he *holds*, that means there's a chance," Lowenstein says.

There are also myriad problems in Chicago. The phone system has broken down completely, with an assist from Mayor Daley and Illinois Bell (Daley's motto is no communications is good communications). In the lobby of the Hilton there are about twenty beautiful plastic house telephones all in a row. They rarely work. "It's all electronic but they get overheated and burn out," laughs the desk clerk.

Lowenstein spends the morning darting in and out of meetings, trying to keep troops in line, and most of it is spent at a Coalition for an Open Convention meeting where fourth-party rumblings are more than rumblings. They are ready to march, people like Marcus Raskin of the Institute for Policy Studies, and Sanford Gottlieb of SANE. But there is a defeated quality to the meeting. Everyone is physically and emotionally spent. They have run out of money, and out of unpaid volunteers, and out of gas.

Lowenstein tells them they are $16,000 in the hole, "but it's really much more." A good many people at the meeting want to break out of the party right now and issue their fourth-party statement. "This party means nothing," one of them says, "and the sooner we get on with electing Richard Nixon the better. You people are still talking about 1968. It's a mistake—1968 is over. So let's start working for a new party and 1970 and 1972." Someone gets up and says the only problem about the fourth party is whether to draft McCarthy right now or wait until after the convention. Otherwise we let all the discontent with Humphrey and Nixon get funneled to Wallace, and the politicians will read all the wrong signs from what happened during the year." Lowenstein holds them off. "If we do this now it'll be like issuing a statement saying McCarthy can't win. It will be an admission of defeat and it will strengthen Humphrey and I don't think we're defeated yet." He holds them off; a decision is delayed until after the convention.

We drive off to another meeting of McCarthy people. Raskin rides with us. He is talking about his new party, "the young third-tier labor leaders, and the radical farmers." It sounds very far away. The next meeting reflects more of the same frustration: how to be heard on the floor without damaging McCarthy. If they protest too much, won't that solidify the Humphrey people? McCarthy disdains leadership while these people spin around in the vacuum. They don't know where to go and who is to lead them. Lowenstein gives brief advice and hustles off to lunch with Ronnie Dugger, the Texas liberal. To Dugger, Lowenstein delivers a long lecture on the liberal possibilities of Amarillo. *Amarillo*. The possibilities are very great, it seems, and have long been neglected by other Texas liberals. "All over Amarillo they kept asking me, Why doesn't someone come up and integrate us with that liberal crowd from Austin." The subject of the fourth party comes up. Lowenstein is edgy about it. When he was running out on Long Island the Liberal party heard he might favor a fourth party and it called him in to question him about this and other stands he was taking.

"How do you feel about fourth parties?" one of the Liberals asked him.

"Some have done very well and have contributed a great deal to this country," he answered.

There was a gasp. Lowenstein was turning out to be just as bad as they had heard. "Which ones?" he was asked.

"Well, for example, the Liberal party," he said.

By Sunday evening it has become somehow clear that a Humphrey nomination will not bring sad tidings to just Waverly, Minnesota, but that it may well mean a disaster of consummate magnitude, bringing down the party's best Senatorial and Congressional people, purging the state house of Democrats, costing the towns their aldermen "and many of our best dogcatchers," in the bitter words of one Kennedy backer who had been warning all year of this and was now being believed. "There must be about three or four Humphrey people who've come up to me and told me that I was right about Humphrey and the fact that he wouldn't be able to change back to the old Humphrey overnight." The polls reflect Humphrey's weakness; but it is more serious than that. There is an intuitive sense that in the six weeks that he has been campaigning he has not caught fire because he cannot catch fire. His style is hopelessly outdated, and he does not, cannot perhaps, sense the new styles, the new issues and the seriousness of the objections to him.

There is talk about Mayor Daley wanting Teddy; Daley is clearly unable to go for McCarthy. He may be better in the polls and he may even be a winner, and Daley likes winners above all else, but he is just too irregular, too unpredictable, he does not know the language. Today Daley and Illinois caucus and delay their decision three days, which starts an escalation of rumors. This makes an interesting situation because of Daley's dual power. His police are already behaving like thugs and pushing everyone around, but everyone is quiet about it; the Kennedy, McCarthy, and Humphrey people, because his votes are still too important. He may be an SOB, but he can deliver the convention, or come very close to it. Right now, on Teddy, he appears to be playing an interesting game. He is hinting at it, without committing himself. Daley and Jesse Unruh meet, spreading even more rumors. Lowenstein starts to grow more and more optimistic. That night, on the way to dinner, he is interrupted by a man from Wyoming who comes over to introduce his wife. "This is the fella I told you about, Margaret. The one who came out last year and made that speech about Johnson. Said it could be done and by God he was right. Well, young fella, you're all right." Lowenstein protests that it is people like the man from Wyoming who did it. He is growing euphoric: Teddy seems ready to go. "Everyone will now act according to character. Johnson will try to screw Humphrey, because he's Johnson. That coalition will shatter. McCarthy will hold his strength but not pick up. Then they will turn to Teddy."

Monday, August 26, 1968

The first Teddy buttons begin to appear. *Draft Teddy*. Done so quickly they are made of paper. Dick Tuck, the prankster, is distributing Humphrey-Connally buttons designed to terrify the liberals that are left in the Humphrey camp. Lowenstein is chasing from caucus to caucus. The New York caucus is a particular zoo. It is filled with reporters and hangers-on, nearly doubling its size. So they ask all non-delegates to stand up and no one stands up. So they ask all delegates to stand up and everyone stands up. So they make everyone leave the hall, then let them back in, one at a time, delegates only. So the caucus starts, three hours late.

Lowenstein heads for still another private meeting and I slip downstairs to have lunch with three McCarthy friends, upper-middle rank. The conversation is filled with the kind of love-frustration-anger which has marked the entire McCarthy campaign. While caucus after caucus of varying states are dying to see him, he is aloof and proud (he will attend only five caucuses finally); the last chance to take the convention, to storm in and flex some might, some polls, and some determination in caucus after caucus is ebbing. Some of his people in these delegations are pleading with him to give it one more try; the Humphrey thing is coming unstuck. But he cannot do it.

Those qualities about McCarthy, observable early in the campaign, the loner, the individualist, the mocker of the American system, have now hardened. There is the quality of brilliance when he wants to be brilliant; at his best there is no one quite like him in American politics, his very detachment allows him to soar above the pettiness and the old blocs and to talk of real visions, of appeals to individual conscience. But there is arrogance bordering on perversity and more, the pride, the ferocity, the refusal to do anything he disdains, even if it is for a larger end. He did not like Robert Kennedy while alive, he will not say anything gracious about him in death. He can go before the California delegation, a delegation he needs, in a private meeting, a Kennedy delegation, and not mention Robert Kennedy's name. Nor will he glad-hand. Or pander. Every man chokes on something; Eugene McCarthy chokes on pride.

So now at lunch the varying McCarthy stories are being told, told in the frustration and the irritation and the numbness of this convention.

"He took us a long way. He went alone and we went a long way with him," one of the people says. "He gave us back something of ourselves."

But another interjects: "Yes, he took us a long way. But he screwed us. We gave him a lot. We invested a lot in him, a hell of a lot of us. He owed us more than he gave us. It wasn't enough. Oh sometimes he even laughed at us."

"I'm not going to leave this thing bitter," the first man says. "He took us further than anyone ever took us before. What the hell would we be like this week if we were here and he hadn't tried? How would we feel about ourselves? Look, you can't expect him to change. He's this kind of man. That's all there is. He isn't going to change for you. For him this convention is like taking out the garbage."

"But it isn't changing for us. It's changing for the issue which brought us all into it."

Then a quick discussion on how McCarthy views man: he does not believe man is perfectible. He thinks man has failings, and God looks down from on high and maybe good things can be done and maybe they can't and you can't push it too far.

A Kennedy man with a touch of bitterness suggests that it is too bad that McCarthy had such a protective press at the end; that the warts on Bobby were always exposed, but that McCarthy's weaknesses were often hidden, discussed only in the inner circle, but not written about.

"Look," said the first man, "I'm not going to feel badly about what was written about Bobby. Gene went in first and he did the right thing. Some of the things you're complaining about, kissing this ass, and kissing that ass, going to this caucus, are going to look pretty damn small fifty years from now and a lot of the things he did are going to look pretty damn big if anyone's left around to judge."

We discuss the security situation. It is oppressive. Security is unpleasant in the first place, no one likes it; but the better the security people are, the quicker and more clinical they can make their job. But this is another thing. Daley's people, particularly his plainclothesmen, are pushing everyone around. The Mayor is clearly mounting a disaster; he does not think the Yippies have the right to protest, since they are not in the party. (In the middle of the Ribicoff demonstration, when Ribicoff came of age and told Daley how hard it is, one of Daley's people, fourth row of the phalanx, turned to another and said, "He ain't so much; I hear he ain't even organization.") Worse, they do not have votes. So there is no point in compromising with them, giving them Soldiers Field.

Daley looks at them and gets angry; he listens and it is worse. It is all changing so fast. (When one of his chief deputies in a suburban area lost his area to a peace candidate, Daley was perplexed: What went wrong? Was the garbage collected? Did they need garbage pails?) There is something ominous about the entire police setup, the vast hordes of them around the Hilton, the arrogance of them at the Amphitheatre. Lowenstein, for instance, was arrested and detained for more than thirty minutes because he walked in with a copy of the New York *Times*; he was creating a fire hazard, it seems.

Tuesday, August 27, 1968

A convention is not sane at all, and it does not test rationality. It is not a matter of who is the best-informed person, or the best-organized, or the most creative; it is a matter of who functions best at 2:00 A.M., who bears best the lack of sleep. At 3:00 A.M. everyone is still trying to react to the events of the previous day, or more accurately, the rumored events of the previous day. Better men may have fallen, the way is open to those men of greater endurance. ("This all wouldn't have happened," Robert Kennedy once said of the choice of Lyndon Johnson as Vice President, "except we were all too tired last night.") Everything is disorganized; either one has not eaten at all, or one eats lunch three times as a means of seeing three different sets of people. There is a sense of touching everything and touching nothing; one is at the center of action and yet feels that the action must be elsewhere. Are you at the convention hall? Then the action must be with the Yippies. Are you with the Yippies? Then it must be at the hall. If you are with McGovern, then it must be with McCarthy. New York? Then with California.

Lowenstein naturally thrives on this. The rest of the world has come round to his way of living. He lives like this all the time and he is at home here, spinning off people, wheeling and dealing. ("God, am I glad to see you. I've been looking all over . . ." And then he sees someone else over *this* person's shoulder, breaks contact, and rushes off.) He is surrounded by coteries of young men. Can they all be student-body presidents? He dispatches them on their many missions of mercy, one to look for James Wechsler, the New York *Post* columnist, and to hold him ("he's rather short and wears bow ties . . ."), one to call Dick Goodwin's room, one to find Mark Raskin, one to find chocolate malts, and, yes, one, to find his wife.

On the way to the Amphitheatre that night he is optimistic and getting more so. The tough Vietnam plank dictated from Washington that Humphrey has accepted does not bother him. "Clarifies the convention. It's clear now. Connally is Humphrey's Thurmond. Humphrey's going to pay a heavy price for this." He is fairly optimistic about the peace plank, supposed to be voted on that night. The Teddy boomlet is still in the background but it is surfacing fast now. Events are starting to get ahead of themselves. Behind Lowenstein's optimism is the belief that Teddy will accept a draft under certain conditions, and he senses that those conditions will be met, that McCarthy will make the move. The thirst for Teddy, the craving for him is very real and it reveals, if nothing else, the party's bankruptcy (the fact that it has the sitting President is largely disguised here). It is badly torn, disorganized, factionalized, and its leadership is largely in the past; most of the men who have made reputations have made them on issues that are increasingly irrelevant; in the cities where new reputations might be made, the Democratic leaders are more often than not tied to corrupt, corroded machines, or at least neutralized by the machines. The party looks for fresh blood; it finds a thirty-six-year-old Kennedy.

The Teddy boomlet reflects the desperation of the moment. Teddy rumors swirl, from the floor to TV, back to the floor, then fed back again to reporters. In a press room, a reliable friend grabs me, and says, "*Teddy's on his way here, I know it and that is a fact*"; whereas, of course, Teddy was on his way at that moment across his Hyannis Port living room. Meanwhile there are other rumors. McCarthy has *conceded.* Around the hall it goes. *McCarthy concedes.* Someone in the McCarthy camp is screaming, *How can he do this to us?* Goodwin is holding a press conference to deny it. On the floor the same old anachronistic procedures are in full force, and the convention goes its dreary way, two different worlds swirling around each other, the old one, used as a base from which the modern electronic one can operate. The floor seems to be quieting down. One senses that the Teddy boomlet is ebbing. Kennedy will once again ask that his name not be presented.

Late this night, I have drinks with an old friend. What are you doing, he asks me. Covering Lowenstein, I answer. "Oh that guy," he says. "Isn't he the one who's been working behind the scenes for Terry Sanford for Vice President?"

Wednesday, August 28, 1968

The Teddy boomlet died last night, and the reasons are still a matter of some confusion. McCarthy met with Steve Smith, who was serving as Teddy's eyes here. Both sides have different versions of what happened. What is clear is that they talk different languages; the Kennedys' is sharp, blunt. McCarthy more opaque, more mystic. What he does not say is almost as important as what he does say. McCarthy gave what he felt were clear and present signals. Stephen Smith did not thus interpret them. Probably had he spent the entire year as a McCarthy lieutenant he would have understood that McCarthy was implying that he knew he could not win and he was releasing his delegates, if they wanted him to. They thought that somehow he was insisting upon a pure and complete draft and for them to make the first step. In addition, word of the meeting soon leaked out; it was bound to; Chicago for a week is a city without secrets. But the Kennedys, who were very edgy about this whole thing, believed McCarthy had deliberately leaked it, as a means of making the whole thing messy. The leakage did make the thing messier, and above all the Kennedys did not want a messy fight. They really did not want the nomination at all. They did not think this would be a particularly good year, they were still shattered from the assassination, and they were worried over post-assassination turbulence. Yet the pressure for Teddy to go, to save the party, was intense, and growing stronger all the time, and the Kennedys are not great waiters. Given an option of waiting their normal turn for some race, as everyone else has done, and going at a precocious age against all normal odds and tradition, they will go for it. If it could be done quietly and sprung at the last minute they would accept (it really would have been a draft), sensing that despite all the factionalism, their young fresh face could defeat Richard Nixon's stubble-lined face in a close race. The role of Daley in all this is at best devious. He was a figure in it; he did in a way encourage the boomlet by holding back on Sunday. Yet when it seemed ready to go (and it would have gone; Teddy Kennedy was very nearly nominated in the party's desperation) he quickly moved to deflate it. Daley later claimed that Teddy would have to ask for it, something of course he knew Kennedy would not do. The more likely explanation, and one believed by the Kennedy people, is that Daley was trying to flush Teddy out in the open and then spring the Vice Presidency on him, having first proven his availability. Either way Daley would have emerged as the kingmaker. Teddy did not bite; the young Irish are as shrewd as the old Irish.

With Teddy goes the last of Lowenstein's hopes. The night before, he was elated, the impossible seemed possible ("the greatest miracle of our time is about to happen," he told one friend who needed a little bucking up). Now he lacks both the votes and the candidate. Even the peace plank is in trouble. Though the Administration plank is hard-line and Humphrey is swallowing it, the Humphrey people have come up with a slick defensive move, an amendment to the main plank put up by more moderate Humphrey forces (Clark Kerr, Victor Reuther, etc.). Anxious to see Humphrey elected, the war ended, and the party healed, they are now pre-selling their amendment, which is more dovish than the Administration position.

The idea is that the Administration position goes through and then the Humphrey forces join the peace forces and come up with the good moderate position. Some of Lowenstein's people have been saying that the amendment looks good and he is trying to hold the line. "I spent two years of my life fighting this. We didn't want it then, and we don't want it now," he tells a Negro woman. "I'm not going to give these people respectability. Tell them they won't have our votes. Tell them they can get their votes from Texas." It is the first time I have seen him angry. The proposed moderate amendment has changed the basic balance on the Vietnam plank; some big states, such as Ohio, Michigan, and Pennsylvania, which might have gone for the peace plank are now swinging the other way. "They won't have our votes," Lowenstein says. "They've just bought the hawk amendment." And the moderate amendment never comes to a vote; its sponsors realize they cannot bring the peace people around. It takes the steam out of the peace plank. It will now go down to defeat.

Now, steadily, the entire convention becomes a scenario of the party's bankruptcy. Even in the Vietnam plank debate the emptiness is obvious. Most of the men arguing for the peace plank have been silent for four years, brought to the podium now to rekindle the Kennedy flame; they are men like Theodore Sorensen who felt in March that the issue was not worthy of Bob Kennedy making the race. It is one more sad note for the party that even here, among its dissenters, there is little in the way of fresh young leadership. One listens to Sorensen and senses that in some ways the radicals are right, that the Cold War put the liberals of this country too much on the defensive, that for some the price paid in fending off the right wing, fighting with conservative forces for minor victories, proving one's basic anti-Communism, took too much out of them. In the years the Democrats have been in power—and thus in a sense the liberals—the power of the Pentagon has grown to the point where it is to a younger generation *the* issue of American life. One senses that one era is ending for the party; perhaps slowly, in the embers here, another is beginning. There is no guarantee of it.

At almost the same time, Daley's police unleash themselves against the Yippies, cracking heads indiscriminately. It is, like the convention itself, a symbol of the inability to handle real problems. The Yippies have come here and failed; their turnout was far below what they expected and needed. The radical Left accuses Lowenstein of manipulation, though of course that is their own game: manipulation and provocation. And who in Chicago have they manipulated? Why Richard J. Daley, of course. For it is true that they have shouted foul words (in unison and in cadence) against the President and the Vice President, worse, even against the Mayor. And the Mayor, the Mayor whose face turns red at off-color stories and who does not like his deputies to play around (though alcohol is a permitted vice, indeed almost an expected sign of weakness of the flesh), the Mayor sent the cops after those kids. He would show them; if their protests were meant to provoke, why, the Mayor would honor that protest, he would be provoked. If the Democrats had shown that they could no longer cope with the country, the Mayor would use their convention to prove it.

All of this has taken place while Hubert Humphrey is being nominated. The dream of all those years coming home, finally so tarnished, and Humphrey was unable to stop it, or worse to *try* to stop it at least; to say something. He was offering himself, he would deal with Brezhnev and de Gaulle and the Joint Chiefs though he is too weak and eroded to deal with Daley *even after the nomination*; perhaps he would go to bed that night telling Muriel that he could not understand why the young no longer loved him and why the liberals had turned on him.

On the floor Lowenstein is trying to get to the podium to make a motion to adjourn until the city does something about the police (an interesting motion which, given the anger of delegates, might have carried; enough had been roughed up by then). In the New York delegation, John Burns refuses to let him use the microphone (which is probably not turned on anyway) so he has to go to the podium. But no one can get near the podium. The Illinois delegation blocks it, and the Illinois delegation is blocked by great circles of plainclothesmen. As Lowenstein moves forward he is hemmed in by the plainclothesmen. They refuse to let him move forward. "I'm a delegate from New York trying to make a motion," he says. "No, you're not," one says. "You're not going to make a motion."

He pushes forward again. "Listen, sonny. Be a good boy. Push off," one of them says. "There are federal agents here and they know what you're doing and you're going to be in trouble."

As he leaves the floor he is grabbed by a New York reformer, an angry one.

"Why isn't Teddy being put in nomination?"

"Because the big shots don't want it," he answers.

"The big shots didn't want Lyndon Johnson beaten and it didn't stop you. Why don't you do something?" she screams at him.

"I don't know who appointed me Jesus Christ. Isn't there anyone else here?"

Later he is grabbed by a series of television reporters, and he gives them something. To one: "This convention elected Richard Nixon President of the United States tonight. That's like electing Arthur Goldberg Mayor of Cairo. I never thought it would happen." On it goes; he heads toward a final meeting of all the McCarthy delegates. (They would meet, pledge themselves to come back again, and then hold a candlelight walk back to the city.) As he goes off to the caucus, the fatigue finally showing, I remember what Ronnie Dugger said about him, recalling a visit Lowenstein made to Texas last August. "He didn't even have a candidate at that time. But he came down and he was organizing and putting it together, telling us it could be done, that we were not alone. That was very important, that we were not alone. And then I remember taking him to the airport afterwards and watching him walk up the ramp, and I thought, my God, there goes one man trying to take on the entire system alone, and I felt a certain chill. It was pretty damn impressive."

Thursday, August 29, 1968

The full recognition of what has happened spreads all over the city; if there is one thing that binds people here, it is a desperate urge to get away from Chicago. (What do you think of the convention, Mr. O'Dwyer? asks a radio reporter, shoving his little beeper at Paul O'Dwyer, and O'Dwyer, bless him, does not analyze the role of the Left, or the Right, or the Center; he says very simply, "It's a horror.") Even Lowenstein is dejected. He runs around from meeting to meeting, arguing fourth parties and Vice Presidential nominations (shall they use nominations for the Vice Presidency as a means of attacking the convention?). But it is all gone. He is still bothered about whether or not he should have put Kennedy's name in nomination, even without the great powers; he is convinced that the support was there, that they could have done it without Daley. But can you inflict the nomination on a man who does not seek it, the surviving son of a tragedy-riddled family in such a particularly violent year? No, you can't, he thinks, and then he talks about all that was riding on it this year, how much work by so many people had gone into it, what the consequences may be, and he is uneasy.

In the afternoon, McCarthy's farewell and it is excellent. He is at his best: "But what of the great issues which we raised—the war and the question of priorities for this nation? Because that was the substance of our commitment. The other reforms of procedure and process and party were secondary. It would appear that we lost on the platform fight. And in a quantitative sense, any kind of numerical measure, you would have to say that we did lose at this convention. But that was not the measure of the judgment which was passed in this country. So what we can do is go on to continue to present to the people as best we can for judgment between now and November the issues we have been raising for nine

97

months in this country. . . . I think that the outlook is one that must be reassuring: one of confidence and of optimism—not really of our own making but by virtue of our having discovered it to exist in the minds and in the hearts of the people of this country. I think we can say we were willing to open the box and to see what America was. We had that kind of trust and that kind of confidence. And when we opened it, we found that the people of this nation were not wanting."

It is very good stuff; he is speaking extemporaneously and yet the words have a precision and a finality to them. They will be around a while. I mention this idea to a boy who has worked all year for McCarthy. And the kid says, "He's a great loser."

Then downstairs to wait for Humphrey's press conference. He will announce his Vice President. He is forty minutes late, and this is a busy day. We are all restless. I ask one reporter who covers him if he's often late. "He's *always* late," says the reporter. "He's incompetent. He can't stop talking. Right now he's upstairs talking to someone he's already convinced." McCarthy said of him yesterday in a long interview with the Chicago *Daily News*: "Hubert's all right on decisions. He usually makes good ones. It's when he starts to talk that anything can happen. I remember in 1954 when everyone was talking about the new Humphrey and how mellow and tempered he was. And he went out to speak to a labor group in Ohio and suddenly it's in the papers about Ike being a canary in a gilded cage while back in the kitchen the blackbirds were eating up the public pie, and upstairs everyone was sunny and light, while downstairs in the cellar there were white creepy crawly things everywhere. So I asked him, 'Hubert what happened to the new Humphrey?' and he answered: 'I heard the whistle blow.' "

Tuck's parody and satire paper claims that Humphrey will nominate Agnew "to dispel the reports of the Eastern Establishment press that there are serious differences between him and Nixon." Finally he arrives. It is Muskie. It will be the "most exciting and challenging race since Franklin Roosevelt." I am nervous but the lightning fails to strike.

Thursday night, riding to the convention hall, the impossible happens. Allard K. Lowenstein—after 18 months of 2,367 speeches in 1,392 cities, 70 percent of them under 50,000 population, 288,021 miles of travel, and 678 missed meals—has laryngitis. He cannot talk. He writes messages to friends. He has a sprayer for his throat. His aides have asked the TV commentators what they use for their throats and the answer is nothing. Nevertheless he sprays and swallows. His wife, Jenny, finds this very amusing. She is a woman who bears her burdens well, the thousands of young people swarming in and out of her home, wearing her clothes, tending her child. Or at least she did until 5:00 A.M. today. Lowenstein, taking pity on the weak, had promised to turn their room over to McCarthy kids to sleep in. By 5:30 the kids had not come by and the Lowensteins went to sleep. But at 6:30 the kids come by and demand the room and Lowenstein gets up, Jenny with him, she very angry, protesting, "I don't care if they're wounded. I don't care if they're dying." Then they give the room up. "He kept introducing them to me," she recalled later, "and I kept refusing to be introduced. Perhaps I'll never be a politician's wife."

"What do you think he's running for?" someone asked her.

"Some minor deity," she said.

"Are you sure it's minor?"

On the Floor

The local Jewish War Veterans post calls up, demanding that Lowenstein apologize to the Chicago police. (This is a typical Daley move; he calls his man with the Jews, who calls his man with the JWV, and thus the Jew is reprimanded, not by Mayor Daley, the Mayor is never touched by this criticism, he is above it, but by people of, yes, his own *ethnic persuasion*). Tonight Daley is making a comeback. Somewhat bruised by all the attention he received Wednesday, he is making a Thursday comeback. On the way to the hall the street corners are crowded with Daley supporters and in the hall itself the claque is at the ready. This is the age of television and perhaps a more subtle man might disguise his claque, make it look like a spontaneous claque, but not Daley; a claque is a claque and a convention is a City Hall meeting. They are all there, they sit together, wear the same clothes, carry the same signs, have the same faces, sitting there row on row, and at signals from the floor below, they cheer. "We Love Daley." No impact. Had he dispersed them through the hall and left out a few signs he might have fooled someone.

During the session, they show the film on Robert Kennedy; it would always be hard to bear, but in this setting, following these events, it is too much, the view of this good and decent and strong young man. It underscores the emptiness and the ugliness of the rest of the week. On the floor the movie touches off a deep-rooted emotion and demonstration. People begin to sing "The Battle Hymn of the Republic." Singing for Kennedy, against Chicago, angrily and bitterly.

Carl Albert, who was working for Humphrey (they had, after all, the peace plank and the Presidency and the Vice Presidency, and the Credentials, they had already won, for whatever it was worth), Carl Albert is a stylish man, and so he relentlessly gavels it down; after five days of banality he realizes that five minutes of singing is too much, and he moves to silence it. It goes on for nineteen minutes. It takes We-Love-Daley demonstrations finally to silence it. Now the dissidents are trying to nominate Vice Presidential candidates but this is difficult; you have to reserve time in advance, and they cannot get time. The whole evening begins to repeat last night. Reports keep coming in of delegates arrested and tear-gassed. David Hoeh, the chairman of the New Hampshire delegation, is arrested for using a credit card in the security machine. It flashed green. His arrest at the end seems symbolic; I had last seen him December 4 in Manchester, New Hampshire, pleading with McCarthy to enter the state. Only twenty-one days, he pleaded. McCarthy shook his head. Okay, only fourteen days then, he pleaded, we can do it, and then finally grabbing me, asking me to convince McCarthy to do it; somehow his arrest seems to end it as his pleading had begun it. On the floor, Wisconsin is nominating Julian Bond and asking for Allard K. Lowenstein of New York to second it. Like Edward Kennedy, Julian Bond is too young, even legally too young, and it would not work. Allard K. Lowenstein has laryngitis. But even so Carl Albert is afraid and Hubert Humphrey is too weak, and they will not let him speak. And perhaps they are right.

THE KIDS AGAINST
THE GROWN-UPS

Calvin Trillin

The New Yorker, November 16, 1968

Lowenstein was deeply engaged in Dump Johnson activities through most of 1967. Early in 1968, he decided against a U.S. Senate race in New York and continued to campaign for McCarthy in New Hampshire. When the antiwar coalition broke into factions, Lowenstein looked for ways to advance the antiwar cause and avoid the rift between the McCarthy and Kennedy forces.

After a debate on the war on Long Island in January, he had been approached about running for Congress by a group of pro-McCarthy Dissenting Democrats. Over the next two months he considered the possibility, and on March 31—the day of Johnson's withdrawal—he was nominated at a Dissenting Democrats convention to be a candidate from New York's 5th District.

Buttressed by appearances by Paul Newman, Richard Goodwin and others as well as endorsements from Senator McCarthy, Southern Christian Leadership Conference leader Ralph Abernathy and John Kenneth Galbraith, Lowenstein marshaled a legion of community and student volunteers. But his candidacy was opposed by most of the Nassau County Democratic Party organization, and he was not expected to win the primary, let alone a general election in the heavily Republican district.

LOWENSTEIN: ACTS OF COURAGE AND BELIEF

One of Lowenstein's favorite film moments was the scene from The African Queen *when Katharine Hepburn and Humphrey Bogart emerge from an unnavigable jungle river. Told that the stream is clearly impassable, the feisty Miss Hepburn raises her head and replies, "Nevahtheless . . ."* Newsweek *saw something analogous in Lowenstein's congressional race: "At the moment, the odds are against him. But Lowenstein has spent his life supporting underdogs and it seems fitting that the same should hold true now that the cause is, for once, his own. . . . Now, in his race for Congress, some people are telling him that he hardly stands a chance, that he would need a miracle to win, that the miracles he wrought for others he cannot achieve for himself. Nevertheless . . ."*

An article in the New Yorker *examined the campaign.*

In discussing the awesome level of political activity maintained by Allard K. Lowenstein as a student, those who knew him at Yale Law School sometimes insist that when people called New Haven information to ask for his telephone number they got an instantaneous reply, as if they had asked for the number of the New York, New Haven & Hartford Railroad. Several years after that, in the late fifties and early sixties, Lowenstein's friends and acquaintances—a group that, according to some calculations, is large enough to be expressed as a percentage of the American population—often joked about his being the oldest living student politician in the United States. In those years, Lowenstein appeared to be about the only adult in America who believed that the college student of the American Dream—healthy, exuberant, basically right-thinking—was either politically interested or politically interesting. Whether Lowenstein was officially working as a dean at Stanford or as a foreign-policy adviser in Washington, he continued to spend a lot of nights sprawled in the second-hand armchairs of college-dormitory rooms, arguing with equal intensity about the evils of South Africa or the role of the fraternity system. Even in New York or Washington, Lowenstein always seemed to be accompanied by a couple of clean-cut young men who would be introduced as, say, a recently returned Rhodes Scholar and the president of the University of North Carolina student government—a pair of Wasp outriders, ready at any hint of trouble to shake hands hard, call their elders "sir," and talk about commitment to the democratic process. The events that caused other adults to take such students seriously came about largely because of Lowenstein's efforts. The participation of hundreds of Northern white college students in the Mississippi voter-registration project of 1964 was the outgrowth of Lowenstein's having induced a number of Stanford and Yale undergraduates to go to Mississippi the previous year to hold a mock election; the students who went to New Hampshire last winter to work for Eugene McCarthy and the Impossible Dream were, like McCarthy himself, present partly in response to the urgings of Lowenstein, who was once almost alone in believing that the Vietnam-war policy could somehow be changed by the electoral process. It was not surprising that when Lowenstein himself decided to run for Congress this year in the Fifth District of New York— a collection of middle-class bedroom communities that extends into Nassau County from New York City along the South Shore of Long Island—he attracted hundreds of weekend volunteers from colleges like Yale and Harvard and Smith, and put together a full-time staff so young that his official campaign manager, a middle-aged man named Horace Kramer, sometimes seemed to be playing the role of token grownup. Although some of the weekend volunteers had worked in the McCarthy or Kennedy campaigns, most of them appeared to be students who had never been involved in politics before; a large number of the Yale volunteers were freshmen. When staff members were asked one day how they had been able to persuade so many students to devote autumn weekends to the house-to-house canvassing of Nassau County, they suggested that some of the more politically involved students might have wanted to make one last attempt at working for social change through the electoral process, and that some of the girls might have decided to settle for the Saturday-night canvassers' party in Lawrence or Long Beach because they hadn't been invited to New Haven for the Dartmouth game. "To tell the truth," one young man said, smiling, "I think most of the kids who came think they're personal friends of Al's."

Many Nassau County citizens who saw Lowenstein on television as a leader of those opposing Mayor Daley's regulars at the Chicago Convention identified him not just with the respectable campaign volunteers who have always formed the core of his following but with the Yippies in Grant Park and the S.D.S. occupation forces at Columbia and the depraved acid-heads who threaten to offend grownups in the street—or, for all a grownup knows, might be living under his own roof, cleverly disguised as his children. American voters have never been scrupulous about precise categories; Lowenstein is a leader of kids, and the campaign in the

Fifth District eventually concerned the suspicions harbored by adults about all kids. Speaking one day before a Lions luncheon in Long Beach, Lowenstein offered an eyewitness account of how young people who had gone to Chicago to work for McCarthy's candidacy had been beaten by the police while they were sitting quietly in the McCarthy campaign suite. When asked what seventeen-year-old girls were doing in a Chicago hotel in the first place, Lowenstein said that adults ought to be grateful for the young people who were willing to participate in the political process, and that the channelling of young people's dissent into such activities was the only way to avoid the disruptive politics of confrontation that he, along with most other Americans, deplores. "They went there for trouble," a man down the luncheon table muttered. "That's what—for trouble."

Lowenstein's opponent—Mason Hampton, Jr., a conservative lawyer—is thirty-seven, two years younger than Lowenstein, but he made it clear from the start that he was on the side of grownups. He spoke of the breakdown of law and order as having been caused by "the permissive view gone wild." Because Lowenstein is a vice-chairman of Americans for Democratic Action, Hampton could have confronted him with any number of A.D.A. resolutions that Nassau County voters might consider at least unwise and perhaps treasonous; the one Hampton chose was a resolution against treating the use of marijuana as a crime. Lowenstein kept repeating that he was opposed to the legalization of marijuana, but that still left him far less militantly grown-up on the issue than Hampton, who for a while seemed to be proposing capital punishment for marijuana sellers—a position that prompted one of the jollier members of Lowenstein's staff to put up a sign in the office reading "Mason Hampton is a junkie." The Hampton forces occasionally claimed to have their own influence with the young. ("We have students, too, only ours don't use obscene language," a Hampton campaign worker told me.) But a week or so before the election Hampton predicted that he would win because his polls showed that he was getting the support of sixty-five per cent of the voters over forty-five. One of the Hampton campaign pictures that appeared in local papers showed him flanked by four or five middle-aged women who were dressed completely in white—white tennis shoes, white skirts, white sweatshirts with Mason Hampton bumper stickers stuck on them—and were waving what looked like cheerleaders' pompons. The caption identified them as "Mothers for Hampton."

One of Lowenstein's primary-campaign posters described him as the man who had "helped bring America's young people home," and his general-election campaign was based partly on the premise that there are some American young people worth having at home. In high schools of Republican towns like Rockville Centre and Freeport and Baldwin, straw votes showed that even students who favored Richard Nixon supported Lowenstein—as if they realized that their reputation was on the line. The visits of polite young men and women to the residents of the South Shore were designed not merely to bring word of Lowenstein's candidacy but to demonstrate to the citizenry that polite young men and women actually still exist. Senior-citizens clubs that invited Lowenstein to speak were delighted to find him accompanied by a courteous young friend named Franklin Delano Roosevelt III; in the last weekend of the campaign Lowenstein was joined by Wendell Willkie, Jr. During that final weekend, in the West End of Long Beach—a lower-middle-class neighborhood, where Hampton is treasured as a man who first came to public notice as the lawyer for some Long Island parents who were opposing a plan to integrate schools by busing students—Irish Catholics who had almost shouted Lowenstein off the platform a couple of nights before were astonished to open their doors and be handed some Lowenstein literature by earnest young men who had come in for the weekend from Notre Dame.

"Regardless of the preparations you've made for a dialogue, you'll find that most of these people don't want to talk," a Lowenstein staff member said to a group of students from Boston while briefing them for a Saturday of canvassing. A congressional race in Nassau County is not a crusade for peace. A year or so ago, Lowenstein, as the leader of a movement that set out to end the war by replacing the President, might have been considered a bit of a traitor by the residents of Nassau County, but almost everyone is against the war now in one way or another. For weeks after the Chicago Convention, Lowenstein resisted the demands of local Democrats that he support Hubert Humphrey, going no further than to say, after mid-October, that he had decided to vote for Humphrey himself. But the long weeks of campaigning gradually submerged Lowenstein's role as a lone dissident to the extent that the issue stressed by his campaign workers in the final days was that Hampton was not a regular—being a founder of the Conservative Party who had managed to get Republican endorsement, rather than a proper Republican—and that Lowenstein was therefore the only candidate in the mainstream of the two great political parties. Most people visited by the canvassers didn't want to talk about any issue—even the burden of taxation on middle-income families. Many of them didn't know who was running. Except that someone seems to have persuaded a particularly large number of residents that there is something classy about having house numbers written out in script, the South Shore looks like any other collection of suburbs. An area known as the Five Towns is largely well-off, Jewish, and liberal; the communities that are strung along the Long Island Rail Road a bit farther from the city are mainly middle-income, Republican, and Catholic. Except for that rough division, the towns seem to have no more distinct identities than the district has. People read a jumble of New York and suburban newspapers. A political candidate who wants to buy television time can buy only the ruinously expensive time on New York metropolitan channels. Canvassing door to door is about the only reliable method of campaigning. In a sense, the student volunteers—energetic, articulate, delighting in producing computer print-outs that indicated precisely when each of the hundred Yale volunteers would arrive and leave during the weekend—served merely as the only available bearers of campaign propaganda to the Fifth District's close-mouthed residents. Usually, volunteers didn't need preparation for a dialogue in order to hand out campaign brochures—any more than Lowenstein needed a Vietnam policy in order to shake hands with housewives at the Big Apple supermarket in Freeport. "They're just bodies," Hampton said of the students. He claimed that in a district with a four-to-three Republican edge in registration, a strong Republican organization, and a Democratic organization hostile to Lowenstein he could outnumber the students easily with the grown-up bodies of Republican committeemen.

At first glance, Lowenstein's full-time staff seemed to differ from the weekend volunteers only in being, on the average, two or three years older. They were mostly intelligent, good-natured young people from colleges like Yale and Stanford—the same kind of young people who had followed Lowenstein to Mississippi and to New Hampshire. (Lowenstein has always maintained that stories of students in New Hampshire shaving beards to be Clean for Gene were exaggerated, since almost all the students were clean-cut types to begin with.) Many staff members had worked against the Vietnam war in the Presidential primaries or in Chicago, and they could have viewed the President's announcement of a bombing halt and new negotiations as a tribute to their efforts and a personal triumph for Lowenstein. But on the night of the announcement there was an air of dejection around Lowenstein headquarters. The members of the staff had felt Lowenstein moving closer to an endorsement of Humphrey all week, and although they agreed that few weekend volunteers would care much one way or the other, they were less certain of their own feelings.

A few staff members were more or less non-ideological people whose concern about an endorsement was based on whether or not it seemed to be good politics. In general, though, the staff members were dismayed at the prospect of the endorsement because they have a harsher view of the American political process than the view held by Lowenstein or by the weekend volunteers. "I think we have much less faith in America than Al does," one of them had told me a couple of days before. "And it's not just one or two issues that bother us—it's the whole stupid framework of thinking in this country." When Lowenstein did announce his decision to endorse Humphrey, he had to defend it in a long emotional staff meeting; a few people said that only personal affection for Lowenstein kept them from leaving the campaign. Lowenstein insisted that the important fact about the President's announcement was that, no matter what kind of face-saving rhetoric it was couched in, it meant a reversal of the war policy and an end to the bloodshed. Some of the staff members were not persuaded that the announcement really did herald a significant change in policy; the attacks on Laos caused some of them to refer to the new policy as "a relocation of bombing." More important, they thought that the tone of Johnson's announcement—his inability to acknowledge that the government had been wrong and that the protesters who had been called traitors for so long were in fact right—was another indication that those in control of the country had learned nothing from Vietnam. To these staff members, the attitudes of the leaders of both political parties meant that even if the war in Vietnam ended, a war someplace else would take its place. "Al argued that the American people have shown that they won't stand for another Vietnam," one girl said later. "But we just don't believe that's the way things work. We might as well get new signs ready and just leave the name of the next country blank."

The following day, volunteers began to arrive for the final weekend of canvassing, and, as had been predicted, none of them seemed particularly concerned about the Humphrey endorsement. On Saturday night, Lowenstein spoke to a gathering of hundreds of high-school and college volunteers, devoting some time to an explanation of why he believed that he had been committed to endorse Humphrey as soon as a bombing halt was announced. The students listened respectfully, and after the speech only one person came forward to state his objections and announce that under the circumstances he could not continue to work in the campaign. A few nights later, even more students jammed a ballroom in Baldwin to await the election results. As the returns were phoned in from Lowenstein headquarters, where the candidate and a number of his young campaign workers were manning telephones and adding machines, Horace Kramer, the campaign manager, read them out to the huge crowd—occasionally accompanying the figures with a request to hold down the noise a bit or an admonition about standing on chairs or a reminder that if he didn't love them all quite so much he might find them somewhat exasperating. Lowenstein seemed to run slightly ahead all night; about midnight, the band began to play "Mrs. Robinson," and everyone joined in. Finally, about one in the morning, with a narrow victory assured, Lowenstein arrived—to almost hysterical cheering from the kids, and chorus after chorus of "The Impossible Dream" from the band. "Part of our constituency," he said. "has to be that the point of view of young America has to be heard in Congress as it hasn't been heard before."

"I think the main thing it'll prove if we win is that we've run a good campaign," one of the staff had told me earlier in the evening. It was a point of pride with the Lowenstein staff that in sheer technique—in organization and mechanics—the kids could outclass the grownups. The extraordinary amount of time and energy that the staff had put into the campaign may have accounted for some of the emotion in their response to Lowenstein's endorsement of Humphrey, but the difference in attitude between the staff and the part-time volunteers was too deep to be explained by strain or fatigue. Lowenstein's recruiters had found that many college students who had worked for McCarthy wanted nothing to do with a campaign in Nassau County or anywhere else. Quite a few Lowenstein staff members were people who had stayed with electoral politics long enough to see a change in the policy they opposed, but after the primaries and the Chicago Convention and the dreary realities of a congressional campaign, some of them no longer had enough faith in the system to believe that the change made any difference. Lowenstein's critics on the New Left have argued that he prevents students from recognizing the kind of revolutionary changes really needed in America by channelling their dissent into attempts at minor reforms within the established political system. But it's possible that the reaction of a lot of intelligent young people to any sustained exposure to the American political system is to turn against it—and that the weekend volunteers retained their relatively hopeful view only through lack of experience. After all, some of Lowenstein's New Left critics—now among those who have come to believe that the established political system is hopelessly fraudulent and corrupt—were themselves, only a few years ago, the healthy, exuberant, basically right-thinking young men from colleges like Yale and Stanford who went to Mississippi with Allard K. Lowenstein.

STUDENTS AND ACTIVISM IN AMERICA

Harvard Class Day Address,
June 6, 1969

In mid-1969, the campuses were smoldering as hundreds of Americans each week were killed or wounded in Vietnam. The stormy trial of the Chicago Seven was underway, and many young people felt they were on trial with the defendants. To numerous students, President Nixon seemed alternately oblivious and condescending to their concerns.

Deprived of the fruits of their 1968 electoral triumphs, more and more young people seemed willing to tolerate or support violent attacks on authorities and officials, whether policemen, ROTC cadets, or campus administrators. Others grew cynical or "dropped out."

As a member of Congress, Lowenstein had hoped to reduce his campus activities and focus more heavily on the legislative front. The renewal of campus polarization, however, returned him to the scenes of previous battles. As the turmoil grew, he began appearing at more and more colleges, not just to speak, but to talk and listen. Often, he would end his visits in dormitory lounges, exchanging views with dozens of students into the early-morning hours.

His appearances were again often attacked by some on the Far Left, who charged him with extolling a "bankrupt" electoral system and co-opting the potential for revolutionary change. In addition, his uncompromising opposition to campus violence and his criticism of sectarian politics drew fire from some student groups.

Students and Activism in America

In the spring of 1969, Harvard, like many other institutions, had been the scene of disturbances and rancor. A student-administration confrontation had led to a sit-in at the administration building, and the demonstration had not subsided until police forcibly evicted the occupiers.

The graduating class invited Lowenstein to give the annual June Class Day address in Harvard Yard. The speech he delivered was a classic expression of themes he had been preaching around the country. Directed at parents as well as students, it attempted to elicit a sense of the goals around which different generations might unite.

As I stand here in this troubled place, in this anniversary month, three extraordinary Americans seem everywhere present. All three were worshipped and detested by their fellow countrymen, were committed to, and made legend by, disinherited men everywhere.

Dr. Martin Luther King, Jr., was to have made this Class Day speech last year. The others, shaped by Harvard and New York, are Franklin D. Roosevelt and Robert F. Kennedy, men whose lives were joined in remarkable ways, perhaps none more remarkable than the fatefulness of their last June 6ths.

On June 6, 1944, twenty-five years ago, a long quarter of a century ago, Franklin D. Roosevelt spoke the heart of America in a prayer for our soldiers as they crossed to France:

"Almighty God: Our sons, pride of our Nation, this day have set upon a mighty endeavor, a struggle to preserve our Republic, our religion, and our civilization, and to set free a suffering humanity. . . .

"They fight not for the lust of conquest. They fight to end conquest. They fight to liberate. They fight to let justice arise, and tolerance and good will among all Thy people. . . .

"O Lord, give us Faith. Give us Faith in Thee; Faith in our sons; Faith in each other; Faith in our united crusade. Let not the keenness of our spirit ever be dulled. Let not the impact of temporary events, of temporal matters of but fleeting moment—let not these deter us in our unconquerable purpose.

"With thy blessing, we shall prevail over the unholy forces of our enemy. Help us to conquer the apostles of greed and racial arrogancies. Lead us to the saving of our country, and with our sister Nations into a world unity that will spell a sure peace—a peace invulnerable to the schemings of unworthy men. And a peace that will let all men live in freedom, reaping the just rewards of their honest toil."

111

It was left to Jack Newfield, the brilliant journalist from New York, to speak the heart of America on the second of these June 6ths, twenty-four years later, in one of the most powerful paragraphs to appear in years:

"Now I realize what makes our generation unique, what defines us apart from those who came before the hopeful winter of 1961, and those who came after the murderous Spring of 1968. We are the first generation that learned from experience, in our innocent twenties, that things were not really getting better, that we shall NOT overcome. We felt, by the time we reached thirty, that we had already glimpsed the most compassionate leaders our nation could produce, and they had all been assassinated. And from this time forward, things would get worse: our best political leaders were part of memory now, not hope. The stone was at the bottom of the hill and we were alone."

Now we meet at the bottom of the hill, to face the questions raised by a troubled and growing majority of Americans—to wonder what has happened to us as a people in this crowded quarter-century, to ask how we got from there to here, to ask what has gone wrong, and to ask if we can do anything to set it right.

I'm part of the generation that grew up under Franklin and Eleanor Roosevelt, a generation given courage by the boldness of his innovation and elevated by the nobleness of her gentle strength; a generation whose optimism grew from great gains made and great tasks done, a generation whose heroes grew old and died of natural causes in their beds. We were wrong to think that things would inexorably get better. But maybe because I remember when it seemed so certain that they would, I'm not prepared to agree now, after so short a time, that inevitably they won't.

Which should itself tell us something about the difference in the relative hopefulness of my generation and of this new generation. They have never experienced a war which made them proud of their country. They have yet to experience an America facing up to her problems, however tough, at home. Their choices in presidential elections have been as inspiring as the sum of Johnson, Goldwater, Nixon, Humphrey, and George Wallace; the greatest political events of their formative years have been the assassinations of their heroes.

This is not, all in all, the sort of political history that gives reasonable men much cause for optimism, and it ought to surprise no one that a generation that has grown up with this history is vulnerable to cynicism and even despair. But hope is one thing this country needs desperately from its young people. So we've got to remind them and ourselves, that it is, after all, barely a year since ordinary people, working without precedent, working at first without money or visible leadership; since ordinary people, at the beginning most of them students, undid the political mythology and reversed the course of history for their country.

The major goals of two years ago, so remote and heretical then, are now the accepted national goals. The problem is implementation. But what a triumph it would be by any ordinary standards to have achieved so quickly what was achieved. But, these are not, of course, ordinary times, as each new casualty list reminds us.

Nonetheless it's important to realize that the confusion about whether we can affect our future arises not because we failed, but because we didn't fail. It arises from the failure to consummate success with the election of a president who would now be implementing the policies dictated by the new goals. And the judgment seems fair that that failure arose from the events of last June 6th, not from any permanent inevitable immobilism in the political process.

Nor does this judgment constitute flight into a personality cult. It is, I think, simply accurate reporting. No country, not even one far less troubled than ours, could lose its greatest public figures in time of crisis without facing severe new difficulties. We lost two of ours in as many months, and lost them in a way that cost us not only their unequaled capacity to inspire energies and handle problems, but much of our confidence in the process of self-government itself.

What would have happened to the United States if Franklin Roosevelt had been murdered in 1933? Could we have coped with John Nance Garner and the Depression? I don't know. But I do know that nothing so betrays us, and our country—and God knows, Martin King and Robert Kennedy—as the presumption that hope and possibility ended with their deaths.

So I'm not prepared to accept as final the judgment that we shall not overcome, that from this time forward things will get worse.

The only thing that seems certain to me is that nothing is certain; that inevitabilities are myths, that how we behave will profoundly affect how things come out, that the dogma that things cannot get better is suitable only for those who hope to make such prophecies of doom self-fulfilling.

There is, in fact, great danger in the arrogance of final assertions about the future, hopeful or gloomy.

113

The Class Day speaker two years ago. Greg Craig, described the state of mind of his contemporaries as follows:

"This generation of students," he said, "has become tough-minded and seasoned idealists. Their commitment to social justice outweighs institutional or social loyalties. It is a generation that is up for grabs, for their hope could easily turn to hate, and their passion for building a more equitable society could easily surrender to the temptation to tear down an unjust and oppressive society.

"It is a generation whose skepticism was born with the murder of a president, nurtured by the bitter frustrations of the civil rights movement, and perpetuated by the brutality of a senseless war."

Has anything occurred in the two years since that speech that so modifies its indictment or answers its challenges that we can say its skepticism is undeserved?

The war drags on and on. So do the poverty and injustice that learned commissions remind us make increasing violence unavoidable. And while the Kerner Commission recedes into a period piece, more politicians get elected on the fears and hates that come with violence, as if incantations to law and order will fill empty stomachs, or trap rats, or heat buildings—or will in any other way help cure what's wrong in this society.

But anyone who says that the events of the last two years have established as fact that we cannot change this country by democratic process misreads these events too. Isn't it nonsense to decide now that we are impotent, when a year ago anything seemed possible?

This doctrine that we are impotent to make things better is especially pernicious, for it gives a kind of spurious credibility to the idea that the only way to remake America is to help make things worse—to predict and encourage events that lead to repression, and then to gloat when repression sets in, as if somehow that guarantees some kind of eventual victory. Victory for what, for whom? If there's one thing you can be sure about, it's that there will not be a unilateral disarmament of everyone in this country except the out-left.

And in the meanwhile, if we turn this country into an armed camp, we will have to live in it. And if we burn it down, we will have to live in what's left of it.

We are already paying a terrible price for silence about things we know are wrong. Some people have even gotten themselves trapped into a kind of rear-guard defense of people's "right" to do things on campuses that they know no one has a right to do—as if the more outrageous the act the greater the test of virtue that inheres in one's willingness to defend it.

And it is precisely this kind of double standard that can split us away from that majority of decent Americans who have showed in two presidential elections and countless other ways that they, too, want to right wrongs and end wars—a majority that includes not just the young, the black, and the poor, but the middle-class, the middle-aged, the Middle West, the middle everything.

For our cause is the cause of Middle America too, and last year showed the power of this political fact, if only we don't throw it away.

I must say something more about the violence that has come to so many campuses, including this one, for it is this as much as anything that threatens to throw that power away.

As you know, much of this violence is imported by embittered little groups. It comes wrapped in high-sounding excuses, and is all too often incubated by confused and disorganized majorities. Sometimes the wrong done by a particular act of student coercion has been quickly overshadowed by far greater wrongs done by administrators or police in the name of restoring order, but this fact does not help very much with the general public, which judges the response of constituted authority far more benignly than it judges student provocations.

And there have been provocations: deans and professors pushed around, speakers shouted down, and unarmed people bullied, buildings ransacked and some burned.

It is past time that we asked what principle or pragmatism is served by this kind of behavior. Will someone please tell me how it hurts racism in South Africa to assault the president of Cornell? Do we really help end the war by shouting down James Reston or hurling profanities at Mary Bunting? Are we contributing to the downfall of the military-industrial complex by burning down ROTC shacks or pitching deans out of random buildings? Will gutting the First Amendment make it easier to create a republic with liberty and justice for all?

There's certainly plenty that's wrong with the educational system in this country. There's a great deal that needs to be changed, and there's a great deal that needs to be protested until it is changed. But there seems to be a strange new doctrine abroad that no tactics exist between committee meetings and riots, that the only things one can do are either parliamentary or coercive, almost as if the vast creative pulse that courses down our history from Thoreau to Martin King and Norman Thomas did not exist.

It's a waste of time—and self-deceiving—to argue with people who have different goals that their tactics are counterproductive from the point of view of your own goals. That, of course, is the point of their tactics—to achieve their goals, not yours. So these remarks are not aimed at those who seek to destroy universities or who want to tear down the country, for whatever reason—to start over in whatever direction.

Some even claim that it would mean nothing to end the war in Vietnam. They may not be comfortable working with those of us who believe that to end the war in Vietnam would mean a great deal.

As for those of us who would reform and restructure the educational system, we ought, to use a current phrase, we ought to get our priorities straight. There are plenty of things that can be done to improve education without damaging what is, after all, the central effort: the effort, in Edward Kennedy's phrase, to right wrongs, to heal wounds, and to end war.

It's as harmful as it is stupid to take out on universities all one's frustrations and resentments about social injustices. Scapegoating may be becoming a national pastime, but closing a college won't end the war. It probably won't even improve the college.

They don't understand, and I think Coretta King had this in mind when she spoke here in place of her husband last year: "I've sometimes thought that the best of our young people," she said. "do not always understand the extent to which our great universities are authentically the most liberal of our institutions. But," she added, "universities, too, must face up to very hard questions which they have thus far avoided."

Basic questions, not footnotes: questions from governance to relevance, questions to which the answer that they are "not negotiable" is no more rational—no more relevant, no more accurate—from university authorities than from agitated students. One hopes we have learned this spring, if nothing else, that nonnegotiability in campus situations is not a statement of policy but an announcement of bankruptcy.

I noticed enthusiastic applause from older people when I said it's terrible to throw around a dean. I think it is terrible to throw around a dean. (I once was a dean.) But I think it's time we understood that buffeting people about, even deans, seems a rather minor offense to a generation faced with the decision of whether to go off to shoot and get shot, in a war they regard as immoral, or to go to jail or into exile. Those faced with this decision find appeals for patience about ending the war more insulting than persuasive.

And then there are all those people whose devotion to nonviolence on campus is so oddly arranged that they roar in horror about buffeted deans, but find nothing whatever to yell about when the governor of California tear-gases a community and has 141 unarmed people shot in a street.

But the greatest inducement for thousands of students to tolerate disorder on campus is the contrast between the great outbursts of indignation about campus violence and the endless excuses and muted protests about endless killing in Vietnam and endless poverty and injustice at home. The towering hypocrisy of this contrast blows like a gale of political halitosis across the land and sours everything in its wake.

So I must ask—especially, I must ask the older people here—is there any reason left on this earth why there should be one more month while American boys—these boys, and others like them less likely to find ways out—while American boys are mowed down and squandered in a succession of irrelevant Hamburger Hills? And if not, what are you willing to do about it?

The House voted the other day for another appropriation of $1.3 billion for the war: Will you help us to get congressmen to vote NO on supplemental appropriations for supplemental Hamburger Hills? Will you tell the President to start bringing the troops home in large enough quantities so the Saigon government knows the party's over, and they will have to accept coalition or do their own fighting after all this time?

The Congress is not a collection of evil men, what it really is at heart is a group of people more anxious about holding onto their jobs than Ivy League assistant deans. So when the House votes money to continue the war, it does so because a great majority of the members believe that the country wants that money voted—because these political seismographs think the tremors registering from their constituents make it necessary for them to vote this money.

And the reason people are assumed to want this money voted is not that they approve of the war but that they think that if we don't appropriate the money, we will be killing American boys who won't be able to defend themselves. So our job—your job—is clear: to explain in every community that this is not the case, that at this point in the war it is those who vote additional money that are sending kids off to die. And to explain that anyone who casts such a vote will be held accountable for that consequence.

Applaud for this, you old folks, do this, and then maybe students will applaud reasonable measures to stop violence on campus. As Professor George Wald put it, the greatest antidote for student unrest is adult unrest. Goodness knows there's enough to be unrested about.

It seems necessary to say at this point what should be obvious: that America owes much of what is hopeful and best about her to this wondrous new generation. For one thing, it has forced us to face questions we have always pretended didn't exist—questions it turns out, we have evaded because we had no idea how to answer them.

For openers, it has rejected the Churchillian nostrum that democracy is the worst form of government ever invented except every other form, and has posed instead the questions no nostrum can answer: Is democracy a racket? Are we coming closer to government of the people, by the people, and for the people, or have we been kidding ourselves all these years?

After all, the "system" people talk about "staying in" or "tearing down" is supposed to be democracy. And if democracy is simply an unending repetition of unfulfillable promise, a device to make people believe they can affect their lives when in fact they can't—if the "system" is largely a manipulative contraption that preserves an unjust status quo, then it is no longer good enough, if it ever was, and no one should urge anyone to "stay in" to be manipulated. We should, rather, join a search for a better way of doing things.

I don't think democracy is either automatically a racket or automatically not a racket. I think that matter is, in Greg Craig's phrase, up for grabs.

But if democracy in America is not to be a racket, we had better understand why so many now doubt that it is not a racket—understand, and then change both the procedures and the attitudes that have produced so much doubt. We know what the American dream means to those who have achieved it; the problem is, what does it mean to those who have not, who seem forever excluded from it, who go hungry and grow bitter in the midst of the greatest affluence the Lord has ever bestowed on any place in the history of the world?

I guess what troubles me most, this year of all years, is how much we are losing by not trying, how costly is the despair that tells us we can't succeed, that tells us democracy in America is forever a hoax, and that then leads us into behavior designed to prove the premise.

America must not be forced to choose between the change that comes with violence and the violence that comes with no change. And that is precisely the choice America faces if so many of us continue to assume that these questions about democracy have already been answered, or that we cannot affect how they will be answered.

You who are about to graduate—and your contemporaries around the globe—have confronted us with another question—by your dress, by your speech, by your search for "relevancy" in education; by your rejection of the sterile in personal relationships and careers—a question more upsetting to many of your elders than questions about democracy. Can't we, you say, can't we develop a life style that liberates instead of cripples?

I think most older people understand, if only privately and uncomfortably, that the life style that has enveloped America since the Second World War—that that life style is not, after all, very satisfactory. Given what we've got, we've made pretty much a mess of things.

The two cars from every garage turn highways into parking lots, and join the unlandable airplanes and uncontrollable industrial wastes to poison the atmosphere and pollute the water, to close the beaches and destroy the open places. We have discovered to our great confusion that affluence does not necessarily bring happiness, that leisure can mean boredom, that greed and corruption are contagious and are not limited to lesser breeds in distant places.

The melting pot seems to be producing a nation of undigestible, depersonalized lumps, a nation of barriers and gaps—gaps not just between races and generations and economic groups, but within these categories as well: husbands from wives, friends from friends. We struggle to "communicate" and then all too often find there's nothing to communicate about. The concept of "neighbors" fades into an announcement of distance. We are better at hating than loving, more at home watching than doing, more admiring of ostentation than compassion. Our personal values, in short, are as screwed up as our national priorities.

A people in this situation would, I think, be wise to welcome instead of fear those who question its style of life. They would, one would hope, be eager to join the quest for something better.

Finally, our young have made us face the self-deception of our most cherished illusion: the notion that whatever is wrong will surely get better, if we just keep patient and believe our traditional rhetoric with sufficient faith.

But, they keep saying, if so much is so wrong in this country, both for those who have made it and for those who have not; if, in fact, the trend is more often than not in the wrong direction—then isn't there something wrong with our strategy, with the way we've been going about trying to change things? And, of course, they're right about that, too.

Some new tactics have of course emerged, new approaches, new initiatives, many of them helpful, some of them promising if inconclusive. But more new tactics, new approaches, new initiatives, are desperately needed. And someone must keep reminding us that there are limits to tactics, if we mean what we have said about goals.

As Martin Luther King once said, "Returning hate for hate multiplies hate, adding deeper darkness to a night already devoid of stars. Darkness cannot drive out darkness, only light can do that. Hate cannot drive out hate, only love can do that. Hate multiplies hate and violence multiplies violence in a descending spiral of destruction."

It is not too late to show that those of us who love this country next only to liberty and justice themselves—who are proud of the work and sacrifice and miracles that have produced America, and that America has produced—it is not too late to show that we are determined not to abandon this country but to reclaim it, not to leave the arena to those who would force a choice between Ronald Reagan and the SDS, but, rather, to pick up where we were a year ago this weekend.

What we must have, then, is a resurgence of people determined to reverse the lockstep that has undone so much that was so good—the lockstep that has wasted lives and resources as if there were nothing better to do with them, that has incubated violence and hate instead of isolating them.

So I finish today with one of those haunting, prophetic epitaphs that were left us by Robert Kennedy during the last and greatest months of his life.

This is what he had to say in the hours after the assassination of Martin King, some of it to a black audience in Indianapolis. But we read it today and know all of it was said as well to steel workers in Gary and students at Harvard; and, in fact, to all Americans everywhere:

"Some Americans who preach nonviolence abroad fail to practice it here at home. Some who accuse others of inciting riots have by their own conduct invited them. Some look for scapegoats, others look for conspiracies, but this much is clear: violence breeds violence, repression brings retaliation, and only a cleaning of our whole society can remove this sickness from our soul.

"For there is another kind of violence, slower but just as deadly, destructive as the shot or the bomb in the night. This is the violence of institutions; indifference and inaction and slow decay. This is the violence that afflicts the poor, that poisons relations between men because their skin has different colors. This is a slow destruction of a child by hunger, and schools without books and homes without heat in the winter. . . .

"We learn, at the last, to look at our brothers as aliens, men with whom we share a city, but not a community, men bound to us in common dwelling, but not in common effort. We learn to share only a common fear—only a common desire to retreat from each other—only a common impulse to meet disagreement with force. . . .

"What we need in the United States is not division; what we need in the United States is not hatred; what we need in the United States is not violence or lawlessness, but love and wisdom, and compassion toward one another, and a feeling of justice toward those who still suffer within our country, whether they be white or they be black. . . .

"My favorite poet was Aeschylus. He wrote: 'In our sleep, pain which cannot forget falls drop by drop upon the heart until, in our own despair, against our will, comes wisdom through the awful grace of God.' . . .

"So let us dedicate ourselves to what the Greeks wrote so many years ago: to tame the savageness of man and to make gentle the life of this world.

"Let us dedicate ourselves to that, and say a prayer for our country, and for our people."

TYRANNY IN
WENCESLAUS SQUARE
Newsday, August 26, 1969

*During the congressional recess in the summer of 1969, Lowenstein
made a self-financed, three-week informational trip to Europe and
Southeast Asia. He had visited Eastern Europe several times before, and
following a late August stop in the Soviet Union, he arrived in Prague,
Czechoslovakia. The date was August 21, the first anniversary of the
Soviet invasion of that country. Shortly thereafter, he filed this report.*

Like most Americans, I was outraged by the Soviet occupation of
Czechoslovakia last summer.

Of course, Soviet officials have always insisted that the Western press
distorted the situation. As recently as last week, I was told in Moscow
that the Red Army was sent into Czechoslovakia at the request of the
Czech people.

If this were the case, August 21, the anniversary of the arrival of the
Red Army, would be quite a festive occasion in Prague. I decided to go
there and see for myself. Tom Engel, a student from Port Washington
now at Columbia Law School who has done some work for me this
summer, came along. We each paid our own way.

The 21st turned out to be a lovely enough day in Prague, if loveliness
can be said to survive what men do to it, but the situation was tense and
ugly. We spent several hours going from place to place, talking with

people, as many as we could, in the crowds that were gathering in the inner city. We were careful to avoid doing anything that might get us involved in any kind of demonstration. In the afternoon, in order to cover more ground and be in more places, we traveled about separately, and arranged to meet at six o'clock to go to a reception at the American ambassador's residence.

At 5:35 P.M., Tom vanished, though it was hard to be certain that he had vanished for some time after that. I spent much of the time from 9:30 on through the night with members of the embassy staff, trying to find some trace of him, in hospitals and police stations and on the streets. It was a fascinating way to see Prague that night, but there was no sign of Tom. As it turned out, no one was to hear from him until he turned up at seven o'clock the next morning with the news that he had been arrested while walking—alone—on the Pariske, a street near the old town square where the statue of the martyred fifteenth-century religious leader Jan Hus was looking down on another of the sad events that have made such a wretched mess of this beautiful old city.

Tom had been pushed into a paddy wagon and ended up at a police station with some 100 other people, all but three of them Czechs and most of them young. The arrests seemed random. Guards beat heads, shoulders, and knees until everyone was off-loaded at a police station. There, Tom established the fact that he was an American. After that, he and two Italians—a Communist journalist-photographer and his wife— were spared further roughing-up.

No one, however, was allowed to phone or contact anyone outside the station, and the Czech prisoners were abused and threatened, sheared if they had long hair, and beaten fiercely from time to time. The noise of small-arms fire and tear-gas explosions came through the windows. For three hours all men in the group were forced to stand erect and were prodded with clubs if their posture displeased a guard.

At 3:30 A.M., Tom was moved across the city to the visa and consulate section, where he was interrogated for three and a half hours in English. He was told he would not be released or allowed to telephone anyone until he signed a statement and the interrogation was concluded. He dictated a statement in English, which was translated and presumably transcribed.

At 6:30 A.M., he was presented with a typed document that was described as his statement. The document was in Czech. Tom speaks no Czech. He asked for reassurances that the typed document said, in fact, what he had said in English. He was assured of this and signed the statement.

What Tom experienced, as frightening and upsetting as it was, of course, was nothing compared to what was endured by thousands of Czechs during the anniversary period. Several died, hundreds were injured, thousands were tear-gassed or arrested without charges (and without the relative shelter of a foreign passport).

No one knows how many people were shot at, but sixty tanks and thousands of armed men in uniform made sure everyone knew guns were for shooting. The state radio said all this was necessary to maintain law and order in the face of provocation by a few "counterrevolutionary hooligans."

"The worst thing about the whole night," Tom said later, "was the wholesale terror that the police exercised over everyone crowded into that room. Every few minutes some policeman—usually young and more than a little sadistic—would walk around and rough someone up. No one knew who would be next, or why. The gunfire outside and the tear gas coming in through the windows added to the terror, because you never knew what was happening to the city outside.

"From time to time, more Czechs would be brought in and beaten savagely. You could hear the slap of the truncheons and the cries from the next room. Everyone wondered, silently, when would all this stop. We felt very much together—united by fear, but also by the most basic hate I've ever felt."

It has been reported that I was tear-gassed several times during the long hours of August 21. That is true. So was virtually everyone else who was in the streets or by an open window.

Trams and other public transport were all but deserted in support of the boycott appeals circulated clandestinely by opponents of the government. The Soviet Embassy and Communist Party headquarters were cut off from public access and guarded by tanks, trucks, and heavily armed men. Thousands of people lined the streets to stand up and be counted. They chanted "Gestapo" when they saw uniformed men, and whenever they could, they sheltered their young, who, doing the most to protest the occupation, were most in need of protection from the occupiers.

The behavior of the authorities confirmed everything the Czech people wanted the world to know: that this government exists only by using force against its own people, and that the Soviet invasion of Czechoslovakia stinks as bad now as it did a year ago.

124

It is the great fortune and the curse of Bohemia that sky, hills, soil, and river blend there to make a fertile, rolling countryside, hospitable to a sensible and friendly people and inviting to greedy, bigger neighbors, east and west, who constantly find pretexts to march in and take what they want.

Nobody questions the good sense and good will of the Czechs, or the good use they have made of their countryside. Some have questioned their courage. But it was not Czechs who caved in at Munich, and it was Czechs who died in Lidice. Jan Masaryk was a Czech, and so was Jan Palach, the former a foreign minister, the latter a student who set himself on fire last year. Both gave their lives to damn the traducers of their pleasant and productive land.

And on the anniversary of the latest intrusion, thousands of their countrymen risked police retribution to overwhelm their graves with flowers and candles. The rest of us would risk nothing to curse the darkness that makes it necessary for people to light candles at martyrs' graves to say that they want to be free in their own land.

I have been asked if it was worth going to Prague in such circumstances. Clearly, it would not have been if Tom had ended up in prison for a long time, or if something worse had happened to him. But we were lucky, and I am very glad we went.

It was useful, too, to be reminded that against Communist tyranny, as against any tyranny, decency has a life of its own that gives strength and hope to the victims of brutality.

It was useful, too, to be reminded in so personal a way how unacceptable life is in a police state. One wonders if America is entirely immune to the siren call of those who would "maintain law and order" by causing people they disagree with to vanish, by saying who will wear their hair how, even by shooting at unarmed people on whim. Today, the Czech government announced that more police than civilians were injured during the anniversary festivities, thus proving that the police were not at fault. There was not a word of thanks to Mayor Daley for using this line.

Prague on August 21 would have been good medicine for any American who might be tempted to think that somehow we would be better off if we could cut the First Amendment, whether by official arrogance or by citizen anarchy.

I am also glad we were there because I am glad there were Americans, Italians, and others who stood with the Czechs, even if only as spectators; who shared briefly a few of their risks, if only because bystanders were not allowed to be bystanders; and who shared briefly their detention, if only until passports separated those who could leave from those who could not.

August 21, 1969, was an atrocious day for everyone concerned—for all men who want justice and peace on earth; for the leaders of the Soviet Union and for Communists generally, who profess to abhor imperialism, and who cannot possibly believe their cause is helpd by displays like this; and, above all, for the Czech people, who have already suffered far too much during the past three decades.

I left Prague sickened and angry that my country's credentials to cry out against the horror I had seen there have been so badly eroded by our own conduct in Santo Domingo and Vietnam, by the tear-gassing at Berkeley and police wantonness in the streets of Chicago.

I left grateful again for the remarkable unity and energy of the rising generation, throwing itself everywhere into the effort to change attitudes and practices that have hobbled men as far back as we know our story.

It is often said that using billy clubs on American campuses radicalizes students. Using billy clubs in Prague anti-Communized students. There ought to be a lesson in that, if anyone can see a little further than the end of a billy club.

Finally, I left Prague wondering if the central fact is not simply that it's high time all of us showed how tired we are of people being beaten, gassed, and shot because they want to breathe free, whether they are in Orangeburg, Johannesburg, Madrid, or Prague.

IN THE FINAL ANALYSIS, IT IS THEIR WAR

Remarks in Congress,

September 30, 1969

In his first nine months in office, Lowenstein spoke and worked intensively around the country for an early end to American involvement in Vietnam. In Congress he vowed to vote against appropriations for the war unless U.S. policy was reversed.

In March, he spoke in the House against the "original defective premises" of the Vietnam policy, asserting that "our people have, in two presidential elections, voted as clearly as our system made possible for a change to policies in the direction of peace." He also hosted a press conference at which 253 campus leaders or their representatives pledged their refusal "to serve in the military as long as the war in Vietnam continues." Lowenstein himself did not publicly advise either resistance to or compliance with the draft, but he voiced his respect for young men's decisions to refuse service for reasons of conscience.

While the Administration was shaping its policies, he sought to heighten public and private pressure for a withdrawal from Vietnam. Administration officials responded only with vague assurances and requests for patience and time. After Lowenstein traveled to Vietnam in August, his last hopes for voluntary reversal of policy vanished and he threw himself into the antiwar opposition with renewed urgency.

In September, he delivered a repudiation of Nixon's war policies in a speech that marked a final break with the Administration. It is reprinted here from the Congressional Record.

Mr. Speaker, it is now 8 months and 9 days since President Nixon's inauguration. It was said quite reasonably at the time of his inauguration that the new administration would need time to get its bearings, to determine a policy, and then to implement it. But it was thought at that time—also, I think, reasonably, in view of statements during the campaign and of the mood of the country—that the goal of the new administration's policy, whatever its details, would be the early termination of American military involvement in Vietnam, whether by the negotiation of an overall political settlement or by the withdrawal of American forces.

There is no way to know how many Vietnamese have died since the inauguration, but almost 10,000 more Americans have, and more than 56,000 have been wounded. More than 16.8 billions of the dollars of American taxpayers' money have been spent directly on the prosecution of the war. The cost in inflation, in domestic bitterness, in deferred and desperately needed programs in this country and elsewhere in the world, is of course, incalculable.

I was among the many Americans who believed that the Midway declaration meant that the United States intended to withdraw its Armed Forces from Vietnam on a set timetable over a relatively short period. I was prepared to support that approach, reserving the right to differ on details of the timetable. I believed that "Vietnamization of the war" was the rhetorical canopy under which the new policy would be sheltered. It seemed not unreasonable that, after 8 years and 7 months, $75 billion and almost 300,000 American casualties, the Government of South Vietnam should have been almost prepared, if not long since overprepared, to stand on its own feet in its own country.

Then I went to Vietnam. What I was told and what I saw there persuaded me that "Vietnamization" is in fact a canopy being hoisted to shelter—perhaps, more accurately, to conceal—our staying in, not our getting out. In effect, last year's heresy, which was supposed to be this year's policy, turned out to be this year's vocabulary. But the policy remained essentially last year's policy. The lyrics had changed, but the melody, if a dirge is a melody, lingered on.

128

I found no prominent American or South Vietnamese, military or civilian, who thought the present Government of South Vietnam would be able to maintain itself even in 2 or 3 years if our armed support were withdrawn. And the new South Vietnamese Cabinet, far from offering hope either for a negotiated settlement or for broader support for the present Government, represented a further diminution of prospects for either. In the face of these facts, the notion that we should protract our military presence for any additional period of time seems to me utterly untenable.

What would we gain for the price we would pay for extending our presence? What would we have bought that would be worth the lives and resources spent?

We are told that if we pulled our armed forces out precipitately, the Saigon government would collapse. But if it is going to collapse whenever we pull out our Armed Forces, should we not face the possibility of such a collapse now? I believe that when we face it, we will find we can live with it with a minimum of national discomfiture.

We have said for many years now—beginning with President Kennedy's comment in September 1963:

In the final analysis, it is their war. They are the ones who have to win it or lose it. We can help them, we can give them equipment, we can send our men out there as advisers, but they have to win it, the people of Vietnam.

—that we cannot fight this war to keep governments in power that do not have popular support; governments that do not respond to the popular will. We have been in this particular orbit, this very bloody orbit, for many years now, and it is time to come home.

It is time to stop saying, "If the Saigon government does not gain public support, if the Saigon government does not free its non-Communist prisoners and institute land reform, if the Saigon government cannot field a fighting force willing to take over the brunt of combat—if, in short, the Saigon government cannot sustain itself in power after all these years—then we should leave." Surely it is clear by now that the Saigon government cannot, or will not, do these things, and therefore it is time that we left.

I would as soon expect the Statue of Liberty to lower her arm as I would expect the Thieu-Ky government to accept a political settlement that would not keep itself in power. There is in simple fact neither the intention to negotiate itself out of power, nor the capacity to maintain itself in power unless the United States is to keep a substantial number of troops there in perpetuity.

So I am convinced that the national interests of this country require that we cease all offensive military action and initiate the withdrawal of our Armed Forces immediately.

We do not seek to "impose a solution" on the South Vietnamese by doing this; we seek to stop imposing a solution on them. We do not "violate our commitments" by leaving Vietnam; we demonstrate belatedly that we intend to keep them. We do not "lose face" by leaving Vietnam; we might, in fact, begin to regain some of the face we have already lost by our behavior there. We do not risk turning other independent nations in Asia into "dominoes" by leaving Vietnam; we risk turning them into "dominoes" by insisting on military alliances where they are of no use to us and provoke fears in others.

I do not know if the President has no policy or two policies, or if he has a policy in Washington that is being undercut in Asia. But I do know that to make our withdrawal contingent on the behavior of the North Vietnamese makes us a prisoner to the wishes of the Communists, and to make our withdrawal contingent on the behavior of the Saigon government is to make us hostage to that very group which loses most if we leave. Neither of these is acceptable as a basis for determining American policy. We must be neither prisoner nor hostage to either Saigon or Hanoi.

It is, therefore, especially disappointing when honest, troubling, and widely shared questions about national policy in Vietnam are disregarded, and those who seek to discuss them are impugned. Neither does such an attitude on the part of the President or his supporters add to the confidence of the American people in the way their affairs are being handled. I hope President Nixon will reconsider his response to questions and suggestions about the course we are on in Vietnam. I hope he will reconsider his explanation of that course. I hope he will reconsider the policies that have put us on that course, so he can carry out the promise of his inaugural address and become blessed as a peacemaker.

This at last is the Christmas by which American boys must be on their way home. If the President is unable to implement policies that will bring this about, the American people will have to break with their President on his conduct of the war. It will not be the first time that this will have happened in recent American history.

Lowenstein supported the massive Vietnam Moratorium in October and denounced as "dishonest and deceptive" an Administration-sponsored House resolution calling for "peace with justice" in Vietnam. But Nixon was publicly impervious to the October demonstration, and to a second one, in November, and no ready means of forcing a change in policy was apparent.

DEMOCRACY IN THE HOUSE?
Remarks in Congress,
October 3, 1969

Once elected to Congress, Lowenstein came face to face with the encrusted legislative procedures of the House of Representatives.

Debate on major issues was restricted; amendments to critical bills were barred; the seniority system lavished sweeping power on members whose chief accomplishment was outliving and politically outlasting their colleagues; speeches on major bills were limited to one minute; votes on important issues were unrecorded. In an interview during his first summer as a member, Lowenstein remarked that "Congress is like Calcutta —nothing prepares you for it. Absolutely nothing can prepare you for the extraordinary difficulty of getting anything done."

When the Safeguard Anti-Ballistic Missile System came up for House consideration in early October, many of these frustrations came to a head. Not only was debate sharply limited, but also House leaders blocked a direct vote on the weapon system's construction. Amid a heated scene of charges and recriminations, Lowenstein rose briefly to address the underlying issues.

Mr. Chairman, many of us have sat through this debate in increasing sadness and disbelief.

We are dealing with huge sums of money, with the security of the country, with the future of the planet. All of us were elected to deal with these matters by similar numbers of citizens, in procedures designed to give an effective voice to the voters and to gain respect for representative government as the way that a free people should conduct their business.

I am sorry the debate has been punctuated by explosions of personal animus among Members, for I am one of those who has come to have great respect and affection for all the Members involved, including the chairman of the Armed Services Committee, who has always treated me with consideration and fairness.

It is my view that what has been wrong during these past few days is what is wrong generally with the way the House operates, and that is not something that can be blamed on individuals or cured by expressions of personal hostility. The fault is in the way we view ourselves, the way we take our responsibilities. This ought to be a place of high debate. There ought to be a clear record of how elected representatives voted on great issues. The proceedings ought to be relevant to the pulse of the Nation, ought to reflect some of the mood and concern of the world around us. Sometimes these things happen here, but more often they do not. I love this place. To be elected to it is as high an honor as I expect to attain. But we demean this place—and ourselves—when we allow procedural tricks to throttle debate on the greatest issues facing the country and to prevent our votes being recorded on these questions. I think it is fair to say that for many Members the last few days have reinforced the determination to begin soon to correct the rules that produce situations like the one we are in now.

Can anyone justify rules that make it impossible for us to have a record vote now on whether or not the ABM should be deployed? Does anyone think it adds to the prestige or effectiveness of the House of Representatives when we are literally not permitted to vote on proposals that are supported by half the Members of the United States Senate? Does it add to our prestige or effectiveness when men elected to represent millions of Americans are not allowed to speak at all, or are told to confine their remarks to 45 seconds?

What it does do when these things occur is to deny the House the opportunity to hear the views of millions of Americans in even remote proportion to their strength outside the House. So the House deludes itself that it reflects the feelings of the public, and increasing numbers of citizens doubt that representative democracy is functioning in this country. This does little to weaken the efforts of those who prefer government by decree, or government by confrontation, or government by democratic legislative process.

We have heard speech after speech today supporting the national policy in Vietnam. But to conclude from these speeches that the American people are united behind this policy, one would have to be oblivious to what is going on in the country. I do not rise at this moment to discuss whether there should be unity behind this policy. I simply want to observe that we fool no one but ourselves when we allow this sort of discussion to create that sort of illusion.

Similarly it is not primarily the merits of deploying the ABM that are in question in this situation. What is in question is a procedure that says we cannot vote on deploying the ABM so the people who elected us will know where we stood on this issue. Can anyone suggest that doing business this way will increase faith in, or respect for, either this House or the concept of representative democracy?

What, in fact, is wrong with letting the American people know where we stand? The ABM was an issue in many of our campaigns. We have a new Member from Massachusetts, just elected, and his opposition to deploying the ABM was a part of why he won. Can it be that the people who favor deploying the ABM are afraid of a rollcall, or because they are afraid of being on record for deployment when they come up for reelection? And in any case should their fears—whatever they may be—be determinative of our procedures?

Surely we can find ways to protect the public from this kind of transgression of democratic process, even if we do not respect ourselves enough to protect ourselves from it.

Too much that happens here simply reminds everyone that we are not conducting ourselves as we should, that we are not conducting the necessary business as this decade, this period of trauma for the American people, requires us to do. We have greater obligations than we have met by our behavior today, or during this session generally, for that matter. Everything in our rules and traditions that impedes the efficient operation of democratic process—everything in committees and on the floor, everything from minority rights and seniority to how we determine if a quorum is present and how we record what occurs—all these things ought to be reexamined and overhauled soon.

The House of Representatives need not continue in its present condition. It dare not. I hope that if nothing else constructive comes of all the frustration and irritation of the past few days, a greater incentive—and resolve—to revise our procedures will survive. That would be an important gain, much more useful than acrimonious personal attacks.

"For a moment," one member recalled years later, "the House was hushed. Al managed to touch the best in each of us. For a moment, we were able to remember that there was a privilege of public service, of being a participant in the American political system and that there might be a duty of reasoned debate to accompany that privilege."

NEW MEMBER

Flora Lewis

The New Yorker, January 10, 1970

Lowenstein's difficulties with House legislative practices and disappointment with Nixon's foreign and domestic policies grew. As Congress continued to accept the President's lead on many issues, he was interviewed about the tide of events during his first year in office.

On January 3, 1969, two weeks before his fortieth birthday, Allard K. Lowenstein rose, with four hundred and twenty-nine other persons, on the floor of the House of Representatives and was sworn in as a Member of the Ninety-first Congress. For the swearing-in ceremony, Lowenstein, who frequently wears a rumpled beige windbreaker, slacks, and no necktie, was dressed with more care than usual; he had on a freshly pressed gray suit and a plain dark tie, and his hair was neatly combed. This was not the first time that he had come to Capitol Hill to work. In 1949, he had been an aide to Senator Frank Graham, a North Carolina Democrat, and in 1959 he had worked as a foreign-policy assistant to Hubert Humphrey, when Humphrey was a senator from Minnesota. Lowenstein had long been interested in politics, but his appearance on Capitol Hill in 1969 was not the result of any political ambitions developed during his days as a legislative aide. It was, rather, a by-product of a campaign he had engaged in to end the war in Vietnam. In 1967 and 1968, he had led the movement to prevent President Johnson's renomination, first urging

Senator Robert F. Kennedy to oppose the President, and then, when Senator Kennedy hesitated, urging Senator Eugene J. McCarthy to take on that task. As an additional contribution to the reformist, anti-war movement, Lowenstein decided to run for the House from New York's Fifth Congressional District, which was once a part of the First District, then a part of the Second District, and later a part of the Third District, and which takes in most of the Southern third of Nassau County. In a sense, Republicans might be said to have held the seat from 1914 to 1964, when Herbert Tenzer, a Democrat, won the office, and now, having served two terms, he was retiring, leaving the seat vacant. The local insurgent Democratic anti-war group asked Lowenstein to run in the primary, and after several weeks of wavering he made up his mind to do so. "The most persuasive argument for running was that the direction of the country was wrong, and if we didn't have candidates who said so and won we would have no way of showing that the country wanted to change direction," Lowenstein said later. "The value of running was not just that you could do a good job if you won. It was also the fact of winning an election on the issues of the war and the reordering of national priorities—the phrase was new and sounded sort of highbrow and vague then—in a district that was supposed to be resistant to this point of view."

Lowenstein, having won the nomination by a considerable margin in the primary, defeated the Republican candidate, Mason Hampton, Jr., by 99,193 votes to 96,427 on November 5th. A few days after the election, he told me that, in a sense, he was not prepared to take the seat in Congress. "I have a certain awe about elections," he said. "The fact of being elected is high in the hierarchy of things I was raised to think of as a great honor, and I had never really seen myself as doing that. By the end of the campaign, I expected to win, but I had never sat down and thought about what would happen next. It seemed to me that that was best, because if I didn't win I wouldn't be as disappointed, and if I did— well, there would be plenty of time to work it out afterward. So finding myself in the House had something of an Alice in Wonderland quality about it—something amazing, because it was unexpected and because I felt this great awe for the electoral process."

After his first week in Washington, Lowenstein returned to New York less amazed. He came to my apartment one evening, wearing his windbreaker and a pair of baggy pants. I asked him how the week had gone, and he told me that at the end of his second day in Congress the Majority Leader, Representative Carl Albert had made him Acting Majority Leader—a job that carries with it the right to adjourn the House. The appointment, which is made almost every day and carries responsibilities that last only for a few minutes, is one of the courtesies that the House leaders extend to their less influential fellow-representatives—a mark of recognition and a sign of welcome. Lowenstein was not as deeply impressed by the gesture as perhaps he was supposed to be until a colleague, congratulating him, mentioned another congressman who had been given a brief turn as Acting Majority Leader—in his case, only after many months in the House. The newspapers of his district—so the story went—had been so struck by this swift rise that they publicized it sufficiently to make it a factor in his subsequent reelection. Lowenstein did recognize a touch of irony in Albert's awarding him a microphone, however. It was Carl Albert who, as chairman of the 1968 Democratic National Convention, had turned off the floor mike when Lowenstein, a delegate from New York, tried to second a motion to recess the Convention while violence was going on in the streets of Chicago. Once Lowenstein had become a member of Congress, Albert made a point of telling him, "You're not a bit like they told me. You're not a long-hair-and-beard type at all." At any rate, it came about that on his second day in Congress Lowenstein spoke his first words there, and spoke them as Acting Majority Leader of the House. He was chided by his wife, Jenny, when he emerged. "How is it that when Carl Albert finally gives you a mike, all you can think of to say is 'I move that this House do now adjourn'?" she demanded. But that was the scope of the appointment, and those first words were the initial gesture in what Lowenstein came to call "the charade."

Later that week, Lowenstein attended a bipartisan briefing session for new representatives. Little was said about legislation or about the purpose and power of the House. The session consisted of a series of tips on the special political etiquette of favors that members expect from each other and should be prepared to repay, on how to get one's name on a bill, and how to impress constituents—in sum, helpful hints about how to get reelected. Lowenstein was both amused and distressed. "That's the trouble with most politicians," he told me. "This slogan that getting yourself reelected is the first rule of politics can lead to a really pernicious attitude. The notion of being elected is inherently virtuous, if you believe in it. We don't believe in royalty and inherited office, or in office as the result of trial by combat. We're raised to think democracy is the best way, and democracy means elections. But if you add the general human ambition to make the most of your own future to the state of mind of people raised to believe in elections, you can end up with a dangerous combination. There is nothing inherently immoral about trying to succeed, and in politics this society's idea of success is to get yourself elected. But once that has become the goal, all the other values and goals can be forgotten. The test of virtue becomes success, and people measure success by whether you get more votes. So why shouldn't you think first about how to get more votes? So that becomes the 'first rule' of that kind of politics. It's also what makes the whole process so much less productive and honest. If you don't want to fall into that trap, you have to say no, you won't accept that view of things. My first rule in Congress is that if I don't do more by being there about the things I would if I weren't there, then I shouldn't be there. That rule will help make a lot of decisions much easier."

The week of the briefing session, Lowenstein went to the Democratic caucus, the organizational meeting of all House Democrats, at which he hoped to raise a question that he and a number of other representatives had discussed in the interval between the election and the swearing-in. Lowenstein and the others wanted to open the rules of the House to debate and amendment, including those on how committees function, how bills can be brought to the floor, how debating time on the floor is assigned—in effect, the very workings of the institution. He and his friends did not have the slightest expectation of winning, but they did hope to provoke a vote in the caucus on whether or not Democrats should seek a debate on the rules instead of adopting them automatically—the traditional way. When the caucus chairman brought up the question of rules, however, it was simply to say that the rules would be passed. The question of debate was never considered. Lowenstein was astonished. He and his friends hadn't even been defeated—they had just been ignored.

Next, Lowenstein attended a meeting of the Democratic Study Group, a less formal body, consisting of about half the House Democrats, all of whom profess some degree of liberal leaning. There, too, he found that nothing outside the routine happened, or, evidently, could be made to happen.

In the months that followed, I saw Lowenstein from time to time—at an airport, in a snack bar, in the corridors of the Longworth House Office

Building, and even at his desk in the Longworth Building, after midnight, but he was always too busy working on his dozens of projects to provide me with any real idea of what they amounted to. He was commuting to Long Island and was also making trips to Biafra, Ethiopia, Vietnam, and Czechoslovakia, and to what seemed to be every state in the Union. By the time we could meet again for a long, uninterrupted talk, he had been in Congress for more than six months and his perspective had changed somewhat. The time for our talk became available when Lowenstein came to New York to pay a long-deferred visit to his mother-in-law, who lives in Sagaponack. I was to meet him at the Westbury station of the Long Island Rail Road one August day around noon. Lowenstein didn't come on the train he was supposed to be on, or the next one. When I went to telephone his home—he lives in Long Beach—all the booths were occupied, and I waited nearby. In one booth, a slim, distraught young woman tried simultaneously to extract information from somebody on the line, keep track of a child, and explain to a young man who was standing beside the booth that there had been a mixup. "Al is in Albertson," she said to him after completing her call. "No one knows where that is. He's trying to get a taxi. I suppose we'd better wait here."

I guessed that she had something to do with Lowenstein, and introduced myself. The three turned out to be Jenny Lowenstein, the Lowenstein's son Frankie, who is now two years old, and Steven Engstrom, a University of Arkansas student who had heard Lowenstein give a speech at a college in North Carolina, had asked the university if he might use a foundation fellowship to spend the summer as an aide of Lowenstein's, and had eventually been accepted. Engstrom lived in the Lowensteins' house in Long Beach, helped run Lowenstein's district office in Baldwin, drove Lowenstein's car (sometimes as chauffeur), babysat with Frankie, and joined the Lowensteins in such other activities as writing speeches, washing dishes, arranging schedules, and doing research on local issues.

The four of us waited at the station, and at last Lowenstein, wearing windbreaker and slacks, arrived in a rattling taxi. He paid the driver, remarking proudly to his wife that, by a miracle, he had thought to put some money in his pocket the night before. Lowenstein explained to us that he had been delayed at Albertson, a stop on what is surely the slowest of the Long Island Rail Road's run. We all piled into the family car, and Engstrom drove. Lowenstein and I were in the back seat, and Mrs. Lowenstein sat in front, clutching Frankie, who kept trying to wriggle over the front seat and onto his father's lap. Mrs. Lowenstein asked her husband if he had eaten. He said no, and she peeled waxed paper off a squashed cream-cheese-and-jelly sandwich she had brought along for Frankie. Lowenstein ate it hungrily, remarking between bites that Albertson was near his district but, thank goodness, nobody there had recognized him. (Presumably, he was grateful to be left alone for an interval.) "That's the advantage of not looking like a congressman," he said.

We all asked at once what a congressman looks like.

"Well, sort of ponderous, I guess—in a good suit," he said. "I never think of myself as a congressman. I'm sometimes surprised when people remind me that I am one. Outside Washington, congressmen aren't a dime a dozen, and people sometimes think it's quite something to meet one. When you go into somebody's house, you have to adjust to the realization that your being there may mean something to people. I think that when you realize that, you should try to be responsive to it. If people act as though they are honored by your being somewhere, you want to try not to let them feel let down or taken advantage of. Some people want to tell you what they're doing for you, how they helped in the campaign—that kind of thing. I've had to work at overcoming a long-standing aversion to publicity. For a long time, it seemed to me that doing things with publicity somehow put the motive for doing them in doubt. When I toured migrant-labor camps on Long Island, I thought I should go alone, but that was the last thing the people who were arranging the tour wanted. They wanted to publicize the conditions in the camps. That's why they wanted me to come—to attract some press and maybe some TV coverage. Often, people who want you to do things want you to do them for the publicity, so if you agree that the cause is a good one you have to work that out and live with it. You can't do much in Congress if you aren't prepared to try to spotlight some of the problems you're concerned about. More often than not, of course, the problem is how to spotlight them effectively. Then, too, you have to get used to a lot of hostile stuff—you know, jealous or bitter people who want to hurt your reputation or get your goat by impugning your motives or inventing malicious tales. If you were to let that sort of thing bother you, you couldn't do very much else. All in all, I'm glad to be in Congress. It's a good time to be there—there's so much that needs to be done. The day-to-day work is a good test of your patience, but I'm used to the long pull—to burrowing along for a while before you can see any results. People make a great distinction between being on 'the inside' and being on 'the outside,' and now I get asked a lot how it feels to be on 'the inside.' Well, I wouldn't know, because where I am is not 'inside' very much, and it hasn't made much difference in the way I try to work. It does make it easier to be heard—at least, outside Washington."

Lowenstein doubts whether he has had much success at being heard in Washington, and, particularly, in the House itself. "My view of how to be an effective congressman has changed a lot since I got there," he told me. "The biggest single difference is that I've learned that all the tests people normally use to decide whether you're a good congressman have almost nothing to do with whether you *are* a good congressman. They are really tests of whether you're keeping up a good façade—things like attending roll calls, getting your name on bills and in the *Congressional Record*, appearing active in the House. If you work at the façade, it can preclude doing what you should be doing; it can determine how you use your time and energy, and even remove the incentive to do the real job. What nobody understands is that the façade is irrelevant to what Congress ought to be and what it ought to be doing. Some people who make a real effort to follow what you're doing take what they read in the *Congressional Record* as evidence of what you've done. Well, it's nothing of the kind, since almost everything that appears in the *Record* has been what is called 'revised and extended.' Or they look at your roll-call attendance, which is in large part a measure of how many times you've interrupted something you should be doing to do something pointless. It means running over to the floor and answering to your name. Which is fine if you are voting on something, but most roll calls are taken to see if a quorum is present—another part of the charade, since people leave as soon as they've answered to their names. Why would you stay to hear everybody else answer to his name? The fact is that even though the House spends more than a quarter of the time it's in session listening to everyone's name being called, there is still no clear record of how members have voted on most things that really matter. Something of great significance may be brought to the floor under what is called a closed rule, which means that you can't offer any amendments and the proposal must be voted up or down precisely as it emerged from committee. That's just plain wrong, and on basic issues like tax legislation it is outrageous. And even when a closed rule is not invoked, the House procedure prevents a recorded vote on many questions of wide interest. For instance, when most of the bills that matter are reported out to the House floor the House sits as a committee of the whole to consider them.

And votes in a committee of the whole are not recorded, so on many crucial amendments there is no way to tell how anyone voted. The recorded vote on final passage often tells nothing useful, because by then the bill may have become virtually non-controversial, or may be such a hodgepodge that a simple yes or no becomes a very complicated vote to cast. The basic fault is in the way the House views itself, the way it takes its responsibilities. There ought to be a clear record of how elected representatives vote on great issues. There ought to be a way to vote separately on separate questions—that is, there ought to be a way to offer amendments. And, as far as debate or discussion is concerned, most self-respecting high-school student councils would stage sit-ins rather than operate under rules like the ones that apply a good deal of the time in the House."

Almost from the moment of his swearing-in, Lowenstein allied himself with a bipartisan group of younger members who had been working to bring about fundamental changes in House rules and customs. "It took a while to realize how bad some of the procedures are and how hard it is to change them," he told me. "It also takes a particular kind of guts to challenge what have come to be almost gentlemen's agreements—to risk the disapproval of those who control committee assignments, floor time during debates, and so on." In fact, after his motion to adjourn on the second day he said virtually nothing on the floor of the House for several weeks. "I learned a lot about how the place works," he said, "and my admiration grew for this small group of people who had thrown themselves into the effort to get changes at least considered."

The car was rolling through Suffolk County now, and Lowenstein sighed. "Of course, there would be a revolt if members had no way at all to go on record about things that are important to their constituents," he said. "So there are escape valves, such as the unanimous consent that the leadership always gets, just before debate on a legislative proposal ends, for every member of the House to put in the *Record* whatever he'd like to put there, as if he had spoken during the debate. Then, there are what are called the 'one-minute rule' and the 'special order.' Every day that the House meets, any member can speak for one minute on any subject. You use your minute to get up and say, 'I ask unanimous consent to revise and extend my remarks and include extraneous matter.' In the *Record*, it looks as if you'd taken on the space program, or pollution, or hunger, or anything else, but you don't have to say a word. You can just hand in a paper. If you're especially conscientious, or you feel very deeply

143

about something, you can actually speak about it for sixty seconds, to an empty House and empty gallery. For a while, I decided never to use the one-minute rule. It seemed phony and somehow deceptive. Gradually, I came to realize that that wasn't a very sensible kind of protest, since it had no effect on anyone but me. And there is, of course, some value in getting things in the *Record*. It is read by some influential people, and it can be distributed widely. The special order is another escape hatch that eases resentments. Any member can ask for a special order to discuss anything that's on his mind when legislative business is finished for the day. This, too, has almost nothing to do with influencing the House, but the speeches go into the *Record*. You can see that, if you play the game and accept the charade, you can give the appearance of being a very diligent congressman with relatively little difficulty. Conversely, if you're doing what you should be doing, it can look as if you were doing nothing. But more important than the effect of all this on individuals is the cumulative effect on the legislative process, and on House morale."

Lowenstein paused to think. "Another thing you have to understand is that the House, in some ways, isn't very representative," he went on. "There's almost never anyone there under thirty. Think what it tells about the place that I'm considered very young! And, of course, there are only nine blacks, when, proportionately, there should be about fifty. Almost a fifth of the population of the South is black, but there are no blacks at all among the hundred-odd Southern members, and on votes that would be of greatest concern to blacks we're lucky if we pick up half a dozen Southern votes for the position the blacks would take if they were there. And this kind of built-in unrepresentativeness is made much worse by the seniority system, which gives enormous extra power to whoever lasts the longest. The people who last the longest, naturally, are the people who come from districts least affected by the two-party system and most removed from the normal swings and political pressures that affect everyone else. The degree of dissatisfaction with all this is a measure of a generation gap as much as anything. The average member now has been in for something over five and a half terms, and that is the line that tends to divide members, more than party or ideology, on questions of congressional reform. And this reminds me of a hopeful political drift in the Congress which hasn't been noticed much yet by the press. There has been a good start toward a kind of spontaneous coalition that is not the traditional conservative one of Northern Republicans and Southern Democrats. In the country at large, this coalition would be regarded as very moderate and rather middle-aged, but in Congress it passes for liberal and young. It's made up largely of newer members from both parties, who don't have much seniority, but if it keeps growing, one of its effects could be to make seniority less significant. That, in turn, could have a very healthy effect on the workings of the committee system. As things stand now, the committee chairmen have enormous power—they can pretty much decide on when committees meet, and if and on what to hold hearings; they create sub-committees, approve members' trips, push whatever bills they want to push, and so on. Since almost everybody on a committee wants favors from the chairman, in most committees he can run things pretty much as he likes. The majority of bills that are important to a member—because they give him prestige and convey the impression that he's doing a good job for his district—are not, in fact, controversial. Out of the more than twenty-nine thousand public and private bills introduced in the last Congress, only six hundred and sixty-two private ones were passed, and of those that were actually considered relatively few were fought over. Which of the non-controversial bills that are proposed get to have hearings generally depends on the whim of some committee chairman, and that often means they depend on his good will toward the sponsor of the bill."

Lowenstein went on to discuss what a congressman should be doing, as opposed to what he is expected to appear to be doing. He divided the job into four major parts, the first of which he likened to the functions of an ombudsman. "Since we don't have that kind of official—one who deals with problems that are separate from political and general issues—every elected official has to help communities and individuals with all sorts of difficulties that have to arise in a society as complicated and impersonal as this one," he said. "Some people think that an ombudsman's functions are somehow unworthy of a congressman—that they are kind of a vote-buying device, and cheapen the office. My view is that if you aren't prepared to do that kind of work for people—who should have an ombudsman somewhere—then you shouldn't run for office. Think of what can happen to individuals in a country that suffers from bureaucratic elephantiasis. Like this morning—I was on the phone about a fellow who's in the Army. He was shot and hospitalized and hasn't got much of a stomach left. But instead of getting a disability discharge he's on orders to Vietnam. You can't find out why—it's the gigantic military machine grinding away. We got him stopped in Oakland as he was about to board a plane for Vietnam. Now he'll be held back for a month while they

145

make another investigation. If they decide to send him after that, you can't do anything. But holding it up this long means that there's a chance this particular absurdity won't go through, and that would be to the advantage of the Army as well as of the boy. When things like this happen—things involving a miscarriage of justice—you should be glad if you can help. Of course, people are sometimes disappointed, because they think you can do more than you really can. And if people want to do something that is improper, you don't do it if you're working the way you should. But I've found that, most of the time, when people know you're committed to a certain view of public functions they don't ask you for improper things. Maybe they're afraid you'll react by exposing them."

We were running through Manorville now, and Lowenstein paused to look out the car window at a group of children at play. Then he resumed. "One big problem is finding time. The second part of a congressman's job—it overlaps with helping individual constituents, but it's a completely separate business—is to do what you can about community problems that come up. If a bridge collapses or some housing doesn't get built or a racial crisis develops, you have to try to help ease the situation. Sometimes that means just being there, because sometimes you can't do much more than that. Holding forums, as we have been doing in my district, can be helpful. It's important at this time in our history for people to have opportunities to express and hear different points of view about things that bother them. In Nassau County, we invite everyone to these forums, and all kinds of people come, either as speakers or just to participate from the audience. Mr. Joseph M. Margiotta, the Republican chairman in Nassau, said that Republicans mustn't come; it would 'lend dignity' if they came, he said. But he's given to making suggestions that nobody pays much attention to. We've had meetings on the war, on taxes, on the ABM, on campus disturbances, on how to finance education, and so forth. They must be interesting, because people keep coming—even Republicans, despite poor Mr. Margiotta. Some Republicans come because they believe in the principle of open forums, or, at least, want to use them if they're going to happen anyway; others come because they want you to do something for them, or because they're friends. We have had some bad racial incidents in a number of towns—people beaten up and hospitalized. When something like that happens, you go to the groups and individuals who are the angriest or the most deeply offended and try to help work things out so that difficulties can be eased without further violence. Of course, where the problems cover a wider area it's

146

harder to do anything effective about them. But the city and the suburbs, for example, do have many similar interests, and if someone were to
bring people together to work regionally—to lobby in Congress, and so
on—that could be helpful. However, most of the time everyone is feuding
with everyone else. Politicians are afraid of potential rivals. So there's
always the problem of who should lead this kind of effort.

"That gets into the question of how the parties affect government. So
many of the complications created by partisanship are pointless, but I
guess in our kind of setup they're natural, and maybe unavoidable. Republicans and Democrats both tend to be all for bipartisan or non-
partisan efforts to do things they'll get credit for doing, and very
unenthusiastic about bipartisan efforts that won't help the party, or some
official the party likes. That may seem obvious, but it can make difficulties. For instance, if the Republicans are in power the Democrats will be
reluctant to help the Republicans get credit for doing something non-
controversial, since that may strengthen the Republicans and enable
them to do things that are controversial. There's another twist to the
non-partisan business. The White House is very anxious for us Democrats not to criticize Administration policy in Vietnam. Its people want
us to help cool everybody down who is upset about the ambiguities and
pace of the withdrawal; they say that we should give them time in Vietnam, that we shouldn't be 'partisan' about Governor Rockefeller's trip to
Latin America or about the surtax, and so on. You know the argument—
we've only got one President, and if we criticize his defense or foreign
policy, that's partisan, and politics stops at the water's edge and anything
else is not worthy of Americans, et cetera. But when we find Republicans
who privately agree with us about problems that ought to be just as non-
partisan, like poverty or campus disorders, the Administration all of a
sudden discovers the virtues of the two-party system. So it's O.K. for
them to put pressure on other Republicans not to work with us for
programs the Administration doesn't want, on the ground that Republicans shouldn't be working with Democrats. I guess it's all supposed to be
clever politics—to get us to support what the Administration is doing and
still try to be sure it doesn't look as if there were bipartisan support for
what we're doing. What makes the whole partisan approach especially
senseless now is that neither party makes enough sense as a party to
justify using the traditional distinction of party label to prevent cooperation among people who essentially agree with each other. Conservatives
of both parties generally seem to understand this much better than mod-

erates and liberals. Still, as things stand today, it seems to me there's no real question but that the Democratic Party is worth fighting for. It's come a long way in the last year or so. Do you know anyone who's hankering for a restoration of Johnsonism? I feel more hopeful about the direction of the Democratic Party than I have in a long time, and more loyal to it. On matters of conscience, though, I don't think either community opinion or party should be decisive. You should follow your conscience and do what you think should be done, then try to explain it to the community, which has a right to reject you at the next election if it feels you've gone against what it wants. I get lots of mail saying that my position on the war doesn't represent the district and I should resign, and so on. I wish there were some way the public could express itself directly on a matter as preempting as the war—it would reduce that feeling of being unable to influence policy which is the cause of so much disenchantment with American democracy these days. Perhaps some kind of referendum could be worked out, or an electoral test of some kind. A year is a very long time for people to go before they have a way to say what they want to do about Vietnam and everything that flows from it. Consequently, my office sends out questionnaires periodically to try to find out how people in the district feel about things like troop withdrawals, the federal budget, the draft, student disorders, the surtax—that sort of thing. I can't promise to fit my views to the results, but I do want to know what people are thinking. Then we can discuss why we differ, if we do. Where there's a substantial disagreement between a representative and his constituency, it seems to me important for both to have the chance to rethink their positions, even though no change may result on either side."

Lowenstein leaned back and stretched. "Another thing a congressman finds he should do is attend a lot of functions," he continued. "Some people think it adds prestige to have a congressman present—or, at least, it shows that a congressman is interested. You try to attend, since people usually can't get a senator or a governor to come. That's part of the problem of time. Do you go to one more church function, one more bar mitzvah, one more meeting of a veterans' group, one more historical-society meeting? There's always more to do, so unless you deliberately set yourself to hack out little enclaves, your personal life can become nonexistent. Droopy is going to say we don't hack out enough." Droopy is Lowenstein's nickname for his wife, and also her nickname for him.

Near Riverhead, we stopped at a roadside restaurant for lunch. Lowenstein had canned vegetable soup, a hot dog, a root beer, and an ice-cream cone. "That's the way he eats," his wife said. "He doesn't even notice that it all tastes like plastic." A few minutes later, the Lowensteins dropped me off at a friend's house, and we parted for the day. As it turned out, I had to wait quite a long time to learn what Lowenstein considered the third and fourth parts of a representative's job.

The next morning, I arrived at the house of Mrs. Lowenstein's mother and found all the members of the household except Lowenstein sitting around a back-yard swimming pool. He was indoors, telephoning. When he came out, he was ready to start for his district headquarters in Baldwin, and we had arranged that he would drop me off at the railroad station there. Again Engstrom was at the wheel and I shared the back seat with Lowenstein. As we rode along, the talk turned to money, which for Lowenstein is a problem second only to the problem of time. His parents once owned a series of restaurants in Manhattan, but neither he nor his family is wealthy. He graduated from the University of North Carolina and from Yale Law School, put in two years in the Army, practiced law briefly in New York, and then taught law at Stanford, North Carolina State, and the City College of New York. Now he earns forty-two thousand dollars a year, but he says that not much of his salary stays with him. "I spend a good deal more on office expenses each month than we get in allowances," he said as we drove along. "I paid my own way to Vietnam, Biafra, and so on, so even though neither my wife nor I drink or spend much on clothes, money is not our long suit. I sleep in friends' rooms in Washington to save renting an apartment there. The forums I was telling you about cost seven or eight hundred dollars every two weeks, what with the printing, the expenses of whoever speaks, and receptions before and after. I send out a newsletter every few months, so that people know what I'm doing. This costs between thirteen hundred and fifteen hundred dollars each time, and that's without anything fancy. Money is one reason most congressmen don't try to do much about national issues. They tend to limit themselves to local questions, plus maybe one national issue they can work on through the committee they're assigned to. That's not a criticism. How much can anyone do with limited staff, and all the mail and whatnot to cope with? If you aren't independently wealthy, you can't have a staff that's capable of putting things together much beyond what you can come up with from the sources available to everyone—the executive departments, the lobbies, the staffs of congressional committees, the Library of Congress. That's one reason lobbies can be so influential. They have people who are able to spend all their time collecting data on why pollution is good for River X. What congressman can match that? And what are congressmen supposed to do about explaining the intricacies of a tax bill? So most members make their peace with the situation—they get active on some issue that is big in their district and will help them there. Another thing about money. Some members bolster their income by leaving their name on a law firm. I would find that difficult. To my mind, the question would arise. 'How come you can do both?' If you aren't too busy in the House to maintain a law practice, then it's hard to believe you're doing all you should be doing in Congress. And if you aren't practicing, why should you have your name on a law firm? Isn't that trading on the name of the Congress? Of course, some men would like to give up outside arrangements of this kind but are afraid that if they did they'd lose their financial independence—they'd be too dependent on staying elected or getting appointed to some political job. I'm not sure I should say all this until I have worked out specific proposals for dealing with the whole mess—conflict of interest, campaign expenses, the adequate financing of staffs, and the rest. It's not just the question of names on law firms. There's the problem of owning stock. Lots of congressmen get money out of things that Congress legislates about. But to limit conflicts of interest between proposed legislation and private sources of income you have to get into everything that is regulated by government agencies. So what should you do? Right now, I have to find some way to meet these expenses—the office, the trips, and so on. You can use a lecture bureau, but I'd hate to wind up speaking to the highest bidder. I made a rule when I entered Congress that I didn't want to know which speech invitations were for a fee, let alone for how much. In the long run, I guess it's better to give lectures than to be in a law firm, and better to be in a law firm than to have a source of income that might influence how you vote. As you can see, this whole problem is very complicated. And it has been ignored too long."

Shortly before we reached the station, Lowenstein, who was dressed much as he had been the day before, rubbed his hand across his chin, which was stubbly, and said, "I can't go into the office like this." He asked Engstrom to drop him at a barbershop for a shave, and we said goodbye.

The next time I saw Lowenstein long enough to have a solid talk with him was at my apartment on a recent Sunday night. He had told me that he had to attend one of his district forums and two other meetings that evening but thought he would be free by eleven-thirty. A little after midnight, Mark Arnold, a Dartmouth senior who had taken Engstrom's place when the summer ended, arrived to pick up Lowenstein and drive him home. I told him that Lowenstein hadn't shown up yet, and asked him to wait. At one-thirty, Lowenstein arrived. When I asked if he had had any dinner or supper, he said no, so I got some food from the refrigerator, and we settled down near a coffee table to talk about what he thought a congressman should do outside his district—the two remaining parts of the four parts of a representative's job, as he saw it. But he had something else he wanted to talk about first. Since our last conversation, he said, the "procedural horrors" of the House had made his earlier comments seem far too mild. Indeed, he seemed a great deal more steamed up than he had been during our discussions in the car. "Do you know that we were not allowed a roll-call vote on whether to deploy the ABM?" he said, "And that on the Vietnam resolution the President wanted passed because it was so vital to his plans for peace, there were no hearings, and discussion was limited to four hours—which averages out to thirty seconds a member—and there was no way to introduce amendments? And we've voted on amendments to bills that appropriate billions of dollars without having amendments *explained*, let alone discussed. Half the votes on bills that matter occur after debates in which most of the newer members get forty-five seconds or a minute to speak. If only the country understood what goes on! But the whole procedure is designed to make that impossible." He pulled some papers out of a briefcase. "Here, I brought you a couple of statements I made in the House," he said. "They're pretty low-key, but they tell a little of what I feel."

I looked at the material he had handed me, which was from the *Congressional Record*. One statement was about the Vietnam resolution. "We mock democracy when we treat this resolution as if it were a footnote to a bill about fishing rights on Mars," it went. "If we do not have the opportunity for adequate debate and to consider amendments on this of all resolutions, we will simply subject these proceedings to further ridicule. Members not permitted to speak here will not thereby be silenced. They will be angered. We are becoming increasingly what we treat ourselves as if we already were . . . second-class citizens with dwindling relevance to the awful events that surround and soon may engulf us."

I asked him if he felt that indignation over such procedures was rising generally in the House, and he said that he thought it was—that the response to statements like the one he showed me had been encouraging. He said that one of his most outspoken protests had come about almost by accident, because he had been recognized unexpectedly at the end of the acrimonious debate on the military-appropriations bill. By then, it was clear that no vote on deploying the ABM would be allowed. House members had begun the chant of "Vote! Vote!" that always arises when the dinner hour is approaching and a roll-call remains as a block to leaving the hall. Several friendly members had counselled him not to speak, Lowenstein said, in view of the mood of the House. He could put his remarks in the *Record*, they reminded him, and no one would know he had not spoken them. "But I decided to speak," he told me. "I got up and asked if anyone thought that behaving the way we were behaving would increase respect for the Congress or for the concept of representative democracy. I asked if anyone could justify rules that concealed our position on something as vital as the ABM. I ended up by saying that the House wouldn't dare to go on in its present condition—that basic procedures would have to be revised soon. I thought at the time that what I was saying would mark the beginning of a kind of ostracism in the House, but that hasn't happened. Some of the younger members were enthusiastic, and this was perhaps predictable, but the reaction of several venerable figures was most unexpected—some all but embraced me in the well of the House, and others made a point of phoning me later on to congratulate me. Whatever the reason for all that, it's clear that the potential for revolt is far greater than it was a while ago. The groundwork was laid by some really good people over the years, and now it has been reinforced by concern about the war and matters growing out of the war. It looks as if we'll finally get a reform bill out of the Rules Committee sometime soon. There probably won't be much basic reform in the bill, but just getting the whole thing opened up that way will be a start, and if we can build a national awareness of what's at stake in something that sounds as dull as 'reforming Congress' we may really get somewhere eventually. I think lots of members would like to see some changes made."

Lowenstein was nibbling at an apple now, and I managed to get him to discuss the two remaining aspects of his job.

"If you simply deal with individual and local problems, you're not doing a very good job, because you've been elected to a national legislature, and that means you ought to be concerned about national needs and the national direction," he said. "That's especially true at a time like this, when very few local problems can be solved if we don't reverse the country's lockstep toward disaster. In that sense, it was particularly useful to have been elected from a Republican district after taking unequivocal positions against the war and for deep reforms at home. But how can a representative function effectively on great national questions? It's completely inadequate to say, 'Well, I'm going to vote right.' That's not the end of your obligation. It's barely the beginning. You have to be willing to take the fight outside your district, because one district isn't going to change things. You must go wherever you're able to rally support that can affect the way Congress or the President will act on these issues. About student violence, for instance—you have to go to the campuses to try to explain why it's both wrong and damaging. You could put yourself on record as opposing campus violence by denouncing it in Rotary Clubs or in the well of the House, but that would be playing out the charade again. Now, I'm not saying that giving speeches around the country makes you a better congressman. But, if you can, you ought to help to build strength around the country against policies you oppose, so that when a related issue comes to a vote some public opinion has been aroused."

Lowenstein was now sipping a glass of root beer. "Fourth, you can also do something about things that trouble you inside the Congress itself. It can be useful to talk to members about the war and the national priorities. And you can also talk to 'them about things that may be more important to your district than they are elsewhere. Take jet noise—not many districts have jet airports to harass them. But the congressional custom of 'You help me on this and I'll help you on that' can be brought into play and a few interested members can build a lot of support for a bill to decrease jet noise. The best place for this kind of lobbying is on the floor of the House. One member got very big on the idea of prohibiting the sale of switchblade knives by mail, and he worked so hard lobbying one by one that he got seventy-five members to back his bill. Rallying public opinion and lobbying individual members are the greatest contributions you can make to influencing the legislative process in your first term. In the House, as elsewhere, personal relations make a great difference if you want to get things done. A member may want you to speak at some function that one of his constituents has organized, or meet a delegation coming to see him, or simply come and have a drink. Then, too, if you're going to somebody's district, you try to tell him ahead of time and perhaps chat with him about your trip afterward. A while ago, when I marched in Charleston with the hospital workers, who were on strike, I called up Representative Mendel Rivers beforehand to tell him what I intended to do. It's no great secret that our political views are about as far apart as views can get, but our relationship has remained cordial. I'm not much good at hating people, and there are lots of people in Congress—and out—whom I like a great deal more than I agree with. One of the unexpected things—to me, anyway—about the House is how affable the leadership is. For instance, Carl Albert and Speaker McCormack show a great deal of interest in the new members and are patient and helpful about the little things that confuse you at the beginning. Of course, if you have a great interest in getting a particular bill passed, you have to have the help of the committee chairman concerned."

I was somewhat surprised by Lowenstein's mention of Representatives Rivers, Albert, and McCormack, because it had seemed to me that throughout our conversations Lowenstein talked about the intimate workings of the House of Representatives as though it were composed of Lowenstein and four hundred and thirty-four nameless members. I asked him about this.

"Well, one of the common-sense customs is that you don't discuss other congressmen in a personal way," he said. "You can see how doing that would undermine the kind of relationships we've been talking about. Sometimes you may have to do it, but the general rule—and I think it's a good one—is to talk about the issue or the approach instead of about individuals."

"At least, one can assess congressmen in general," I suggested.

Lowenstein nodded. "They're more like seismographs than you'd expect," he said. "Most of them are rather timid, considering their relative eminence. There's a real desire to represent their districts accurately on major issues, but there's also a tendency to misread the country, partly because the cumulative effect of being in the House is like that of being in a rather pleasant cocoon. There's a serious underestimation of what leadership, including their own, could do. Most members see themselves as leaders only in local matters, and the result is that that's what they tend to become individually, to the detriment of the House collectively. It's one of the sad consequences of believing the old saw that the first rule of politics is to get reelected. But even if Congress should now start to do much better—if the rules are changed and members begin to show more guts—the quality and direction of the President's leadership would still be the most critical element at this particular turning point. When President Kennedy died, the country was in relatively good spirits and was moving forward. We had great problems, but people were hopeful, and the spirit of hope was contagious. I was in Mississippi in the summer and fall of 1963, with the civil-rights movement. Life was a nightmare, but nobody doubted that we were going to win—that America would come to the rescue of her downtrodden. America was going to be something good, and even Mississippi would come around. Who feels that way now? The awful change in the national mood is the result of something more than Vietnam and the defense budget. It is the result of President Johnson's over-all conduct as well. People in a democracy get sour if they feel they are being deceived. If the top leaders of a democratic society use words to conceal, or to mislead and divide, a mood of revulsion sets in among the people—revulsion against the government and against each other. So few people are in a position to reach the country quickly, to change this kind of mood. That's why Franklin and Eleanor Roosevelt meant so much—far more than all their specific programs and statements put together. And that's why the double loss of Martin Luther King and Robert Kennedy was so totally devastating. It's why I hoped that Nixon would do well—that he would seize the opportunity presented by succeeding Johnson. It's why I was so reluctant to criticize Nixon once he was elected. Presidential leadership could have made it so much easier after the nightmare of 1968. Everyone wanted to help him. If he had set the right tone and tried to move in the direction we needed to go in, the country would have moved quickly. There was really an eagerness for guidance and impetus from the top. It could have been contagious; it could have touched so many people so quickly. People wanted almost pathetically to trust a President. But Nixon seems to be frittering his moment away. He's buying popularity now at a terrific future price by promising things that are inconsistent and therefore cannot all be delivered. He has started this sad business of saying one thing and then saying another, and is thus risking the same kind of disenchantment that Johnson incurred. All this talk that Nixon can carry this state or that state in 1972 is so silly. The same kind of prophecies were made about Johnson. They mean precisely nothing three years ahead of time. People are going to judge Nixon by whether they feel that the things they are unhappy about have been changed. If he would begin, even now, to tackle the tough things candidly, to move away from the mistakes of the past, a lot of people would rally to help him. I know I would. But the impression is growing that we're all watching a juggling act—a skillful juggling act but still a juggling act—which sooner or later has to end with things crashing to a halt."

Lowenstein leaned back and became silent for a few moments, and then went on. "If the President won't lead the country toward basic change, our job is to put together a majority coalition to work for the kind of changes that will make things better. Change in *some* direction is inevitable. What is not certain is whether it will be in a Robert Kennedy direction or a Spiro Agnew direction. In the Depression, such enormous numbers of people were hungry or out of work that you could put together that kind of coalition, based on the reality of the needs people felt. Now, even with the war, a majority of the country lives comfortably. The people who are disaffected over their economic situation don't come close to a majority. In a sense, this country suffers from its own great material success. The fact is that economic rights and opportunities are withheld from the people who are outnumbered. Out of the frustration of having no way to get things changed, or even to get represented adequately, the unhappy people who are consigned to a permanent minority can turn to upheaval and disruption. We have to make a new majority for change that will include them. And will include the middle class, too, which is miserable about inflation, taxes, overcrowding, pollution. We must make middle-income people understand that solving the problems is related to solving the problems of the poor. It's not the poor who are getting the money out of the middle class—it's the war, the so-called defense budget. The middle class pays a disproportionate amount of taxes not because of welfare but because of oil companies. And what is collected unfairly is spent absurdly. What the McCarthy and Kennedy campaigns were doing—and I think everyone knows this by now—was bringing together the poor, both black and white, and the lower-income middle class, and the Spanish-speaking people, and the great numbers of relatively well-off Americans who are upset about the war or discontented with the quality or style of life in this country. All those people together would make up quite a majority, and that was the basis of the 1968 alliances. It was what elected me. If there were effective national leadership for that kind of alliance now, it would carry the country. But, given the urgency of our situation, I am not optimistic about where the country is headed if the President can't soon be made to realize what's going on and so try to do the things that are so desperately needed. First of all, I think we are going to come apart as a people if we don't get out of Vietnam soon, and that would mean paying for this extended national stupidity with an eternity of awfulness. What might be worst of all about that would be realizing how close we came to getting started in the right direction. You might almost say that the margin was one bullet. I wonder what would have happened to us if Franklin Roosevelt had been killed in 1933. Could we have coped with John Nance Garner and the Depression at the same time? It's frightful how much more this country needs and misses Robert Kennedy now than it did even a year and a half ago. But saying that simply underscores how much harder we must work than we have been working."

It was now nearly 4 A.M., and Lowenstein and Arnold had to go. In a few hours, Lowenstein would be back in Washington. Just before he left, he said, "I don't know what I will do if the effort to bring change through electoral democracy fails. The far left thinks—really, hopes—that an explosion is inevitable. You know the line: the whole society is hopelessly sick and Vietnam is only a symptom. I think that's untrue. But if enough people came to believe that—came to feel that it no longer mattered what they said or did—the belief could lead to our undoing. The only thing I'm sure about is that we must not fail simply because we didn't try, and try with all the energy and brains we can muster. If we did fail, would I join the revolution? Would I leave the country? After all, I would be obsolete. But I don't engage in the luxury of wondering what I would do if the effort shouldn't work. I'm committed to the notion that it *will* work."

LET THE PEOPLE DECIDE
Press Conference Statement,
February 16, 1970

Lowenstein continued looking for ways to dramatize antiwar senti-
ment. He believed that Nixon's claim of a "silent majority" in support of
the war was empty, but there seemed no way to pose the war issue
squarely to voters.

A few months after he had taken office, Nassau County Republican
Chairman Joseph Margiotta made the first of several demands that he
resign from Congress. Margiotta claimed the new lawmaker's antiwar
activities had been so extreme that he had forfeited the right to repre-
sent his district.

In 1969, the New York State Legislature began revising his district's
lines, thus threatening to deprive its voters of the chance to test Mar-
giotta's claim. The revision was part of a statewide redistricting prior to
the 1970 census. One October story in Newsday *was headlined* GOP RE-
MAP AIMS AT LOWENSTEIN.

In January, the legislature completed its redistricting, removing major
centers of antiwar strength from Lowenstein's district. At a press confer-
ence the following month, he responded to the resignation outcry and
the gerrymander by issuing a challenge to his opponents.

I think it's fair to say that when I was elected to Congress, everyone
knew pretty much where I stood on the war, and in fact on most other

major issues. But for many months now, Mr. Joseph Margiotta, the Nassau County Republican chairman, among others, has been demanding my resignation on the grounds that I do not represent the views of the people of the 5th Congressional District on the war and on problems related to the war.

Demands like those of Mr. Margiotta could ordinarily be discounted the way that most political statements are discounted, but these are not ordinary times. The war grinds on, and so does inflation, poverty, pollution, and a host of other curable ills. Meanwhile the nation waits in vain for leadership with guts, brains, and programs to cure these ills. Instead, it gets nostrums and name-calling from the national administration, and the spirit of the people grows more troubled and querulous while the national will seems almost paralyzed.

Vietnam remains at the heart of these difficulties. I cannot support the President's policies there, for I am convinced that these policies will lead to many more years of war, with all the horror that entails for the United States and for Vietnam. Mr. Nixon may feel that 5,000 more dead Americans—and God knows how many more Vietnamese killed by Americans—are small numbers. I don't.

In these circumstances, I believe there is much to be said for the kind of electoral test that could occur if I were to resign, as Mr. Margiotta and others have suggested, and let the voters decide if they want me to continue as their representative.

I assume that Mr. Margiotta and the others who have asked me to resign don't intend to have the 5th Congressional District unrepresented in Congress. If I resign, the only way the 5th Congressional District can be represented would be to hold a special election to fill the vacancy. So if Mr. Margiotta's demands for my resignation are not pure grandstanding, I expect him and his associates to join me in asking the governor to assure that a special election would be held promptly to fill the vacancy that would be created by my resignation.

The moment the governor agrees to call a special election he will have my resignation, and the people of the 5th Congressional District can then say who they want to represent them for the remainder of the term to which I was elected in November 1968. Since the state legislature has dismembered the 5th Congressional District, there will be no other way that the people of this district can make such a choice. And while I disagree with Mr. Margiotta about what choice they would make, I agree that the issues are too critical to deny them the right to choose.

Let me make it clear right now that a special election would fill my seat only for the rest of my current term. Even if I were to win such an election, I would have to run again in November under the new district lines if I wanted to stay in Congress next year.

I have hesitated to take this step for personal reasons and for reasons of precedent. To begin with, one doesn't lightly put one's family or one's community through extra campaigns for offices fairly won. And mid-term resignations are not generally desirable in our system of government.

But America is in the kind of crisis that makes usual politics unacceptable. We play politics as usual now at our own grave national peril.

The division about the President's war policies is very deep. His claim that a majority of the American people support these policies should be subjected to the best test available, which is, in the last analysis, an election. In America, the people must speak on questions like these, not the politicians.

My action today then should be welcomed because it can achieve three useful results. It can assure that the people of the 5th Congressional District will have a spokesman in Congress during the next ten critical months who will represent them properly on the great problems besetting the nation. It can provide a clear test of how the American people feel about the President's leadership on the war and on the crisis at home in a district in which the President obtained a higher percentage of the popular vote in 1968 than he did in the nation at large. And it can help reinvigorate in some small way the electoral process itself, so more Americans will see that they can, in fact, influence the national policies that affect so profoundly their lives and the future of their country.

I take this action today in the spirit of the late Senator George W. Norris of Nebraska, who opposed steps he believed would involve the United States unnecessarily in the First World War. Senator Norris warned that a member of Congress who ignored his conscience on a matter as basic as war and peace "becomes only an automatic machine" requiring "no patriotism, no education and no courage."

Instead, Senator Norris decided that he must "do what in my own heart I believe to be right for the people at large," and "let my constituents decide whether I was representing them or misrepresenting them in Washington." So he wrote to the governor of his state offering to resign his seat in the Senate and urging the governor to call a special election. In this letter he said he had "no desire to represent the people of Nebraska if my official conduct is contrary to their wishes."

"I will not . . . violate my oath of office," he wrote, "by voting in favor of a proposition that means the surrender by Congress of its sole right to declare war. . . . If my refusal to do this is contrary to the wishes of the people of Nebraska, then I should be recalled and someone else elected to fill the place. . . . I am, however, so firmly convinced of the righteousness of my course that I believe if the intelligent and patriotic citizenship of the country can only have an opportunity to hear both sides of the question, all the money in Christendom . . . will not be able to defeat the principle of government for which our forefathers fought. . . . If I am wrong, then I not only ought to retire, but I desire to do so. I have no desire to hold public office if I am expected blindly to . . . be a rubber stamp even for the President of the United States."

This republic is stronger for the contributions of men like George Norris, who understood that in a free country no public office is more important than obeying one's conscience and then being prepared to abide by the decision of the people.

Some may suggest that it is "grandstanding" to offer to resign rather than simply to resign. I would, in fact, prefer to resign outright. The United States Constitution says: "When vacancies happen in the representation from any state, the executive authority thereof shall issue writs of election to fill such vacancies" (Art. 1, sec. 2, (4)). But the New York State statute leaves the decision about filling vacancies to the discretion of the governor, and the work of a congressman is too important to his constituents to risk leaving them unrepresented for ten months. So I have concluded that I cannot resign until it is certain that the 5th Congressional District will not be unrepresented as a result of my resignation.

I want to repeat that I urge and expect Mr. Margiotta, and those who have joined with him to demand my resignation—I urge and expect them to join with me now in urging the governor to agree to a special election.

Otherwise it will be perfectly clear that it is Mr. Margiotta and his allies who have been grandstanding—that they are, in fact, unwilling to submit our differences to the people. In short, it will be clear that they know the majority of the people in the 5th Congressional District approve of the kind of representation I have been giving them.

May I add that if no election is agreed to, one might suspect that the President and the Vice-President have also been grandstanding with their claims that they speak for the "silent majority," because they ought to be able to win an election in my district if they could carry the country. At least they'd have a very fair battleground.

Some will object that a special election adds to the burden of the already-overburdened taxpayer. As far as I can find out, the cost of a special election would run around $75,000. That doesn't seem very much to me, representing as it does the cost of about seventy-five seconds of prosecuting the war. But if cost is a problem, I would be glad to split it with Mr. Margiotta and the Nassau County Republican Party so it need cost the taxpayers nothing.

In any event, in Congress or out, I will continue to oppose the President's policies in Vietnam, and the deranging of our national priorities that has resulted from these policies and those of his predecessor. I hope it is clear that my position on this matter is not based on partisanship. We have opposed presidents, equally, regardless of party.

I am convinced that as a nation we are on a disaster course. I am convinced too, that more and more Americans will want to change policies as they understand where we are headed, and at what a terrible price to all we hold dear.

In my judgment, the only thing that could be worse for America than the continuation of these policies would be their continuation because those who believe them to be wrong have not done everything humanly possible to change them. That means carrying our views as effectively as we can to the people, in whom after all the power of decision ultimately resides.

I believe we can do something useful to strengthen democracy in the United States by holding a special election in the 5th Congressional District at this time. And, win or lose, I know I can do more to help move America toward the goals that are growing more distant by submitting my record and taking my case to the voters than I possibly could by staying in Congress safely for the rest of this term.

So I am sending the governor a letter today urging him to assure us that a special election would be held within sixty days of my resignation. I hope that assurance will be forthcoming today, so I can submit my resignation and we can start right away to find out how the American people feel about the war and about the problems so closely tied to it.

The resignation proposal was described as "absurd" by the Republican chairman, but a Newsday *editorial entitled "The Judo Master" said*

162

Lowenstein had "neatly used the force of the GOP attack to send Nassau GOP Chairman Margiotta to the mat with his foot lodged firmly in his mouth." Governor Nelson Rockefeller refused to comment on Lowenstein's request, and no special election took place.

UP FOR GRABS

Speech, Stanford University,
May 24, 1970

By early 1970, the antiwar movement, still sometimes punctuated by violence, began to lose steam. In the spring, the Vietnam Moratorium organization disbanded, citing apathy and the declining appeal of large-scale protest movements.

Then, on April 30, the United States invaded Cambodia. Suddenly, the fading antiwar movement was revivified. Massive protests erupted on campuses across the nation. President Nixon responded to the renewed activity by visiting the Pentagon and by denouncing "the bums . . . blowing up the campuses."

The protests expanded, resulting in more violence. On May 4, four students were killed by National Guardsmen at Kent State University in Ohio. On May 8, a student antiwar demonstration on Wall Street in New York City was broken up in a planned attack by hard-hatted construction workers, representatives of whom were later invited to the White House. On May 9, tens of thousands of persons marched in Washington to protest the expansion of the war. On May 10, eleven black students were shot following unrest at Jackson State University in Mississippi.

In one bizarre episode, Nixon emerged from his White House cocoon to mingle at dawn with antiwar demonstrators on the grounds of the

Lincoln Memorial. Meeting a student from Syracuse University, he praised the school's football program, a remark that for many came to symbolize his insensitivity to the deep-seated concerns of youth.

Throughout this period of turmoil, Lowenstein worked in Congress to develop a new legislative drive to cut off funds for the war. He also spoke on many campuses, and once again his speeches were often disrupted or assailed by some on the Far Left. Following a trip to schools in the South, he addressed a student meeting at Stanford University.

I have come from Tuscaloosa and Jackson, and it strikes me that some of the things that I would like most to discuss were made more pressing on my mind by events there.

I went to the University of Alabama in Tuscaloosa because I was called by the student-body presidents of the law school and other places, plus the editor of the paper, who said that the police in Tuscaloosa had responded to a protest about the Cambodian attack by arriving on the campus and then beating everybody at random, arresting very large numbers of people, and clubbing kids that they found in fraternities and in dormitories and in eating places on the street, and that nobody would do anything about it. They seemed to be at their wit's end.

It was quite a state of affairs for white Southerners to be in—to find that their own police had suddenly turned on them and were now dealing with them as they had dealt previously with blacks. And the two distinguished public figures running for governor of Alabama had been vying with each other on television to see which could impress the state more enthusiastically with the virtue of what the police had been doing in repressing anarchy and insurrection on the campus. Therefore the state was under the impression, since nothing else was reported, that the police behavior was justified. And they didn't really know what to do.

Well, I went to Tuscaloosa. I really hoped that these reports had been exaggerated and that one would find out that some of the things that had happened were in fact misstated, but that wasn't the case. We had eight hours of hearings in the Student Union Building, which seats a couple of thousand people. During this period of time they would come by one by one and tell what they had been through, the experiences they had either endured themselves or had observed at first hand. It was quite an outrageous story.

The Alabama papers did cover it very intensively, and just as I left to come out here this telegram came, and I thought I'd share it with you. It's addressed to me at the House and it says:

I resent very much and protest your recent trip to the University of Alabama to hold a completely unofficial and uncalled for investigation. I fail to see your qualifications to hold such and of course it is ridiculous. It's extremely easy to understand why you chose to make such a grandstand play. The popular thing to do in case of confrontations with law enforcement officers is immediately to send up a howl of police brutality. . . .

I noted among other pearls of wisdom which you so graciously gave the people of Alabama was the profound statement that "What we need to do now is to redirect the energies of this country because the Republic is in grave peril." I agree with you, the republic is in grave peril, because we have allowed people like you on our campuses. Today we stand on the brink of a bloody revolution in this country.

I have conferred with the Alabama Sheriffs' Association, and I am speaking for them as well as for all of the law enforcement officials in this state when I say that if you must give someone the benefit of your expert advice, we would respect it if you would do that in New York. . . . In short, Mr. Lowenstein, we do not need or want you meddling in the affairs of the state of Alabama.

Yours truly,

Sheriff Jerry Crabtree
President of the Alabama Sheriffs'
Association

Now, the relevant parts of this telegram, of course, are the parts where someone authorized to speak for the Alabama Sheriffs' Association, and, according to the telegram, for all other law enforcement officials in the state of Alabama, finds it possible to send a telegram saying that the country is on the brink of bloody revolution because people like me have been allowed on campuses and that we are going to have to deal with this accordingly. Now, other than the insolent tone of the telegram, what it says, of course, is that you can create the impression, as in Alabama has been done, and as in other places has been done, that there is some kind of bloody revolution being planned and organized by groups, whoever they are, so that you don't need to answer for what you do at all.

Eight hours of testimony by white Alabamians to the rain of atrocities that showers down on them in Alabama doesn't even merit a pause, because, in fact, the country, by this view, can be convinced that all of this is in response to the sort of bloody revolution being planned by small groups of fanatics—"radicals" or whatnot. I should add that in Tuscaloosa I met with the university officials, none of whom denied any part of what the students said had happened. They simply said they couldn't do anything about it, because if they intervened in the situation, they would be in fact damaging the university very badly in the state of Alabama, so they couldn't take sides.

Unfortunately, when you get to Jackson, the situation is worse. In Jackson, what the police and the patrol did was to go out to the campus of Jackson State and there to proceed to murder two people and to send others to the hospital, some of whom may die. There isn't any verb you could use but "murder," because what they did was to go out with automatic weapons and use these weapons on buildings where unarmed people were clustered until some of them were killed.

The girls' dormitory is on Lynch Street, which is the main street in the part of town Jackson State is situated—the heart of the black area of Jackson. And as the girls' dormitory fronts onto Lynch Street, these automatic weapons were used to shell—I don't know what else you would call it—the front of that building so that the windows are all gone, the walls are pockmarked with holes, and there are two people dead and others who may die.

And again, the interesting thing is that the mood that you find is one that condones this kind of behavior on the grounds that the alternative is that there would be bloody takeover by people who are trying to impose minority rule on the country.

Now, if you come from Tuscaloosa and then Jackson, in sequence, and you understand the events on Wall Street, you perceive the degree to which a very large part of the United States is confused about these events, because of their own genuine fear that things are falling apart in a way they don't understand. They think that therefore we've got to rely on some authority to bring it together again. In this way, you get one glimpse, one very brief glimpse, but a very clear glimpse, of where we could go with the approval of the majority of the country.

I mention these things to start with simply because there is a certain degree of rather astonishing naiveté among some people, including people at Stanford, that suggests that there is some hope for a better country out of a kind of random violence and incendiary misbehavior on the left.

Apparently there are some people who really believe that there is going to be a general disarmament of everybody in the United States except those people who are clothed in great virtue because they are in fact against the war and against the causes of war; in their own mind they're against the evils of the society. If that philosophy, if that concept, ever had any potential credibility, it would seem to me it disappeared sometime in the last six months, because what we've seen occurring is, of course, the reverse.

We now condone outrages committed by authority with an imperturbability that would have been undreamed of a year or two ago. We have events in Mississippi which could not have occurred any time after 1964 when Mississippi was pried open by the beginning of national concern about it. And instead of Mississippi turning out to be more like the United States, as we had hoped at that point, we are having the United States turn out to be more and more like Mississippi, which is a very queer kind of conclusion to come to for a country that had been on such hopeful paths some years ago.

Now the effect, of course, of this sort of activity by very small groups of people is going to be, and has been, to precipitate the kind of confrontations which result in changing the nature of the central question disturbing this country from the causes of all distress in the country to some of these very difficult symptoms that erupt.

If the issue can be changed from the war and results of the war at home to the question of whether small groups of people should be tolerated when they go around creating disruptions and throwing rocks and burning buildings, you'd better understand precisely where the country is going to line up. And it's going to line up there not merely in terms of public-opinion polls and electing people. It's going to end up there also in terms of who gets killed by whom and in what numbers.

You can, in this process—no question, take a few with you. But very few compared to who will be taken. There are six dead people in Augusta, shot in the back. There are four at Kent State. There are two in Jackson. All within a very short period of time, with a decreased revulsion each time from the country.

So I would hope that we could begin understanding precisely how endangered all the things are that we want to see happen in this country, the kind of country that we would want to have created, by the kind of tolerance and silence that has so often greeted acts of disruption and violence from the Left by so many others of us who have an obligation to remember precisely what comes when you poison a society by violence, and who have to understand that not only in principle, but simply in pragmatic fact, what happens if we go that way is that the things that we think we are achieving get further and further removed from possibility.

Now there is something to say that is very hopeful, despite Tuscaloosa and Kent State and Jackson, and Wall Street, and that is that even with these disastrous events that have been etched into the history of this country now—even with the invasion of Cambodia and the rest of it—the mood of the country is visibly moving away from supporting the substantive policies of this Administration.

And so we have a very curious kind of crossing of currents, and at this moment it's not very clear which current is going to prevail. But just as we have this increased tolerance of the misuse of force by authority in the name of repressing what this telegram calls "incipient bloody revolution," just as the polls will reveal that 76 percent of the country believes that the Black Panthers constitute a great danger to the future of this country, and just as there is the abhorrent discovery that most of the country doesn't understand that there were murders committed on Panthers in Chicago which are unacceptable in any society worth the name of civilized—you have the paradox at the same time that overwhelming numbers of Americans do not accept and will not support a continuation of the policies that have led us into the war in Vietnam and that continue that war.

So the only way the President is able to continue having any kind of support is to pretend he's doing things he's not doing. Therefore, while we're in despair and have the sense of frustration that comes when you see these awful things going on, any detached assessment of what's going on should also include the fact that the retreat that we feel from our point of view has to be a very minimal retreat compared to the pell-mell retreat from old goals that are being abandoned right and left by the Administration and those who support it in the effort to keep the country confused as to what they're doing.

Can you imagine where we would be now if public opinion hadn't arisen as it did over Cambodia? We'd be liberating Rangoon by now.

Is there any question in anybody's mind what the miscalculation was when the move into Cambodia was made about the response of the country? Is there any question in your mind that if it wasn't for the fact that the President discovered that he couldn't deal with the country the way he was dealing with it that we would never have had the tolerance of the Hickle letter, that we would never have had the President in his extraordinary effort to redeem his human qualities appearing at the Lincoln Memorial at dawn and chatting about football at Syracuse in his effort to communicate?

So you have a very peculiar thing going on now. They know that they are in retreat. They know that the only way they can hold their country, to hold the support they need, is precisely to have the escalation of disruptive protest reach the point where the country sees that as the central question instead of the substantive issues.

If these two currents are meeting just now, as they are in my judgment, then it should be clear that we are very specifically up for grabs right now as a people, and that the tunnel that we're entering or the corner that we're turning is going to have a tremendous impact on what goes on in the next decade and, so far as one can foresee, in the rest of the history of this country, with all of the impact that has on the history of the world.

And it's for that reason that it seems to me it's worth making the effort that is going on now around the United States, to see to it that the energies of people are channeled into something that has the possibility of bringing a change for the better. I think it was Hannah Arendt who once remarked that you don't know what's going to change when you change things through violence, but the one thing you can be sure of is that at the end of the change through violence things will be more violent.

There are times and there are places when it is, in fact, in my judgment, not only necessary but moral to seek change through violence. I have been involved, as some of you have, I am sure, in events in South Africa, where anyone who talks about nonviolent change hasn't been aware of the history of the realities of the situation, and where violence as a tactic over the long run even has some prospect of success. Certainly there's no prospect of success in trying to reason with the Portuguese or reason with the South African government.

But you're dealing with a situation where in fact the ingredients in this country for change seem clearly to be present more effectively if in fact we make the effort not to destroy the Constitution but to implement it. And that goes, I think, into every area of public activity in this country now.

We had a bill in the House for stopping crime—crime is a big issue in the United States, as you doubtless have heard. And the proposal was that we should pass what is summarized as a preventive-detention provision. Now, it passed overwhelmingly. It was very, very difficult to vote against it, because it's considered to be a very popular thing to support preventive detention.

Well, one problem with that, of course, is that we already have preventive detention. By any standard I know of, this country's system of justice is such that people who don't have a great deal of money can't afford to post bail and are in fact preventively detained. What happens is that it takes up to twenty-four months for a trial. If you can't post bond, you're kept for up to twenty-four months before you're tried. And you spend that period of time in prison without any reason to be there under our system of jurisprudence, because you can't get out. Then you're tried, if you're tried.

In the meantime, you're in prisons which are unfit for anyone to live in. If anyone thinks you can be rehabilitated in any prison in this country, it's because you haven't examined prisons. So what happens is that you spend your time in prison without even being tried, let alone convicted, and when you come out of prison after a long period of time in prison, the likelihood is that you're a criminal if you weren't before you went in. And so the statistics show that people are recidivists when they come out of prison, and those statistics are then used to show that they should have been preventively detained. Where in fact it's the fact that being preventively detained has as much to do with the recidivist rate as anything.

And the paradox, you see, is that the facts in that situation are not in support of preventive detention. They are, in fact, in support of the view that we should be implementing the Constitution, which guarantees to people a speedy trial and reasonable bail. So that when we put ourselves in the position of eroding further the constitutional guarantees that have been neglected so long, we're not helping to make things any better at all. What we're doing is making it less likely that they'll get better.

That problem produces the enormous obligation that seems to me to rest on people who feel deeply about what this country should be and which so many of them aren't meeting, and that obligation is to become sufficiently informed and sufficiently zealous about what we want that we go outside of our own ranks to talk about it. Maybe that's beginning again in the last two weeks, but for two years it didn't happen at all. People were convinced of their own virtue but the virtue that they were convinced of was a virtue which escalated the stridency of their frustrations in dealing with other people equally convinced of their virtue. It never reached out to anybody else. So all over the country we were in retreat, even though we were right.

It would be a tough situation if in fact the evidence was that the country supports imperial adventure in Asia or it supports starving children while it wants to give oil companies exemptions from paying taxes.

It would be very tough to know what to do then, because you'd be in a situation which was almost permanently unchangeable through any kind of democratic effort. But that's not what the evidence is. Look at the evidence wherever you can find it.

What happened in 1968 is only two years ago. What happened is that it wasn't just in Berkeley or in Greenwich Village that we beat these people without any money at the beginning, without any visible leadership, without any precedent, without anyone who really even thought it could occur. Two years ago the whole thing was turned around in three months. We beat them in Nebraska, we beat them in Indiana, we beat them in New Hampshire. We got 89 percent in California. I'm oversimplifying it because obviously not everybody on that side voted for all the things we care about, but in a democracy what we're talking about is not reducible to ideological questions.

Why do you think so many people went from Robert Kennedy to George Wallace? It wasn't inconsistent if what you felt was that things were going wrong and you wanted someone who cared about you and who seemed to understand that things were going wrong and wanted to do something about them and seemed to talk straight about what he was going to do. That transformation of people from supporting the most progressive kind of candidate to supporting the most regressive and racist kind of candidate can occur in a country in which people are freed of the usual party shackles and see themselves voting on the basis of what *they* think is their own self-interest as it identifies itself with people whom they see on television and think they can almost psychoanalyze. They know them very well. They decide this guy really means what he's saying, he really represents change, and that guy doesn't.

So the job you've got, and it's a very important thing to perceive it accurately, is not to convert the whole country to the same ideological position. The job is to get enough information out about why things have gone wrong so people stop fighting each other as enemies when in fact they should be allies, and then to put candidates up who can convey the sense that they care enough and will work enough to change the things that people are frustrated about, because once you get that kind of candidate, the package comes together.

Inflation and taxation are ruining the middle class—why? Not because we're doing a lot for black people and poor people, but because we're *not* doing enough for them in order to get this country moving toward unity. Because we're in fact squandering 66, 70 percent of all the money we

172

appropriate for a budget which makes no sense in terms of security. That's the fact. And in 1968 people rejected the leadership that wanted to go on with the program of the war, forced the reversal of escalation, the ending of the bombing, the entering of negotiations, and it would have had, I think, without any real doubt, the presidency of the United States. Without the assassinations, we would have been moving in a different direction.

You talk about democracy, you talk about leadership, you talk about the meaning of the individual. When you don't have the inspiration out of the top, because the people who could inspire people from the top are killed at the point when they're most needed, what happens, of course, is that the despair is contagious. People stop trying, and you can sense it every place you go. And when everybody stops trying, when "the best lack all conviction," in Yeats's phrase, and "the worst are filled with a passionate intensity," what happens is that things don't move. The system grinds to a halt, and when it grinds to a halt, that's taken as proof that it can't function. All it's proof of is that we can quit it. We've done that.

If you take as proof that you can't change the United States the fact that you can't change the President in the next several years, then of course you will watch Tuscaloosa and Jackson State and Kent State and Wall Street become the order of events. That will be the pattern, because there are some people who are not going to stay out of it. They're going to continue out of desperation, or fanaticism, or conviction, or all three—or out of neurosis or compassion—or anything else that motivates them to not stop when you stop. They're going to go on. And then, of course, you have the country thinking it's choosing between Abbie Hoffman and Spiro Agnew—and guess who they'll choose?

And then everybody will say, "Ah, the country's going fascist." Well, you can produce a situation in which this country could go fascist. Quite true. But isn't the evidence just as clear that you *can* produce a situation in which it goes the other way? It won't end all injustices overnight, but neither will burning a building or dropping a bomb someplace. These injustices are going to have to be ended with all the speed we can muster but with some sense of reality that human institutions, being what they are, have to be changed in a way that makes them change for the better.

So here we are at this turn. When I was in Connecticut the other night campaigning for Joe Duffey against Tom Dodd, SDS tried to break up the meeting because they said there's no difference between Joe Duffey

173

and Tom Dodd, and it was an outrage that I was being allowed to speak because I was misleading people into thinking they could make a difference. And there was a great shouting contest. Well, it's an interesting concept that there's no difference between Joe Duffey and Tom Dodd, but it happens to be a palpable lie, because one difference you should remember it would have made is that there would have been no ABM deployed. We lost by one vote. And if we could have stopped the ABM in the Senate last year, that would have meant that out of that extraordinary wastage of money, 12 billion dollars, which is now going to be 21 billion, you would have had the beginnings of a reversal of the notion that every time they want money for the military it's got to be voted. And you would have been able then to fight to get some of that money used for the things that we can't do. And, of course, you would have had a different rung on the whole arms race and the whole approach to whether we're ever going to control weaponry before we blow the whole globe apart.

So it is not proper to say that it makes no difference whether there's Joe Duffey or Tom Dodd in the United States Senate, just as it is ludicrous to say, as I heard someone say, that there's no difference whether it's Robert Kennedy or Richard Nixon. It happens to be the difference about whether a lot of people are dead in Vietnam and killing other people in Vietnam or whether they're not. And the difference about whether a lot of people in this country find that the whole movement of the country is toward solving the problems which have made life so difficult for them, or whether it's away from that.

Did Robert Kennedy do bad things? Of course he did. Does any human being do everything you want him to? Do you? Do I? But the question of the direction of the country, the question of how we move out from this dreadful place that we have gotten to is something that deserves much more serious and honest answers than simply to say that nothing is going to change overnight and therefore we're going to opt out of making this long-haul effort for change at the fastest rate possible. Because that's what the choice is. If you burn it down, you have to live in what's left of it. If you turn it into a police state, you live in that. And if we come to the point where the choice is between the violence that comes with no change or the change that comes with violence, you're going to end up with that kind of nightmare to choose between. But that isn't what has to happen if we work at what we know we can do, what we saw we can do very recently.

It's much pleasanter to have one sunny demonstration and be done with it, standing around with everybody that you already like and agree with. That's much pleasanter than it is to go into areas where it's not clear people agree with you, to try to find a way to talk to people who don't agree with you, to explain and digest enough information so you've got something to say to them that makes them reexamine questions they haven't thought about. But that's the route which has hope in it, because the other route leads to exactly nowhere except worse and worse hatreds and fears.

During his two years in Congress, Lowenstein's efforts against violence were widely regarded as a major factor in averting campus explosions. For years thereafter, attacks from the Left would continue, and he remained a prime target of groups whose strategies he had helped frustrate.

In the following decade, however, many who had criticized involvement in the electoral process during the sixties would reverse their positions. Tom Hayden would spend hundreds of thousands of dollars to win a California State Assembly Seat and David Harris would run for Congress. For many, these and similar metamorphoses would be a telling commentary on Lowenstein's position during this turbulent period.

ON SUBSIDIZING OPPRESSION IN SPAIN

Remarks in Congress, August 6, 1970

As a young boy, Lowenstein had closely followed the course of the Spanish Civil War and even collected donations for the Republican cause on the street corners near his parents' Manhattan apartment.

His first active involvement in the Spanish cause came while he was working as a foreign-policy assistant to Senator Hubert Humphrey in 1958. He traveled to Spain, where he quickly established contact with the anti-Franco opposition. Over the next two decades, he kept abreast of political developments there and offered what help he could. Throughout this period, he was a frequent critic of U.S. support for foreign dictatorships, not only in Spain but also in Brazil, Taiwan, South Africa, Greece, and elsewhere. His efforts against the Franco regime were a prime manifestation of this commitment.

In Congress, he was in a better position to focus attention on the government's Spanish policy and possibly even to help shape a new one. Early in his term he visited Spain, and one of his first major House initiatives was the organization of a debate on the expiration of the U.S.'s agreement with Spain on military bases.

In July 1970, Lowenstein addressed the House again on Spain and urged Congress to assert a role in the decision on the future of the U.S. bases there. A month later, however, Nixon unilaterally renewed the pact. Shortly thereafter, Lowenstein rose to address the Administration's performance on the issue.

Mr. Speaker, I rise today in dismay and anger over the administration's decision to extend our agreement to maintain bases in Spain.

The decision itself is outrageous enough. The way the decision has been arrived at is inexcusable.

Thank God for the courage and persistence of that appropriately named giant, Senator Fulbright, who brings such distinction to the State of Arkansas and to the U.S. Senate. If it were not for his exertions, the administration might have tiptoed virtually unnoticed into this newest of its misbegotten foreign overcommitments. I salute him on behalf of many of us in this House who admire his dauntless efforts to restore some measure of constitutional balance in the making of foreign policy.

In the Spanish agreement just concluded, this administration has once again short-circuited proper constitutional process by proceeding from clandestine negotiations into arbitrary executive agreements without congressional hearings. The treaty responsibilities of the Senate have been ignored. Congress should assert its authority in this situation—as it should in Southeast Asia—by refusing to appropriate the funds necessary to carry out these unnecessary and unauthorized military and economic commitments. It will do us no good to go on protesting about the way national priorities are ordered and about the undercutting of the legislative branch by the executive branch of Government if we are not willing to do more than protest in situations as flagrant as this one.

The bases in Spain are not needed for our security. The money to be spent on these bases is badly needed at home. No conceivable national interest is served by supporting this particular dictatorship against its own people. Why then are we extending—it would be more accurate to say "expanding"—our commitment to this government? What a peculiar time to be getting ourselves more deeply involved in the ugly business of helping to preserve unpopular military juntas.

The Spanish decision is more than just wrong in principle and wrong in procedure. It is specifically and dismally wrong in practice. The Spanish Government is opposed by the overwhelming majority of the Spanish people. That is why elections are not allowed. A government that has the support of the people allows the people to vote. In fact, at this precise time repression in Spain has taken another of its periodic turns for the worse.

Not long ago the brilliant and uniquely respected Count of Motrico—a man who has been, among other things, General Franco's Ambassador to several countries, including the United States—was punished for speaking out against the repression by having his passport withdrawn. It says a lot about a government when it has to prevent its former Ambassador from leaving the country.

So at considerable expense to the American taxpayer and at the price of further erosion of proper constitutional procedure, the administration has gained the great privilege of using unnecessary bases for a while longer, and of defending yet another unsavory government. Now who might the Franco government need protection against? Who but its own people? Who else might attack the Spanish Government? The Soviet Union, with whom it engages in increasingly friendly intercourse? Portugal? Mainland China? Last year we were told there was a threat of a so-called people's revolution from the Spanish colonies in Africa, but now there are no Spanish colonies in Africa.

What then is all this about? We are retaining bases we do not need in return for money we cannot afford and for pledging to defend a government almost no one wants, against the possibility of attack by its own people.

The terrible suspicion steals across the mind that maybe the U.S. Government actually prefers a dictatorship to a democratic government in Spain. Why else are we continuing to meddle so blatantly in the internal affairs of this unhappy country? Does the "self-determination" we tout as the basis for various others of our interventions around the world not apply to Spain? Are the Spanish people inferior in character or rights so they should be denied what thousands of Americans have died in the name of giving to Vietnamese?

Ultimately, in a democracy like the United States, the people are supposed to decide whether their foreign policy is consistent with the principles and the security needs of the country. How are they to do this if secret negotiations are to lead to hidden agreements, and if even the elected representatives of the people are not consulted as prescribed by the Constitution?

I do not believe a persuasive case can be made that our Spanish policy is consistent with our principles or our needs. If the administration believes a persuasive case can be made, someone in authority—the Pentagon, the State Department, the President—should try to make it, and then the people should decide in the manner prescribed by the Constitution.

The notion that the survival of freedom at home depends on the survival of various malodorous regimes around the world is as repugnant as it is incorrect. Let me say as simply as I can that it brings discredit on this Government to pretend that the freedom of the American people depends on the enslavement of people abroad. I can think of nothing more arrogant and few things as shameful as the United States continuing to prop up a dictatorship in Spain in the name of defending freedom elsewhere.

The truth is that one side effect of our undercutting democracy in Spain is that we weaken it elsewhere in the process. We weaken it here at home, when to implement our Spanish policy the administration must do things furtively that ought to be done in the light of public discussion. We must deceive ourselves about national motives and reinforce archaic and dangerous views of the world. And, of course, we must go on wasting money desperately needed for programs that would help us where our security is in fact imminently imperiled—at home.

We are evidently able to overhaul the Spanish Air Force every year or two, but to do anything about the safety of Americans riding on the Long Island Rail Road, or about the pollution of our water and air, or about bad housing and continuing hunger in our midst—these things we seem unable to do anything about. Have we learned nothing from our misadventures in Southeast Asia?

I want to conclude by saying a word about the Spanish people, in whose name we have committed such sins against our own best interests and theirs. No people have fought more courageously or suffered greater privation in the defense of liberty than the Spanish people. Yet here they are, 31 years after losing their liberty to a dictator who could gain power only through the massive intervention of Hitler and Mussolini, and who has held power only with the massive assistance of the United States. Free elections are as remote as ever, and many of the finest of her people are still in prison or in exile because they care for freedom.

I, for one, want to tell the Spanish people on this ignoble occasion in our history that there are millions of Americans who are ashamed that their Government has made possible the continued intimidation and persecution of Spaniards whose values and hopes are the same as ours. We apologize today to our brothers in Spain, to that great suffering mass of Spaniards who hate totalitarianism, left and right, Russian, Chinese, Greek, or Spanish—the people in whose hands lies the future of Spain, because ultimately freedom will prevail there, as it must everywhere.

It is fitting today to remind ourselves and the Spanish people that thousands of gallant young Americans have volunteered and died in the cause of freedom for Spain, and others have toiled for that cause through these long decades. Our allies in Spain are those who care for democracy, not those who oppress it, and we hope they know in their darkened circumstances that their plight will not be forgotten wherever men care for freedom and justice until at last things are brought right again in that glorious old country to which everyone in the new world owes so much.

Allard K. Lowenstein in the early 1950s

Campaigning with Eleanor Roosevelt, 1960

With Norman Thomas, 1966

Note to Lowenstein from
Robert F. Kennedy

*for Al who knew the lesson of Emerson
and taught it to the rest of us*

*"They did not yet see, and thousands of young
men as hopeful now crowding to the barriers of
their careers do not yet see, that if a
single man plant himself on his convictions
and there abide, the huge world will
come round to him"*

for his friend

Bob Kennedy

Campaigning, 1968

Chairing community
issues forum on Long
Island

In his congressional office

Lowenstein as seen
by David Levine, 1970

September 9, 1971

White House "enemies list,"
1971

MEMORANDUM FOR: JOHN DEAN

FROM: CHARLES COLSON

I have checked in blue those to whom I would give top
priority. You might want to check someone else although I think you will find this is a pretty good list.
Right on!

6. STEIN, HOWARD
Dreyfus Corporation
New York   ✓

Heaviest contributor to Mc Carthy in '68. If Mc Carthy
will receive the funds.

7. LOWENSTEIN, ALLARD
Long Island, New York   ✓

Guiding force behind the 18 year old "dump Nixon"
vote drive.

8. McGOVERN, GEORGE
Leading executive at Common Cause   ✓

A scandal would be most helpful h

Conversation
with Brooklyn
voter

Photo by Sheila Harkavy.

With family on
front stoop in
Brooklyn

At ADA National Convention,
1972

Campaigning with Herman Badillo

Photo courtesy National Review / FIRING LINE.

With William F. Buckley, Jr., on "Firing Line," 1975

Campaigning for Jerry Brown in presidential primary in Maryland, 1976

Photo by Peter Barry Chowka.

Photo by Kenneth McCumiskey.

With Warren Beatty, Andrew Young and Coretta King, 1976

In his office as United States ambassador to the
United Nations for Special Political Affairs, 1978

FOR U.S. S

FRANK G
Champion of D

Photo by William Suttle.

Photo by Ira N. Brophy.

Allard K. Lowenstein

LAME DUCK

Hendrik Hertzberg

The New Yorker, November 21, 1970

After the Nassau County redistricting, many urged Lowenstein to seek a more winnable district or run for the U.S. Senate. Instead, he chose to stay and fight. What followed was a pitched battle matching the Margiotta organization and national Nixon-Agnew forces against Lowenstein's battalions of community workers, Democratic Party backers, and student volunteers.

Denounced at the time by a prominent student radical as "the greatest threat to the movement," Lowenstein found himself paradoxically accused by his local opponent of "echoing the line from Hanoi, "voting for the smut peddlers," and "coddling the leaders of violent confrontation." On Election Day, he was narrowly defeated. The following piece discussed the campaign.

One of the noteworthy results of this month's elections was the defeat of Allard K. Lowenstein, the freshman representative from this state's Fifth Congressional District, in Nassau County. Mr. Lowenstein, a Democrat, is best known for his activities in 1967 and 1968, when he set in motion the events leading to the "Dump Johnson" movement, the Presidential candidacies of Eugene McCarthy and Robert Kennedy, and the Children's Crusade. He was in politics in the broad sense—mostly as a kind of one-man civil-liberties committee, with branches in South Africa,

Spain, and Mississippi—before he ever thought of public office, and he is certain to remain in politics in the same way.

We've been over the returns for the Fifth District in more detail than the Election Night television bulletins permitted, and the figures show that while Mr. Lowenstein lost the election, he ran a considerably stronger race than he did in 1968, when he won. What happened between 1968 and 1970 was that the Republican-controlled state legislature redrew the boundaries of the district, eliminating the heavily Democratic Five Towns area and adding heavily Republican and Conservative areas, including the village of Massapequa. Had the voting followed the pattern of two years ago, Mr. Lowenstein would have lost by twenty-five thousand votes; as it was, he lost by about eight thousand, and he ran some twenty thousand votes ahead of the Democratic ticket. His vote on the Democratic line exceeded by about five thousand that of his opponent—Norman Lent, a state senator—on the Republican line. Mr. Lent's margin of victory came from his votes on the Conservative line, where he was helped by the extremely strong showing of that party's successful candidate for the United States Senate, James Buckley.

We had a talk with Mr. Lowenstein a week after Election Day and asked him what he thought the consequences of his defeat would be. "The fact that I lost worries me less than the possibility that the results in my district will be misread," he said. "One of the most satisfying aspects of the campaign for me was that I had the opportunity to go down to Washington in the middle of it and vote against the crime bill and the military-appropriations bill. A lot of people came up to me on the floor and said, 'For God's sake, don't vote against these bills, Al! You'll never survive.' I think the figures show something quite different, which is that you *can* stand against the war and against the Administration's way of dealing with the so-called social issue and you *can* survive in the face of that. My physical presence in the House, continuing to vote as I voted before, would have been the best reminder of that, but if the message can be got across that I was not in fact defeated because of the stands I took, the danger that what happened will weaken people's backbones will be less."

"How about the students? Did they help you?" we asked.

"Enormously," Mr. Lowenstein said. "Two of the great myths of this campaign were that the students weren't interested and that where they did take part they were a liability, especially in blue-collar areas. A lot of the very considerable resistance to the Republican-Conservative tide in

182

the Fifth District is clearly traceable to the fact that day after day hundreds of extraordinary kids were out canvassing. I think the campaign demonstrated the falsity of the notion that kids and blue-collar workers are somehow natural enemies."

We asked about the character of the campaign, and Mr. Lowenstein said, "There was an ominous warning in this campaign, and that is that the ugliness can get so intense that it confuses great numbers of voters."

Having followed Mr. Lowenstein's fortunes off and on through the fall, we remembered that his opponent, Mr. Lent, had taken his cue from the Nixon-Agnew campaign against "permissiveness" and the like, and had carried the theme to limits not exceeded anywhere in the country. Among other things, Mr. Lowenstein found himself accused of being "an echo of Hanoi," "an inflamer of youth," and "the chief apologist for the Black Panthers"—odd accusations all, since Mr. Lowenstein is a convinced anti-Communist, the leading advocate of student participation in electoral politics, and a critic of the Panthers' infatuation with violence, and since these stands have resulted in much ill feeling toward him on the extreme left.

"The possibility exists that the same thing might happen that happened in the nineteen-fifties, when people were swept away by distortions," Mr. Lowenstein continued. "The fact that this approach was used here in the suburbs of New York City this year was a surprise to me. In the case of the Fifth District, I think it's important to stress that while it hurt us in areas where we weren't able to get the facts to people, it wouldn't have worked without the gerrymander. It didn't work in the country at large, and I don't think it will work in 1972. You just can't gerrymander the whole country."

"How do you account for Buckley's victory?" we asked.

"I think what the Buckley thing shows is that people are looking less for a specific program than for a certain kind of approach. People would come up to me during the campaign and say, 'I don't know who's right about the war, you or Buckley, but you both stand up for what you believe in and I'll vote for both of you.' Maybe that's why Buckley and I carried a lot of the same election districts. The Buckley vote has been interpreted as a vote for Nixon, but to a great degree it was a vote against the status quo. Buckley's slogan 'Isn't it about time *we* had a Senator' had racial overtones in some people's minds, but I think its effectiveness was due to its anti-Establishmentarian tone. As far as 1972 is concerned, the point to be made is that Nixon is not Buckley. The kind of appeal

Buckley made—the personal charisma, character, and image of courage that he substituted for programs—would be out of the question for Nixon. The lesson of the Buckley victory is that we can't run away from the positions that have to be taken. Not only would that be morally wrong; it would also be politically stupid, because the voters can sense that kind of cowardice, and it's exactly the opposite of what they're looking for."

"What about your own plans?" we asked.

"In personal terms, I don't really have any, beyond attending the lame-duck session of Congress. The lame-ducks like me will quack, and the lame quacks will duck. In political terms, I'm going to work, beginning right away, to see to it that the ugliness that was unleashed all over the country is turned out of office in 1972. We have taken the measure of these people, and they can be defeated."

MAN TO WATCH

Newsweek, August 23, 1971

Following a fact-finding trip to Southeast Asia in December-January, Lowenstein opened a community office on Long Island's South Shore and accepted appointments as a lecturer at Yale University and at Harvard University's John F. Kennedy School of Government. He also continued to speak around the country against President Nixon and the war.

"In my view," Lowenstein said on "Meet the Press" early in 1971, "the general feeling in this country for basic social change is greater than at any time since the bottom of the Depression." In May, he was elected chairman of Americans for Democratic Action, but he continued work on a movement to harness the potential of newly enfranchised eighteen-to-twenty-one-year-old voters. A massive infusion of issue-oriented youth into the political process, he believed, could not only reshape the political landscape of 1972, but also affect politicians at all levels for years to come.

The national kickoff for the youth-vote movement had come in April in Providence, Rhode Island. Senators Birch Bayh and Edmund Muskie, along with Representatives Paul McCloskey and Bella Abzug, exhorted a giant turnout of young persons to evict Nixon with their votes in 1972. Similar events had swiftly followed in California, Indiana, Minnesota, and New York as the movement picked up steam. The ratification in July of the Twenty-third Amendment had added to this momentum, and the following month, Newsweek profiled the growing campaign.

About a year before re-election time, there are several things that an incumbent President must begin to keep a wary eye on: among them, the cost-of-living index, the unemployment rate and Allard K. Lowenstein. Lowenstein is the energetic New York Democrat who in 1967 organized the "Dump Johnson" movement which, to the astonishment of the experts, helped to do just that. This year Lowenstein, having in the meantime won himself a seat in Congress and been gerrymandered out of it again, is back at his old line: he is leading a campaign to dump Richard Nixon.

Actually, he is trying to do more than that. His goal is to mobilize the estimated 25 million young people who will be voting next year for the first time to encourage them to use their immense electoral power to bring about the changes in American life that many of them insist are necessary but currently despair of achieving through "the system." This is not, according to conventional wisdom, a very promising project: apathy and cynicism are said to have returned in force to the campuses this year. But Al Lowenstein has never paid much attention to convention. He is, for example, chairman of Americans for Democratic Action, but some of his best political friends are Republican. He is 42 but displays an enormous appeal to the under-30 generation. and he is an unreconstructed liberal at a time when an increasing number of liberals have struck their colors under attack from the left and right.

His technique for President-busting is essentially the same this time as last, though with a far heavier accent on youth. Lowenstein projects himself into national orbit, achieves a rate of spin that defies the norms of human metabolism and gradually, through a combination of personal magnetism and gravitational tug, sets tides flowing across the political map. Last week, for instance, Lowenstein popped up in Austin, Texas, to address a student-sponsored conference on voter registration, went on to New Orleans to speak at the Southern Christian Leadership Conference convention, hopped over to Mississippi to campaign for black gubernatorial candidate Charles Evers, surfaced in Washington to talk to 200 young Congressional summer interns, rejoined his family briefly in Long Beach, N.Y., attended an antiwar rally in Suffolk County, then headed off again to Chapel Hill, N.C., for another student-registration conference.

The Austin and Chapel Hill events are part of a drive Lowenstein has helped organize called "Registration Summer." Some 60 student "interns" have been dispatched to eighteen states where they help local student groups put together youth-vote campaigns. They are paid $50 a week, $75 if they are graduate students; some of the funds come from the

ADA, the bulk from private contributions. In a few cases, these campaigns feature a mass rally addressed by Lowenstein and one or more Presidential candidates, real or potential. But the core of the effort is the student conference, where young people are taught how to get their peers registered, how to become registrars themselves (in some states, such as California and Texas, almost any accredited voter can become a registrar), how to pack precinct caucuses so as to influence—or even control—the delegate-selection process for next year's party conventions.

The drive is billed as bipartisan, and so it is—in the sense that both Democrats and Republicans are welcome and involved. But the campaign is hardly nonpartisan: its three main themes are opposition to Richard Nixon, to the war in Vietnam and to the tactics of violence for achieving change.

Only such an "issue-oriented" effort, Lowenstein contends, can rekindle young people's interest in electoral politics—mere registration drives are not enough. The turnout in Texas last week—640 student leaders showed up though only 500 had been expected—gives him heart, as does a rising tide of inquiries from student groups in other states. "Gradually the mood is switching," he told Newsweek's Kenneth Auchincloss. "It used to be fashionable to say 'we can't do anything.' Now people are beginning to say, 'OK, we'll take a look, we'll give it a try.' It's very encouraging to see how quickly this supposedly unchangeable despair can be changed."

Lowenstein is fully aware that the gloom could set in again, perhaps more intensely than ever before, if none of the antiwar candidates catches on with young people. He himself carefully avoids expressing any preferences, though one gets the impression that he is watching John Lindsay's fortunes with more than casual interest. As for his own ambitions, he would like to run for Congress again, but further redistricting in Long Island has dimmed that prospect.

Democratic Party regulars worry that his efforts might lead to a fourth-party movement, but he contends he is trying to prevent just that. One top Republican strategist scoffs that, in stressing the war issue, he is playing with "an idea whose time has gone." Above all, the pros remain skeptical that young people, even with their strength increased by the 18-year-old-vote amendment, are any more apt to vote as a bloc than they have in the past. As usual, Al Lowenstein is defying convention but, as a number of people learned in 1968, he bears watching.

FOR AS LONG AS IT TAKES
Toothing Stones, 1972

Lowenstein continued to press for nationwide youth registration and to work in the effort to oust Nixon and his cohorts throughout the summer and fall of 1972. Student conferences and rallies were held in twenty states, and included such political figures as Senators Edmund Muskie, George McGovern, and Fred Harris, Mayor John Lindsay and former Senators Eugene McCarthy and Charles Goodell.

The "Dump Nixon" campaign was directed at issues rather than specific candidates. Lowenstein spoke favorably about all the antiwar Democratic contenders, although he had some private reservations about their effectiveness as candidates. His efforts continued to cause anxiety in some quarters. A memo from White House operative John Caulfield about the Republican presidential candidacy of Congressman Paul McCloskey, an antiwar ally of Lowenstein's, advised, "Because of Lowenstein's success in 1968 with the McCarthy forces, an alert should go up if he surfaces with McCloskey."

In an introduction to Toothing Stones, *a book on political activism published during this period, Lowenstein sketched some political opportunities and dilemmas.*

Perhaps the first thing that might be said is that all the problems that have borne down on us for so long as a people now are at some turning. When we consider the lawlessness and violence on our campuses and in our streets over the past several years, I think that it is important to clarify the sequence of that lawlessness which the President and Vice-

President have seen fit to condemn. While I imagine that I have condemned lawlessness as much as any person, I think it's important to remember that, in fact, what has produced the kind of atmosphere in the United States that can turn young people against their government in such bitterness that they would march on other young people wearing its uniform, which has become a sadly common affair, is not something planted from some alien place. It's not conspired into or organized by "kooks." Rather, it's something done to our people, to our young people especially, by our government. And that's an atrocious fact, which our government ought to recognize and remember. It isn't something that could have been done by anyone but our government. Because our kids, our people, grow up loving this country, caring about it as much as any generation ever has, and more than most; and they find themselves in a situation where all the things that they love, and all the things which they are told are true, seem not to be true. And so, their tremendous sense of gratitude for being American, and their fidelity to the traditions and heritage of this country, are precisely what lead to hostility, resentment, and frustration and, finally, to outbursts of protest and, occasionally, even of violence, which then produce a wave of repression and even of killings, which are then justified as necessary and appropriate responses to arbitrary violence. And that's the sequence.

It wasn't random children gone crazy under foreign sedition that ran up against guns at Kent State and Jackson State. They were not lunatics who were poisoned by money to turn against their own people. Those young men and women, whose disillusionment and depression resound all over this country, in every university and most schools, are the most dedicated, the most concerned, the most generous, the most hopeful of our own future generation, who have somehow, in the period since 1963, been made to feel so sour about what their government does and says that they are now in a condition that leads to the kind of events that have marked the past few years and have scarred the memory of our people with such moments as Kent State and Jackson State.

Now all of this needs to be understood by the President and the Vice-President, because if they don't understand it, and if all they think that they need do is to pin libellous labels on people they don't care for, people who don't agree with them, then they are, in fact, going to wreak extraordinary havoc on this country. They are virtually going to lose for us our sons and our daughters. They are going to refuse their loyalty, their love of country, their spirit, and their generosity. They are going to

189

turn these into something embittered and negative; they are going to make of our people a country that cannot stand. Because a house divided in that fashion cannot stand.

There was a quote from Vietnam some time ago, after the events at My Lai; a colonel was asked about the complaints of some of the draftees about those events. What he said was: "The young are idealistic; and they don't like man's inhumanity to man. But as they get older, they will become wiser and more tolerant." I suppose that if one could summarize the horror-show of the last few years in one paragraph, it would be that.

The side of the ledger that we don't talk about enough, the fact that we don't face clearly enough, is the extraordinary, although tangible fact that the feeling of frustration with this country's policies and its failures is now not limited to the groups usually cataloged "young" and "poor" and "black." That frustration reaches now throughout the country; if we regroup and take it on ourselves to explain why things are as bad as they are to all the other people who know they are as bad as they are and who are being misled into thinking that they are this bad because of something that has to do not with the way the country is led, but with the way the protesters complain about the way the country is led, then we can, with rather extraordinary dispatch, I think, change the direction of this country.

On every one of these questions, the war, poverty, racism, pollution, on the questions that afflict the American people, we happen to be standing for what is right, we happen to be standing for the interests not just of the minorities, not just of the young, but for the interests of the American people. That's the fact. We ought to stop pretending it's not the fact; we ought to stop acting as if we have to hoodwink them. It's the Nixon administration that has the problem of hoodwinking the American people. And it was the Johnson administration that had to hoodwink them. And it was the American people who said "no" to the Johnson administration, when they realized that they were being hoodwinked. And why in the world is it necessary now for all of us to act as if somehow we're licked? Why is it necessary to pretend that somehow or other the hope has gone out of the change we sought to make in 1968 and came just up to the point of making? It is nonsense. We need only get the facts to people about the situation. They are not boobs.

Put the facts about the situation into the information booth in every state, and we'll discover how quickly people will come back to where they were in 1968 when they were turning against those who misled them and were trying to find leadership that would in fact end wars and right our serious wrongs. So I hope that in understanding what the facts are and instead of just talking to each other all of the time, escalating our own miseries and frustrations, we will remember just exactly what power is represented by people, ordinary people like ourselves, who did so remarkable a job in 1968. I hope that we don't go on with the self-pity that I hear from every side that says "We've been trying to change the system for years and nothing works" as if we've been storming the Bastille with bare fists. It was three months in 1968; it began in New Hampshire with McCarthy in March and ended in Los Angeles on June fifth. That was what we did then. There were three months of effort, which was not extreme, either. And yet there followed a most profound change in the attitudes of this country, there followed for the first time the possibility of reuniting our people in a program that would make sense. All this was taken away by bullets.

And that's part of the story. For it's obvious that the problem we face now, in near despair, is not because we failed then, but because we succeeded and yet nothing changed. And that's where this terrible gap comes. It was Hannah Arendt who once said that what drives people from being *engagé* to *enragé* is the sense that words have lost their meaning and that nothing one does is consummated, because there is always some way in which it can be distorted. It's that sense, I think, of distortion that interrupts the achievement and makes it all so sour.

It's honest to say that we don't know whether, if the right leaders had come along and not been taken away when we needed them most, we could have salvaged the country. What would have happened in the United States in 1933 if Franklin Roosevelt had been assassinated and we would have had to cope with the depression and John Garner at the same time? I don't know; thank God we never had to find out. But it surely isn't clear or certain that we can't succeed, because, in fact, a measure of success was nearly had a few seemingly long years ago. In a very, very clear way this country turned. And it's my judgment that if we get back into this with the effort that we're capable of making, with the facts that are on our side, we can effect a similar turn again. Are we such summer soldiers that whenever it looks like something will change only slowly and with great difficulty, we immediately opt out of trying to change it at all and leave the state to the things we see happening when we quit? I just don't believe that. There's too much at stake in this whole test, this whole turning that we're at, to allow such a response.

191

In conclusion, I wish to quote two things. The first is from John Gardner who made a very remarkable speech some time ago in which he said:

As we enter the 1970s, there are many curious aspects of our situation, but none more strange than our state of mind. We are anxious but immobilized. We know what our problems are, but we seem incapable of summoning our will and our resources to act. We see the murderous threat of nuclear war. We know our lakes are dying, our rivers growing filthier. And we have racial tensions that can tear the nation apart. We understand that oppressive poverty in the midst of affluence is intolerable. We see that our cities are sliding towards disaster. But these are not problems that stop at our borders; problems of nuclear war, or population, or environment are impending planetary disasters. We are in trouble as a species. But we are seized by a kind of paralysis of the will that becomes a waking nightmare. . . . Systemic inertia is characteristic of every human institution and is overwhelmingly true of this nation as a whole. Our system of checks and balances dilutes the thrust of positive action. Competition of interests inherent in our pluralism acts as a brake and the system grinds to a halt. Madison designed it in such a way that it simply won't move without vigorous leadership.

That's democracy and not a cult of personality. It says that individuals matter and that great individuals can inspire other individuals to do things they might not otherwise do, so that cumulatively individuals can make a difference. That's what the history of this country has shown. And that is, of course, what we know in our hearts is not now happening.

These next words were spoken several years ago in Indiana by Robert F. Kennedy on the day that Martin Luther King was killed. We recall them now with the very haunting sense that everything said then is so much more true now than it seemed to be then.

Some Americans who preach nonviolence abroad fail to practice it at home. Some who accuse others of inciting riots, by their own conduct invite them. And some look for scapegoats, some for conspiracies; but this much is clear, violence breeds violence, repression brings retaliation. And only a cleansing of our whole society can remove this sickness from our soul. But there is another kind of violence, slower but just as deadly, destructive as the shot or the bomb in the night. This is the violence of institutions, indifference, inaction, and slow decay. This is the violence that afflicts the poor and poisons relations between men because their skin is different colors. This is the slow destruction of the child by hunger in schools without books and in homes without heat in the winter. So that really we are asked to look at our brothers as aliens, men with whom we share a city but not a community, men bound to us in common dwelling but not in common effort, men who learn to share only a common fear, only a common impulse to meet disagreement with force. What we need in the United States is not division or hatred or violence, but love and wisdom and compassion toward one another, and a feeling of justice toward those who still suffer within our country, whether they be white or whether they be black. My favorite poet was Aeschylus who wrote: "In our sleep, pain, which we cannot forget, falls drop by drop upon the heart until, in our own despair and against our will, comes wisdom through the awful grace of God." So let us dedicate ourselves to what the Greeks wrote so many years ago, to tame the savageness of man and to make gentle the life of this world. Let us dedicate ourselves to that and say a prayer for our country and for our people.

The President, I think, would do well to note that we who oppose his policies are not bums but men, that we are not cops but neither are we cop-outs, that we are alien neither to this land nor to its Constitution. We are, on the contrary, the heart of this land and the pillars of its Constitution. We are a vital part of the broad, intelligent mind and powerful pulse beat, with reason and compassion, which courses all the way back through our history from a hundred far-off shores and through two hundred extraordinary years. We are Washington, Jefferson, and Madison, the Adamses, Robert E. Lee, Lincoln, and Whitman, Holmes and Audubon, La Guardia and Einstein. We are Woodrow Wilson, Norman Thomas, and Wendell Willkie, Franklin and Eleanor Roosevelt, and, yes, Dwight Eisenhower. We are John F. Kennedy, and we are Martin Luther King; and we are Robert F. Kennedy. We are Ethel Kennedy and Charles Evers; we are Shirley Chisholm, David Harris, and Cesar Chavez. We are grieved, and we are wounded. We are alive and we are tough; and we have just begun to fight. We are in the Valley Forge of the American spirit; but we have been to Valley Forge before, because America has been to Valley Forge before, and we are part of what is best in America. We are going to survive these perversions of America during the past years to become one nation, indivisible, with liberty and justice for all, one nation where we can eat grapes and sing joyous songs and be able at last to love justice and still love our own country. We are the majority; and we shall no longer be silent. We shall march henceforth not to taps but to reveille. And soon our country shall march not to war but to stop war. We are in the battle to reclaim this country that we love so very dearly. And we are in the battle for as long as it takes to reclaim it. We speak both for our children and to them when we say that we shall prevail.

LOWENSTEIN VERSUS ROONEY

Judith Michaelson

New York Post, June 15, 1972

The culmination of the 1971 Dump Nixon drive came in December at the three-day Emergency Conference for New Voters in Chicago. Delegates agreed to form a National Youth Caucus to support antiwar candidates. After the conference, Lowenstein continued to speak widely and pursued his duties as national chairman of ADA.

He was also eying a bid to regain his Long Island congressional seat, but the Republican-controlled New York State Legislature was making that an uninviting prospect. Mindful of his strong 1970 showing, the GOP map drawers excised his Long Beach house from his former district, placing it in new and unfavorable territory represented by Republican incumbent John Wydler.

Democratic Party reformers in Brooklyn then suggested he run against hawkish veteran congressman John Rooney. Two years before, Lowenstein had been one of three New York Democratic lawmakers to endorse Rooney's challenger in the primary. He made clear his interest in the race, and after speaking at reform-club meetings and conferring with political and community leaders, he received their united backing for the challenge.

Lowenstein versus Rooney

The 14th Congressional District ran along the north Brooklyn water-front and was comprised of ethnic Italians, Poles, upper-middle-class pro-fessionals, blacks, Puerto Ricans, and Hasidic Jews. Setting up more than a dozen neighborhood store-front offices, Lowenstein quickly undertook the sizable task of ousting a congressional institution. He enlisted an army of student volunteers and moved with his family to the largely black community of Fort Greene. He also joined forces with other re-form candidates and recruited prominent campaigners, including Aaron Henry of the Mississippi NAACP, singer Tom Lehrer, Coretta King, Dustin Hoffman, and Congressman Herman Badillo. As usual, his wife, Jenny, actively contributed to the political effort and its spirit.

In the face of these unprecedented efforts, the powerful Brooklyn Democratic organization, led by Meade Esposito, counterattacked. At-tempts were made to launch minority candidacies in order to split the black and Puerto Rican vote. Secretary of Defense Melvin Laird visited the district and praised Rooney's support of "national security." AFL-CIO chief George Meany personally endorsed Rooney, and the Diocesan Home School Federation, after promising neutrality, distributed Rooney endorsements in local churches.

As Lowenstein's neighborhood-based campaign cut into Rooney's strength throughout the district, the organization's counterattack inten-sified. Rooney material referred to fictional Lowenstein votes against "military aid to Israel." Appeals to the Hasidic community, written in Yiddish, described Lowenstein as "chairman of the committee to get rid of Yeshivas," and added, "It is interesting to note that he has settled in Ft. Greene with his friends." "If the carpetbagger wins the election," noted one Rooney spokesman, "outsiders and hippies will take over the entire borough."

Here is one newspaper account of the campaign.

There was a chill wind rising in Our Lady of Snows meeting hall as they waited, patiently and loyally, for their Congressman of 28 years, John J. Rooney. Speaker after speaker got up to warn the new "stranger" in their midst, and underlying all they said was a mood of fear: if they did not implore each other to tell their friends and their friends' friends to vote Rooney, Allard K. Lowenstein might win, and all that was left of their own power, and of politics as they had always known it, would fade.

It was so close in the Democratic primary two years ago—only 1223 votes separating their man from Peter Eikenberry, the young attorney;

and here in this very hall on the Williamsburg-Greenpoint border, Rooney had intoned: "Eikel-berry, or whatever his name is . . . not one of us . . . a stranger among us."

Before that it was Frederick W. Richmond, the millionaire industrialist, with a similarly slim margin, but at least *he* was now with Rooney, his co-campaign manager. And if, two years from now, Rooney retired—he'd be 70 with an even 30 years in the House—and the tall, slick, fair-haired Richmond got the Regulars' endorsement, that would be okay. Meade Esposito, the Brooklyn county leader, and Richmond were allies; and they, the people, always followed the Leader.

But now there was Lowenstein, that peripatetic former Congressman from Nassau (1968-70) with the look of the perpetual graduate student, though he is 43, national president of Americans for Democratic Action, and involved in all these Movements—from Dump Johnson to civil rights to youth caucuses. (Irving Gross, who last time polled 1392 votes is also on the ballot.)

The local chapter head of the Italian-American Civil Rights League cautioned: "We will not stand by allowing any outsider to come into our territory . . ." And Assemblyman Chester Straub, steepling his hands, said that, just as when you see a car that needs towing away you call not the Mayor's office but your local leader, so when you need "help for Poland, Italy or Israel" or "hard dollars" for the 14th, you go to Rooney.

But it was Rudy Zimmerman who drew the most excitement. Lowenstein's "a radical, a leftist," he shouted. "Those who support him don't want democracy, they want communism."

(Except for one radio broadcast, Lowenstein this night was not campaigning. It was the fourth anniversary of the death of Sen. Robert F. Kennedy, and Lowenstein, friend and gadfly, who in the fall of 1967 first urged Kennedy to run for the Presidency before turning to Eugene McCarthy, had spent the day at Arlington and Hickory Hill. Twice in 1968 Kennedy asked Lowenstein, his friends say, to run for the Senate.

Then came Rooney: short, portly, dapper with a straight-across handkerchief like a white stripe on his jacket, and pink-cheeked. Coming down the aisle, waving his right hand as befits a Representative 15th in seniority out of 435, aware of the kind of power that makes and breaks Senate, Commerce and Justice Dept. budgets.

"I usually don't need mikes," he began in tough street cadence. "I can roar like a lion when the time comes." But he did not roar. He entertained—to a half-empty house. Fewer than 100 were in the hall including a score of Lowenstein youths from the nearby storefront. The Congressman will not publicize his schedule.

Rooney gave a passing jibe at Mrs. "Zugzug" (for Abzug), and then on to his opponent, "this boy-d," a marriage of boy and bird, who "flies from Newark (Lowenstein's birthplace) to Manhattan to Long Beach."

He details his own Kennedy associations. "When Kennedy was elected President, his father invited me down to Palm Beach . . . I have a letter from Jackie Onassis in which she says: 'the next time you're in New York do come and see Caroline and John and myself. You're one of the first persons to know John . . .'

"And I remember Caroline . . ."

Three days later Kathleen Kennedy, 20, Robert Kennedy's oldest child, would be coming in to campaign for Lowenstein.

Rooney said his opponent never got one bill through the House; that in his two-year term, unemployment in Lowenstein's area went from 36,000 to 59,500; and did you know how much money his student volunteers were getting?

Lowenstein says he co-sponsored the Food Stamp Act of 1969 as well as parts of other laws that increased housing funds for the elderly, reduced oil depletion allowances 20 per cent and raised Social Security benefits 15 per cent. As for unemployment, he says Rooney's "dear friend Richard Nixon" had something to do with that and besides the figures apply to all of Nassau and Suffolk; as for his volunteers, they're lucky if they get $15 a week in food.

Rooney said he's obtained $150 million for the district (Esposito cites $200 million) and so what if he's a friend of Nixon, Mitchell and ex-Commerce Secretary Stans. "That kind of nonsense is for the boy-ds."

"Mr. Low-Esteem," he concluded, to laughter.

Next night Lowenstein whirlwinded the district, which takes in the northwestern chunk of Brooklyn and much of its waterfront. A walking and jaywalking tour in Polish-Irish Greenpoint. Then a small private meeting with blacks and Puerto Ricans in Bushwick, seeking to make inroads against hostility to the white politician, pledging he would not be "an absentee" like Rooney. (Until recently, Rooney had no district office, preferring to work out of one of the local clubhouses.) Lowenstein urged them to get out the vote. "Otherwise we're trapped in the cycle where people think the politician is no good, they don't vote, then they *get* the politician who is no good."

197

Three kaffeeklatsches: in Italian Carroll Gardens, posh Cobble Hill and an integrated one in predominantly black Ft. Greene—the community in which Lowenstein has settled with his wife, the former Jennifer Lyman (of the Beacon Hill GOP Lymans), 27, and their three children.

Gerrymandered out of his former district two years ago by the GOP Legislature—he still ran 30,000 ahead of the Democratic ticket—Lowenstein is now running scared, and hard, again. Despite nationwide fame and an army of the young who keep pouring in—on any given day he has over 300 volunteers, from John Gilligan, 23, son of the Governor of Ohio, to Keith Farmer, 13, son of a Greenpoint truck driver, who likes Lowenstein "because he is against the war"—Lowenstein figures he started 5000 votes behind Eikenberry. To begin with, the 14th C.D. was redistricted a bit.

The well-organized blacks of the Lindsay Park, Red Hook Houses and Lafayette Gardens projects, along with 500 students in Pratt Institute dormitories, were penciled out of the district. Much of Bushwick—Italian, with black and Puerto Rican—which went heavily for Procaccino, was mapped in.

Lowenstein is Jewish. One of Rooney's labor backers—he has 56 unions including Anthony Scotto's politically potent Longshoremen to Lowenstein's 11—said that unfortunately this is a factor. An official of the Smolenski Democratic Club in Greenpoint urged a gathering one night, after Rooney had gone, to "vote the Christian ticket." Ironically one of Rooney's strong areas is Williamsburg, where the conservative Hasidic Jews cite his aid to immigrants and to Israel.

In the end, the outcome could hinge on the fight between the pro-Rooney unions and the oldtime political clubs versus the Lowenstein storefronts. Lowenstein has 17 of them scattered across the 14th C.D., as well as a main headquarters. Rooney has only his air-conditioned headquarters in down-town Brooklyn where last Friday afternoon the press secretary could be seen taking out the garbage. To say this is a hostile campaign would be understatement: One night last week a brick was thrown through the window of the Carroll Gardens storefront.

At the Carroll Gardens kaffeeklatsch Lowenstein told his audience that Rooney is unaware of the district's pervasive poverty. Rooney claims to have saved 2,800 jobs at the Brooklyn Navy Yard, but Lowenstein said Rooney had promised 7,000 jobs.

In the 14th C.D., said Lowenstein, one out of four people is on welfare; in Williamsburg alone 20 per cent are unemployed and 25 per cent under-employed.

He talked of Rooney votes for tax programs that allow an oil company with an income of $1.1 billion to pay only 1 per cent in taxes. He noted that Rooney cast one of the key votes defeating a $20,000 ceiling on agricultural subsidies, paying people not to grow things "while kids go hungry." And that he "always" votes for war funds.

He spoke of his own plans for a Gowanus Canal marina, and asked: "What has Rooney done about getting federal money to get rid of the stench? Hell, he'd disintegrate before he'd drown."

Home about midnight, Lowenstein discussed his differences with his opponent. "We're about as opposite as any two people can be. He has supported policies disastrous for the country: the war, the votes for SST, ABM, Lockheed, votes against $800 million for education . . . the whole mass of economic bread-and-butter bills."

But COPE, the political arm of the AFL-CIO gives Rooney 100 per cent for his voting record on domestic-labor issues. He has George Meany's endorsement.

Rooney at first refused an interview. But at Our Lady of Snows in front of his constituents he laughed: "All right, I'll see you, so you don't have to follow me around Bedford-Stuyvesant. That's Shirley Chisholm's district."

The only inscribed photo in his office is from the late J. Edgar Hoover. "A grand American and the best administrator you ever saw," says Rooney. What is he most proud of in his 28 years in the House? "Oh, the hundreds of millions of dollars I've saved the taxpayers from government waste. Yup."

Any bills? "The annual Appropriations bill. The bills bear my name."

And who's doing the subverting? "Those who don't think the same as I and most right-thinking Americans."

Asked about the President he said: "Nixon misrepresented the war to the American public, he hasn't produced, he has woefully inadequate economic proposals . . ."

His interviewer, recalling that in 1970 Rooney had also co-sponsored a resolution to cut off funds for the Cambodia "incursion" unless Congress approved them, suggested that his views on the Indochina war seemed to have undergone a change in recent years. "My position is the same," he protested. "We have to leave it in the hands of those who know something about it—the President and the Joint Chiefs, etc."

Finally, asked how he got into politics, he expands. He was third assistant district attorney under William O'Dwyer—"I never worked so hard, 16 hours a day. Put Lepke in the chair and all those Murder Inc. guys, then when Rep. Thomas Cullen died, Mr. Kelly, the leader of Kings County, suggested I run . . .

"I found I was working for the greatest corporation in the world: the U.S.A. And I became a member of the Appropriations Committee and I had to visit our real estate—our embassies and consulates all over the world, and it's not hard to like that." He laughed. "Lowenstein wouldn't say that . . ."

Lowenstein didn't. Riding in Williamsburg with Kathleen Kennedy— Coretta King would be in two days later—past empty littered lots ("like it was bombed out, like Vietnam," someone said) Kathleen asked him how he got into politics.

He mused. "As a kid I was skinny and funny-looking and I got beaten up a lot. I got mad. I used to see ugly girls at a dance, nobody would dance with them, and I got mad for them. And at Chapel Hill where I went to school I saw blacks sitting in the back of the bus and I got mad. After that it . . . *happened.*"

Primary Day was marked by an array of election irregularities. Machines in minority and liberal areas broke down, poll-watcher challenges were ignored, and hundreds of long-time voters arrived only to be told that their registration cards were "missing."

At midnight, Lowenstein told an overflow crowd that "John Rooney's claim of victory tonight is as accurate as everything else he has said in this campaign."

TAMMANY HALL REVISITED

Jack Anderson

New York Post, August 31, 1972

Within hours of the close of the polls, Lowenstein and his support-
ers began mapping plans for a court challenge to the election results. In
spite of rampant election irregularities, they faced a formidable task:
reversing an 890-vote margin—out of the 29,500 cast—was almost unprec-
edented.

Over the next nine weeks, student and community supporters worked
painstakingly in the grueling New York summer heat to build a case. The
legal team was assisted by Terry Lenzner, former head of the federal
legal services program, and Adam Walinsky, a former aide to Senator
Robert Kennedy. Thousands of voter cards were laboriously reviewed at
the Board of Elections, and scores of affidavits from voters and poll
watchers were collected. The peculiarities of the balloting were noted by
such journalists as Jack Newfield, Jose Torres, and James Wechsler. Re-
marking that he opposed nearly every political idea that Lowenstein
espoused, William F. Buckley, Jr., nonetheless concluded, "The evidence
suggests that Lowenstein would have won by something like a landslide."

In August, columnist Jack Anderson added his review of the election.

The Justice Dept. must soon decide whether to investigate alleged
criminal violations in the election of Rep. John Rooney (D-N.Y.), who
has immense power over the department because of its tight hold on its
purse strings.

The cantankerous Rooney heads the House Appropriations subcommittee, which decides how much money the Justice Dept. can spend. Thus, Attorney General Richard Kleindienst will face the dilemma of subpoenaing the hand that feeds him.

The election case grows out of the bitter Democratic Primary, which Rooney won by a disputed 890 votes. The loser, ex-Rep. Allard Lowenstein, has been calling for a new election.

He has pressed his case in the state courts. But now he is going into federal court with allegations against the Rooney machine that would make a Tammany Hall ward-heeler blush.

For example, Rooney's nephew James and James's wife Beatrice are both shown on voting records as voting twice. When we reached them at their home across the street from their famous uncle, they insisted they had voted only once. If a second vote was cast in their name, they said, it was not done by them.

"There has been a foul-up somewhere," said James Rooney, a florist.

We also have copies of an official-looking postcard with "Primary Election Notice" printed on it. But on the back is an advertisement for Rooney's slate. The bulk rate Post Office permit was issued not to the Board of Elections, the seeming source of the card, but to the pro-Rooney Pioneer Regular Democratic Club of Brooklyn.

Political ads with no reference to their sponsor violate the federal criminal code.

We have also learned that New York Board of Elections Commissioner Gumersindo Martinez, whose job it is to keep elections fair, boomed Rooney from a sound truck.

He assured us this wouldn't interfere with his impartiality in dealing with the election. He had campaigned for Rooney on his own time, Martinez explained, because his wife ran as a committeewoman on the Rooney ticket.

We also have affidavits telling how supposedly neutral poll inspectors were assigned by the Rooney machine. Rooney himself, according to testimony, belabored Lowenstein poll workers twice when he visited a polling place.

When Lowenstein levers were broken in Puerto Rican and black areas where Lowenstein was strong, there's evidence they were left in disrepair for long periods. Lowenstein plans to charge racial discrimination in his federal suit.

In one Lowenstein area, Rep. Paul McCloskey (R-Cal.) was conducting a get-out-the-vote campaign. He swears the lines were so slow that at least 40 voters simply left.

A special deputy attorney general for New York has sworn that one Spanish-speaking woman arrived at the polls only to find that someone had forged her name on her voting card.

There's no reason to believe Rooney was personally aware of all that his supporters were doing at the polls. But it will be interesting to see what the Justice Dept. does about the allegations. . . .

Footnote: A finding of fraudulent election would mean Rooney must run again. Rooney could not be reached.

ELECTIONS AND CHANGE IN AMERICA
Interview, January 1973

On September 7, 1972, the New York State Appellate Court ordered a new election for the 14th Congressional District in Brooklyn. Reversing a lower-court ruling, the unanimous decision, in Lowenstein vs. Larkin, said that the primary was "characterized by such irregularities as to render impossible a determination as to who was rightfully nominated." Noting that statutory safeguards were "totally or substantially ignored by election officials," the court observed that hundreds of would-be voters were turned away from the polls, 1,300 Democrats with lapsed registrations were allowed to vote, and at least 1,920 "irregular votes" were cast. "Every dictate of fairness and protection of the voters' franchise," it concluded, "demands a new election."

Primary contests often amount to competitions in pulling out the vote, and this was even truer in the resulting special election. With only a twelve-day campaign period and the absence of other races to heighten publicity and voter interest, organizational strength was crucial. The Brooklyn organization, whose manpower had been partially diffused in other contests in June, poured every available resource into the September battle. Lowenstein campaigned exhaustively, but the court challenge had depleted his finances, and it was difficult to mobilize voters for a second turnout.

In spite of elaborate precautions and the presence of congressional observers, many of the June irregularities were repeated or even accentu-

ated on September 19. Lowenstein's formal tally fell only slightly short of his June showing, but the official Rooney count increased. "The second time was even worse in some crucial ways than the first," said Mc-Closkey, who had observed both contests. "A lot of the earlier violations were repeated, but this time many more blacks and Puerto Ricans were denied the right to vote. My congressional colleagues and I had never seen anything like it." In October, the Fair Campaign Practices Committee condemned nine pieces of Rooney campaign literature for misrepresentations and "appeal to prejudice based on race."

Bereft of money, organization, and time, Lowenstein decided against another challenge, and that fall he devoted much of his time to campaigning around the country for presidential candidate George McGovern and other antiwar candidates. After the November election, he set up a Brooklyn community office and continued his local and national commitments. Early the following year, he was interviewed by Walter P. Loughlin, an editor of a law school journal, about the Brooklyn experience and the potential usefulness of elections as instruments of social change.

Q. Walter P. Loughlin. Would you describe the problems you were confronted with on Primary Day?

A. Well, all during the day of the June primary we were inundated with reports of machines breaking down or polling places opening late, or voters not being allowed to vote in areas which I was supposed to carry heavily. So we knew, by the end of the day, that there was a massive denial of franchise to people who were in areas that were favorable to me.

In fact, it was the first time in the history of American elections where people had to wait for a change of seasons in order to vote. Because they went in on June 20 and there were election districts where they were still voting at 2:30 A.M. on June 21.

But, of course, what we did not know on the day of the primary was the degree to which this was intentional. And what we could not tell was the degree of affirmative fraud as distinguished from what would be called negative fraud of refusing to let people vote or of denying them a reasonable process of voting. In this country elections are not supposed to be endurance contests. Waiting on line for four hours is no more what the franchise is supposed to be than requiring people to walk long distances from one polling-place location to another like some sort of shell game.

As I say, we knew during the voting that day that these things were occurring. Nevertheless, it took the following six weeks of very hard work to reconstruct the events of that day—examining buff cards, collecting affidavits, etc.—in order to establish that what had happened was not merely the deprivation of the right to vote for some people, but also the casting of enormous numbers of votes by unqualified or ineligible people. Ultimately, when we went through all the records, we determined, first of all, that 833 more votes were cast than there were voters who voted. Additionally, close to 3,000 votes were cast by people whose registration status was such that they were either unqualified or ineligible—for instance, people who were not enrolled Democrats or whose registration had lapsed.

Even worse was the fact that we discovered that one of the most extraordinary things that occurred was that in Spanish-speaking areas polls were moved to new locations in violation of the law, without notice to the voters, and without any apparent reason. These were polling places where some voters had cast their ballots for twenty years or more. Suddenly they were told they had to go from P.S. 19 to P.S. 200, which was ten blocks away. Of course, they were not told this in Spanish, either, so the total effect was one of sheer confusion.

This happened on a large scale in many black and Puerto Rican neighborhoods. Hundreds of nonwhite voters—many of whom had been voting all their lives—were peremptorily informed they were not registered and could not vote. When that happens, under the present New York law, one's only recourse is to go to the Board of Elections and obtain a court order that allows one to vote. By midevening the night of the primary, there was a massive human traffic jam at the Board of Elections—made up of mostly nonwhite voters all trying to obtain court orders allowing them to vote. At 9:30 that night, Judge Corso, who was in chambers, where he was supposed to be issuing court orders, sent out word that it was late and that people had better just go home.

Q. You assume that these voters were, more likely than not, attempting to vote for you?

A. Well, I assume it and so did Judge Corso, since he provided a corollary to the scenario that night. After the announcement had gone out that it was too late for court orders to be issued and people should go home, a busload of reportedly "Rooney voters" arrived. Evidently their registrations had been irregular. When Corso was informed that some "Rooney voters" were outside, he issued them court orders in blank! And they went back and voted. We weren't able to trace all their votes, but we traced enough of them to establish in court the whole pattern of their trip to the Board of Elections, their court orders, and their subsequent voting.

There are countless examples of the discriminatory pattern we established—much of it not even contested in the testimony at trial. I remember one polling place, which was the First Election District of the 52nd Assembly District, which I carried by about 80 percent. At that location, the polling place had to be kept open until 2:30 in the morning. Of course, a lot of people did not wait until 2:30 in the morning to vote. But the important thing is that that polling place had always had two machines before this election, and this time they only had one. They enlarged the area that had to vote at this polling place; decreased the number of machines; had a longer ballot, and when the lines developed so that there was a two-hour wait at 6:30, we went into court to get an order to have another machine placed there. There were 350 machines sitting in a warehouse two blocks away, and they refused to send a second machine over. . . .

Q. When you went to court to challenge that election, what was it incumbent upon you to demonstrate?

A. That the result of the election had been tainted by the irregular procedures it involved to the point where you couldn't ascertain the outcome. I have touched briefly on the specific occurrences. Generally, I think it is fair to say that almost nothing about that election met the minimal standards set forth in the statute. The statute itself is in my view an unconstitutional statute, because it places all the authority for conducting the primary in the hands of one faction of one party—they pick all the officials; they decide how the law is to be implemented; they are the ones that set the polling places.

Q. If you were forewarned from your experience in the first primary, how could it happen to you again, after you won your suit and obtained a special primary?

A. I think that is worth explaining very clearly. If all the officials are selected by one candidate and his faction, and all the judges are responsive to that faction, and the law gives the officials the authority to decide who can and who cannot vote—you can have everybody in the world you want watching, but it doesn't change the outcome. The election can still be stolen.

In the second primary we experienced a multiplication of the fraud and the deprivation of voters' rights. More people were turned away at the polls; more buff cards were "missing." So more people had to go down to the Board of Elections to obtain court orders. This time we had four judges instead of one to issue court orders. But when the crowds of mostly black and Puerto Rican voters got large around 7:00 P.M. the night of the special election, the four judges went into conference and issued no court orders for two and a half hours. Meanwhile, many people gave up, left, and spread the word that there was no way to get a court order.

In the June election, something like 80 percent of the voting-machine breakdowns and late poll openings occurred in election districts I carried by better than two to one. The second time, something like 95 percent were in election districts which I carried two to one or better. What do you do when a machine breaks down? What do you do when inspectors do not show up to open a polling place? We had six members of the United States Congress and as many deputy attorney generals as we could get trying to insure that the rights of the voters were not violated, but nobody could do anything. So, what I am saying is that being forewarned does no good unless one has a chance to wrest control of the process from one's opponents. . . .

Q. What specific reforms is your challenge to the election law aimed at?
A. There were seventy-four sections of the statute that were either ignored or not implemented—or that on their face are unfair to certain candidates. We are in federal court to get the election law knocked out. You cannot have a fair election under the law if you have a machine running the election procedure. . . . The stolen election has a greater importance, though, apart from the fact that one person was deprived of a seat in Congress to which he was elected. I don't want to leave you with the impression that the history of the republic was significantly altered because I was deprived of the seat which I was voted into by the citizens of Brooklyn. But it is true that the taint on the process of election increases the toxic level of the poison in a community like the one that I was elected from, where the feeling is that the government rips you off, that it is insensitive and unresponsive. An election stolen in that type of community confirms the already negative attitude toward the whole system of government. People say, "We finally want to vote for somebody, we went down and nobody would let us vote." In Brooklyn last year the community did get concerned; it did get involved; and then they were cheated. The danger is that cynicism multiplies. But what was amazing about this incident was that each time, instead of getting discouraged,

the community got angrier. This is the thing that I think you have to say is hopeful. That what was done didn't destroy or discourage; it in fact engaged a very substantial feeling in the community—so substantial that in the general election, when my name was only on the Liberal Party line, I carried about forty election districts. Which is testament to the fact that people are indignant about everything that was done, and are not about to lie down and play dead.

Q. If, indeed, the election had to be stolen because you would have won, we must conclude that you were a white liberal candidate who managed to establish the coalition between usually polarized segments of the electorate—poor, nonwhite voters and white ethnic voters. Do you think that liberal candidates can succeed in building bridges between polarized communities, or will they have to modify liberal positions to be elected?

A. I think it is very clear that you can take the positions which I have taken since I've been in public life and win. You can win in almost any circumstance in almost any district. It is not always easy. It is not always pleasant. You may get called names. You may get a lot of sewage thrown at you. But if you're willing to fight it through and explain tough issues, you can win.

Q. Are busing and abortion included in those tough issues?

A. First, I don't think you should lump together a lot of separate questions, and I don't think that I know anyone who favors busing, if by favoring busing you mean what Nixon makes it sound like—namely, taking children in buses long distances across communities to inferior schools. Why is that considered a liberal position? That seems to me to be conceding the argument. The argument isn't whether children should be bused across communities to attend inferior schools; the question is why are there inferior schools? What have we done in organizing the economics of this country that we still have schools that we don't want? No mother should be expected to send her children to inferior schools in a country where the gross national product surpasses a trillion dollars a year. No country with the wealth we have should debate busing, as if the choice was between sending children to inferior schools or having just black children attending inferior schools, because we are not doing anything about the schools.

The issue is: why was Nixon vetoing money for education? Why were we engaging ourselves in profligate waste in the war and on the military, when we could have been doing what should have been done? Perhaps if we had, then there would be no children going to inferior schools.

209

So, if you are asking can liberals get elected, I say yes they can. You can take the positions that I took—I voted against all the appropriations for the military; I voted against the omnibus crime bill; I voted against the pornography bill—which are stands supposedly impossible under the Scammon-Wattenberg doctrine. I did those things because the legislation was wrong, bad, dishonest, and deceptive, and I ended up running after the gerrymander in 1970, carrying some of the same communities as James Buckley, the Conservative Party candidate for the U.S. Senate. The point is that people were prepared to accept the fact that there is no simple doctrine that defines their position, but they will vote for candidates they think are honest and care about their problems and want to work at them.

People vote on a confused medley of questions. All I'm saying is that you can stand on the positions that I've taken, and it is clear from the results in both campaigns, in Nassau and in Brooklyn, you can carry election districts which include people of all backgrounds without running away from these positions. The tragedy of this election and the national election would be compounded if the lesson people learned from it is that you have to trim and sound like Richard Nixon, George Wallace, or Norman Lent to win an election. It just isn't true.

Q. If you reject the sort of conventional wisdom that liberals have alienated themselves from Middle America, why was McGovern so overwhelmingly defeated?

A. What I said was that one can take liberal positions and win. I did not say that every liberal can be elected and I did not say that no liberals had alienated themselves from anybody. For instance, liberals have alienated themselves from the campus—there are campus precincts that voted for Nixon.

The whole problem is not to make a doctrinaire rebuttal of doctrinaire nonsense that has been peddled. The point is to understand that candidates have an enormous effect on who people vote for. The manner in which issues are couched shapes the answer that you get about what people want done. Nixon's skill in couching questions had people voting on things they weren't voting on. So, the skillfulness of the Nixon campaign, in dissembling and confusing, combined with the failure of the Democratic campaign to communicate effectively what it did stand for, added up to a Democratic defeat. The people, who were deeply troubled, concluded that the Democratic ticket would not be able to govern the country. Those were the things that had enormous impact on communities that might have very clearly voted in a different way if these problems had not developed as they did.

Q. You mentioned that there were campus precincts that voted for Nixon. You have always been associated with the involvement of young people in politics. Have you noticed any trends toward a decrease in that involvement over the years?

A. Well, there are ups and downs. I think to be fair about what happened in the presidential campaign, one must say that a lot of students in the spring of 1972 created a myth about George McGovern. They tried to make him out to be something he never was, and then, when it turned out that he wasn't the myth they had created, they blamed him for changing.

On the basis of this myth they had created they then turned on him. It was really quite a sad phenomenon—to make Edmund Muskie into an archfiend and think Pete McCloskey some kind of fool, as people were doing in the primary, to justify all this fanatical work for George McGovern. It may have been politically useful or politically necessary, but I found it unattractive and was denounced by people when we were doing the Dump Nixon rallies in 1971. It seemed important to me to say that there were several good men and that people could make decisions that they want without trying to pick the alternatives in hostile terms. I did not succeed in conveying this to many people in this period. They remained zealous in thinking that they were right in making this kind of distinction between McGovern and some of the others.

But, then, the same people, six months later were too busy to work for McGovern when he was running against Nixon. And that struck me as being the ultimate absurdity of the whole political season. So it is true that some students and others got uninvolved—found emotional reasons that they were not going to work. And that quite clearly contributed to the magnitude of the Nixon victory. But much as I think that process was absurd, I think it would be a great mistake to think it signals that there is not a potential for deep interest and involvement. I do not believe that has been permanently eroded.

Q. If anyone would be convinced by the argument that the political system won't work—that electoral politics is not the the way to achieve fundamental social reform—it seems that you would be. You were gerrymandered out of one congressional seat. You had another stolen from you. And yet you have not given up. What is the basis for your continuing faith in the electoral process?

A. I think it is oversimplified to say that it is continuing faith. There is always the tendency, in print, to oversimplify. I am constantly quoted as saying the system works. I don't know what that phrase means. I have never used it. I have never, anywhere, said "the system works." What I have said is that the things that have gone wrong with the system can be changed more effectively if you elect people committed to change them.

It isn't that I am convinced that the system as it is today can be fixed to the point where it is as it should be. What I've been saying is that nothing is inevitable. It is not inevitable that we will win. It is not inevitable that we will lose. It is only inevitable that we will win or lose. Given what the stakes are, that should be an incentive to work harder. Dogmatism has no place in the prediction of the outcome, in assuring that something is going to occur that should occur. If I knew a better way, if anyone had come up with a better way, a speedier way, to bring about some changes, then we all would pursue that course of action.

Q. How do you react to the argument that politics may not be the best way to work for reform because the electoral process, in requiring a majority consensus of its participants, may have a built-in conservatizing mechanism?

A. I think there is room for a hundred different ways to try to influence events. I think people who lead good lives, and never get involved in politics more than just as transient participants—people who write, people in the theater, etc.—make vital contributions. There are 100 milieu that contribute to the shaping of society. I am not saying everyone should drop everything and become lifetime political people. I am not sure that I'm not going to want to spend more time on other things beside politics. That is a very difficult decision to make.

All I am saying is that there are some things that can only be changed through politics. Those things include the disposition of the national resources, because that's voted by Congress. Lives are squandered in Vietnam or they are not—depending what the votes are or what the President does.

To say that politics is the only way is nonsense. But to say that politics is not one of the significant ways is also nonsense. The degree to which you combine your activities in politics with your other activities is an individual decision, and it is one that can be made honorably in 100

212

different ways. You can spend relatively little time in politics and be a useful citizen, or you can say that until the war is over we have to stay as active in politics as we can, to prevent it from continuing indefinitely or escalating. How many people would be dead now if we had given in at that point to the Johnson doctrine and Nixon's sequel to it?

So I certainly have no regret about being in politics over this period of time; whether I'm going to stay in it to the same degree I have, I don't know. I am not advocating any one life style. You can spend time with your family and friends; you can teach, write, go into a law firm, sit by a swimming pool, make a debut as a movie star, turn tennis pro. Whatever one's choice, I think you ought to make a contribution in some way in order to achieve the same opportunities for people that you have.

We live in frivolous circumstances—it is easy to forget that there are people who live in less frivolous circumstances, but millions do. We live among people whose whole life may be an example of the gap that exists between what we like to think of America as and what it is to millions of people. You can't see that and say, "This is of no concern to me." Whether you work in politics or not is not the fundamental decision. I do think that to bring about basic changes such as money for housing and hospitals, jobs for people who want to work, fair tax structures—so that Ronald Reagan doesn't go home without paying any state taxes while denouncing poor women as cheats because they gained an extra check for an extra child—is the goal to which we all must dedicate ourselves in some way.

If the government is not going to respond to injustices visited unfairly on people, then there is no reason to say that we are a society that believes in the things we keep saying we do. We are going to have to unravel the contradictions in our society before the hypocrisy becomes too monumental, because people are not going to live two-thirds affluent and one-third in a kind of economic and social servitude. It isn't going to work and it doesn't need to work—the society can be so abundant for everybody and so much fairer.

So what you are talking about is fighting for the future of the country. People now take for granted that their lives are going to be very pleasant for them and their children. But their whole future is in fact imperiled if we don't move the country in a different direction, toward resolving the enormous frustrations that have been allowed to accumulate and embitter, alienate, and divide our people.

213

It is not that the system works or doesn't work, whatever that means. The system is here. There are people who work the system—the milk lobby, the oil companies, ITT—they all work the system. It is incumbent upon all of us who are committed to turning this nation toward its much-needed reordering of priorities to reclaim the system and make it work for the benefit of all Americans.

THE WATERSHED
OF WATERGATE

ADA World, June 1973

Lowenstein was reelected as chairman of Americans for Democratic Action in April 1972. The following year, he touched on some of the implications of the developing Watergate crisis.

The unprecedented events and revelations of the past few months should make it unnecessary to stress that we cannot afford the customary "off-year" period of detachment or disengagement. We must try to influence the course of affairs in this extraordinary situation with all the determination and resources we can command.

One cannot be expected *not* to feel a kind of interior satisfaction over the capsizing of a palace guard whose combination of arrogance, dishonesty, and corruption has done such general damage to the nation and to cherished institutions. But we also must shudder at what all this has done to accelerate the decline of the credibility of all politics and of all government, and to erode further the influence of morality and high purpose in shaping the public's attitude toward its governance. Thus, in addition to exposing wrong-doing and bringing the guilty to justice, we must assess the extent of the damage and search out ways to repair, protect, and improve the fabric of the Republic. We must examine what has happened to us as a people during the cumulative tragedy of the last ten years, and we must think out what we want next: How did we get from

215

there to here? What went wrong? How do we go about setting things right?

Meanwhile, there is the additional task of defending much that is hopeful and good against continuing assault. One might hope that the Administration, with its prestige in tatters, would abandon at least some of the policies which have divided and weakened a country weary of discord and division. But so far there is little to sustain such a hope.

The effort to justify years of horror in Indochina has extended to December-scale bombing in Cambodia, now without a scrap of legal or constitutional sanction.

The national outcry for reordered priorities has been twisted into the excision from the national budget of some of its most necessary and hopeful ingredients—and to achieve this strange end, even stranger procedures are concocted, including the ignoring of laws duly enacted whenever they don't suit the President.

Newsmen who insist on upholding the First Amendment face jail, while special "privileges" are discovered to shield executive bureaucrats who break the law.

The famous "compassion" which Henry Kissinger seeks for liars and crooks in high places is not sufficiently expansive to apply to the unwillingly unemployed, or to Cambodian peasants, or to welfare mothers, or to draft resisters, or to retarded children.

"Strict constructionism" vanishes (and the Constitution reels) under bombings, impoundments, and concealments, while some of the highest law-enforcement agencies and officials in the land rationalize and sometimes organize crimes, burglarize people's files and burn their own, and peddle illegal influence while waving banners touting law, order, and honor.

Meanwhile, vital aspects of the national agenda remain neglected, though not even the current Ambassador to India is now likely to try to describe this neglect as benign.

But this sad, appalling and sinister mess provides opportunities almost as extensive as the dangers. The quality of Presidential leadership is clearer to millions of Americans, and people of all persuasions are disgusted as seldom in the past. It begins to be generally understood that men who lie about buggings can lie about bombings, that those who find "honor" in the Vietnam involvement are the same people who found honor in degrading the FBI, and that some who rode to power exploiting fears of crime have used power, once attained, to commit crimes and to shield criminals. So now it should be easier to focus attention and harness energies to deal effectively with real problems, and to forge new alliances out of shared frustrations. All of those who are determined to end the corruption of the public arena and to prevent the dismantling of much of what has been most promising in America since World War II should now be able to join together.

The end of the fighting in Vietnam should make possible the end of the fighting *about* Vietnam in the Democratic Party and among all Americans alarmed by the attitudes and tactics of the Nixon Administration. To refight the past in the midst of this present is to invite renewed defeat in the future. Wouldn't it be more useful to join together to try to prevent even more privilege from flowing to the too-privileged, and to try to restore constitutional balance and protect the general liberties? And to use the watershed of Watergate to elect a different leadership in 1974 and 1976?

What America needs now is the involvement and unified efforts of concerned and outraged people, not what Burke once called the "lump-ish acquiescence" of a citizenry grown cynical about its capacity to end wrong-doing.

One dangerous side-effect of last fall's election is that some otherwise sensible people now seem to believe that the ideas and programs we have worked for are unacceptable to a majority of Americans.

There always will be moments when people of principle find themselves swimming upstream. There always will be sensitivities that unscrupulous, ambitious people can seek to manipulate to their own advantage. But whatever else November 1972 was, it was not a repudiation of the Roosevelt-Kennedy tradition. The desperate maneuverings of demagogues determined to divert attention and misstate choices show how clearly the President and his surrogates understood this central political reality. We must understand it as clearly, and act accordingly: to clarify what the Administration seeks to confuse, to unify whom the Administration seeks to polarize.

One sad fact underscored by the voting is how many Americans are losing faith in the electoral process. Mandates and coattails, trends and inconsistencies, all must be argued against the backdrop of record numbers of citizens refusing to vote for anyone in an election featuring presidential candidates whose goals and programs offered very real choices. We failed to make those choices clear and compelling to most voters.

217

But that is a very different problem from the problem we would face if most voters had understood the choices and were prepared to vote *for* injustice, and against their own best interests in the process.

So now more than ever we must work to inform and arouse opinion, and to do that effectively we must offset honest and intelligent leadership that can articulate and inspire. This will not be easy, in the face of the wealth and power to distort now concentrated in the White House, and in the wake of bullets that destroyed those best equipped to lead the effort. But the fact that these things are not easily done should propel us into working harder to do them, if we understand the stakes and care as we have professed to care about the outcome.

We are not at a high point in the annals of the Republic. But there is reason for hope, and where there is reason for hope, there is incentive for work. Certainly there is no excuse for quitting when there is so much to do—so many wrongs to right, so many wounds to heal.

Robert Kennedy once wrote, "Our future may lie beyond our vision, but it is not beyond our control. It is the shaping impulse of America that neither fate nor nature nor the irresistible tides of history, but the work of our own hands, matched to reason and principle, will determine our destiny. There is pride in that, even arrogance, but there is also experience and truth. In any event, it is the only way we can live."

What we need now is to end the damaging detour that has led to such waste of lives and resources and has so hobbled the national spirit. Given the urgency and virtue of our goals, we would have to work for them even if they seemed impossible. But we should know they are not impossible— and that knowledge should increase our determination to work to achieve them. In any event, that is the only way we can live.

218

A LONELY INQUEST

James A. Wechsler

New York Post, January 9, 1975

Lowenstein first became aware that serious questions existed about Robert F. Kennedy's assassination in 1973. Until then, he had privately dismissed that and other assassination criticisms without closely examining the issues involved.

As the Watergate disclosures poured forth, though, he grew increasingly concerned about the darker forces affecting the political process in America. He was startled by his ranking on the White House "enemies list," and in July of 1973 a story in the New York Times reported his support for "a deeper examination of a whole range of events, from elections to assassinations, which may not have happened in the way generally accepted." (Ironically, the Times disclosed in a front-page story seven months later that the Federal Bureau of Investigation had, at the request of Congressman John Rooney, investigated Lowenstein and an earlier Rooney opponent during their campaigns against the lawmaker.)

On a visit to Los Angeles in the summer of 1973, Lowenstein was exposed to the major inconsistencies in the official evidence and conclusions of the Robert Kennedy assassination probe. The most apparent problems involved the number of bullets fired, the distance and direction of the fatal shots, and the weakness of the bullet identification evidence.

After questioning critics carefully, Lowenstein concluded that the case deserved closer examination. He met privately with Los Angeles Police Chief Edward Davis and District Attorney Joseph Busch, but found that

their evasiveness and inaccurate recitations of the case further fueled his
skepticism. He carried on additional research and interviewed eyewit-
nesses to the shooting. One of the latter was Paul Schrade, a former
Kennedy campaign coordinator wounded during the assassination, who
now joined the inquiry.

By the end of 1974, when it was clear that officials were unwilling to
reopen the case, Lowenstein and Schrade called a press conference to
raise their doubts publicly for the first time. "We offer no answers today,
only questions," the statement said. "Nor have we any prejudice or pre-
conception about what may ultimately be found to be the whole truth
about the assassination of Senator Kennedy. . . . In short, facts must be
determined free of any dogged precommitment to any theory." They
listed specific steps to help clear up doubts about the case, but it proved
difficult to attract careful attention to the issues they raised.

Columnist James Wechsler took note of these developments.

From a variety of sources, I have recently been subjected to some
version of the same question: "Why is Al Lowenstein involved in the
Sirhan case? Has he flipped?"

The quick answer is that he is alive and well, and in full command of
his senses. But since that reply may seem either protective or glib, I am
setting down some personal knowledge of the sequence that led to his
absorption in the circumstances surrounding Robert Kennedy's assassination.

His lonely exploratory mission was not undertaken with any impulsive
zest, or any expectation of public notices. He has never had any attach-
ment for fanatically conspiratorial theories of history. Even now, he does
not dogmatically advance any blueprint of a plot that goes beyond Sirhan. He is asking questions—and pleading for a diligent effort to get the
answers.

For Lowenstein this has been a long journey. In a sense it began with
an unrelated episode in the summer of 1973 when the existence of a
White House "enemies list" was revealed, and Lowenstein found himself
on a small roster of very special "enemies."

I recall him remarking at that time that the disclosure had persuaded
him to re-examine many seemingly implausible political nightmares. If
the Nixon Administration could thus caricature the grimmest projections
of its kookiest critics, what other apparent fantasies might have some
roots in reality?

Not long afterward he found himself in Los Angeles. He was still uncommitted to any crusading inquiry. What plunged him so deeply into the affair was the "stonewalling" and deceit he encountered among Los Angeles police and prosecutive officials.

He found glaring discrepancies between what they told him and both the Sirhan trial record and the autopsy report. He was troubled by their refusal to release the 10 volumes of the official report on the killing and permit access to other vital evidence. He was impressed and disturbed by the affidavit of ballistic expert William W. Harper raising doubts about whether Kennedy had been killed by the same gun that wounded a bystander. He was perplexed by the disparity between the number of bullet-holes found after the shooting and the official assertion that only eight bullets were fired.

His independent inquiries unfolded new conflicts in eyewitness testimony and strange aspects in the security arrangements.

Despite his deepening skepticism, he remained reluctant to "go public." In numerous private conferences, he implored Los Angeles officials to initiate a full review of the murder story. Only when he and Paul Schrade, the Auto Workers Union leader who was wounded during the shoot-out, became convinced that the cover-up was unbreakable did they finally decide to air their misgivings and call for an investigation "free of prejudice or preconception."

The frustrations Lowenstein and Schrade have encountered were symbolized by a story transmitted on the *Washington Post* wire almost simultaneous with their public move. The dispatch (written by Ron Kessler and published in this and many other newspapers) began:

Pasadena, Cal—The nationally recognized ballistics expert whose affidavit gave rise to a theory that Robert F. Kennedy was not killed by Sirhan Bisharra Sirhan has said there is no evidence to support the claim.

The story said in effect that Harper, whose 1970 affidavit had been cited by Lowenstein and others, had repudiated his earlier statement.

What has not been reported is that Harper, in an unpublished letter to the Washington paper, blasted its account of the interview. Among other things, he wrote:

"At no time did I ever directly or indirectly repudiate my findings in this case. For Kessler to say I did is preposterous. . . ."

"I would like to point out, however, that my original affidavit was never represented as being completely definitive. Rather it was meant to focus attention on some of the gross irregularities in the official handling of this case, and to ask questions that obviously demanded answers. It was these unanswered questions that ultimately caused me to have grave doubts regarding the official handling of this case, questions that have still to be answered . . ."

There is no fatal contradiction between the possibility that Sirhan was "the lone assassin" and that Los Angeles authorities have been primarily concealing flaws and blunders in their own investigative process.

But it is hardly madness to continue asking whether Sirhan was a solitary operative. Lowenstein and Schrade have surely made a compelling case for either a Congressional investigation or an independent commission of inquiry.

In the succeeding months, the questions about the assassination were pursued further by Lowenstein and others. Two key eyewitnesses and four of the shooting victims called for a reexamination of the case, and a special committee of the American Academy of Forensic Sciences reported basic problems with the firearms evidence. That summer, a partial reexamination of this evidence was ordered by Los Angeles Superior Court.

SPAIN WITHOUT FRANCO
Saturday Review, February 7, 1976

Lowenstein's lifelong interest in Spain never waned. He spoke fluent Spanish, his library contained numerous books on the country and its civil war, and he served on the board of a Spanish refugee aid organization. One of the paintings in his home showed a Spanish militiaman and bore the letters P.O.U.M., the initials of a Republican faction in the civil war. He also maintained his contacts through the years with friends in the opposition movement.

When the aging General Franco fell gravely ill in November 1975, Lowenstein returned to Spain to confer with his friends and to survey the prospects for a democratic revival. His published account of the trip received a citation for outstanding foreign reporting from the Overseas Press Club in 1976.

The end of personal rule by Francisco Franco y Bahamonde came as a strange sort of punctuation mark—an inverted Spanish exclamation point on one side and a question mark on the other, a victory in the unfinished war of our childhood, a kind of unearned run evening up the score a little, if scores can be evened up in overtime. The fact is, of course, that the end was coming with no help from anyone who had tried to bring it about. Still, the end of Franco, whatever its cause, doesn't happen every day, and I was wondering how to treat an event so uniquely significant and irrelevant when a call came asking me to Madrid for meetings about the "transition," almost as if somehow my being there to celebrate the end might make up a little for not having been there to resist the beginning.

By this time I had been attending "meetings" in Spain on and off for some 17 years, ever since the son of the chief of Franco's air force, fresh from jail, had made his way to Hubert Humphrey's office, where I was working at the time, to plead that someone come to see the evils of the government that his father had helped to put in power. That was the beginning of my association with some of Franco's new enemies. It had never occurred to me that the risky politics of opposing a dictatorship would attract the pride and heirs of the realm: wealthy, tough, bright young men who were to display a gallantry that would have been notable at the Round Table. Men like these—Juan Kindelán, Carlos de Zayas, and the others—the scions of grandees and dukes and Nationalist generals, with lives of almost guaranteed success ahead of them, impelled by no discernible force but conscience, chose to throw away the most privileged position in a land of protected privileges to languish at times in jails of peculiar inhumanity. Their sacrifices, whispered across a moribund countryside, reminded a drained people of hope and, in the process, wrenched at families whose loyalties to God and Spain were not prepared for a clash with loyalty to Family itself.

And they provided a remarkable introduction to the continuing involvement that led me back to Madrid all these years later.

I arrive in Madrid as Juan Carlos is skittering into the strange upside-down semi-regency made necessary by Franco's refusal to yield authority: everything tentative, a curious uncertainty abetted by medical bulletins announcing that an octogenarian who seems to have every disease known to man is constantly rallying and is planning to resume presiding at Cabinet meetings; but something more than uncertainty, too: not exactly relief from fear, not yet, but an *expectation* of relief, with the familiar fears receding into a soupy uneasiness about what might follow the relief.

The transition is beginning at a moment when the national mood is forcing the moderating of old antagonisms. The economic uplift that spread political unrest has multiplied the number of people with a stake in retaining order, people who, above all, don't want a Portugal or an Argentina or a Chile in a new Spain, and who are part of an unexpected consensus that wants consensus to guide the transition and wants elections to determine consensus. There is a great wish to see an end to political prisons, terrorism, censorship, whimsical governing, and an end as well to conflicts swirling beyond or beneath the governing.

This mood affects everyone who hopes to ride the succession to ultimate power: Communists become devotees of pluralistic democratic institutions, Monarchists accept elections, Socialists accept the throne. The quest is for a way to achieve change without disorder; the worry is that the moment held back too long will be ill used and will somehow end in another 40 years in another wilderness.

Above all, the mood has affected the perceptions of the successor, of the handpicked Prince, scorned all his life as pliable and stupid, an ingrate to his father, a creature of the dictator, too weak to survive once his patron is gone.

From the moment one lands at the airport at Barajas, the attitude is different, the scorn replaced by hope, by an impatience for the patron to be gone so that the Prince can begin. Everyone wants, or at least accepts, Juan Carlos, at least for now. The response is overwhelming; it is in fact astonishing: everyone now wants him to begin—everyone, that is, except Franco, who picked him, and La Señora Carmen Franco, demanding a title for herself, viewing the death of her husband as a cosmic impertinence and the proposal to transfer power before his death as heresy.

Why everyone suddenly wants Juan Carlos and what they expect of him are complex matters with troublesome possibilities. But he arrives at power with an unexpected opportunity to be his own man, to build from support to popularity, and then to use popularity to steer and protect progress—the origins of his rise almost forgotten in the awareness that only in his person does a succession seem possible that will end the past without bloodying the future. He chairs a Cabinet meeting, and the press cheers; he utters slogans, and wise men read wisdom into them.

The Prince—El Principe—the pleasant nonentity from the family of archaic hemophiliacs picked by Franco to give a touch of purple to the gray steel of the real heir apparent, the assassinated Admiral Luis Carrero Blanco, the man designated to perpetuate Franco after Franco; the Principe without known principles, selected because his father, heir to the abandoned throne, had offended the dictator by tinges of open-mindedness; El Principe, the handpicked puppet, now come to power with puppeteer dying and Carrero dead.

He is dying as he has lived, outdated, pious, insulated in his palace at Pardo from his own unpopularity, saint's robes thrown over the bed, enlisted in the battle to stop time; indomitably narrow, clinging to power long after every sycophant around him has wished for a more graceful turnover—every sycophant, but not his wife, the untitled Duchess of El Pardo, or of Plaza Toro, or of whatever. He has outlasted Hitler, Mussolini, Salazar, Chiang, even some, like the Greek Colonels, who didn't get started till he had already ruled Spain for a decade longer than any President has ever ruled the United States. But now ashes to ashes, Madrid at last the final tomb of fascism, if not quite when or how the men who had died to keep it from fascism 40 years earlier had meant it to be.

I chat with two officials, a bureaucrat and a colonel, men who have known each other only slightly, and across a divide of presumed political hostility summarized by one whispering to me that the other is a "hidden leftist" just after the other has warned me by phone that we are about to meet a "rightist militarist." There is a cautious fencing at first, some talk of army officers fat from insufficient activity who might spring into action for its own sake.

"The army will be loyal to the government," the military rightist assures us. "But who is the government?" I ask. "The Prince or the Pardo?" "The *King*," they say, unintentionally together, together even in their embarrassment at being together. We are all surprised at the sound of the unfamiliar title. It is the colonel who resumes first. "Whatever good he did, the old man should have let go. Soon they will have to bury a machine in his tomb; there will be nothing else left. And when the funeral is over, Juan Carlos will be King, and the army will obey the King."

So it goes, on and on: Left militants and Right militants, separated by lifetimes of reciprocated hatreds, denouncing each other—and anyone else who won't give the Prince a chance; courtiers of the father, Don Juan, the legitimate King, if kings are legitimate, recently vituperative about usurpers, now confiding about new virtues found in the son; intellectuals and hereditary Republicans discovering possibilities in constitutional monarchies: isn't Britain a constitutional monarchy? And if you ask whether Juan Carlos is a constitutional monarch, you are told that he can be, that he must be; at least for now there's no other way. Presently the two illegal collections of opposition parties, including among them the Communists, join to say as much formally and publicly.

Then a shiver runs through the city: a Socialist gynecologist just back from Europe has been arrested; again, so soon, the fumes of yesteryear— or rather of yesterday. Students plan a protest: the new regime must know at once that it cannot survive this way. The gynecologist is released—remarkable speed for Spanish political police; it is as if the first message of the new era, intentional or otherwise, is this: you restrain your fanatics, your hotheads; we'll restrain ours.

There is in all this something almost un-Spanish—a voluntary, if transient, unity after so many years of bitterness over efforts to enforce unity. But un-Spanish or not, it is there; everyone feels it, and almost everyone feels good feeling it. Perhaps the mood can't last; the stakes are too high, and hot blood must be poured willy-nilly after blood already spilled; perhaps the bunker mentality of a few high officers or outbursts of Falangists defending a special status or bombings by ideological desperadoes will abort it and trigger new spirals of confrontation and repression.

But maybe, just maybe—the thought glimmers and won't go away— maybe with so many people so determined to try another course, maybe the past can be ended without being relived; maybe a beginning can be made in that direction. Even a beginning would require unusual reciprocal restraint and a general agreement on procedures for deciding what the next steps will be; and it would require a government that could assure fairness in implementing the procedures: Juan Carlos perhaps, Juan Carlos surely, but a Juan Carlos whose intentions are underwritten by a Cabinet committed to fair elections sometime soon.

Simply to state the problem is to spotlight its delicacy. I begin to wonder whether power and privilege could ever accept peaceful transition to a rearrangement that would at least dilute power and modify privilege. Experience, certainly the Spanish experience, does not encourage great hope for such a response.

Perhaps that is why I decide to have my first post-Franco dinner at the residence of an elderly aristocrat, a woman used to having her own way except with her own children, children now in their 30s, whose courage and intelligence are like hers but whose politics are not. Managing her blend of bluntness and graciousness, she is glad, she says as I appear, to see me again, even at this sad juncture in the affairs of Spain, a juncture that no doubt accounts for my unexpected appearance, not entirely unlike a vulture's. She sits serene amid the exquisite artifacts and Castilian heirlooms of her living rooms, an unembarrassed and unreconstructible Fascist, contemptuous of charade; a gentle woman—there are gentle Fascists as there are gentle Communists, perhaps not too reliable in a shootout, but believers in authoritarian rule, in a corporate state, a state ruled without disorder by one man for as long as God wills: Francisco Franco. She prays a great deal, delicate hands clasped in faithful, believing prayers, and cannot understand why any thinking person would want votes instead of prayers to guide the State.

Elections are not for Spain, certainly not for "street sweepers." "I do not know what your street sweepers in America know that qualifies them to tell the government what to do, but here they know nothing." She recalls 1936 with a grimace, a slight shudder, the last Spanish government picked by street sweepers: disorder, churches burned, two first cousins shot by the Reds; Reds dominant and everywhere, she herself taken to prison to be shot, rescued at the last moment. (By Reds? "Reds shoot, not rescue, people who worship God.")

Now, she asks, is there to come again the day of the street sweepers? Already it is coming to Portugal, brought on, inexplicably, by the army— you see what has already happened to Portugal in a year; is it to be Spain's turn next, no lesson learned from the mess next door?

There is a madness loose in Europe, she says—Europe shouting about Franco executing Basque murderers of policemen, nobody shouting about the policemen; the Church grown soft, its murdered priests forgotten; and now foreigners demanding "elections" in Spain, as if it were their business: do we tell them they must restore their kings? In Spain the malcontents, given too much rein by Franco in his failing years, undermining the universities where they teach our children to be Reds, an undermining that the State should never have put up with, much less have paid for; and now these same malcontents telling Don Juan Carlos, whom they hate and have always opposed, that he must take into the government the *chaqueteros*—Ruiz Giminez, Areilza, all the Francoists-turned-critics: the contemptible opportunists suddenly made into tests of the acceptability of the Prince. In her hostility to them she sounds as unreconcilable as some in the opposition who deny that anyone can ever be trusted who fought against the republic and then worked for Franco; and I wonder whether such divergent antagonisms could possibly find common ground.

The Prince, she says suddenly, almost as if my thoughts are audible— ah, no *chaquetero* he. A loyal and honorable man, religious, the only hope for calm, for order, a man who understands and cherishes the values of the real Spain, the Prince would protect these values, these institutions; there would be changes (changes are life), but there would be security, too. One could sleep at night; the streets would be safe. The Prince is trained; he is fair. He knows the evils of disorder and communism. "We cannot have rioting here; I am too old to run from guns and bombs or to start again in some other country. If Europe accepts Don Juan Carlos, he can hold things together. Why can't they see that and help him? What do they gain if the Bolsheviks bring us to chaos here?"

"Europe," I say, "will not help anyone who resists elections. Juan Carlos needs the people you call *chaqueteros* to show that he intends to allow elections. If you want Europe to accept the Prince, you will have to accept elections."

At that instant the direction of the succession—confrontation or compromise, perhaps war or peace—seemed to hang on her silence. "But will you be as eager," she asks at length, "to rescue me after these famous elections if they put me again in prison for praying to God, as you were to rescue my son when he was put there for plotting against the government? You won't be; nobody will be. Without the Prince we will be forgotten in the prisons while Europe celebrates the elections. So we will have to resist if they try to drive out Don Juan Carlos. They will buy the street sweepers and brainwash the students and frighten the bourgeoisie, and say such 'elections' decide what it is right to do. Then they will do terrible things in the holy name of democracy."

I do not ask her to define precisely who "they" might be. With the distance of time, the experiences of the Thirties have all come together in one horror—the Reds and Anarchists, who had shot priests and cousins, and the Republicans, who had rescued her from the Reds: all subsumed in one giant vengeful "they." Much of the street-sweeper problem she blames on the ignorance of people too young to remember the Second Republic and the Civil War. "My son," she says, "came home from prison after I used all this family's influence to get him out. He stood in this room, the heritage of his family all around him, and he made a clenched fist. Do you know his first words? '*Viva la República*,' he said. If the republic had won, he would have no rooms like this to mock or to come home to from prison. Oh, what a test it all is of even a mother's patience."

And what a tribute, I think, to the efforts of the offspring of privileged parents—parents who spent fortunes and fought wars to save Spain for their children only to find them in prison for trying to overturn the victory of their own mothers and fathers. All over Spain tormented aristo-crats—"ultra-rightists," they are usually called, by themselves and their worst enemies alike—have had to live the same dilemma; and however they have worked it out, attitudes cannot be what they would be if the next generation had rallied to their old banner.

Rearguing history, I say, is no way to a happier future. "There's no proposal for a republic now," I add. "Couldn't you all agree, even you and your children, to '*Viva el Principe*'? Wouldn't that be better than more conflict, more bitterness?"

For a moment I think the old lady is going to accede. Then she says, "I think you must mean '*Arriba el Principe*,' " and there is a stress on the Falangist verb she has substituted for my Republican *viva*. Still, it is a unity of some sort, if only around a proper noun, a noun modified at that by an undefined overused catchword called *elections*; and I depart won-dering whether clashing symbolic verbs can undo overlapping substantive agreement.

Back to the hotel late that first night, through middle-class crowds in streets once filled with industrial workers in shabby clothes, many of them desperate refugees from peasantry. Cafés still open, even bars, young people like young people in London or San Francisco (a bit better dressed, perhaps), rock music, big advertisements urging people to read the "continuing debate" in the Falange newspaper, movie posters with breasts peeking out. I remember when the regime had decided that every-one should eat dinner earlier, and the city should close down earlier—perhaps as broad a resistance as the regime ever brought on itself. But the breasts still only peek out on Madrid posters, I think, perhaps the great-est of Franco's Canute achievements: he kept two or three inches of bosom under wraps for an extra six or seven years. In six more months breasts, too, shall appear.

Then suddenly two street sweepers in front of the hotel—more accu-rately, one man sweeping the street and one hosing it. I greet and am greeted politely, deferentially, as is still the custom among older Spanish workers dealing with visitors from another world. We discuss the weather and the cleaning of the streets. I drift into a comment about the dying Generalissimo. The old reflex: caution, puzzlement, evasion; a stranger talking politics: the Generalissimo dying is clearly politics. I mention the Prince, to ease anxieties. We all wish the Prince well. "*Arriba el Prin-*

cipe," I say absent-mindedly in farewell, "*Viva el Principe*," I hear from behind as I enter the hotel.

A fresh air is settling on Madrid, there is the sense that buds are peeking around to see if spring will last this time. If it does, it's clear that very quickly there won't be much more left of the sullen Madrid that has moped and wriggled under a turgid blanket for 35 years than there is of the defiant Madrid that transformed a proper noun into a rallying cry of several generations. All at once the city is expectant, expectant and calm, the calm not ruffled even by Franco's interminable lingering or by the rumblings from the Spanish Sahara. Fists and stomachs are coming un-clenched in the realization that Franco is irrevocably terminal despite the brigade of peasants one pictures lined up at gunpoint outside the death chamber, ready to provide substitute parts to replace failed organs. For the first time anyone can remember, people think of Franco and smile.

I dine with an assortment of Socialists and government functionaries, once high-school classmates, divided by years of bitterly different experiences, and it is like a reunion. I talk to an official at the American Embassy who is matter-of-fact about the "pleasant" lunch the ambassador fed recently to Felipe Gonzalez, the new young head of the Socialist Party; I think of all the years when Third Secretaries with redundant names like Putnam Lowell felt venturesome every time they slipped off to an unobserved cocktail with an opposition figure, and I know that even the embassy has decided that Franco is dead or close to it. Then word comes that the army has undertaken, of all things, to protect two "personalities" of the Left who have been threatened by "off-duty police."

It is announced that Franco is eating while his stomach bleeds, and I go off with old Spanish friends to the Valley of the Fallen. Here Franco dramatized his peculiar notion of the way to restore unity to Spain by forcing Republican political prisoners to rebury Republican war dead under Nationalist flags and slogans. And here, when the country was desperate for housing and schools and hospitals, Franco spent billions of pesetas erecting a cross 495 feet high and hacking the world's largest church and his own tomb out of the hard rock of a mountain.

We stop at the gate, and the guard asks for the entrance fee. That's very inexpensive to see Franco's grave, we say, and realize the remark would have made us nervous not long ago. "Even though he's not in it yet?" the guard replies and waves us in free.

In the vast, empty mausoleum, surrounded by buried soldiers and the smell of votive candles burning, one finds it hard to shed an attack of history. One is overwhelmed by thoughts of loss, by wonderings about what might have been. "*Un sang dont nous ne pouvons pas nous laver les mains*," a French magazine called the Spanish Civil War, and surely few scars have lasted as long or remained as raw for as many people in as many distant places. I find myself humming "*Madrid, que bien résiste*," feeling a little triumphant and a little silly, and feeling again the wound at the heart that brought me to this improbable spot.

I realize how odd it is to feel something so sharply after all these years, but terrible things have kept happening since it began, way back, in Guernica decimated, in children dead from mass bombings of open cities, in the massacres of Majorca and the bull ring of Badajoz. After that there was Franco heiling in tandem with Hitler, reviewing goose-stepping troops about to go off to try to finish the conquest of the world; and then the decade of democracy renascent, Mussolini hanging by his ankles, the bunker burying its evil, the Emperor of Japan becoming mortal, while through it all Franco's prisons overflowed, the Spanish people silenced, Spanish refugees starving and forgotten in foul camps far from home. And then the last chapter, perhaps the least comprehensible: Franco alone, Franco vulnerable till rescued by America, the triumphant fresh new world protecting the last partner of Hitler, the unrepentant bully-ghost of the old, without even trying to moderate the oppression of Spaniards who had fought on our side in return for the rescue. So one feels even now the needless suffering, and the guilt of knowing how much one's country has contributed to it, and the concern that that contribution may not yet have been concluded.

Needless suffering? It is not, of course, given to us to know what would have happened if what happened had not happened, if the republic had been allowed to win, or if Franco had not been allowed to survive his allies. A Stalinist dictatorship would have been as bad or worse for most of the Spanish people, but it is hard to see how a Stalinist dictatorship could have survived for long in Spain—yet it is hard to see how a Fascist dictatorship could, and it did.

If we had helped when so many Spaniards bought time for Western democracy at such dreadful cost to themselves, might Prague have been spared, or Paris or London or Bataan or Guadalcanal? Was Munich inevitable, and Dachau, and the Hitler-Stalin pact, and so on to Hiroshima and the Berlin wall and the bridge at Andau and the Bay of Pigs and Vietnam? Could Communist misbehavior in Spain and Poland have been avoided or tempered if ours toward Spain and Czechoslovakia had been, and so perhaps some kind of understanding if not cooperation preserved that would have minimized the post-war ordeal of Eastern Europe and the polarizing of the post-Hitler planet?

If it is foolish to underestimate the chasm that separated Western and Soviet attitudes so fatefully in the Thirties and Forties, it is also simplistic not to wonder whether the paranoid viciousness of emergent communism might have been modified had the Western democracies resisted sooner the calculated viciousness of emergent fascism.

But even if nothing anyone could have done in or about Spain would have averted World War II or the Cold War, what if democratic countries had helped the republic during the Civil War instead of driving it to dependence on the Soviet Union? Is it inconceivable that democracy triumphant in Spain could have headed off extremes of anticlerical misconduct and thus defused the antagonism over Franco that poisoned relations between American Catholics and liberals at a time that was so critical?

What a difference it might have made if McCarthy and Nixon had not been helped in their rise by the extravagant emotions about Spain that led so many Catholics to suspect liberals of being soft on communism, and so many liberals to suspect Catholics of being soft on fascism: isn't it just possible that a different Spanish experience, perhaps even a concern shared as it is now about Portugal, could have spared America the unhappy period of the exploited neurosis that led first to such destructive mistrust at home and then to such devastating consequences in Indochina? Maybe Cardinal Spellman would not have attacked Mrs. Roosevelt (after all, she had been rather good about Al Smith); and maybe John F. Kennedy would have been nominated for Vice-President in 1956, thus perhaps ruining his career, or perhaps saving him from assassination so that we could have him now. But we wonder too far—that way lie screenplays or madness.

What is clear is that this has been a long and dark passage for the Spanish people, who did more than most people to keep their freedom and who have suffered more than most people because outside forces were visited upon them. And it is hard to see how their suffering has helped us, even if our own needs could be said to justify making the lives of others more difficult.

On the other hand, the United States has not paid the conspicuous price for its misconduct in Spain that it has paid elsewhere. With our help, the repression outlasted several generations of potential anti-American rioters; and there will be those who say that even if the American bases are closed soon, they will have served their purpose: we had them when we needed them—and at the minimal cost of an insurance policy whose existence may have helped avert the fire it never had to be used to put out. The policy, it will be argued, thus succeeded: Franco survived, Spain is not Communist, American investment flourishes; even the American Embassy is not bombed.

Had the gamble failed, had the dictatorship fallen despite all the United States did to sustain it, it would have been a spectacular failure; but to argue that the gamble was not worth the risk of failure is to argue theory against results. To argue that nations pay for immoral misuse of power is to argue theology; to talk about costs of policies in global intangibles is to sound fuzzy in a discussion with people who pride themselves on their pragmatism.

Furthermore, one's personal assessment of American behavior in Spain must be affected by the long hurt of feeling years of hate directed at one's flag by one's friends. My thoughts fly to an old bishop, 90 and blind, returned to his village at the end of life from exile for opposing Franco in the war, spitting at my American accent, "What has become of the soul of your country? Even my church has learned that to lie with tyrants is to stink of tyranny."

The bishop of course is dead; two decades of angry students have graduated into careers where private distaste for American policy will not affect their purchasing habits, and whom they boo privately on newscasts affects nothing at all.

But there have been other consequences, wider costs if less tangible ones, that should at least be noted before we conclude that unclosed bases and an unbombed embassy equal a successful foreign policy.

I still wonder at times whatever got into otherwise thoughtful people like Adlai Stevenson where Spain was concerned. Political considerations can explain many things, and there was certainly a price to pay in the United States in the Fifties and Sixties for outspoken opposition to

Franco; the few who were prepared to pay the price were people like Herbert Lehman and Eleanor Roosevelt, people who were extraordinary in any event. But Adlai Stevenson twice chose to go to Spain and pose with high officials after his elective career was over, both visits coming at moments of special difficulty for the opposition; and the second visit was even less understandable than the first, because it took place after Walter Reuther, Norman Thomas, and I had sent him a petition signed by Socialist and Christian Democratic leaders whom he had refused to meet on his first visit, pleading that he not "damage" Spanish democrats in the same way again.

The "damage" referred to was two-sided: it helped the Spanish government at a rough moment; and it helped the Spanish Communist Party, perhaps even more than it helped the government. These were the concerns of the people who sent the petition; they were of course concerns of mine, too, but I had another: the drain on what Wendell Willkie had called the "reservoir of good will" for America around the world.

Global results are, after all, the only practical measure of foreign policy. And the feeling of the world about the United States is not hard to measure. Anyone who lived through the glory of being an American during and early after World War II knows that that glory resulted not only from strength and wealth, but from an almost universal sense of fraternity as well. We have retained the strength, squandered the wealth, and ended the fraternity. Except where Communist misconduct is blatant and immediately at hand, the reservoir is dry or close to it. Our isolation is unsolicited and inverted: we retain bases, we crave approval, we lobby for votes at the United Nations; almost everyone wants the bases out, intellectuals see in us the wave of the past, and fewer and fewer countries vote with us at the United Nations even as our position becomes more and more sensible and justifiable.

How easy to dismiss it all as inevitable or as the result of national jealousies or Communist plots or Arab oil—or to decide that world opinion is inconsequential in any case. But to refuse to examine a 25-year erosion is no way for practical people to measure the effect of a policy designed to be pragmatic, and is certainly no way to determine future policy.

The questions basic to any realistic assessment of the results of American foreign policy since the first aid to Franco was voted over President Truman's opposition are almost never asked: is it really desirable to have arrived so quickly at so lowly a place in world esteem? And if it is not desirable, was it really necessary?

In so grand an overview, Spain is clearly a small factor; but Spain as symbol and Spain as consequence of general attitude are not. Our sins in Spain seem minor compared with some we have committed. They do not seem minor, of course, to Spaniards, who come from 35 years of darkness blinking uncertainly, and noticing not very sadly that the sun that radiated energy into their oppressor seems to be sinking.

And from the point of view of our national well-being, were bases in Spain, and assistance to Salazar, and make-believe about China, and toleration of apartheid, and intervention in the Dominican Republic, and war in Indochina, and lecturing new countries steering a wobbly course between polarized titans about the immorality of not "aligning" themselves with us—were these, and the rest of the policies that derived from what was thought of as hardheaded realism, were these wise policies, even if measured only by the standards of those who set the policies?

If a program devised to contain Communists ends up somehow containing the containers, is it really fuzzy to judge the policy a failure? Might we not have done better to worry more about other people's sensibilities and priorities if we wanted them to worry about ours? Are we to reap a disagreeable and perhaps unnecessary harvest of our own planting, and never even notice that we planted it?

As I left Spain, there were sad signs of old times, or rather signs that there was not yet an end to old times. Some political arrests occurred, and the sense of instant replay almost drowned out the possibility that these were the actions of intransigent subordinates rather than government policy. Men conditioned by long repression saw a pattern emerging for the new regime in what might have been individual acts of harassment, much as a pin-prick may seem a sword wound to a body running a fever. Sober men and women began to talk of the inevitability of upheaval, of greater acceptance even of acts of violence, if the government decided to ignore the general yearning in deference to particular pressures.

It seemed that buds were retreating from an atmosphere once again weary, the air murky, the odor familiar. One realized how quickly fists and stomachs could reclench when nervous systems had not had time to develop new reflexes, how inescapable was the lurching between fear rooted in memory and overblown hopes, how fragile is everyone's trust in government and in everyone else's motives—and how essential such trust is if protest and repression in escalating counterpoint are not to undo the Prince before anything better could possibly replace him. There arose in the mind the image of a man negotiating a high wire over an abyss with a coronet teetering on his head while ideologues with knives in their souls and teeth crept toward both ends of the wire, the man inexperienced on high wires, balancing his way along, fighting against time measured on a blurred clock while a throng of well-wishers inhaled and prayed below, shouting encouragement, whispering advice, trying to warn about the knives.

Melodramatics, to be sure, but not much farther from reality than the flow of bulletins from the imaginative parade of physicians, surgeons, and mind readers that kept reporting Franco always lucid through his various comas, Franco issuing edicts as he rallied to one more call to duty, Franco receiving the tribute of thousands through the cordon of plugs and devices that suggested at least a limited deathbed conversion to modernization. It occurred to me that it may not be precisely the kind of miracle he would have planned, but Franco had managed to make Spain the only place on Earth where the restoration of the Bourbons could be described as a giant step forward in 1975.

For everyone concerned it is a remarkable moment: for Juan Carlos, the most improbable of kings, born in the second third of the 20th century of a royal house whose thrones had been abolished, the unearned opportunity to overrule history's judgment that his is a family that learns nothing and forgets nothing; for Spain, the overdue opportunity to heal wounds and right wrongs without renewing wars; for America and democracy, once more the opportunity to help a battered and deserving people to find their own way, knowing that if that is finally permitted to occur, a great symbol of past misconduct may at last be replaced by an example of democracy resurgent. In an age of humanitarian values in disarray, such a replacement may do almost as much good today as the defeat in Spain did damage 35 years ago.

It is true that the last Bourbon citizen king departed the throne of France generally unmourned, as it is true that healing wounds is not a procedure found to have occurred frequently in Spanish history—and above all, as it is true that nothing in America's conduct toward Spain during our lifetime gives precedent for our behaving as we should. Still, it is a remarkable confluence of opportunities, and maybe everyone has at last learned something—Bourbons, Spaniards, and Americans. What is certain is that this moment, this confluence of opportunities, is evanescent, is passing even now, and cannot be summoned back if squandered.

"It was in Spain," Albert Camus wrote, "that men learned that one can be right and yet be beaten, that force can vanquish spirit, that there are times when courage is not its own recompense. It is this, doubtless, which explains why so many men the world over regard the Spanish drama as a personal tragedy."

And why so many men the world over pray that now the Spanish tragedy may finally be ending.

A RARE COALITION

James A. Wechsler

New York Post, October 22, 1976

After the 1972 election, Lowenstein continued to live in Brooklyn and to maintain a community office there. He also served on the Democratic National Committee and aided several reform candidates in Brooklyn. But he continued to believe that he could most effectively fight for change as a member of Congress.

In 1973, he began exploring the chances of making a race for the U.S. Senate. The following year, his Senate bid picked up important strength with endorsements from the New York State reform movement and the state ADA. In June, he received 40 percent of the vote for the Senate nomination at the Democratic State Convention, which assured him a place on the September primary ballot.

But Meade Esposito and other Democratic-organization powers in New York City adamantly opposed him. Limited to a shoestring campaign budget and facing a costly and divisive primary, Lowenstein bowed out of the race.

Meanwhile, a federal court had abolished the 14th Congressional District, ruling that it had illegally diminished the strength of minority voters. The decision largely ruled out a second race from his prior Brooklyn district.

With the Senate option scratched and his home district obliterated by remapping for the third consecutive election, Lowenstein was offered the

*Democratic House nomination from the district containing his home in
Long Beach. The overwhelmingly Republican district was represented by
John Wydler, a six-term incumbent who had decisively turned back past
Democratic challenges.*

*Against the backdrop of Watergate and Nixon's foreign and domestic
policies, Lowenstein felt it was critical to pose the issues unmistakably to
voters. Though advised by many that it was an unwinnable district, he
waged a tough campaign emphasizing economic issues and the Watergate abuses of power. Though he cut his opponent's previous margin of
victory by 51,000 votes, he still fell short.*

*Lowenstein remained on Long Island after the 1974 race, worked on
community issues and played a leading role in the presidential primary
bid of Governor Edmund Brown, Jr., of California. In 1976, he mounted
a second powerful bid in the 5th Congressional District, drawing unexpected support even from conservative quarters. In late October, columnist James Wechsler looked at the campaign.*

In the course of modern human events there have been few occasions on which Bill Buckley and I have found ourselves on the same side
of the political barricades. But that historic circumstance, if I may so
describe it, is only one manifestation of the remarkable coalition rallied
behind Allard Lowenstein in his uphill battle to unseat an undistin-
guished, uninspired Republican-Conservative Congressman named John
Wydler in Nassau County's Fifth District.

I doubt that there is any other contest in the country in which such
divergent voices as Rep. Andy Young and Leonard Garment, Coretta
King and Rita Hauser, Sen. Henry Jackson and Gov. Jerry Brown, the
Patrolmen's Benevolent Association and Americans for Democratic Action—to name only a fraction of Lowenstein's broad spectrum of sponsors—have joined hands to support a candidate whose commitments to
Democratic progressivism have never wavered. Equally startling have
been expressions of support from Republican notables in the area.

Clearly neither Bill Buckley nor others on this roster who differ with
Lowenstein on many issues have modified their own convictions. What
has brought them to his side is a generous recognition of his rationality
and decency and, to quote Buckley, "his extraordinary integrity and sense
of justice." During the term he served in the House (before he was gerrymandered out of office and later defeated in dubious fashion by the

Rooney machine in Brooklyn), he similarly earned the esteem of conservative adversaries.

For Lowenstein this is not a campaign lightly undertaken. He had been defeated before in the same district, known as "safe" Republican territory. His financial resources were sadly limited. He was keenly aware that another setback, no matter how explicable in terms of the unfavorable battleground, would almost certainly be construed as his last hurrah in the conventional political arena (at age 45). There was no issue comparable to Vietnam, which catapulted him into national headlines.

Ironically, however, he has mobilized an infinitely wider degree of support than before. The clearest evidence of its impact is the frenzy of the counter-attack mounted by Wydler's camp. While Wydler has steadfastly refused to engage in direct public debate, his managers have conceded that the contest is now a horse race.

Rocked by Bill Buckley's endorsement of Lowenstein, they hastily produced Sen. Jim Buckley to engage in fraternal argument, but that predictable move primarily underlined the jitters of the Wydler forces. Subsequently they have waged a campaign of smear and fear that may backfire; it is too reminiscent of an era of "dirty tricks."

Thus Lowenstein, for example, has been portrayed as "anti-Israel" because, on complicated votes in the House dealing with the Pentagon budget, he refused to let appropriations for Israel be used as a cover for handouts to oppressive tyrannies. But Sen. Jackson's appearances on Lowenstein's behalf have largely deflated that spurious issue.

Wydler's literature has also branded Lowenstein a "professional agitator" guilty of seeking to return to Congress "so he can travel around the country looking for ways to foment discord." It is, in fact, a matter of record that in his crusade to end the U.S. involvement in Vietnam, Lowenstein was the frequent target of ultra-leftist attack because he firmly rejected tactics of violence and disruption.

But he admittedly cannot plead innocent to the charge that he has been deeply involved in great national debates often transcending the immediacies of the district. He has never viewed the affairs of Nassau County's 5th C.D. as separable from the state and fate of the nation.

Wydler certainly cannot be accused of any comparable vision. He has been a mediocre, largely inaudible Congressman through seven dull terms. In larger affairs he may be remembered most for his last-ditch apologies for Richard Nixon long after most men had recognized that the moment of truth had arrived. He was similarly slow-witted about detecting the dimensions of the Vietnam disaster.

A journalistic footnote to the contest seems warranted, especially in view of the closeness of the race.

Some time ago *Newsday* announced (in conformity with a decision of its parent corporation, the Los Angeles Times) that it would abandon the practice of endorsing candidates. Its explanation was that editorial neutrality was vital to public confidence in its news columns.

My own view at that time was that the decision was a form of abdication. It seems to me a newspaper's responsibility is to declare itself where it believes real issues have been drawn. The notion that a failure to endorse insures the incorruptibility of news reports is at once an innocence and a pretension.

But even if non-endorsement remains a matter of policy at *Newsday* (the *Long Island Press* has endorsed Lowenstein) the level of Wydler's campaign and his flight from debate are surely valid subjects of comment—especially in a newspaper that has often generalized about lofty campaign standards. When does "neutrality" become absurdity?

The "rare coalition" was not enough to carry the district. A late deluge of charges that Lowenstein supported "unilateral disarmament," "campus radical movements," and assorted subversive activities had an enormous impact. Although these two races were the closest ever waged against Wydler in the district, they failed to return Lowenstein to Congress.

SUPPRESSED EVIDENCE OF MORE THAN ONE ASSASSIN?

Saturday Review, February 19, 1977

The test-firing of Sirhan Sirhan's gun in 1975 marked a short-lived high point in the efforts to reopen the Robert Kennedy assassination case. But over the ensuing months, serious evidence against the official theory of the case continued to build. Early in 1977, Lowenstein reviewed the record and argued for renewed inquiry.

One day in the summer of 1973 I agreed to meet in Los Angeles with some people who insisted that Robert F. Kennedy had not been killed by Sirhan Sirhan acting alone. Nothing seemed clearer to me at that time than the absurdity of this notion. Everyone had *seen* Sirhan shooting at Senator Kennedy, and at Sirhan's trial his lawyers had argued only about his mental condition, not the accuracy of his firing.

That I went to any meeting about any assassination was due primarily to the persistence of Robert Vaughn, the star of a popular TV spy series called *The Man from U.N.C.L.E.* But even my esteem for Robert Vaughn couldn't totally wash away a furtive and unworthy suspicion that maybe he had hopes of transporting a successful dramatic role onto the duller stage of real life.

The truth is that I finally went to that first meeting chiefly because in my closed-mindedness I believed that spending half an hour with people who had gone gaga about the Robert Kennedy case would both prove my open-mindedness and help me persuade a good man to avoid further involvement in such foolishness.

That afternoon at Robert Vaughn's house I saw the autopsy report and discovered that Robert Kennedy had been hit from *behind* by bullets fired at point-blank range—that is, from a distance of several inches or less. I thought I remembered that Sirhan had been *facing* Senator Kennedy and had shot him from a distance of several *feet*, so I assumed that either the autopsy report or my memory was in error. I soon learned that neither was.

The police report agreed with the coroner about the range (point-blank) and direction (from behind) of the bullets that hit Senator Kennedy; so I proceeded through the grand-jury and trial records, searching for testimony that placed Sirhan's gun to the rear and within inches of Kennedy. There was none. The distance mentioned most frequently was two to three feet. Eyewitnesses can be depended on to be unreliable, but this information was unsettling: it seemed unlikely that everyone could be wrong about something so visible and significant as the difference between inches and feet. I set out to talk to the eyewitnesses in person: maybe, I thought, the transcripts were misleading, or maybe the witnesses were uncertain or confused. Not so. Everything was consistent with the earlier testimony, and people were emphatic about what they had seen. All the eyewitnesses thought it was wacky to doubt that Sirhan had killed Kennedy—*until they heard what was in the autopsy report.* Few of them thought so afterward.

My involvement in the RFK case had started late; it now developed slowly, pushed along by discoveries and events that made no sense, things that could not be explained by established facts or old theories. Early skeptics like Lillian Castellano, Ted Charach, Jonn Christian, Gerard Alcan, and Betsy Langman introduced me to an assortment of questions raised by the official version of the case, the most puzzling of which had to do with the physical evidence.

A firearms expert named William Harper had executed an affidavit asserting among other things that the relatively undamaged bullet removed from Senator Kennedy's neck could not be matched to Sirhan's gun (a conclusion to be confirmed four and a half years later by a panel of other experts). That was disturbing enough, but I was most troubled by the question of how many bullets had been fired. Sirhan's gun could fire only eight shots; if there had been more than eight fired, there had to be more than one gun, and arguments about whether bullets matched or did not match would then become superfluous.

Seven bullets had been recovered during surgery, one from each of the five bystanders who were hit and two from Senator Kennedy. Another bullet had entered Senator Kennedy's back and exited through his chest, and still another had passed through the right shoulder pad of his jacket (the left sleeve of his suit disappeared sometime after the shooting).

In addition, three bullet holes were found by the police in ceiling tiles that had subsequently been removed and booked into evidence, and there were indications of still other bullet holes in doorframes that had also been removed and booked. One thing at least was certain: if all the holes in the tiles were entry holes, at least ten bullets must have been fired. Nobody could add seven to three and get eight.

I did not want to add to the public controversy about the case, so I went to Joe Busch, then the district attorney of Los Angeles County, with a list of questions about specific problems that seemed troublesome. I assumed the DA's office would be able to give satisfactory explanations. In fact, I felt a little as if I were about to discuss unfounded fears about flying saucers with scientists who could lay the fears to rest. It became clear early in that first session, however, that my fears were not about flying saucers, and that they were not being laid to rest.

The official response to my questions was as peculiar as the contradictions in the evidence. As I remarked later on, every official I saw at the DA's office was polite and talked about cooperation, but nobody did anything much with my list except periodically to request another copy.

When a question was answered at all, the answer often turned out to be untrue—not marginally untrue, but enthusiastically, aggressively, and sometimes quite imaginatively untrue. I was not prepared for that, and I was to waste a lot of time before I realized that Ron Ziegler himself might have gawked at some of the statements that officials were making about the case—not just to me, but to the public as well.

As events moved on, I found that propaganda campaigns were being concocted that peddled the precise reverse of the facts. Two of these were especially daring and effective: it was repeated constantly that "every eyewitness" had seen Sirhan kill Kennedy (so how could any rational person doubt that he had done it?); and it was said almost as frequently that there was "only one gun" in the hotel pantry where Kennedy was shot (so how could anyone have fired a second?)—this de-

245

spite the fact that everyone connected with the case, if very few other people, knew that there was at least one other gun in the precise area from which the bullets that hit Kennedy were fired.

Joe Busch simply took to announcing the opposite of whatever facts didn't fit. In this spirit he said on the *Tomorrow* show: "Every eyewitness that you talk to, *every* eyewitness . . . there is nobody that disputes that he [Sirhan] put that gun up to the Senator's ear and he fired in there. I then asked him to name one such witness, and he replied: "Would you like Mr. Uecker, the man that grabbed his arm? Would you like any of the fifty-five witnesses?"

When John Howard, a less flamboyant personality, became acting district attorney, he claimed only "twenty to twenty-five" corroborating witnesses. Pressed to name one of this formidable collection, he also cited Uecker.

I could not imagine why Busch had selected Karl Uecker as what he called his "star witness," since Uecker's testimony about the matters in dispute not only contradicted the official position but had been repeated several times. Could he have changed his mind since 1968 about what he had seen then? And if he had changed his mind, why had he?

Karl Uecker was indeed a key witness, perhaps *the* key, the only person who was standing between Kennedy and Sirhan when the shooting began, the man who, as Busch put it, "grabbed his arm"—the imprecise "his" being applicable both to Kennedy (before the shooting started) and Sirhan (after).

Uecker had gone back to Germany some years before, and perhaps it was assumed that would put him out of reach. When I located him and was en route to see him for the first time I found myself hoping he would uphold the official story and thus confirm what Busch and Howard were saying about him. If he did that without apparent duress, what a great relief it would be—a kind of justification for accepting other official explanations; furthermore, the implications of the alternative were particularly unpleasant to me.

Karl Uecker turned out to be a solid, intelligent man. His recollections were unwavering, consistent with his grand-jury and trial testimony, and explicit: "I told the authorities that Sirhan never got close enough for a point-blank shot, never." It irritated him that he was being misquoted, but he felt that nothing could come of my efforts: "It was decided long ago," Uecker said, "that it was to stop with Sirhan, and that is what will happen." He reconstructed the sequence of events in the pantry for myself and two reporters from the West German magazine *Stern*, and it emerged that he is utterly certain that Sirhan had fired only two shots when he, Uecker, pushed Sirhan down onto a steam table.

And that, for Karl Uecker, is that. At least four bullets hit Kennedy; if Sirhan was on the steam table after firing two shots, he could not have fired all four of these shots, since that would have required him to put the other two bullets into Kennedy from behind, at point-blank range, while struggling on a steam table several feet in front of the Senator and with a distraught crowd flailing around between them.

The Uecker statements went virtually unreported except in *Stern* magazine. They had, therefore, limited impact on public opinion in the United States. They had no impact whatever on officials in Los Angeles, who still quote Karl Uecker as their star witness. But then, they have been unable to find another credible witness to quote, and it is unlikely that anyone will go to Germany to check with Uecker again.

The Uecker flimflam was modest compared to the official handling of the eight-bullets problem.

There was a period of confusion after I asked how so few bullets had caused so much damage, but eventually I was informed that a bullet had penetrated a ceiling tile, bounced off the floor above, ricocheted back down through a second tile, and ended up in Elizabeth Evans Young's head. What complicates this proposition is that Mrs. Young, who was some 20 feet down the pantry from the shooting, had lost her shoe at about the time the shooting began. She had stooped over to put it on when the bullet entered her forehead, traveling *upward* into her scalp, where some of it remained even after surgery.

But even if the Young bullet had achieved everything ascribed to it, there remained the shot that went through Senator Kennedy's shoulder pad, the shot that exited through his chest, and the third bullet hole in a ceiling tile, a hole that meant the eighth and unrecovered bullet had to be "lost in the ceiling interspace" (as the official summary put it), unless, as I commented at the time, a bullet went up through one tile, bounced off the floor above, came back down through a second tile, and then decided in midair to go back up and make a third hole.

And if Sirhan's eighth bullet was "lost in the ceiling interspace," there were no bullets left to be found anywhere else. Which brings us to the problem of the doorframes.

On June 5, 1968, the Associated Press sent out a photo of two policemen pointing to a door "near Kennedy shooting scene." According to the caption on the picture, a "bullet is still in the wood."

Few people could have known at that time the potential import of that photo. It was ignored in the turbulence of events and might have gone unnoticed if it had not been for a remarkable Los Angeles institution named Lillian Castellano. From the moment Mrs. Castellano read the wirephoto caption she began telling everyone who would listen that if a bullet had been found in a doorframe, there had to be at least nine bullets. She and an associate named Floyd Nelson wrote an article pressing this point, and it appeared in the May 23, 1969, *Los Angeles Free Press.* Two weeks later, a local reporter asked Evelle Younger, then district attorney of Los Angeles and now attorney general of California, about the photo and its implications. Younger promised that "tons of information over at the LAPD [Los Angeles Police Department]" were going to be "made available."

But nothing relevant had been "made available" to anyone four years after that, and I therefore attached a copy of the wirephoto to the list of questions I submitted to the authorities. Question II-3 read: "Who are the police in the AP wirephoto examining bullet in 'doorframe'? Why did they say there was a bullet there if there wasn't one?" It tells a lot about my state of mind at the time that I accepted the official assurance that the policemen had been misquoted in the photo caption. When repeated requests for a study of the doorframes ran into unpersuasive evasions, I was irritated at what I took to be bureaucratic delays rather than suspicious motives. And that is where the matter rested for almost two years.

Then, in the summer of 1975, Paul Schrade, a close friend of Senator Kennedy and one of the bystanders who had been shot on the night of June 4, 1968, brought an action for damages against Sirhan and anyone else who might have been involved in the shooting in the hotel's pantry area ("Does 1-50," as California legal terminology puts it). Schrade was represented in this action by former assistant district attorney Vincent Bugliosi and myself. This procedure was designed to get the investigation of the RFK case "out of politics and into the courtroom"—a step long advocated by officials who refused to do anything to reopen the case through more accessible channels.

The county board of supervisors, prodded by a feisty, public-spirited member named Baxter Ward, joined in the effort to get a court to accept jurisdiction, and eventually seven experts impaneled by Judge Robert

Wenke of the Los Angeles superior court conducted a series of tests on firearms involved in the case. The experts then answered some questions, added mystery to others, and concluded that on the basis of tests conducted to date they could neither support nor preclude the presence of a second gun. Beyond that, their opinions varied widely. They disagreed among themselves about two thirds of their findings and tended to disagree as well on how to interpret what they did find.

But they unanimously reached one conclusion that must have rattled the authorities, at least until it was clear that almost nobody had noticed it: the panel agreed that there was no possible way to determine whether the bullets recovered from the victims had or had not been fired from Sirhan's gun. What this meant in plain English was that DeWayne Wolfer, the LAPD criminalist, had sworn to an impossibility when he had testified under oath at Sirhan's trial that the bullets had to have been fired by Sirhan's gun.

A finding by these nationally recognized firearms experts that a critical part of the testimony of the LAPD firearms expert could not have been true has implications that go far beyond the RFK case. But its significance in the RFK case is not obscure either.

Most of the panel said or implied that, on balance, the absence of specific evidence of a second gun decreased the likelihood of two people having fired in the pantry. On the other hand, the expert selected by CBS, which was one of the parties to the litigation, was perhaps the best-known member of the panel. He testified under oath that the question of a second gun was "more open" now than it had been before the tests, a conclusion that, for whatever reason, not even his employer saw fit to report. And all the experts agreed that if there were evidence of *more than eight bullets*, matching or failing to match bullets could not reduce below two the number of guns involved. But the panel was not allowed to hear about, let alone study, material dealing with the number of bullets fired.

It was after this standoff and while the Schrade matter was still in court that Bugliosi located the policemen in the wirephoto. It turned out that neither of the officers knew he was supposed to have been misquoted by the AP photographer, and both still believed they had been pointing at a bullet in the doorframe. This bullet, they thought, had been "removed" soon after the photo was taken.

The official reaction to these developments may seem a bit odd for men who kept announcing their determination to do everything possible to resolve doubts about Senator Kennedy's murder. The LAPD suddenly leaped into action and caught one of the policemen in time to dissuade him from executing an affidavit; and the next day the representatives of the district attorney and the state attorney general cooked up such a procedural storm in the courtroom that the policemen could not be subpoenaed to testify under oath.

All this activity generated some publicity about the question of bullets in doorframes, and soon four more reputable individuals materialized who had seen, or thought they had seen, bullets or bullet holes in doorframes shortly after the assassination. One of these was the maître d' of the Ambassador Hotel, a man with substantial military experience. Presently, a fifth witness came up with the news that he had heard police officers discussing the removal of a bullet from a doorframe.

Apparently none of this aroused the curiousity of those charged with law enforcement in Los Angeles, despite the fact that the doorframes had been booked into evidence, presumably for some *reason*. I finally inquired if someone in the LAPD had taken to collecting doorframes as a hobby.

And then, as new information stretched the dimensions of possible useful inquiry, the new district attorney and the former district attorney of Los Angeles moved together to extinguish the judicial proceeding that for years their office had insisted was the only legitimate way to inquire into the case. "We shouldn't bury any kinds of questions that are raised," proclaimed the new district attorney, John Van de Kamp, as he sought to dismiss the matter from court. "There are plenty of bodies that can continue to follow that inquiry."

As part of the effort to quash the court proceedings, Attorney General Younger's office had objected to proposals of some of the firearms experts that further tests be conducted at the scene of the crime. Use of the Ambassador Hotel pantry for any investigation, the attorney general's office warned Judge Wenke, would constitute "an egregious invasion of the rights of private property," one that should not and legally could not be permitted.

Seven days later, on December 10, 1975, several assistant district attorneys and a score of police officers, accompanied by much of the LA press corps and a search warrant, arrived at the Ambassador "to search the pantry area for bullets or bullet holes which might be evidence in the murder of Robert Kennedy." To this end, it was announced that the search would concentrate on doorframes, key parts of which had been replaced more than seven years before, after the originals had been removed by officers of the LAPD!

"The significance of the examination, as far as I am concerned," Deputy District Attorney Stephen Trott said of the pantry raid, "is the fact that it again shows that we are taking every step to unturn, as Mr. Van de Kamp said, every stone in this case to get to whatever bottom there may be in this continuing matter."

"No other bullets were found last night," an official spokesman announced the next day and was quoted deadpan in the media. It was nowhere commented that to locate "other" bullets or bullet holes at that time in that place would have been remarkable indeed.

Of course a more sensible way to settle these questions might have been to conduct the standard scientific tests customarily used in such situations on the doorframes and tiles then presumably in police custody. The requests for such tests that had been addressed to the police, the district attorney, and the Los Angeles police commission for several years got nowhere until August 1975, when a number of public officials began to wonder out loud why the bullet-holes issue could not be resolved by suitable tests. It was then revealed that the frames and tiles could not be tested because *they no longer existed.* There were a variety of explanations for the fact that they had been destroyed (one official said they couldn't fit in the filing cabinets available), but the date of the destruction was set as June 30, 1969—a date shortly after Lillian Castellano's article had appeared and Evelle Younger had promised that "tons" of material would be "made available."

The fact that these items no longer existed and the fact that that fact had been concealed was troublesome at best, but the statement that they had been destroyed *in 1969* raised an additional difficulty: the report of a police board of inquiry in 1971 stated that "an inspection of the ceiling tiles removed from the pantry" had refuted a tangential claim about bullet angles. It has yet to be explained how such an inspection could have refuted anything if the tiles had been destroyed two years before.

In late 1975 one Thomas Kranz, the district attorney's special counsel for the RFK case, wrote a report in which, among other things, he commented on the destruction of the doorframes, ceiling tiles, and various critical documents that had also turned up missing. Special Counsel Kranz, who was paid by public funds, says he submitted his report to the DA more than a year ago. In a lengthy preview that appeared in March

1976 in the *Los Angeles Times* Kranz supported the official conclusions, but proceeded to describe the LAPD's scientific research as "sloppy," denounce the destruction of "potential evidence" as "wrong" and "idiotic," and complain that "a major aspect of the prosecution's case . . . isn't substantially documented."

The Kranz report may have met the same fate as the doorframes and ceiling tiles. In any case, it is still not available. People who ask for it now are told that it is being "revised," and that the new version will be available in "a week or two." It is not clear when the original version will be available, or why it was necessary to spend a year "revising" it after the man who wrote it had retired to private practice.

Meanwhile, the significance of another group of remarkable documents has somehow been lost in the shuffle. Dr. Robert Joling, past president of the American Academy of Forensic Sciences, has released the reports of the FBI agents who examined the pantry area after the assassination. These reports were obtained by Bernard Fensterwald, a Washington attorney, under the provisions of the Freedom of Information Act and include photographs of doorframes with what the FBI agents describe at least twice as "bullet holes."

Perhaps these photographs did not startle law-enforcement officials in Los Angeles, who tended to boast about exchanging information "freely" with the FBI during the investigation. But if they knew about the FBI reports all along, the concealing of the knowledge is not reassuring.

So we have reached a stalemate. It has been very hard to get information against the wishes of a wily, uncompromising, and entrenched law-enforcement establishment supported by the only newspaper of general influence in the community. But no reasonable person who knows the facts can now profess to believe that the question of who murdered Robert Kennedy has been resolved. There are too many gaps and inconsistencies in the evidence, too much covered up for too long by those who should have been most eager to pursue leads instead of ignoring or concealing them.

Despite all the obstacles, new facts have come out about what FBI agents, policemen, and other reputable persons said about the matter of bullets in doorframes, and it seems fair in view of these facts to say that there is now a rebuttable presumption that more than one assassin was involved. But what is even clearer than that is that nobody is making a serious effort to rebut that presumption. The notion seems to be that the presumption can be waited out, that unanswered questions will fade, given time, and that the best way to deal with awkward new facts is to ignore them until they can be denounced as "nothing new" and then dismissed; as if awkward facts somehow become less awkward or less pertinent with age.

There were people who kept advising Richard Nixon during Watergate that if he would just tell everything, everything would be all right. By the time he left office, presumably everyone except Rabbi Korff and Julie Eisenhower understood that this was not exactly so.

I do not know why those responsible for law enforcement in Los Angeles decided to stonewall the RFK case. But once they had made that decision, the rest followed: facts had to be concealed or distorted and inconvenient evidence done away with; inoperative statements had to be replaced by new statements, until they in turn became inoperative; people raising awkward questions had to be discredited, preferably as self-seeking or flaky.

"If you listen to these idiots long enough," Joe Busch once announced, "they'll convince you that John Wilkes Booth didn't really kill Abraham Lincoln." An LAPD spokesman with a gift for simplicity tried to dismiss questions with the explanation that the "TV footage" of the shooting resolved any honest doubts, apparently assuming that nobody else would realize that no such footage exists.

The behavior of the police commission may be even less excusable than that of the LAPD and the office of the district attorney. The police commissioners are estimable and independent people, appointed by the mayor, who have no vested interest in the original investigation. They do, however, have jurisdiction over much of the critical material, as well as specific responsibility for the integrity and competence of overall police operations. And they have the stature and authority to act on their own initiative.

Even the Warren Commission published most of the exhibits on which its conclusions about the assassination of President Kennedy were based. The police commission, on the other hand, has refused access to anything in the ten volumes collected in the RFK case, despite the flow of pronouncements by high officials that all relevant information, including the "work product" of the investigation, would be made public.

The commission invoked high principles about civil liberties in detecting a threat to the "right of privacy" in proposals for testing physical objects within its jurisdiction, but the discovery that these same objects had been illicitly destroyed aroused no discernible interest. At one point, in a flurry of responsiveness to public pressures, the commission announced that it would accept and reply to written questions, but that announcement stands as the only reply that has been given to any question. Whatever its motives, the commission has lent a kind of respectability to the cover-up, and it has done so with a clumsy arrogance that leads one to wonder if it took lessons from the Hapsburgs, who are said to have ruled Austria by tyranny tempered only by incompetence.

I began my activities in this case with no doubt at all that the authorities would be as eager as anyone else to investigate any legitimate questions that might arise. I persisted in that belief, and kept acting on it, long after there was any basis for it. But there comes a time when official dissembling should impel everyone else to pursue the unanswered questions with more vigor than ever. The American people should have learned that from the events of the past four years.

I do not know whether Sirhan acting alone murdered Robert Kennedy. I do know what happened when we tried to find out. Eventually, reluctantly, against all my instincts and wishes, I arrived at the melancholy thought that people who have nothing to hide do not lie, cheat, and smear to hide it.

It is possible that the small numbers of people in key places who have worked to head off inquiries and cover up facts have done so simply because their reputations or careers are at stake; but the fact that this is a possibility does not make it acceptable to allow the situation to rest as it is, for there are other possibilities, too.

For a long time now, we have been trying to explain that what commands the reexamination of the Kennedy and King murders is not ghoulish curiosity, or vengefulness about dishonesty or incompetence, or devotion to abstract concepts of justice, or sentimentalism about the men who died, but simply the urgent question of whether disasters may loom ahead that could be averted if we found out more about disasters past.

Years have been squandered in ugly stupid brawling about whether to face legitimate questions about seminal events. One result is that some people have come to see conspiracies everywhere, and some invent them where they can't see them. Some who have poked around these skeletons for a long time have capsized somewhere along the way into a kind of permanent overwroughtness that makes them easy to ridicule. Matters that require dispassion and open minds have become polarized, while everything hangs in limbo and suspicions keep oozing around that things are more sinister than may actually be the case. It may turn out that the hardest part of dealing with the new realities of the arrangement and use of power in America is to modify our sense of what America is without modifying the sense of what it can and should be.

Sensible people keep asking if it is really worth the time and effort to dig into the difficult past in this difficult way. Some time ago, near the beginning of this long journey, I tried to explain my own reason for pressing ahead. "Assassinations of national figures are not ordinary murders," I wrote. "When bullets distort or nullify the national will, democracy itself has been attacked. When a series of such events changes the direction of the nation and occurs under suspicious circumstances, institutions seem compromised or corrupted and democratic process itself undermined." It was Robert Kennedy's special gift that he understood the new realities of power in this country and could make people believe that if they roused themselves to the effort they could, as he liked to put it, "reclaim America." Perhaps that helps explain why the pain of his loss remains so great after so long a time.

We have made a good start toward preventing the repetition of some past abuses of power, especially government abuses, because we have learned about those abuses and have set out to guard against them. But there are other abuses we cannot yet guard against because we do not yet know enough about them to know *how* to guard against them. It seems elementary, for example, that if groups do exist that can eliminate national figures and get away with it, they are unlikely to spring into existence only on occasions of state murders: How are they occupied between-times?

James R. Hoffa did not vanish after a rendezvous with a James Earl Ray "acting alone," loose nuts did not do in the Yablonskis, new editions of Lee Harvey Oswald or Sirhan Sirhan did not murder Sam Giancana in the basement of his home while he was under twenty-four-hour guard by the FBI. It is time to accept the fact that the question is not whether groups with such power exist, but how these groups use their power, who their allies are—in and out of government—and what if anything can be done to protect democratic process against forces and alliances that operate out of sight and often beyond the limits set by the law.

That is a fitting question for the elected representatives of the people

255

to deal with, since nothing less than the strength of government of, by, and for the people rides on the answer. And finding out all we can about the assassinations is an important part of trying to answer that question.

When finally released in 1977, the Kranz Report criticized the official investigation, but generally supported its conclusions. Soon afterward, Lowenstein, Schrade, and Joling provided a point-by-point rebuttal to the document in testimony before the Los Angeles Board of Supervisors. Though pressed into other arenas, Lowenstein continued to monitor the case. Additional disturbing evidence has since emerged, but no public agency has actively pursued it.

IS THERE HOPE FOR THE U.N. AFTER ALL?

William F. Buckley, Jr.

Washington Star, March 15, 1977

Following Jimmy Carter's election, Lowenstein was approached by long-time friend Andrew Young to become the U.S. representative to the United Nations Commission on Human Rights.

He regarded the offer with a mixture of interest and skepticism. On the one hand, he respected Carter's general foreign-policy intentions and was impressed by his campaign emphasis on human rights. Moreover, as a friend and admirer of Young, he was hopeful about the impact the new U.N. ambassador could have on U.S. policy, especially in the Third World. On the other hand, he was uncertain about the chances of reversing the recent decline in U.N. effectiveness. He was also wary about his ability to operate usefully in the slow-moving State Department bureaucracy. Ultimately, though, he concluded that the chance to help press for major foreign-policy reforms deserved at least a fair test.

The annual plenary session of the Commission on Human Rights was held in Geneva in February and March 1977. The commission itself had seldom been a body of great importance or impact, but its charter suggested much greater potential. Before the conference convened, the Carter human-rights policy had been broadly articulated but not specifically applied in an international forum. Lowenstein had that chance, and he left the meeting feeling that some new ground had been broken in the struggle to find specific openings for effective human-rights diplomacy. Soon after his return, William F. Buckley, Jr., examined the developments in Geneva.

In Geneva every year for about one month, a body called the Commission on Human Rights meets for the purpose—one would assume on surveying its historical record—of reiterating its disapproval of South Africa, Chile and Israel. To the astonishment of the nations assembled, our representative this year, Mr. Allard Lowenstein, brought up the subject of human rights violated elsewhere, specifically in the Soviet Union and in Uganda.

For a couple of convulsive weeks the Commission was agitated by this fracture of complacency. It looked as though it might actually be forced to take a vote on the possibility of an inquiry into the human rights situation in the Soviet Union, which has been protected from such impertinencies by the perpetual hostility of the vast Soviet enterprise toward any country that tells the truth about it; and Uganda, protected by the fraternal solidarity of the Third World, which suspects that any criticism of any of its members is a criticism of them all.

It is disappointing to record that, in the end, the initiatives were blocked, or more specifically withdrawn, by their sponsors. But several points are worth making.

In the opinion of Mr. Lowenstein, huge strides were made. *Le Monde*, which appears to be the historian of the Commission on Human Rights, recorded that Mr. Lowenstein's initiative was the first taken at the prospective expense of the Soviet Union in the Commission's history over the past two decades.

Mr. Lowenstein, a folk hero of the American liberal-left for his captaincy of the movement to unseat Lyndon Johnson in 1968, has always been a consistent anti-totalitarian. He arrived in Geneva sharing the almost universal despondency over the possibilities of achieving anything through that vermiform appendix, the Commission on Human Rights, whose function has been the ritual denunciation of the conventional enemies of the dominant coalition of forces. That he succeeded in persuading a majority merely to discuss probing the Soviet Union's war on human rights may not strike us as much of an accomplishment. But there is no question that it is a step in the right direction.

Mr. Lowenstein pointed out that the Third World is not the only concentration of parliamentary cowardice. When time came to vote the usual condemnation of Israel—as a genocidal, totalitarian, imperialist, colonialist, war-loving power—the United States argued quite correctly against the resolution. But what did our western allies do? They sat on their hands. Why? Because they are afraid of displeasing the Arab world.

Mr. Lowenstein's point: Those of us quick to criticize the pusillanimity of the Third World, which is fearful of antagonizing the Soviet Union and its own confederates within the Third World, should pause over the behavior of west European countries. To be sure, they abstained, declining to vote against Israel. But they did not reject the preposterous arguments leveled against Israel. Have we any right to expect more courageous behavior from Kenya than, say, from West Germany?

Mr. Lowenstein infers from the experience of the past four weeks that the machinery of the United Nations might yet be revived to good ends. It is of course too early to say—for one thing, we cannot know whether Mr. Carter's enthusiasm for human rights as an objective of U.S. policy can survive *realpolitik*. . . .

HUMAN RIGHTS AND AMERICAN FOREIGN POLICY

Congressional Testimony,

May 19, 1977

After his return from Geneva, Lowenstein continued his diplomatic work at the U.S. Mission to the United Nations. In May, he testified in Congress on the meeting of the UN Commission on Human Rights, as well as the overall role of human rights in American foreign policy.

Mr. Fraser. Today the subcommittee [Subcommittee on International Organizations] is considering the recent session of the United Nations 33d Commission on Human Rights which was held in Geneva from February 7 through March 11, as well as other developments which have occurred subsequently.

At the Commission session, a number of issues of special concern to this subcommittee were considered, including the procedures for reviewing human rights complaints, as well as the human rights situations in southern Africa, Chile, the Soviet Union, the occupied territories in the Middle East, and Uganda. . . .

We are delighted to have as today's witness the Honorable Allard Lowenstein, U.S. Representative to the United Nations 33d Commission on Human Rights. Mr. Lowenstein served as a Member of the House with great distinction and has long been actively engaged in the defense of human rights both in this country and abroad. It was a great personal pleasure for me when I learned that Mr. Lowenstein was appointed as our representative to the Commission. . . .

Mr. Lowenstein. I am grateful for the chance to appear before a subcommittee chaired by Don Fraser, who is one of the few public figures who gets better the better you know him. His presence in Congress is a national blessing, and his chairmanship of this subcommittee is proof that even the committee structure of the House of Representatives can produce dazzling results now and then. . . .

Perhaps the most useful way to proceed would be for me to begin by saying a few things about what I learned in Geneva, and to indicate some of the significant things that happened that nobody expected to happen. I think there are important lessons in our experience in Geneva that ought to be understood in shaping American policies about human rights, and in working out our attitudes toward international agencies and toward the United Nations itself.

I went to the meeting of the Human Rights Commission with a sense that I think is shared by most Americans who follow these things—the sense that it was a rather hopeless endeavor, that the Human Rights Commission was part of an international machinery that has come to be increasingly hostile to the United States and certainly increasingly irrelevant to human rights. I expected to encounter a kind of monolithic bloc structure that would keep useful discussion to a minimum and produce propaganda at escalating decibels on questions which are mostly designed to further particular ideological interests.

In short, I didn't go there with any notion that there would be much useful we could do for human rights or for specific concerns of the U.S. Government.

I was wrong about that. The results of the Geneva meeting are much less important, if you measure them by specifics, than if you measure them by what they show is possible in international meetings if we understand the complexities and are committed to a quest for ways to maximize cooperation without abandoning our basic convictions. We have tended at some points in the past to wander between withdrawal and a sort of bellicose self-righteousness. Neither of these seem to me the most useful approach.

By any objective yardstick, some useful things happened in Geneva. But much more important was the discovery that President Carter's approach to human rights, the support for that position by the Secretary of State, and the remarkable achievements of our Ambassador to the United Nations, Andrew Young, have made a different atmosphere possible. Disagreements don't disappear but they don't have to preclude finding areas of cooperation. And I must say that I found greater candor than has always been customary in trying to deal with problems which have for a long time been trapped in a quarrelsome impasse.

So my sense of Geneva, Mr. Chairman, is that it was an example in miniature, and under rather difficult circumstances, of what can be achieved in the new period now starting. It was much more hopeful than I expected. Clearly the distance covered was small compared to the distance that needs to be covered. But the fact that that kind of beginning was achieved suggests that the notion that we are unable to work effectively in international organizations for the goals that are part of our heritage and that are set out in the charter and Universal Declaration of Human Rights is not correct. Something very much more hopeful is correct, and it is up to us to use that opportunity as effectively as we can, understanding that there are risks in any human activity and that we will make mistakes as we go along.

But not to try to utilize that opportunity at all would be the greatest mistake and would, above all, increase the great risk of wasting this moment. Another such moment may not come anytime soon, and it would be a terrible mistake not to try to reverse the disintegration of the world community and the increased irrelevance of multilateral agencies to many of the problems that afflict human beings everywhere. This effort should be a high priority of any government that understands what technology has done to the world and what the pressure of injustice does to people exposed to it.

I believe that Congress and the administration can cooperate, that we have a coalition of domestic political concerns that can come together to work in unity on issues where we were divided for some years. I think basic division is no longer necessary on questions of direction and purpose.

There will always be disagreement among people who have independent judgments about tactics and degrees of activity here or there, but I think there is a chance to sculpt an approach to foreign policy that will have very broad support involving human rights as a major component. Human rights can't be the only component, of course, since other factors must affect foreign policy decisions. But the new approach can include a much greater effort in the U.N. Human Rights Commission and other international bodies, and much more effective moral leadership generally to decrease human suffering than we have provided in some years past.

Finally, let me mention how lucky I was in the quality of the people who were my associates in the U.S. delegation in Geneva. Warren Hewitt, and Lois Matteson, who is in the U.S. Mission to the United Nations; Brady Tyson, who is also serving there; and Gloria Gaston, who is in the Mission in Geneva, were all tremendously helpful, really quite wonderful people.

I think everyone in the delegation came to respect the contributions of everybody else. The total effect was greater than the sum of the individual parts.

Mr. Fraser. Well, thank you for that overview of the experience that you had. If you are willing, maybe we could sort of start with some elementary facts just to help me, because I don't remember these things very well.

The U.N. Commission of Human Rights does not include all countries. It has a limited membership. Do you remember what the size of the membership is approximately?

Mr. Lowenstein. Thirty-two countries are elected from ECOSOC, the Economic and Social Council of the United Nations. The United States has just been reelected to the Human Rights Commission in the voting at ECOSOC, and we will continue to be a member of the Human Rights Commission. . . .

Mr. Fraser. Now, what happened [at the Commission meeting] with respect to Israel?

Mr. Lowenstein. The first thing that happened was that an outrageous telegram was sent to Israel regarding conditions in the occupied territories, particularly in the prisons.

The text of the telegram contained assertions and conclusions that went far beyond anything that there was any evidence to support, and we opposed it in rather a novel way—we argued specific content and tried to get a debate going, instead of just reading a formal statement of protest and dissent.

We agreed that the Commission had an obligation to discuss conditions in the occupied territories, and proposed a wording for the telegram which we could have supported. Our wording was rejected, and most of the debating against the telegram as put before the Commission was left to us. Many Western European countries remained virtually silent on this question.

Now, I may sound Pollyanaish, but it is my view that had we discussed the Middle East later in the session instead of as the first item, some of the attitudinal changes might have carried over even to the Middle East discussion. Be that as it may, there was a brisk debate in which we spoke as strongly as we could against the dominant view.

Despite that—I would almost say partly because of that—we were able to work quite well on other issues with some of the most militant supporters of the opposite position. I think the understanding that developed as a result of the frankness of our disagreement over the Middle East resolution was useful in developing working relationships. In fact that was my experience in general at Geneva, not just on the Israel issue.

I think being very clear about what we believed in was tactically as well as morally right. We didn't duck controversy, which I believe added to the effectiveness of the U.S. position. We weren't bellicose, but we weren't silent or supine either where fundamental principles were concerned. We were frank about the Soviet Union and ourselves, and we declined to join in the usual lockstep of routine rhetoric. I think our spontaneity helped bring some flexibility to discussions in Commission sessions and to informal talks outside the sessions, some of which were at least as valuable in the effort to change the atmosphere.

So our outspokenness about the Middle East may actually have helped our efforts on other questions, in addition to being right in principle. We made it clear to the Arab countries that we wanted to cooperate with them on other matters, and hoped they felt that way too. But such cooperation could not occur if the price were silence about matters we felt very deeply about. If the Commission were to have any utility for resolving disagreements, disagreements would have to be recognized and discussed. Otherwise, we might as well go home. In short, disagreement on some questions could not be allowed to prevent working together on others.

The same thing was true on the Soviet issue. If we had not pursued the Soviet initiative, we would never have been able to make credible our commitment to universal application of the declaration. We would have looked like we were playing games.

I think that one of the two or three most significant moments of the session occurred when we raised the Soviet issue under Agenda Item No.

11, Detention and Arrest. On that occasion, at a Friday evening session, four Western European and other countries spoke out in support of what we were doing: Canada, Italy, the United Kingdom, and the Federal Republic of Germany. Not a single unaligned member state supported the effort to block the discussion, which was made by Bulgaria on behalf of the Eastern European countries.

It was a moment of rather high drama when, despite the great exertions of the Soviet Ambassador, Valerian Zorin, not one unaligned member of the Human Rights Commission joined the Soviet attack on the American initiative.

That unprecedented situation had a considerable emotional impact, and meant that we would resume the discussion of possible human rights violations in the Soviet Union on Monday morning.

At that meeting we got into the question of specific arrests in the Soviet Union, including the arrests of Orloff, Ginsberg, a Baptist minister named Vins, Dr. Stern, a Jewish activist, and so on. I am convinced that those discussions on Friday night and Monday morning were essential if the atmosphere of the Commission were to be changed and if the U.S. Government's position on human rights were to be credible.

I want specifically to emphasize that point, because there are some generally sensible people who insist that pursuing this question in the Human Rights Commission is somehow counterproductive, either because it jeopardizes some larger notion of détente or, alternatively, because it shows how ineffectual discussion is. I don't think either of those things is true.

It is certainly impossible to achieve détente if the price of détente is to give the Soviet Union immunity from even talking about questions which are of great concern to a very large number of Americans, and which are legitimately a concern of the international community under the charter, the declaration, and the Helsinki Final Act.

Furthermore, I don't see how you can give immunity to the Soviet Union without throwing away a crucial ingredient in the effort to decrease human suffering in the world.

There will always be suffering of course, but to see needless suffering inflicted by governments and be silent about it seems to me unnecessary, unacceptable, and hypocritical. I think it hurts us and hurts the international machinery we talk so much about improving, and it certainly doesn't help people who look to us for moral support when they act with great courage to protest denials of basic human rights.

We tried to be balanced in discussing human rights problems, but we did not try to woo support by abandoning basic convictions. You have to make tradeoffs of course, but those should occur as part of—and not in place of—speaking out for what you believe in.

Mr. Fraser. And the resolutions on Chile—I think there were—I guess they were in the form of asking the subcommission to take action. One was to review consequences of aid to Chile; the second was to consider giving humanitarian, legal, and financial aid to those arrested or forced to leave the country.

What was the U.S. position on that? Do you recall?

Mr. Lowenstein. For the first time, we cosponsored the general resolution on Chile, which was organized by Sweden. That resolution was reasonable, and if we had not cosponsored it we might have been confronted with one that would not have been acceptable to us but which would have had the support of most other delegations.

So we worked with the Swedish delegation to produce an acceptable resolution, and that resolution carried with only Uruguay voting "no."

Our dilemma on human rights issues in Latin America is complicated. Discussing these problems without Latin leadership risks reviving or strengthening anti-gringo emotions, and could produce a reaction that would not help human rights anywhere.

Just as it is clear that Uganda, for example, is dealt with more effectively if Africans take some leadership, dealing with human rights violations in Latin America requires sensitivity to regional, cultural, and historic factors. Spain and Portugal could be helpful in this regard.

None of this means that the United States should be silent about or acquiesce in human rights violations in Latin America. But we will have to accept and understand the force of regionalism at this stage in the evolution of the human rights machinery. The world is at the same point in its history, but every country is at a different point in its own history. So situations vary very greatly regionally, economically, historically. And vary enormously among countries within the same region, as well.

All these matters are complex enough that anyone who thinks the United States can—or should—do the same thing about each country or region, simply hasn't tried to figure out what is effective or reasonable.

I felt that our concern about human rights in Latin America had to be clear in Geneva, but that the extent to which we could press our views depended on finding other countries that would join in and take some leadership. That, of course, is almost a truism which would apply in every part of the world, but the situation is made more difficult for us at this point in Latin America because of the spread of repressiveness there. Once you go beyond Chile, it is not easy to know what priority to set.

For these reasons, we tried to figure out a way to raise general problems of human rights violations rather than to press ahead on single country questions, and the problem of Desaparecidos seemed the most immediately important one.

People don't always want to understand or accept the fact that in the Human Rights Commission there is very little distinction between many of the positions taken by leftist oppressive governments from positions taken by rightist oppressive governments. Beyond ideology, they tend to want to protect themselves—and hence each other—from having too much done about oppression. This produces a coalition of governments that don't want to strengthen the machinery for human rights, that don't want to extend the agenda to include additional countries. Left and right oppressors tend to become allies when faced with the possibility of a spotlight being focused on oppression.

So you are walking through minefields when you try to get countries to work together. In that sense, Chile and South Africa have been helpful to the cause of human rights, because in the case of both Chile and South Africa, enough countries have supported international efforts so precedents have been established for dealing more energetically with other oppressive situations. If you have the precedent, you don't always have the votes, but you have at least a base to argue and build from. . . .

Mr. Fraser. In terms of the way our own Government is organized to address matters that come up at the U.N. commissions and our ability to be effective there, within the inherent constraints [that] exist, do you have any recommendations?

Mr. Lowenstein. Yes. I am not content with the way that the human rights component works its way into foreign policy decisions. I am not even certain that the basic lessons of the Geneva meeting have been understood. One of those lessons, maybe the most important one, is that there is tremendous potential for desirable changes in the world situation at this juncture. The confluence of the remarkable personal achievements of the President and Ambassador Young with a number of other events, including the emergence of democratic governments in India, Portugal, Spain, and Greece, give the first chance in a long time to make progress toward achieving a much more satisfactory atmosphere in the United Nations. That in itself would be useful, but it would also open the door to dealing more hopefully with a lot of very difficult economic and political problems.

In short, I believe that what is called the human rights issue touches on almost everything of consequence, and that this moment in world history, if we use it wisely, could produce some valuable and long-overdue results. But that will require high-level decisions, intelligent use of personnel, and some long-range planning. We might even begin to make the United Nations function in a way that would gain back some support and respect for the United Nations among Americans who have written it off for quite understandable reasons. That could lead to greater support in Congress for funds for aid and development programs and to increasing U.S. influence within the United Nations. And that, in turn, could produce more sensible actions by the United Nations. We might in this way reverse the spiral that has eroded our effectiveness in the United Nations and the United Nations' effectiveness in general. . . .

In any case, as I said before, overhauling the U.N. machinery depends on, and is less pressing than, overhauling attitudes.

Suppose, for instance, the Human Rights Commission met three times as much and all it did was to go back to discussing Israel, South Africa, and Chile. One would sit there wishing one could figure out a way to get everyone to go home.

We have to work to develop an approach that will utilize our enormous resources, private and public, to contribute to a diminution of suffering around the world. That is, after all, what a "human rights" policy should be about, when all is said and done. Structure will follow along.

One starting point, which the President has endorsed would be to ratify the covenants. But we are not going to ratify the covenants if there isn't a major effort to explain why they should be ratified.

Some people are really concerned primarily about the so-called political and civil rights. They believe that with these rights people can get "other" rights. But in much of the world political and civil rights seem quite remote because people don't have enough to eat. Now obviously the urgency of eating does not justify torture. It does justify a great concentration of effort on obtaining and distributing food.

The position we took in Geneva is that there ought to be a prioritizing of concerns about human rights, whether they have been labeled traditionally "political and civil" or "economic and social."

Ambassador Young also talked about setting such priorities both at

ECOSOC and in Guatemala City. But to implement programs dealing with some of these priorities will require much more than the rhetoric which is easier to deliver than the programs.

So just as human rights cannot be the only component in a sensible foreign policy, neither can it be limited to discussions of human rights issues which are then excluded from decisions involving economic policy and other matters affecting social justice.

Mr. Fraser. Mr. Smeeton.

Mr. Smeeton. Thank you, Mr. Chairman. I might preface my question by making an observation. I have before me a press release of the last session that lists the membership of the Commission. And I would say almost three-fourths of the members sitting on the Commission are themselves accused of violating the rights of their own citizens. For example, Uganda, the U.S.S.R., Cuba, and Uruguay are all members. That is a real political irony and helps explain why the Commission frustrated some of your efforts to push more vigorously for inquiries regarding Uganda and the Soviet Union.

Mr. Lowenstein. May I expand a little on what you are saying? Your first impression when you discover that you are sitting near the Minister of Justice of Uganda and the Soviet Ambassador who was in Prague at the time of the coup—as well as other stirring defenders of human rights—is to think that now is the moment to fly to that thin red line of virtue which is somewhere about.

Perhaps it was my experience in the House of Representatives—I don't mean to make invidious comparisons, but one learns in the House of Representatives that human hypocrisy is not unknown in legislative bodies—anyway, if one is to be effective in any legislative process, dwelling on the iniquities of everyone else may be less rewarding than acknowledging one's own iniquities, and then attempting to find common ground that may reach out to something decent, or at least cooperative, in everybody. That approach does not suggest that you should be naive about the hypocrisies and mixed motives that are so prominent in determining what goes on.

Of course in international bodies there are national as well as personal contradictions to take into account. I tried to take that fact into account in my first statement to the Plenary in Geneva. I said that I represented a people who had given the world one of the most electrifying battle cries for human rights in history—that all men are created equal and are endowed by their Creator with certain inalienable rights, among which are life, liberty, and the pursuit of happiness; and I observed that we had given the world this battle cry for liberty at a time when we had slavery. That is a part of our history, I said, which, like the history of every country, is a mixture of glories and tragedies. I said we had better get past the attitude of using everybody else's shortcomings to excuse our own, and try to figure out some way to start moving forward.

So your comment is exactly on point. But if your first thought when you go into a commission meeting is: "My goodness, where are Gilbert and Sullivan?" Your second should be: "How do we get around the fact that governments are the cause of most of the oppression that we have to do something about?" . . .

At one point this year, when the Russians were arguing that we couldn't discuss arrests in the Soviet Union because that would invade their "internal affairs," I reminded everyone that in 1947 the NAACP had come to the Human Rights Commission with a petition about American blacks being segregated and discriminated against. The Soviet Union was very enthusiastic about the Human Rights Commission investigating that; they didn't see any "internal affairs" objection at all. And Mrs. Roosevelt agreed that any people who feel they are being deprived of human rights anywhere ought to have the right to bring their complaint to the Commission, if they follow the proper procedures. I said that the United States had made great progress with its racial problems in 30 years, partly because we have been conscious of the pressure of the rest of the world, which was judging us by what we did about racial injustice in the United States.

I said:

I want to thank you for that help in improving conditions in the United States. While I don't expect the Soviet Union will thank us tonight for assisting them in dealing with some of their human rights problems, perhaps in 30 years they too will perceive that they were very fortunate that there was outside pressure to make them do better.

I think almost everyone now realizes that Mrs. Roosevelt and those who worked with her were right to plow ahead and get to an agreement despite the vocabulary problems and all the other vagaries. . . .

There is one statement I would like to add to the record. I want to say why I think that what Andy Young has been doing has been so enormously important, so valuable for the United States, and to the world for that matter. His personal qualities, I believe, are indispensable to the efforts which have made it possible to hope for better days at the United Nations and in the international community in general. His great warmth and spontaneous candor have broken through the rigor mortis that so often dooms diplomatic activity to irrelevance.

I do not minimize the complications that may be caused by media hoopla over this or that statement, but that is a small price to pay. And that is a topic I would like to discuss with responsible newspeople. For instance, the central drama of our time is not the fact that Brady Tyson uttered two unauthorized sentences in Geneva—sentences which he said were not authorized immediately after he said them. By rational standards, those sentences could have been perceived as worth perhaps three or four lines in the midst of reports about some rather significant other actions that were never reported at all. And if we end up trapped by fear—of occcasional public disagreements, or of flaps in the media—into saying nothing that hasn't been orchestrated by committee and weighed through 16 filtering processes, so nothing is said that doesn't meet high standards of nonspontaneity—don't we sacrifice a great deal more by that kind of restrictiveness than if we accept the virtuoso achievements of people like Ambassador Young and of Senator Moynihan during his tenure at the United Nations? One may disagree with some of the statements made, but there is an important value not in contradicting established American policy but in adding spontaneity and openness to diplomatic discourse.

I believe there is a great advantage in encouraging the right people to use such latitude—that is to say: Don't appoint people to these positions if you don't feel they are the best people to further our national interests. But if they are the best people to do that, if they have the intelligence and integrity and commitment and sense of responsibility that should go with appointments to these jobs, let them use these qualities to further our policy goals. Your report on your term as a U.S. Delegate to the General Assembly and Bill Buckley's book on his service at the United Nations both make that point powerfully. The best talents we have, regardless of ideology, need to be used in these situations. The best talents, the best spirits, the people who are best at communicating ideas to other people—we need representatives at U.N. meetings who can empathize with other points of view, who can work comfortably with people from all parts of the world. To try to homogenize everything is to reduce the efficacy of our representation.

What Andy Young has achieved, and what in limited circumstances we tried to achieve in Geneva, is the impact of spontaneity in debate and conversation. That carries the risk that not every word will be exactly as you might later wish, and that some things may be said at times that you wish you had said differently.

You may have to say afterward: "Wait, I made a mistake on that," or "I wish I could have explained my position because I see now it was misinterpreted," or "That statement does not reflect the ultimate position of my delegation."

Those are not great tragedies for individuals or for the national interest. If one says something and discovers that it is inaccurate, one says: "I made an inaccurate statement."

I found in Geneva that, if what you say is always sculpted in advance, you can't have the back and forth that is so valuable, for example, in Congress. And if you can't draw people out and try to understand what they are saying and make them reexamine things, everything tends to fall into a kind of tedious ritual drill that affects almost nothing. Instead of that, we tried to discuss and argue without getting into accusatory polemics, if we could avoid it. We took that awful Middle East resolution almost sentence by sentence: What does it mean to say Israel is an aggressor, and why is it the business of this Commission to decide that? Then we argued that point and others like it.

Now, traditionally, that is not what happens. Everyone makes speeches which are mostly written by somebody else often weeks ahead of delivery. Everyone reads canned speeches; nobody listens to anyone else if they can help it, and what you have at the end of it all is not an exchange of ideas but a kind of verbose trench warfare from fixed positions.

So I think it is most helpful to the United States that people all around the world know that our Ambassador to the United Nations speaks feelingly about things so many people feel very deeply about.

He doesn't undermine fixed American policy decisions. he simply uses the opportunity to discuss what factors should go into making that policy. He has made countless people everywhere begin to think: "Wait, maybe the United States really isn't what we have always been told. Maybe the caricature isn't real." Andy Young's freshness and independence reflect his own remarkable experiences and compassion. He has reached great numbers of people that no one else could have reached, and I can't for the life of me see how this triumph is somehow damaging to what is called the "unity" of American foreign policy.

I understand there can be a problem if the public or other nations were to get the impression that there are major conflicts in our foreign policy, but it seems simple enough to make sure that everyone knows that this is not so. Soon it will be realized that dialog is not dissension, and that spontaneity is not irresponsibility. . . .

Of course, we all understand that when you sit behind a sign that says "United States of America" there are things that you cannot say because you are speaking for your Government. But at the same time you are useful in that seat, instead of having a robot sitting there, precisely because of whatever you bring to it. That should be part of the reason you are appointed to that seat in the first place.

For instance we benefited in Geneva from an odd coincidence that no one could have anticipated. It happened that in 1959, I was asked to go to a place called Otjiwarongo in South-West Africa to see a man called the Reverend Chirimuji. If you are ever asked to go to Otjiwarongo and find a man called Chirimuji, you will remember it.

I went there, but I didn't find him. The South African police got wind of our presence and we had to hide, since we were there in an African area illegally. I suspect our whole trip to South-West Africa was rather awkward for the U.S. Government at the time. Cables must have flowed for weeks about that odd enterprise.

Then years later, there we were, in Geneva. I am speaking for the United States, and suddenly the Reverend Chirimuji emerges from South-West Africa and appears in Geneva as a leading spokesman for his people. You will understand the considerable emotion of that delayed meeting. There we were in a distant city years later, to discuss human rights, Namibia now a high priority on the agenda of human rights concerns in the world. We gave a reception for Reverend Chirimuji and his colleagues. It was an event that said something helpful and perhaps even poignant about where America stands, and it occurred because the U.S. delegation brought some unusual personal experiences to its work. And Andy Young brings not only his own remarkable qualities, but his close association with the preeminent figure of our time on matters of human rights.

The point is that President Carter, Secretary Vance, and Ambassador Young have achieved a great deal already to reverse the trend toward the United States becoming a rather isolated voice dealing increasingly ineffectually in international forums with things even when we are right, which, may I add, increasingly frequently we are.

I know there will be moments when what Andy says, or what I or someone else may say, will produce disagreement. This kind of disagreement is as healthy as it is inevitable.

The last thing Andy Young expects is that everyone will agree with everything he says. But something quite extraordinary is beginning to happen in world affairs, and we ought to understand it and be grateful.

At times the President himself makes some people nervous because he has rattled some ancient notion of propriety, or has spoken out candidly at an unexpected moment. Adlai Stevenson once observed that diplomacy consists of alcohol, protocol, and Geritol. We ought to be pleased that we are helping to make it something better than that, that we need not be locked in that way. . . .

I was at a human rights seminar at Notre Dame where many people from private organizations were still acting as if the U.S. Government were their enemy. They are so used to opposing whatever the Government does in these areas that there is a resistance, or maybe it's just a delayed reaction, to understanding that now the Government wants to do many of the same things they do. There will be confusion and bungling, but the will is there. Can we get the energies that were spent during the disputes over the war and in the efforts to obtain and protect citizens' rights—can people got together to help make a new start? If we can get past old conflicts and find a way to work together without easing up on the obligation to disagree with any officials when we think they are wrong—if we can do that, those things that we have wanted to achieve over the years can in my view begin to happen. I would hate to see us lose this opportunity out of a reflex rigidity that keeps everybody repeating their old slogans in the same old way as if nothing had changed.

So I hope that a measure of unity to work toward one overall shared goal—to try to reduce human misery—these goals will be preserved. I know it won't be preserved if there isn't some effort to communicate, as well as a lot of tolerance of independent judgments and differences over strategy and tactics.

ANNIVERSARY OF AN ASSASSINATION

Washington Star, June 5, 1978

The following article by Lowenstein appeared on the tenth anniversary of the assassination of Robert F. Kennedy.

And now suddenly it is 10 years since Robert Kennedy was killed: another anniversary in a season of little-noticed 10th anniversaries that remind us, when we think about them at all, how much a country can change in a decade, and how inadequate a substitute nostalgia is for hope.

How long ago it seems since the three most beloved and promising figures in America all died within five years, all murdered strangely, all having lived only half their lives. And how easy it is to think that what has happened to us since then was somehow inevitable, to forget that those deaths changed the national mood and direction, and that much that has happened might not have happened were it not for this series of events that left us haunted by great absence through years made difficult in part by those absences.

Perhaps because Robert Kennedy was the last of the three to die, his death seemed the cruelest—bearing the cumulative freight of what had gone before, multiplying the doubt that there was any place for hope in a society where the best spokesmen for hope could not survive.

He was not a prophet like Martin Luther King Jr., not a president like his brother, but he touched his countrymen in a special way, reaching large numbers of people who were least sure that they belonged, and so were hardest to touch. That was a boon to this country, and to democracy itself.

Robert Kennedy meant as much as he did to as many as he did partly because he was his brother's brother, and his death hurt as much as it did partly because he died so early and so wrongly. But the totality of loss was far greater than these parts, for with him went the spirit of a generation.

When he was killed, so was something generous and electric in us and in the nation, something not yet reborn and possibly not to be reborn in our lifetime. We were left instead with a scar too close to the heart and with leaders whose bleakness was to remind us continually through a damaging decade of what might have been.

As a politician, Robert Kennedy was less than heroic, and as a hero he was uncomfortable and uncertain. But by the end he was blending in common purpose not just the rich and poor and black and white and young and old that he invoked too often during his last campaign, but toughness and gentleness, and the pragmatic and the uplifting as well.

More than anyone since FDR, he brought people together at the price of driving others away. But in a time of great divisions he brought more people together than any of his contemporaries, and he made more people believe that they could, as he liked to say, "make a difference."

He wanted everyone to see what seemed so obvious to him: that if people couldn't be roused to try to make a difference in the effort to "reclaim" their country, they would make a difference anyway by not trying.

Before and better than anyone else, he understood the realities of power in the United States. Almost alone he saw the nature of the lassoes that were hobbling the machinery of democracy, and he set out to weaken the hobblers and strengthen the hobbled.

And somehow, through all the commotion, he managed to keep growing, to become a presence as well as a politician, an American resource beyond the glitter of mere celebrity. He was the midwife of the uncertain arriving future, trendy, moody, in motion, but he called us as well to the abiding values of stabler times.

The Robert Kennedys enjoyed it when they played together and meant it when they prayed together, and they made us want to enjoy each other and to believe that we could pray together too. Their grace through devastating grief helped everyone with lesser griefs to endure, and Robert Kennedy's words after Martin Luther King's death would turn out to be among those few words whose power increased as their immediacy faded.

And then Robert Kennedy died too, just when the sense of promise that he inspired was overtaking the resentments and suspicions that he aroused. He was getting better as the nation's problems were getting worse, and in retrospect almost everyone would realize that he was needed more than anyone had understood until he was gone.

I was never close to Robert Kennedy. Our relationship was political, and started out in rather adversary circumstances at that. Of the only year I knew him at all well, it would be accurate to say that I spent one half arguing that he should run for president when he wouldn't, and the other half supporting an opponent when he did. Yet he meant more to me, as to so many others, than any other public figure of the time, and the awful fact of his unnatural death will shadow events as long as we are a part of them.

And in that shadow we still struggle with the problem connected to so many others—the problem of how to revive enthusiasm and excite energies, of how a spirit once aborted can be born again. Old battle cries drift back, but they are harder to hear now through the years of My Lai and wheat deals and Elizabeth Ray and Spiro Agnew and Tongsun Park and expletives deleted.

The mind wanders past jaded words, there is no radiance, nothing is clear-cut. We have learned that Camelot was not quite Camelot, and that America is neither as innocent nor easily changed as we once thought. It has become sensible to be cynical.

But anybody who thinks about it knows that it is sensible, too, to remember that great sophistication is not the same thing as greater wisdom, that an immobilizing cynicism is no cure for what has gone wrong.

And anybody who finds himself wishing on this occasion that Robert Kennedy were still around knows what Robert Kennedy would be saying if he were—knows that we have dallied long enough, and that it is past time to try again to do better, to make a difference; past time to dream again of things as they ought to be, and to ask again why they are not.

WHY I QUIT
New York Post, July 14, 1978

In August 1977, Lowenstein was sworn in as one of the U.S. ambassadors to the United Nations. In that role, he represented his country on the Economic and Social Council, traveled to Africa, Europe, and Latin America, and lobbied Congress on behalf of Administration policies. He also defended President Carter and Ambassador Young and worked with black and Jewish groups to promote common fronts on some human rights issues.

He soon grew increasingly doubtful, however, that he could effectively contribute to human-rights policy from within the Administration. He was frustrated by working in the slow-moving and sometimes indecisive foreign policy bureaucracy, and was also troubled by a shortage of new and creative diplomatic initiatives.

"I'm here because of Andy Young," he told one interviewer. "He's the best part of my job." But although his regard for Young remained high, the two men differed on some questions of strategy. At one point, Lowenstein was told by a foreign diplomat, "It isn't so much that I mind your government constantly arguing with itself about what its foreign policy is—it's just that I wish someone would win the argument." The remark summed up some of his own frustrations.

Early in 1978, Lowenstein notified Young that he would soon leave the UN, and his departure was announced in May. In this article, he outlined some of his reasons for leaving.

Resigning from the Carter Administration is a tactical judgment, not a moral imperative. In appointive office, as in Congress, I have tried to follow this precept:

If you can't do more about the problems you care about by being in office than you could if you were out, don't cling.

Since I have not been able to influence policy much from inside the Administration, I think it's time to try to influence policy from outside.

Take the Middle East.

The President means it when he insists that the U.S. commitment to Israel is unequivocal. But Israel was born of a thousand years of experiences that override unenforceable promises. Arrangements that give lethal weapons to hostile autocrats in unstable nearby countries remind Jews everywhere of Jews who are no longer anywhere because they lived in a world that sent the *St. Louis* back to Europe and let the *Struma* blow up and sink in the Bosporus.

Israel was promised F-16's in return for a withdrawal in Sinai. Whoever reattached these previously promised planes to a "package" that includes planes for Saudi Arabia ignored history and flunked psychology. Breaking promises to people seared by broken promises is no way to build confidence in new promises.

At best the package made it harder for the Administration to attain its own goals. Then a tactical blunder was turned into a test of loyalty, which polarized old allies and encouraged a mistrust that will last long after people have forgotten its origins.

In this situation, as in others, I found myself agreeing with the Administration's stated goals and unable to understand how you can achieve goals by asserting them and then pursuing policies that lead elsewhere, if anywhere.

What was wrong with the plane package may not have been motives but consequences, but everything this Administration does in the Middle East now bears the additional freight of fertilized mistrust. White House receptions for rabbis and airborne pilgrimages with the Vice President can't explain why a Saudi Arabia that will not even publicly acknowledge Israel's right to exist is to get advanced American weapons, or what will happen to those weapons if Saudi Arabia should go the way of Afghanistan and South Yemen.

Some policies fail simply because decisions get stuck in the cotton candy of bureaucratic rigor mortis, though you can't always be sure when bureaucratic rigor mortis is the cause of something and when it's a scapegoat.

FDR's most perceptive observation may have been about animals in heat rather than about fear itself. Decision-making at the State Dept., he said, is like watching an elephant get pregnant: everything takes place at a very high level, there's a great commotion, and then nothing happens for 22 months.

Still, after a while an Administration is accountable if its programs get stuck in the cotton candy that it was elected to cut through. Which brings us to "Z-R."

The United Nations resolution defining Zionism as racism multiplied the number of people who dismiss the UN as a kind of radicalized Lewis Carroll contraption filled with leftist mad hatters who might next announce that slavery is freedom or that Jews are Nazis, or who for that matter might direct the Mississippi River to flow uphill.

But the UN cannot be dismissed. The world, not Lewis Carroll, created the UN and the UN reflects and affects the world in which we must go on living, like it or not.

A world as interconnected and imperiled as ours desperately needs a credible functioning world organization. To abandon the UN would be dangerous and self-defeating; to abandon the effort to improve the UN makes no sense at all.

Opposition to racism is one of the world's great and just emotions, and the UN is in the midst of a "Decade Against Racism." What "racism" is, therefore, becomes strategic, and Z-R is a poisoned dart aimed at eliminating Israel.

Since just about everyone is against racism except white South Africa, if Zionism is racism, Israel is equated with South Africa and the Arab countries with everyone else. Which makes Sadat's mission to Jerusalem the equivalent of Africans negotiating to preserve apartheid.

Some governments that can distinguish between Golda Meir and Ilsa Koch, including our own, refused to get involved in a "Decade Against Racism" so peculiarly skewed. That encouraged lots of people, especially in the Third World, to believe that we are indifferent to racism, or worse.

So the same stinking little resolution that gave anti-Semitism a grand new respectability impugns our credentials while discrediting the UN and helps racism as well, by splattering the unity against racism (rationally defined) that might otherwise have been effective, if only because of its novelty.

Thus, freeing the UN from Z-R is as important for the UN as it is for Israel, and as I believe it is for the U.S. Government. That is why the U.S. delegation set out at the Human Rights Commission in Geneva in March to reverse the Z-R spiral—a goal regarded as noble but hopeless.

Then to everyone's amazement, a U.S. proposal for a "Year Against Apartheid," with no contaminating additions, was adopted. A UN body had actually approved an American proposal that meant Israel and the U.S. would be able to participate in programs dealing with racism.

And then the same Commission did something utterly unprecedented and even more astonishing: it supported us against angry Russian pressure when we insisted that the Soviet Union could not be exempted from discussions about Human Rights violations. The events of the past few days should remind us how right we were to take that position, and how important it is that we stick to it now.

These were only the first steps on a journey of a thousand miles, but they were steps in the right direction for a change.

And that is where this story ends—just where it should have begun. The opportunity provided by the turn of events in Geneva evaporated in Washington some time before the General Assembly, where the next and first major steps would have had to occur. An effort to disentangle Z-R at the General Assembly would have required a decision to make that a major priority in the give-and-take that characterizes international negotiations. It would be inexact to say that someone decided against making Z-R a priority, more likely the matter was never really resolved at all.

I don't know if the President was ever aware of the decision, or non-decision, that cost his Administration its best chance to do something valuable simultaneously for human rights, Israel, American influence, and the UN itself—something that would also have gained the Administration credibility and gratitude among millions of Americans.

I do know that despite the urgency of the moral and practical imperatives involved, and despite the efforts of Rabbi Alexander Schindler and other major figures, the high hopes of spring had foggy-bottomed out by fall, with nothing to show for the loss.

Despite disagreements and disappointments, I applaud many things this Administration has done, and I'm grateful to President Carter for the chance to have worked with Andy Young and other fine men and women for the past year and a half.

An administration less genuine in its desire to decrease human suffering would not have sent me and others with similar views on Human Rights visits to countries like Chile, Poland, Nicaragua and South Africa. Those trips were helpful to brave people in difficult situations, and in ordinary times it might be enough to settle for making occasional contributions in an administration with good intentions.

But the times are not ordinary. East-West, North-South, all around the globe, clouds darken, good folk falter, deadlock reigns. We despoil the planet, and kid ourselves that the rational alternative to nuclear weapons is nuclear power for peace. We drift into unacceptable options in Africa, and address the disarray of democracy as if the Wizard of Oz will rescue us if only we skip on down the yellow brick road.

At home we haggle and ramble, trapped in economic disquiet and political charade. California at the polls shouts the nation's frustrations in a sort of middle-class Watts, but the response is as barren as the response to the Wattses of a decade ago.

Everybody is frustrated, but nobody seems to be able to figure out how to limit government without ignoring social injustice, how to pursue a more humane society without destroying the goal in the name of arriving at it. As Dorothy Parker once remarked, you can't teach old dogmas new tricks.

No one seems to have noticed that almost everyone now agrees on lots of things that need to be done, and that what we ought to be seeking is ways to do them.

But instead of searching for the delicate balances necessary to work through the dilemmas presented by valid competing values and difficult experiences, politicians dive into old trenches and shoot tired slogans past each other, while everyone else tunes out. We worked to reform politics so everyone could participate, only to discover that nobody much wants to any more. So now we must deal with the problem connected to so many others—the problem of how to revive enthusiasm and excite energies.

I cannot do much about that problem either—the problem connected to so many others—if I too get stuck in the cotton candy.

A LIBERAL INDULGENCE

William F. Buckley, Jr.

Newsday, August 15, 1978

When he had taken his ambassadorial post in 1977, Lowenstein had moved into a Manhattan apartment near the United Nations headquarters. Following his resignation, he made what would be his final bid for Congress, in the East Side congressional district formerly represented by Edward Koch, who had been recently elected mayor of New York City. Perhaps fittingly, it was a district in which Lowenstein had been active in the reform movement battles of the fifties and sixties.

In the campaign, he continued to argue that both rigid liberal and conservative doctrine were inadequate to deal with the basic political challenges ahead.

Lowenstein's race was beset with difficulties from the start. He was confronted with the fast-breaking candidacy of millionaire resident Carter Burden. Unable to raise adequate campaign funds, he was eventually outspent by a wide margin. The Executive Committee of the New York Liberal Party denied Lowenstein its backing and, moreover, blocked a party primary in court. A final hurdle came six weeks before the election, when the first city-wide New York newspaper strike in twelve years began.

One month before the primary, Lowenstein was endorsed by his friend and frequent forensic adversary William F. Buckley, Jr.

In the Silk Stocking District of New York City, the ganglion of so many of the miseries of the republic, and not a few of its glories, the congressional race for the seat once occupied by Mayor Ed Koch and former Mayor John Lindsay goes largely unnoticed. This is odd because the two Democrats contending for the nomination are interesting to write about, and the district one of them will represent, if he defeats the incumbent Republican who last January in a special election defeated Bella Abzug, thus qualifying for national gratitude and relieving him of any future obligation to the republic, is the most vibrant in the United States.

I came close to granting a plenary indulgence to John Lindsay for all his sins when, as a congressman from the district, he replied years ago to a reporter who asked why he had on that day voted both against an anti-obscenity bill and an anti-subversion bill, that subversion and obscenity were the principal industries of his constituency. That is hyperbolic, but so is everything in Manhattan, and it is fitting that the district should be represented in Congress by one of the outstanding young men in the country, Allard Lowenstein.

Twice in seasons gone by I have written about Lowenstein, infuriating many of my friends because, you see, Lowenstein is a liberal Democrat. Why should a conservative Republican advocate the election to Congress of a liberal Democrat? In the past, pressed on the matter, I have permitted myself, out of polemical fatigue, to reply simply: "It is a personal indulgence." One should try to do better.

Lowenstein is independent, thoughtful in respect of not a few matters, an opsimath whose belated recognition of, for instance, the inherent rights of parents to select the schools their children may attend could lose him the editorial support of the New York Times.

But most appealing is Lowenstein's ability to talk to people who disagree with him without inducing a shouting contest. As U.S. representative in Geneva to the UN Human Rights Commission two years ago he actually caused that commission to consider—however briefly—the question of human rights in the Soviet Union.

There is in Lowenstein a quality of innocent good will that makes the conventional defenses appear fustian and contrived. Recently, having been banned from traveling there for 20 years in punishment for writing an unfavorable book about the race laws, Lowenstein was invited to visit South Africa. There, over the airwaves, he spoke simply and eloquently about the fraternal imperative, and lo, high officials in the South African government, instead of looking the other way and shooing him out, invited him to return, on the understanding that he would be free to continue to speak out against apartheid, but confident that his palpable integrity distinguished him from the fanatics who desire in South Africa less the restoration of black rights than the shedding of white blood.

There is, in Lowenstein, a hectic idealism which it is impossible to fail to be moved by. There will be quite a few liberal Democrats in the next Congress. So why not one whose integrity and warmth will at least re-pristinate a movement grown cynical, bureaucratic and ineffective?

The liberalism of the Eastern Establishment is grown hoary and bu-reaucratic. Its idealistic vision, filtered through conservative forms, would be an improvement on the existing situation. "Christianity without the crucifixion," Whittaker Chambers once meditated, "is liberalism." Allard Lowenstein belongs in Congress as demonstrably as Rudolph Nureyev belongs on the stage.

Because of the newspaper strike, the Buckley column did not appear in any daily paper in the 18th Congressional District. In the five-way September primary, Lowenstein lost by a 4-percent margin. In November the Republican incumbent was narrowly reelected, in one of the highest-spending congressional races up to that time.

TOWARD MAJORITY RULE AND PEACE IN ZIMBABWE

Congressional Testimony,

May 14, 1979

*While at the UN, Lowenstein had worked with the Carter Admin-
istration to help end the bloody Rhodesian civil war and move that
country toward majority rule.*

*For years, the conflict between black political leaders and guerrillas
and the white supremacist regime of Prime Minister Ian Smith had
raged. Despite the imposition of international economic sanctions,
Smith still exercised power over the overwhelmingly black population.*

*In 1977, Carter had won congressional approval to reimpose the em-
bargo on the importation of Rhodesian chrome. The U.S., along with
Great Britain, also called on all parties to the struggle to negotiate a
resolution. Neither Smith nor the Patriotic Front, a loose coalition of
the two black guerrilla forces, accepted the proposal to open talks.*

*Early in 1978, Smith, Bishop Abel Muzorewa, and two moderate black
leaders engineered what they called an "internal settlement" of the conflict. They formed a transitional government, in which whites played a
major role, and scheduled biracial elections for April 1979, to be followed
by a transfer of power. The settlement was opposed by Robert Mugabe
and Joshua Nkomo, the leaders of the Patriotic Front, as well as by the
governments of the black-ruled "front-line" states bordering Rhodesia.
The Carter Administration also opposed it, insisting that the elections*

would be meaningless as long as whites continued to control key military and government posts and a transition to full equality had not been achieved.

The Administration asked Lowenstein, early in 1979, to visit southern Africa to explore ways to break the diplomatic stalemate. He held meetings with some leaders of the front-line states and with Smith, Mugabe, and Nkomo, from which a formula emerged that included Smith's resignation, a liberalized constitution, and internationally supervised elections. A key element of this approach was the possibility that the U.S. would consider lifting sanctions against Rhodesia if fundamental progress toward majority rule was achieved.

Some of the parties to the dispute reacted favorably to the formula, but it was not pursued in Washington.

In April, Lowenstein went to Rhodesia again, to observe the April elections. "It was extremely moving," he later recalled. "You saw old people who traveled hundreds of miles for days. . . . The feeling reminded me of Mississippi after the Voting Rights Act. The important thing was that the people were voting less for the government than for the election process to go on."

Reacting to the relatively free elections and the limited concessions made by whites in the internal settlement, some members of Congress began to push for termination of U.S. sanctions. Lowenstein thought an immediate end to sanctions would be a mistake and would drastically reduce U.S. leverage needed to force continued progress. Shortly after returning from Rhodesia, he testified before the two House foreign-affairs subcommittees involved with the issue and outlined an alternative to a rigid prosanction or antisanction choice.

Mr. Solarz. . . . In the next few weeks, the Congress and the President will once again face the issue of sanctions against Rhodesia, and we begin today with a series of joint hearings on Rhodesian sanctions. We also plan to have hearings on May 16 and May 21, which will focus on the question of whether or not the United States should end its policy of enforcing U.N. sanctions against Rhodesia.

Today's hearing will focus on the recent elections in Rhodesia. Last year, as I am sure most of you know, Congress adopted the Case-Javits amendment which stated that the United States shall not enforce sanctions against Rhodesia provided that the President determines that:

One: The government of Rhodesia has demonstrated its willingness to negotiate in good faith at an all-parties conference, held under international auspices on all revelant issues; and

Two: That a government has been installed, chosen by free elections in which all political and population groups have been allowed to participate freely, with observation by impartial, internationally recognized observers.

Today's hearing will focus on the extent to which the second condition has been fulfilled by the recent Rhodesian elections.

My own feeling is that the question of what to do about Rhodesia is likely to loom as one of the major foreign policy issues confronting the Congress. Congressman Bonker and I both felt very strongly that a firm, factual foundation should be laid for a responsible congressional decision on this subject. . . .

Mr. Lowenstein. Mr. Chairman—both Mssrs. Chairmen—I am very grateful to you for this opportunity to appear.

The difficult part of discussing this particular issue is that the terms of reference, as Lord Chitnis has pointed out, vary a great deal. Before the voting began, there were a great many statements announcing that the voting was *ab initio* invalid. Those statements were made by serious supporters of democracy in Africa and elsewhere. I quote just briefly from one or two so that we can set the context.

The general elections which the Smith regime is proposing to organize on 20 April will, if they take place at all, be held amidst a climate of desperate and uncompromising purges by the security forces and intense political repression. There are really no objective grounds for arguing that if nothing more the election should at least be taken to indicate the internal settlement retains some measure of popular support in the African community, and that the result should therefore be taken into account in any subsequent negotiations involving Zimbabwe's future. On the contrary, the election arrangements that have been put in hand by the regime indicate that voting will be a traumatic experience for the great majority of the black population.

That is from a publication called *Focus* on March 21, a publication which I subscribe to and admire. I have been involved with the people who put it out for many years.

Similarly, in letters that were sent out by dear friends of mine, people whom I admire very much, Members of the Senate and of the House, statements were made, the mildest of which were things like:

The United States and Great Britain have consistently taken the position that no solution nor any election can work if it does not have the support and consent of the people of Rhodesia as a whole, and that the exclusion from that electoral process of the Patriotic Front meant in advance it was not going to be a fair test.

Others have stated repeatedly that the Constitution itself eliminates any potential for a fair and free outcome and that therefore the election is disqualified because of the Constitution. So it has gone.

We were told, those of us who were planning to keep an open mind on the elections, that in fact to keep an open mind was to prejudice the elections because there was no basis for an open mind, the outcome was going to be impossible to determine, intimidation was assured by the martial law situation in 85 or 95 percent of the country, and so forth.

Ambassador Young has said since the elections, consistent with some of those views, that the elections were stolen a year ago.

Now, I cite all of that simply to say that if one's position is, in fact, that the elections were stolen a year ago or that it was impossible under that constitution to have fair and free elections, then I am at a loss as to what we are talking about. If that is the fact, then we are not looking to see what occurred; we are saying that what occurred had had no chance of validity.

The letters sent out by Senator Kennedy and Senator McGovern, in which questions were asked as to whether the elections gave one-man one-vote in its ultimate sense—the kind of impact that ideally would have been attained—clearly dictate the answers that those letters will get, because nobody could pretend that the Constitution equalized the voting power of everybody in Zimbabwe.

So, I have to start out, just in brief, by saying that if I believed that the issue in this voting was, has perfection of process been achieved, is the Constitution as I would have written it, I assume that we would have spared people the time of these hearings and spared the people in Zimbabwe the hypocrisy of saying we are going to study the process to see whether it had any merit as an effort to find out what they felt.

I do not think that is what the issue is. I think if our problem is with the Constitution, we ought to say that a Constitution, to be ultimately valid, ought to be voted on by all the people. I think we ought to say that. I think it is clear that that is a basic concern which people ought to express about the way the Constitution was adopted in Zimbabwe.

If we do not like provisions in the Constitution, as I expect most of us do not, we ought to have the modesty of experience not to try to dictate what those provisions would be, but to assert that, whatever they are, they have to be acceptable to the Africans whose rights we have been concerned about.

So, I want first to say that I cannot understand the notion that we can consistently claim that these elections had no validity because of the Constitution, or because of other circumstances preceding their being held, and then hold hearings and have the President assert that he has to wait until June 16 to determine whether, in fact, those elections were sufficiently compliant with the statutory requirements they can affect our policy.

In the event itself, a number of things occurred which, I think, were potentially valuable to people who want to have academic or legalistic arguments about the effectiveness of the procedures, and I would be glad to discuss those if I am asked about them. But, again, I think that is not terribly useful. What, it seems to me, is significant about the elections has to do with the only question which I think can be measured with any accuracy by that process, and that is: What is the mood of the people of Zimbabwe? That, one can measure. I am sure there are people in this room who have had much greater experience than I, but many of us have had experience in observing and participating in elections in many different countries, in democratic countries—in my case in the Dominican Republic and Vietnam and other places where there was a war situation attending the voting. And I think that the honest conclusion that virtually everyone who was present during the voting in Zimbabwe reached is that the mood of the great number of Africans participating in that voting was, they wanted that process to go on.

Anyone who says they did not know what they were voting on, it seems to me, is condescending, perhaps imperialist. Anyone who says that the African people of Zimbabwe have not known how to express their feelings in the past ignores the impact on the Pearce Commission of the expression of the African viewpoints some years back. [The Pearce Commission, created by the British, went to Rhodesia in 1972 to canvass black views on a proposed settlement of the conflict.] This is a great people in a great place, who have made great sacrifices to have the opportunity to speak about their own future.

The contributions made to that future by the Patriotic Front have been enormous. Without the effort of those who have been fighting to end white supremacy over the years, there would have been no elections like this. Anyone who tries to put a "cold war" overlay on this misses the point entirely. I cannot believe that the idea in this situation is that one group is more in tune with our thinking in global terms, or another group is more in thinking with the views of some other power, and, therefore, we should accept those overlays in lieu of the central issue about these elections.

The central issue of those elections is: What do the people of Zimbabwe want? If you look at the elections, I think you have to see that what they are saying is, they want elections. Does that mean they endorse the Constitution? No. Does that mean they are committed to the present government that emerged in those elections as the ultimate expression of their views? No.

What it does mean is something which I do not believe anyone can say with individual anecdotes of incidents occurring in any part of that country, because we can match anecdotes all day and not challenge the question of mood. What it does mean is that the electoral process in Zimbabwe, in the minds of the vast majority of the people who live in Zimbabwe, ought now to replace the war as the way of deciding their future. They did not feel that when the white supremacy relics were so powerful that African rights were subordinated with no hope of change except through violence.

It is in that context that I want to proceed for a few minutes to discuss policy as it results, in my mind, from this election.

I was one of those who worked very hard to get sanctions imposed on Rhodesia after UDI [Unilateral Declaration of Independence] in defiance of the provisions of democratic process that I think have to be at the base of American policy in southern Africa. I have opposed American policy in Africa for many years when that policy was indifferent or benign about repression of black people by white people.

But anyone who says today that we are being evenhanded by keeping sanctions on seems to me not to understand that we intended, when we put sanctions on, not to be evenhanded. The precise purpose of the sanctions was not to be evenhanded; it was to say that we cared about the rights of black people. That is in fact why we worked for sanctions. We attempted to get sanctions imposed because we wanted to say that, without violence, without war, without bloodshed, injustice of a racial kind could be ended. We imposed sanctions to achieve that goal.

The test now is, have sanctions achieved that goal? Is white supremacy over in Rhodesia? The answer to that is not clear. I do not say today that it is over. I cannot believe that anyone who knows the situation can say that the ultimate result has been achieved. But what the election seemed to me to be saying was that the rest of the end of white supremacy can be achieved by violence ending and elections taking place through the process that this election was an important step in pursuing.

If that is the case, then it seems to me that we ought to get past the extraordinary potential to have sort of sterile quibblings over the details of the voting. Accept the fact that there were incidents of repression and intimidation; there were. There is a war. Bad things occur in wars. Both sides were doing bad things. I remember for a long time being told that we could not, in fact, discuss the issue of the future of Zimbabwe with Muzorewa and Sithole and so forth because they did not have armies, and the people with the armies were going to determine the future. Then Muzorewa and Sithole got armies. Now we are told that because they have armies they are repressive and cannot be involved because they are no longer reflecting the wishes of the community there, but intimidating the community.

I believe it is fair to say that the intimidation can be canceled out, not because it is not a terrible thing, but because in fact it is not the decisive question. The basic intimidation that we are talking about was not an incident of people being taken off a bus by one side or another, or people being blown up on the way to the polling place by one side or another. Those things occurred. But the basic test, it seems to me, of the intimidation was that it sent people to vote because what they were intimidated by was the war. What they wanted to see ended was the war. Lord Chitnis is right that the massive effort to get them to vote was based on that statement.

Now, if these people who voted thought that they would not see that war end by voting, they would not have voted. They would have done what they did with the Pearce Commission; they would have protested against the process.

But all of us who were in Harare or Heifield or in Quaiquir, any other part of that country from the Mozambique border to the Zambian border, will tell you that where people could, they voted. I remember an elderly man who had walked several kilometers who was hobbling out of the place. I said to him, "Why did you go to this trouble to get here to vote?" and he said, "It is a weapon." I was startled and said, "A weapon to do what?" and he said, "It is a weapon to defeat the other weapons."

Now, it seems to me that sophistication of understanding suggests that, when you begin to have white oppressiveness ending because of the success of the military adventure, you encourage that process. You say: This is a step in the direction we ought to be going, you ought to be going. We cannot dictate what happens next, but we can say that we want to encourage this process. We want to see lives spared. The whole notion of economic power as an alternative to military force has helped to bring about a change. The military force itself was crucial, and now we hope to get on to the next stage which is going to be, we hope, the revision of the Constitution so Africans can say, in fact, whether they want it or do not want it, which can bring the change of personnel that needs to be achieved inside Zimbabwe to make sure this is not just a token change of power.

I think that fits exactly into the legislative history of Case-Javits. I have studied that legislative history, as have all of you. What Case-Javits wants to achieve is not simply the process of an election, but the genuine transfer of power; that is what it is about. To say at this point that that has been finished is obviously not true. For one thing, the Prime Minister has not even been sworn in. It seems to me that the legislative sense which comes out of the history of Case-Javits and the reality of what the African people were talking about in that election is that this is an important step in the ongoing process toward achieving what we have said we believed in, toward achieving what the basis of American foreign policy in Africa has been in this administration.

If that is the case, then we ought to say, "Let us give it time to see if the next step occurs." The way to do that, it seems to me, is to recognize legislatively that this is an important step, not to say it was a fraudulent expression. I do not see that anyone who has seen it can say that. We ought not to say it is disqualified because of a Constitution that needs further changes, but to say that, as an important step and the right process, we recognize its validity, we welcome what occurred. We understand what the African people in Zimbabwe were saying in their participation, in their enthusiasm, in taking part in that election in large numbers.

Now we want to see if the new government exerts authority, if it controls those parts of the administration that will be of concern to Africans. If those things happen, I think we can then say, fine; by this time, by a time fixed—however you negotiate the exact date—we will, in fact, lift sanctions because the purpose of the sanctions was to give the African people the opportunity to select their government, to decide the process for selecting their government, and not to give that right to anyone else, whether it is us or other people in other parts of the world.

Now, just two or three short observations—I do not want to impose on the time of the committee, but there are a few other points I think need to just be introduced into this discussion if we are to understand what the issues are that we are talking about today.

The newspaper today has a headline describing this discussion as having one concern, about trying to save the foreign policy of the Carter Administration in Africa.

I am very concerned about saving the gains made by Andy Young and the Carter Administration. I think Ambassador Young is a great resource. I think much that he has achieved no one else could have, and I have enormous affection and admiration for him and for what has been accomplished by this administration.

It is suggested that, in some way I cannot yet understand, if one recognizes what occurred in Rhodesia, somehow that means one is being soft on white supremacy. Let me make it very clear that the part of the Carter policy that makes sense in Africa is that we will not be soft on white supremacy. I spoke recently at Yale University in support of divestiture of Yale's investments in South Africa because in South Africa there is no sign that the repression is decreasing and because the liberation effort there has to have economic support and moral support.

But if that is why we believe in such a policy in South Africa, if those are what our motives are, if we are trying to save the Carter policy in Africa, then, for heaven's sake, when the situation changes in a place where the whites accept the fact that white supremacy cannot be retained and are haggling over the details of ending it, then let us give the most encouragement we can to that process precisely because that is the consistent role of the Carter policy. The principles of the Anglo-American plan need to be achieved. They cannot be achieved if we do not understand what happened since they were first laid down.

I am reminded by Lord Chitnis' presence that there is supposed to have been a Princess of Wales in the 14th century, I think, who once maintained three priests whose full-time job was to do nothing more than chant prayers for the soul of her departed first husband. There is a point at which one stops prayers for things which have passed by and moves on. I think at this point, if we care about the goals of the Carter policy, we ought to understand that those goals cannot be achieved by pretending what happened in Rhodesia did not happen.

So far as the rest of Africa is concerned, it is a terribly important part of our foreign policy. It is a priority that I have been involved with, Congressman Diggs will recall, almost all of my life. There is not anything that seems to me to be clearer than the fact that, when the public opinion in this country moves toward lifting sanctions because we have selected Rhodesia for sanctions uniquely, we have to recognize in a democracy that we must respond to that public opinion and work out a policy that flows with that opinion.

Those of us who opposed the President's policy in Vietnam and said the Congress and the people ought to be heard on those issues can hardly turn around now and say that it is irrelevant what public opinion says about these things. My view is that public opinion in this country would support a policy that said, "Do not lift sanctions without understanding that more has to happen." But do not say that we cannot lift sanctions if those additional things do occur. I believe that would be the consensus of people of good will in our country, of both races. I think it would be the position that would be most consistent with the stated goals of Andy Young.

Even though it will be difficult to get that policy understood by many people in the world, it is the right policy in terms of what we are trying to achieve. If that is what the people in Zimbabwe are asking that we do through the process that they participated in, it seems to me that the real hypocrisy, Lord Chitnis, is in saying the opposite, saying, "Well, we do not care what they are saying because our global *realpolitik* prevents us from recognizing what they are trying to tell us." I think that is bad *realpolitik*. I think it is bad morality. I think it is bad politics domestically because I do not think it is consistent, either, with the purposes that most of the people in this room have worked for all their lives. If someone can tell me that by continuing to refuse even to look at the issue of sanctions we are going to make elections more likely, I would love to see that argument spelled out.

I would like to know the use of saying that no matter what happens in Zimbabwe, we are going to sit here and wait because there is nothing this Government can do except to wait, keep sanctions on and call it even-handed. That means no encouragement to Muzorewa to make the further changes necessary, no encouragement to the Patriotic Front to come in and discuss anything. But a policy of sitting here and having three priests mutter incantations for the soul of a departed first husband is not going to bring about what the administration has said it wants in Africa, nor what those of us who have worked for liberation in Africa spent so much of our time doing.

What we really need, if I may conclude, Mr. Chairman, is an all-parties conference here. We keep asking them to have an all-parties conference in the middle of a war, which is a terribly difficult thing to do. But there is no American that I know, no member of either of these subcommittees, or the Congress, or the administration, that does not agree on what our goals should be. We all know that the goal is to achieve democratic process with the least bloodshed possible.

Mr. Bonker's comment on the four issues was exactly on point, it seems to me, if you read those four questions that he raised at the beginning of the session. If you read the chairman's, Mr. Solarz' questions in his letter, you know that all of us have the same goals.

Now, if rational people have the same goals, then what you do is to sit down and decide what is the most effective tactic to achieve them. You do not begin with name calling that polarizes and divides and says what is a sellout, that we ought to look at the realities on one side and then have everybody on the other side saying we are ignorant of the issues of the cold war. This is not a question that can be reduced to slogans. It is, however, a question, it seems to me, that could be resolved rationally, if people want to do it, by saying that we have achieved a great deal in the process in Rhodesia because of sanctions, because of the courage of the people fighting that war, because those people living there now said, "Let's move forward in that process." Can we not now sit together and figure out what legislative wording would assist the President so that he is not faced with an up or down choice, which up or down choice, it seems to me, if you look at the meaning of Case-Javits, is not even consistent with the legislative intent? That intent was designed to achieve exactly what we can now do by taking the next step in that path. If we do that, I believe we will be helping the President's policy in Africa and around the world and not undercutting it, as sometimes is said by those who say we should do nothing but simply sit still until events carry the war further and it is resolved in military fashion.

I very much appreciate the time. I know I have gone over my time. If

Speaker McCormack were here, he might say that the 1-minute rule never really meant 1 minute if you were fond of the person who was extending it. . . .

Mr. Bonker. The hearing is intended to deal with reports from those who were on the spot during the elections, so that they could share with the subcommittees firsthand information on the authenticity of those elections. We have from Mr. [M. Stanton] Evans a statement in which he says:

Judging by all the direct evidence we could gather, the elections were conducted on a free and fair basis; secrecy of the ballot was observed; eligible voters had ready access to the polls; ineligible voters were turned away; steps were taken to preclude double voting

and so on. Then concludes by saying that:

In terms of everything we were able to observe, the Zimbabwe-Rhodesia elections were conducted on a free and fair basis.

Following him, Lord Chitnis said that:

The recent election in Rhodesia was nothing more than a gigantic confidence trick designed to foist on a cowed and indoctrinated black electorate a settlement and a constitution which were formulated without its consent, and which are being implemented without its approval.

So, we start with extreme and highly polarized viewpoints on this sensitive issue. Fortunately Ambassador Lowenstein was able to bring to us something that represents a middle position, and I hope that the committees who are involved will be able to sort out some of the commentary and deal more directly and honestly with the issues at stake. If we do not we might as well dispense with the hearing and just start with our biases.

Mr. Lowenstein, the real concern I have with the U.S. position, if it were to lift sanctions based on the recent elections, is how that is going to affect our relations with other African leaders. You mentioned in your opening statement that this administration and specifically Ambassador Andy Young were able to renew our ties with African States, our credibility with African States, and a new sense of trust and confidence has evolved over a period of time that places us in a much better competitive position with our Russian adversaries. They continue to resort to more violent means of achieving their ends. We take a much more constructive, albeit slow means of achieving our ends.

Do you not fear that if we were to lift sanctions at this time, that it would greatly rupture our on-going relations with other African States?

Mr. Lowenstein. I think that if we were to lift sanctions without evidence that the transfer of power which Professor Kintner and others have asserted will occur, and which one hopes will occur without that transfer having been demonstrated—yet if we were to do that immediately without understanding the on-going process, the danger of that result would be very great because the African governments concerned about an end to white supremacy would have a right to say, "This is a prejudgment of the ultimate result that we expected to achieve."

I have spent some time talking to prominent leaders of African governments in the course of the time I was at the United Nations and since. I believe that a substantial number of African governments would understand if we were to lift sanctions in the process that is now going on as part of the inducement to have that process continue. I do not mean to say that they would support it or advocate it, but I think there is a difference between lifting sanctions, let us say, on an Ian Smith government which says, "These elections are the ultimate statement of what people want in Zimbabwe," or lifting sanctions on a black government with different personnel running it and a commitment to the black people having the chance to vote on that constitution before it is considered the ultimate ruling document of the country.

I see here, for instance, Congressman Gray. I do not know how many people know how long he has been involved in the effort in this country to bring justice to people who are deprived of it. I think he would be as much aware of the fight to continue the changes here as any human being alive. What we are talking about is not that there will be an end overnight to the injustices which white people have visited on black people, inexcusably, for so long; but that the process itself needs to be pushed forward as effectively as possible toward ending these injustices, even knowing that we have not yet finished ending them in this country.

So, I would say that the difficulty of explaining to African governments why the mood is for lifting sanctions is a terribly important difficulty. But it is much less difficult if it is clear that the leverage of sanctions is being used to achieve a continuation of the end of white supremacy, rather than that the lifting is taking place simply because of an indifference that appears to have taken over in the public mind of our country. . . .

Mr. Derwinski. One of the recurring questions asked, gentlemen, is the situation in the new Constitution in Rhodesia by which the white population has a disproportionate share of the members of the Parliament. My question is, is it not true that a number of the neighboring states, specifically Kenya, Zambia, and probably one or two others, have in their Constitutions some provisions whereby their white or Indian—there are many Indian minority populations—have membership out of proportion to the actual population.

Would any of you four gentlemen care to comment on what you may know about that? . . .

Mr. Lowenstein. I think Lord Chitnis would agree that if there is ever to be a solution in Northern Ireland that does not entail continuation of violence until there is nobody left there, that it will require some understanding of communal protection.

In the reality of Africa, what we ought to be talking about is what can be done to encourage an end of violence being the only way to end white supremacy. I think that that question dictates an answer which is that you are going to end white supremacy in stages. Either there are going to be stages of increasing bloodshed and hatred, of more and more death and less and less hope of people reconciling and living together, or you are going to show that you understand that the pace of the end of white supremacy must be worked out through means other than violence by the people living there.

Certainly, if one understands the potential for disaster in South Africa itself, the notion that where white people are yielding power in stages, they should be told that nothing they do is acceptable unless it is done immediately and totally overnight simply encourages never doing it until death and destruction become the method that everybody must resort to.

So, my feeling about the Constitution in Rhodesia is that perhaps if Congressman Solarz and I had been negotiating it, we would have done a much more effective job in achieving democracy totally. But on the other hand, considering the talents of those doing it and the circumstances they did it under, it is our job, it seems to me, to encourage that process and not to say that what they have arrived at is unacceptable.

So, I come back to where I started. We have a right, it seems to me, to feel that no constitution ought to be perceived as having lasting validity where Africans are deprived of the right to speak on it. But what the terms of it are should be determined there by the people voting, and those terms will be different in Zimbabwe and presumably in Namibia and in South Africa than they would be under other circumstances elsewhere. . . .

Mr. Bowen. I would like to simply pursue this issue and ask, since the language that we are looking at in Case-Javits talks about a government being installed, the question is, how long does that government have to be installed? I mean, do you have to have a cabinet, and you have to have the parliament meet, you have to start rolling out some legislation. Exactly at what point along the trail do you gentlemen feel that it would be appropriate for us to presume that the requirements of Case-Javits have been met? . . .

Mr. Lowenstein. Congressman, that question, if it is answered rigidly, leads to misleading conclusions. So, although the question is a shrewd and brilliant one, the answer has to be very equivocal. Let me explain why.

We are talking about negotiations, and anyone who has negotiated anything knows that people do not want to make concessions unless they have to. I have no illusion that the new government in Zimbabwe is going to want to make concessions along the lines we have talked about today simply because it believes that is the next thing they should do. Nor do I believe that any of the Patriotic Front forces are going to welcome enthusiastically the idea that this process needs to be encouraged.

I do believe it is in the interest of both the Patriotic Front and the new government in Zimbabwe to move along the lines that we discussed today, the first stage of which is to see that the personnel in the new government are in fact not puppets of whites who pull the strings, the next stage of which is to accept as a principle that must be acknowledged that Africans will vote on a Constitution before it has long effect. Those stages need to be negotiated.

If the objection to lifting sanctions were stated privately or otherwise in those negotiations on the basis of the need to accommodate those next steps and others that would be discussed and bargained about, I think that you would end up with leverage and incentive for those steps to be taken by the government inside and to be accepted by the forces outside as part of a good faith process toward new elections which will have to be held at some point, including everybody.

I think the Congress, to fit into that, must pass legislation which will recognize the ongoing process as valid, and which will in fact set some date by which time these further steps can be measured again. I would say that that timetable probably would be 60 days. I think it is, again, subject to negotiation among the various factions and groups concerned about this policy in the Congress and in the administration.

But what I hope comes out of this is a sense in the Congress that the administration is a cooperating partner and ought to participate in deciding the timetable. As I said—not whimsically—at the end of my remarks, this ought to be an all-parties conference in this country, and with Mrs. Thatcher's government and, I hope, Africans in general.

I want to disagree in passing with the assertion that the African leadership in any substantial number would privately welcome lifting sanctions at this time. I do not believe that. I believe there would be a time when that would be accurate, but I believe it would be very difficult to find substantial African leadership that would welcome lifting sanctions simply on the basis of the important process that is now proceeding.

Therefore, I would hope that discussions could be held with African leaders as well, who might then be in a position to say, this is the minimum that is necessary to get to a point where we see this process is acceptable.

So, I would want to see the legislation not so specific as to be a straightjacket, proceeding on the shoulders of Case-Javits with its wise general statement of direction, and then, God willing, to get this administration with its very high purpose in Africa to participate in formulating what the reasonable test would be which, at the beginning or the middle of July would be measured for the final vote on lifting sanctions. That seems to me to be consistent both with the standards we have set legislatively and the pragmatics of our concern about our role in the world. . . .

Mr. Solarz. I was under the impression that your feeling was that, while this was a great step forward, in many senses a significant development, strictly in terms of the question of freeness and fairness, given the right of all groups to fully participate, that you would not personally urge the President to say that these elections were free and fair and, therefore, the sanctions should be terminated now.

Mr. Lowenstein. I would at this moment not vote to lift sanctions. I would vote for legislation which set a time by which, if other things had occurred, I could vote to lift sanctions.

Mr. Solarz. And since, given the ambiguities of Case-Javits, I assume your advice to the President would be, for the underlying policy reasons you have described, you would urge him under Case-Javits because he has to make a determination, and he may have to make it before Congress acts. I gather you would urge him not to make a positive determination that the elections were free and fair and that they are willing to negotiate in good faith in an all-parties conference, thereby requiring the lifting of the sanctions.

Mr. Lowenstein. This is what I would urge, Mr. Chairman. I would urge the administration to utilize the leverage it has in the issue of sanctions to encourage further steps in the Zimbabwe situation—internally and externally—without committing what I would do about lifting or not lifting sanctions.

The worst mistake I think we have made is in fact to assert that we cannot lift sanctions unless everybody agrees that we should, thus removing the leverage that sanctions provide to utilize our good will and our moral persuasion to produce the goals that you want.

Mr. Solarz. Well, I agree with you. But at the same time, of course, you are aware that if the President found the elections were free and fair under the terms of Case-Javits, he would have to lift sanctions even if he thought it was not a good idea to lift them right away because he wanted, as you suggest, to use them as leverage in order to get additional concessions from the Salisbury Government.

Mr. Lowenstein. But if the Congress and the President together were to agree that at this juncture, in the light of events since Case-Javits, further legislation, spelling out the additional steps, was desirable, you would avert this awful moment of "yes" or "no" on something to which the answer is not either "yes" or "no."

Mr. Solarz. Then let me ask you lastly on the question of what those criteria ought to be, you have indicated some. You felt that as one condition for lifting sanctions we ought to ask that a referendum be held which gives the 96 percent of the population, which is black, the right to express their support for this Constitution.

You have also indicated that there should be meaningful manifestations of the reality of black majority rule in the country, which presumably means—although we do not necessarily spell them out in legislation such things as land reform, bringing blacks into the civil service, and to other prominent positions in the government; a demonstration of the fact that the government is doing what you would anticipate a genuine black majority rule government would do, rather than a government that was nothing more than a bunch of black puppets whose strings were being pulled by their white masters.

Let me ask you about one other criterion. Do you think it would make sense to build into this legislation a requirement that the new government indicate a willingness in principle to accept the idea of a U.N. or internationally supervised election under adequate security provisions as a way of demonstrating that all of the political factions in the country would have an opportunity to compete in such an election? . . .

Mr. Lowenstein. First, I think President Carter has done more in his term to make human rights a central concern than anybody since Mrs. Roosevelt, in terms of our foreign policy priorities, and I think that concern he has manifested. With the help of Ambassador Young that has created an atmosphere in which his credibility is involved in making sure that whatever he does now does not look like it is an effort to prevent agreement in the ruse of stating principles that cannot be achieved.

Given that concern that I have about the credibility of this government, I think that it is impossible to require at this point, what we could have required in February, namely, an acceptance of a specific form of internationally supervised elections. We could have done that before the April elections were held; I do not think we can do it now.

What we can do is to require that there be an acceptance of the principle of additional elections under circumstances negotiated among all the parties and accepted as fair in the Congress before we make the next decision on how to proceed. The timetable of that is what Mrs. Fenwick keeps pointing out is the problem. What I am suggesting to you is that I do not think you can legislate the negotiations. One can only legislate the direction and the concern.

If that happens, maybe we can still get what would be ideal in historic terms, the U.N.-supervised elections. But if the time for getting those has elapsed because we have not pursued it before, I would not allow that to stand in the way of accepting the next step, which is the one that you expressed so really extraordinarily clearly, of the Africans in Zimbabwe saying what they feel about the process through a vote on their Constitution. That seems to me the sine qua non at this point, though the other is desirable in the general spirit of the approach.

Lowenstein's proposed approach met with a mixed response. The Washington Post *called it "a promising initiative," and an analysis in the*

New Republic *concluded that "a middle course solution . . . might enable the Carter Administration to salvage its basic aims in Rhodesia and its prestige both here and in Africa . . ." But in some other quarters, it was described as "racist."*

The day after his House testimony, the Senate voted, 79 to 19, for an end to U.S. sanctions. But building on approaches outlined in the testimony, Representatives Solarz, Bonker, Fenwick, and others delicately crafted a resolution giving the President discretion to keep or lift sanctions in response to further developments in Zimbabwe. In a striking display of unity, the resolution was unanimously passed by the House Foreign Affairs Committee.

On June 7, the President announced that he would not end sanctions immediately, but added that he would continuously review them in the light of progress toward majority rule. This modified position closely corresponded to the House resolution.

Throughout June, Lowenstein lobbied vigorously for this flexible approach, meeting personally with many House members. The resolution was eventually overwhelmingly passed and a similar version became law soon afterward.

In September, negotiations between the British, the Muzorewa government, and the Patriotic Front began in London.

FREEDOM SUMMER REVISITED

Address, Tougaloo College,
October 30, 1979

Many disagreements, animosities, and emotional scars were pro-
duced in the crucible of the civil rights movement in Mississippi, lasting
often into the next decade. Some bitterly accused Lowenstein, Joe Rauh,
Bayard Rustin, and others of working to co-opt and subvert the move-
ment, charges that were dismissed by others.

In the fall of 1979, a retrospective conference on the movement,
which was punctuated by disputes over its strategies and achievements,
took place in Jackson, Mississippi. Speaking on a panel during the first
night of the event, Lowenstein devoted part of his remarks to perspec-
tives that might be applied to the meaning of the freedom struggles.

One of the great problems with dealing with the realities of history
is that, as with Rashomon, everybody's version of what happened differs.
But I would hope that everybody who was involved, who took risks with
their lives, and who went through the ugliness of that period, could share
in the sense that there are things that do unite people even when there
are differences as to goals or even achievements.

I think there was a sense we shared in those very peculiar times that
whatever our differences were, there was a unity against a very central

evil, and that evil has, to a degree which would have seemed impossible when we first came, been extirpated in its legal form. That, I think, ought to be understood as something which the citizens of Mississippi, black and white, have benefited from. If we don't acknowledge that those changes have occurred, I think we first arrogate to ourselves the right, which we don't have, of judging for many other people what they feel about their lives. We also mistake what the facts are.

I remember one night that has been for me, through all the events of my life since, a major force in the shaping of what I wanted to do with my life. It was a night on Lynch Street in SNCC headquarters with Stokely [Carmichael] and others, when we were told that we would all be killed, as people circled with guns and shot into the place. And the fact that we all lived through that night together, maybe it's maudlin to say, but it makes me feel that whatever my disagreements are with Stokely and the others, they are forever in my life a band of brothers with whom I share a deep sense of gratitude, affection, and respect. That will not change, however our paths may have gone in different directions since then.

I wish Dave Dennis was here, and many of the early SNCC people, but Bob Moses more than anybody, because in that period, if there had been no Bob Moses there would have been nothing. It was Bob Moses everywhere. It was Bob Moses, the towering figure whose presence gave people, in the face of such fear that they didn't know whether they could go to bed at night, the sense that if he could be calm and strong and wise, we could get through what was going on. Nobody who lived through that experience would ever feel, I think, that there's any way that we could ever repay the debt we owed to those people we found here.

I think every person who came to Mississippi from outside knew that they learned more, grew more, and experienced a kind of love and wisdom from people in Mississippi that they would never have had and they took away infinitely more than they ever could bring. I think all over the world people are better people in their effort to reduce human suffering because they had that tremendous opportunity of being in this state with people who, though oppressed, loved, and though faced with enormous adversity managed to have a community that had happiness in it.

It did raise basic questions to a lot of people, because they didn't find the white community in Mississippi that they came to see. They didn't find that they identified with it, they didn't find that this was what they wanted to be like or have their country like. They found the opposite. They found themselves embarrassed that white people could behave the way these white people were.

They came with a sense that somehow America wasn't that—that was aberrational. They came with the feeling that they wanted to put whatever they could contribute into the pot to try to change that injustice. And the fact that they were able to contribute, even as minutely as their time here might have contributed, was, I think, a tribute to the innate quality in people that Martin Luther King reached for so many years. Because it was something which fundamentally changed the face of the South, not as much as it needs to be changed, not as much as we wish it could be, but a great deal from the time that all of us grew up in it or went to school in it.

That Mississippi experience was a very important process for the United States to go through because we owe to Mississippi, in addition to the personal adventures that were part of our lives forever afterward, some very basic lessons about America that we didn't know before. They had to do with the inherent ways in which the oppression of white people was more a concern than the oppression of black people. They had to do with the political indifference that was visited on people if they didn't have the right to vote. They had to do with what came to be perceived as a necessity to deal with economic as well as political injustices, because that too had to be faced very clearly.

Since that very difficult beginning, ideological differences did become very significant, and those differences occur wherever you have oppressed people trying to change their circumstances. If you think about what was going on in Spain, where people had a common war against a fascist government, there were terrible differences within the opposition to Franco which ended up as a civil war within the republic. There's always the problem when you're facing difficulty, when you're facing a very formidable opponent, that people will blame each other; they feel frustrated, they don't know quite what to do next, they're trying one thing and the other. But I think one ought to understand something enormously important: With all of those complicated, experimental programs and efforts, and with all the enormous antagonisms that developed among people who came with different motives and experiences, we did, in fact, make a difference. And that difference was felt by a very large number of people in this state who might have spent the rest of their lives in fear when walking down a street, or unable to take part in any of the political and economic changes that America is about.

I remember somebody once said that "history is a cross between the frustrations of how far we still have to go and a sense of satisfaction at how far we have come." People will disagree about what that blend is. How far do we still have to go? How far have we come? Well, it's not easy to answer that, and there's going to be dissent about it because people are not monolithic. But there are things about the experience here that are unifying, and when all is said about the many complexities to it, those complexities ought not to eradicate a couple of fundamental and lasting truths. People behaved better than they would have because they cared about each other. There was a tremendous change in the lives and the spirit of people for each other because they were part of something that mattered.

Commitment is a cheap word. It's not very present in the country today. It's a great word, though, because it says something about what people are capable of when something moves them. And people were moved by the wrong in this state, by the evil that they saw here, and they were moved to try to change it. And that's something that is a fact which can't be changed whatever the ideological changes and differences people will have.

The second, I hope, transcendent fact is that nobody who came here, whatever simplistic notions they may have had before, left without understanding that the sophistication they brought in was infinitely less important than the sophistication of the people who were here, than the wisdom and the sense of humanity, the sense of courage and love that was present among the black people who'd experienced this kind of difficulty for so long. And that changed people's assessment of what life was about. It changed not just the political judgment, but a judgment about marriage and about poetry and about history and about politics. It changed things very deep in people in a way that almost no experience ever changes people.

So what is it that we do now together in the difficulties of *this* period, with all the differences that are going to continue to exist, so that people in Soweto, just as people in Brooklyn or here or anywhere else, will have in a world that offers such enormous opportunities for good things, the opportunity to share in those good things in a way that they haven't been able to do in the past?

If we can understand that that priority is still there to unite us, then the differences of opinion and the arguments about how to achieve it will be profitable ones. If the differences about how to achieve it drown out the common sense of what we want to achieve, then we end up doing nothing but helping those who don't want to see suffering reduced because they profit from the suffering of others.

PRACTICAL DIPLOMACY IN ZIMBABWE

Jack Anderson

Washington Post, January 20, 1980

In the fall of 1979, while Lowenstein was continuing his Manhattan law practice and supporting the early presidential candidacy of Senator Edward Kennedy, negotiations in London on the Zimbabwe-Rhodesia government transition continued. Led by the foreign secretary, Lord Carrington, the British applied heavy pressure on both the Rhodesian whites and the Patriotic Front to approve a new, liberalized constitution and plan for a democratic election. In October, a new constitution was agreed on; in November, a plan for a British-administered interim government was accepted; and in December, an agreement for a formal cease-fire was finalized. The United Kingdom and the United States lifted sanctions later that month, and Britain's Lord Soames went to Salisbury to oversee the transition and the new elections.

Following the London negotiations, Columnist Jack Anderson examined somewhat acerbicly the U.S. and British records on Zimbabwe and Lowenstein's early part in the affair.

Jimmy Carter's wavering, waffling response to the Iranian hostage situation and the Soviet invasion of Afghanistan has drawn increasing fire from his frustrated opponents for the presidency. At first cowed by the possibility that criticism would sound unpatriotic in a crisis, they nevertheless are coming to realize that what was first seen as admirable restraint by the president may in fact be the symptom of a basic flaw in Carter's handling of foreign affairs. His policy has always reflected his pusillanimous tendencies when dealing with hard-nosed street fighters on the international scene. . . .

Just such an opportunity to watch Carter in action—or, more accurately, in inaction—occurred last year in Rhodesia. The president was offered a no-nonsense policy to pursue in that volatile situation, but chose instead to do what amounted to nothing.

Feisty British Prime Minister Margaret Thatcher, stepping in firmly where Carter feared to tread, was able to bring the white-supremacist forces of Ian Smith and the black Rhodesian guerrillas to the conference table and hammer out a negotiated settlement.

Though the White House was not reluctant to accept credit for the success of the British-engineered settlement, secret State Department cables make clear that Carter contributed virtually nothing. Indeed, the administration's refusal to play hardball in a tough international situation made the British efforts even more difficult.

The unwelcome suggestion that Carter play a little practical politics to bring the Rhodesian imbroglio to a peaceful solution came, my sources tell me, from former Rep. Allard Lowenstein, an old Africa hand and former New York congressman who served at the United Nations with Andrew Young.

Almost exactly a year ago, Lowenstein proposed a plan that was roughly the same as the successful one used by the British months later. But a Capitol Hill source told my associate Bob Sherman that Lowenstein's plan was disregarded at the White House, the State Department and the National Security Council.

What Lowenstein suggested—and the Carter administration tinkers apparently gagged at—was that the United States use the economic and military sanctions imposed on Rhodesia years before as a means to get both sides to the negotiating table. The black guerrillas would be impressed by a threat to lift the sanctions, which would give the white Rhodesians power to keep control of the country indefinitely. Conversely, the white Rhodesians would be impressed by a threat to continue the sanctions indefinitely.

Playing both ends against the middle is not the Carter way of doing business, at least in international affairs. There is evidence that Carter's politically oriented chief of staff, Hamilton Jordan, may have failed to push this suggestion that a peaceful solution be achieved by knocking the two sides' heads together.

In an "eyes only" memo to the president, Lowenstein said the possibility of lifting—or maintaining—the sanctions "can influence both sides to negotiate in good faith." But the memo was routed through Jordan, and it is not known whether the president ever saw it. What is known is that Carter never acted on the Lowenstein suggestion.

This was no will-o'-the-wisp theory cooked up by a pipe-smoking egghead far removed from the scene. Lowenstein had made an on-the-spot visit to Southern Africa last February to sound out leaders on both sides.

Not only did he clear his "big stick" sanctions policy with President Kenneth Kaunda of Zambia, but he was told by Ian Smith that Smith had "no problem." with renegotiation of the whites-only constitution, its submission to the entire nation—blacks and whites—and elections under U.N. supervision in which the black guerrillas would participate.

But the U.S. embassy in South Africa denigrated Lowenstein's diplomatic efforts, professing in a cable to Washington that Smith's reasonable attitude "boggles the mind." The embassy experts suggested that "Smith [intentionally] and Lowenstein [unintentionally] were . . . talking past each other."

So the administration sat on its hands. Eventually, the British moved along the lines recommended by Lowenstein and brought the whites and blacks to the conference table. . . .

In spite of violence and continuing political disputes, transitional arrangements in Zimbabwe prepared for implementation of the new constitution. Former guerrilla leader Robert Mugabe became Zimbabwe's prime minister following an election in late February, concluding the transition to majority rule.

ROBERT F. KENNEDY
AND POWER IN AMERICA

Essay

1977

Completed in 1977, this essay did not appear during Lowenstein's lifetime.

Not the least of the wonders of Robert Kennedy is that more than almost anyone else he understood both what America had become and what America could be, and that he set out to change not just specific policies but the way policies were made. He knew a great deal about the curious, contorted, nonideological reality of power in the United States, understood it, and decided to try to increase the influence of people, some of whom had never really had any, and others of whom had barely noticed that they were losing what influence they had.

He had managed his brother's transactions with the political warlords whose help was necessary to put together a presidency—the operatives from businesses, unions, city machines, the media, and racial jive artists getting their "share of the action," and the rest. He knew the world of patronage and payoffs as well as he knew the world of slogans and issues and egos, and when he wasn't trying to reform something he was trying to use it. He dealt in jobs for uncles of Democratic committeemen, with dollars for minority ministers and saloon keepers and undertakers to run "registration drives," with estates for properly connected lawyers to probate; dealt with these attractions of American politics with the same magnetic detachment that he reserved for reformers agitated about whatever revisions of the national agenda had currency at the moment.

He said he could breathe better north of the Bronx line where the air was freer, but he knew that even up there the toastmasters of Kiwanis luncheons and hostesses at Hadassah coffees were more likely to support him if they were stroked personally and helped with their sons' problems with the draft.

He made his way through these worlds that we all knew something about, first for his brother and later for himself, the celebrated ruthlessness concealing the reticence and humor that might have seemed weakness to people who experience had taught him responded mostly to power.

But he knew as well about worlds the rest of us didn't know about—worlds situated, as it were, above invisible barrage balloons that shield those below from glimpsing too clearly whatever might be influencing events from far overhead. And the more he learned about these shadowy forces, the more troubled he became.

He respected and wanted power too much to agonize over the necessary accommodations with the corruptions normal to the human condition, but what he discovered about the extent to which hidden influences affected the nation stunned and engaged him.

His early education must have been slow—whiffs from some of his father's associations, McClellan Committee run-ins with intransigent figures invoking constitutional strictures and protected by high connections and endless quantities of untraceable cash.

Bullying and influence peddling, racketeering with roots deep in American life, he understood. Like Tom Dewey and Estes Kefauver, he set out to expose the worst of it, to try to arouse the public and the government, and so to reduce its scope. But somewhere along the way he discovered that the uses of illicit power went beyond buck-chasing, beyond bullying mom-and-pop stores, even beyond owning a few politicians here and there; and he decided that this power had become a threat to democratic process itself. The zeal of his hostility to this threat was to cost him the trust of some who saw in this zeal a greater threat to democratic process than they could detect in what seemed a few corrupt union officials.

He wrote a book, *The Enemy Within*, and those who thought the book was designed mostly to trumpet his own ambitions found in its fury a confirmation of their suspicion that he was in fact not very committed to democratic process, at least not where individual liberties stood in the way of his ambitions.

Even friendlier observers found the book overdrawn, a bit fanatic. A decade later it would sound more prophetic than fanatic; but by then Robert Kennedy knew that the source of the threats to democracy was much broader than he had realized when he wrote the book, and that those threats had become much more powerful over the years. Above all, he had come to know that the word "threat" itself was misleading, because power exercised is not a "threat" but a fact.

Then suddenly he was the attorney general, the chief of law enforcement, and he began to poke beyond the known parameters of illicit power, to become an explorer in the unknown blue yonder above the barrage balloons. Soon he was after Hoffa and Marcello, the capo of New Orleans; and then after other capos, other unions, other institutions—on to Chicago, and Miami, and Las Vegas; and early on, when most people were just beginning to notice the charm and style that were known as Camelot, he was already into the soupy brew of exiles, gangsters, intelligence agents, and ideologues of all kinds that led to and from the Bay of Pigs. Always at hand were the peculiar and sometimes unfathomable workings of J. Edgar Hoover, his field marshal and presumed chief ally in the wars both to secure civil rights for racial minorities and to protect the interests of the general public by whittling away at an amorphous empire whose webs and tentacles stretched across the land and reached equally into its penthouses and alleyways—an empire with many czars and would-be czars, not all of them known even to one another.

From these adventures emerged an attorney general determined to stem the drain of power to mysterious forces, working with a president too new, too narrowly elected, too vulnerable to risk head-on the consequences of his desire to fire Hoover and cast the CIA "to the winds." And somewhere along the way started a new phase in the accelerating education of Robert Kennedy—a stumbling across unexpected people in hidden alliances in high places, the uncovering of overlapping clandestine interests and operations; and so to a dawning glimpse of the full enormity of the unknown, an invisible empire allied to parts of an invisible government. Could anyone, even a president and his attorney general brother, master anything so cloaked, so ubiquitous, so complementary and unreachable—icons and hit men in holy league against Communism; parts of J. Edgar Hoover and Roselli and Giancana and sometimes Allen Dul-

315

les; Howard Hughes and more money than most governments, John Rooney running the House subcommittee that financed Immigration, Commerce, Justice, and the FBI; pension funds and real estate developers, Teamsters and Longshoremen, journalists and entertainers and folk heroes; more paleolithic than monolithic, built on greed and mistrust, battling over turf and spoils, scorpions in spidery embrace for fear of mutual extinction—who knew where it all started or how far it all reached, much less how it could be tamed or its power balanced?

But it was clear where to begin, and Robert Kennedy began: from forty underworld figures targeted for prosecution to 2,300, a 400-percent increase in one year in the Organized Crime and Rackets section of the Justice Department; from marginal staffing of half-hearted or half-baked inquiries to platoons of bright lawyers prying into Nevada and Texas and places between and around.

Not many people, not even all his closest associates, understood this preoccupation, some said his obsession: why so much energy chasing a bunch of gamblers and hoods, why not more effort in antitrust or civil rights? Why this vendetta against a few corrupt union officials? The emphasis seemed disproportionate, an elephant after some gnats.

But he saw it as a problem of the basic health of the republic, and eventually Robert Kennedy tried to do something even more difficult than restructuring intelligence agencies or imprisoning or deporting would-be czars. He tried to build the strength of the democratic counterpoise, of people struggling around in constitutional forums beneath the balloons; and he died when there was a chance that he might succeed.

"Every individual can make a difference," he kept saying; the simplest acts can spread ripples of hope; personal involvement is the only way to safeguard freedom, to make electoral democracy work; we can do better if everyone understands that, and *tries*.

The passion of this greatest effort of Robert Kennedy's came not from a naiveté assumed for political purposes, a willingness to build false hopes in pursuit of personal power, but, rather, from a great optimism about America. It was his central conviction that if people couldn't be roused to try to make a difference in what he saw as the effort to "reclaim" their country, they would make a difference anyway by not trying.

He knew more about the problems of reclaiming the country than any of his contemporaries. He understood the complexities and absurdities and paradoxes; almost alone he saw the nature of the lassos that were hobbling the machinery of democracy, and he set out to weaken the hobblers and strengthen the hobbled. He must have thought of his brother even more than we understood at the time, and wondered if he would be able to do any more in this effort than his brother had. It was inevitable and magnificent that he decided to try.

Robert Kennedy's death, like the President's, was mourned as an extension of the evils of senseless violence; events moved on, and the profound alteration that these deaths and the death of Dr. King brought in the equation of power in America was perceived as random, a whimsical fate inconveniently interfering in the workings of democracy.

What is odd is not that some people thought it was all random, but that so many intelligent people refused to believe that it might be anything else. Nothing can measure more graphically how limited was the general understanding of what is possible in America.

RETROSPECTIVE

ANOTHER NIGHT, ANOTHER ROOM ...AND DEATH

Jimmy Breslin

New York Daily News,

March 16, 1980

It was a night from a long time ago, from the 1960s, with empty coffee containers on a table and William Sloane Coffin talking about Martin Luther King and people singing to a guitar and coats thrown everywhere and children sitting on laps, and death.

This was on Friday night in a room on the sixth floor of St. Clare's Hospital. They had Al Lowenstein one floor below. The blood would not remain in the body and he was trying to live on his spirit. As this was so limitless in the life he led, there seemed no reason to assume it would not carry him through the hours of the night.

Peter Yarrow sang "Puff the Magic Dragon" and Steven Smith Jr. held Tommy Lowenstein on his lap. And you thought of a night in another room and Robert Kennedy saying to Jeff Greenfield or Adam Walinsky, "Did you find Al Lowenstein yet?" And the one on the phone saying, "We're trying. He's out on Long Island." And Robert Kennedy nodding and saying, "I can't wait. I'll try him when I get back here. It's important that I speak to him." And then Robert Kennedy walking out of the room and taking the elevator down to the hotel ballroom to be shot. And now here, on Friday night, the connection had carried across the years and it was Al Lowenstein's turn to be shot.

"Your father was shot five times," a doctor said to Frankie Lowenstein, who is 13.

"Five times?" the boy said.

"Five," the doctor said.

Then the doctor said, "The one that was the worst came in from underneath. It went through the diaphragm and the lung and it clipped the edge of the heart. It clipped the muscle. It didn't go in."

"Does that mean there is no interior bleeding, in the chamber?" the boy asked.

The doctor tried to say no.

Steve Smith came into the room. Arcs the color of dark coffee were under his eyes. From too much practice, he went directly to the kids.

"What are you doing here?" he said to Tommy, the 10-year-old.

"Sitting here."

Somebody was telling a story about a dwarf. Smith said to Tommy, "Do you believe that?"

"I don't know," Tommy said.

"I think it's a lie," Smith said.

"I think so too," Tommy said.

"Don't be afraid, tell him he's a liar," Smith said.

William Sloane Coffin sat on the floor. Somebody asked him how he had met Al Lowenstein and Coffin began talking about the day Lowenstein was married. "There was a reception on Beacon Hill before the ceremony and when I arrived, one of Jenny's aunts, one of these Brahmins, said to me, 'I don't know one of the people who are here.' So I said to her. 'Well, see that tall man over there? I'll bet you voted against him at least 24 times. That's Norman Thomas.' And the aunt said, 'That Socialist!'"

"Did you know the fellow who shot him?" Coffin was asked.

"No, all I know is that he's one of these kids Al picked up when he was the dean at Stanford. There were 16 of them and you know how that loyalty string held with Al. If you were with him once, you were with him forever. He was in Mississippi with Al and then Al lost track of him, but whenever he'd see one of the bunch from Stanford, he'd say, 'Hey, have you seen Sweeney? Where is he, what is he doing?'

322

"Jenny said that Sweeney was at their house in Brooklyn a year ago. He was very mixed up. Jenny said that Sweeney told her that evil was coming out into the world from his teeth. Al felt sorry for him. Al thought that Sweeney had all this trouble because of his time in Mississippi. He wanted to help him."

The talk was of all the places in all the years where Al Lowenstein had been. His politics were those of the parched. He was rumpled and gentle and annoying and one of the very few in the last 30 years who understood that always the true calling is to engage the most popular evil. Al Lowenstein went to Mississippi when he was an outside agitator: he was against the war in Vietnam at a time so early that the nation thought any such stand was treasonous.

Outside in the hallway, Secret Servicemen arrived. Edward Kennedy was flying from Chicago. Lowenstein's brother, Larry, and other members of the family kept going from the room to the hallway downstairs, to wait outside the operating room.

At a couple of minutes after 11 p.m., the room on the sixth floor was nearly empty. Tommy Lowenstein sat on a chair, and Steve Smith's son was talking to him and now there was a crowd at the door, a doctor and a nun and relatives, and the boy's mother came into the room and knelt in front of her son and told him that his father had died.

People grabbed for the coats and left the room as the family came in.

Outside in the hallway, Steve Smith was walking alone to the elevator when a man from the hospital staff, thinking he was one of the Lowenstein family, said, "You know in one of these matters, a shooting like this, there is a procedure that is out of our hands. The body must go to the coroner."

"You're telling me that?" Smith said.

On Saturday morning, the suspect was at the Criminal Court Building. A clerk held up papers bound in yellow, docket No. 13616. The typing on the page said, "Deponent is informed by the defendant that the defendant, with intent to cause the death of Allard Lowenstein, caused the death of Allard Lowenstein by shooting him with a .380-caliber pistol. Detective Vito Verni, No. 537."

Verni, somber and handsome, brought his defendant, Dennis Sweeney, into the seamy room. Sweeney was lanky with a gaunt doomed Irish face and hair becoming gray. He wore a green rainjacket. He stared down and said nothing.

The assistant district attorney said that Sweeney had made admissions, and that he had said that Mr. Lowenstein was one of six people that he had strong feelings against.

Sweeney was put back in a cell and Verni walked out of the room.

"Who were the other names he was angry at?" Verni was asked.

"He didn't give us names," Verni said.

"You know what I'm asking you."

"I know what you're asking me," Verni said. "And I'm telling you he didn't mention any names."

Al Lowenstein's candidate was at the New York Hilton yesterday morning. The night before had brought back the pain of the '60s, and now it brought back the glory: Teddy Kennedy, everything he always should have been, thundered at an audience, "We will not accept a society in which health is a function of wealth . . . we will not accept a society in which houses are boarded up while hundreds of thousands of families wait in rat-infested tenements . . . we will not accept a society in which whole sections of our cities become a blighted wasteland . . . we will not accept a society in which a handgun can be bought today and fired tomorrow to kill a man like Al Lowenstein."

And if Lowenstein himself had been alive, and able to move yesterday, everybody knows where he would have been. Not with Kennedy, but down at the Criminal Court Building trying to do something for Dennis Sweeney. Sometimes you get a guy who goes this way.

REMEMBERING A MAN WHO MATTERED THROUGH THE YEARS

Richard Cohen

Washington Post, March 16, 1980

On Friday, a man named Sweeney walked into the law office of Allard K. Lowenstein and shot him dead. Lowenstein was 51 years old. He has three children and a former wife and several thousand friends and they will all tell you the same thing about him: he mattered.

He mattered in Mississippi and he mattered in New York politics and he mattered in the U.S. Congress and in southern Africa and in the National Student Association but he mattered most—at least for me—when he stopped Lyndon Johnson cold in New Hampshire. It was 1968, and Allard K. Lowenstein had set out to end the war in Vietnam.

I know that one man is not supposed to be able to do that. I know that historians debate whether even heroes—emperors, generals—control events or whether it is the other way around. I know a teacher who thinks that the correct answer to the question "who discovered America" is "the Nina, the Pinta and the Santa Maria." Allard Lowenstein would not have liked that teacher.

Lowenstein helped organize something called the New York Coalition for a Democratic Alternative. It was dubbed the Dump Johnson Movement and it was given no chance of succeeding. No one thought Al

Lowenstein could succeed. No one but Lowenstein. That proved in the end to be more than enough.

In 1968, I was a graduate student. In 1968, I was also a member of the United States Army Reserve and bitterly opposed to the war in Vietnam. I'd already decided that if called to fight, I would not. I would go to some other country—Canada, Sweden. I had told my parents this and they had said simply that they understood.

Lowenstein worked near where I lived. At night, I would walk my dog and see the lights burning late. Several times, I looked up the stairs and thought about going in, but every time I backed out. It was foolish. It was senseless. Johnson would win a second term. The war would go on and on and no one, especially me, could do anything about it. Later, I went up to New Hampshire. I went to write about the primary, Eugene McCarthy's campaign. As a student I already knew, of course, how Lowenstein had gone to Robert Kennedy and asked him to run against Johnson and how Kennedy, anguished, had finally turned him down. In January of that year at the Commonwealth Club of San Francisco, Kennedy had in fact endorsed Johnson.

Lowenstein then went to McCarthy. McCarthy also said no, muting that along the way to a maybe. McCarthy also went west—to Berkeley across the bay from San Francisco. There he gave his standard antiwar speech, but this time called for the resignation of Secretary of State Dean Rusk. The kids went wild. McCarthy became hopeful. He declared for the presidency and Al Lowenstein, working hard once again, cajoled him into that race in New Hampshire.

Much later, of course, Lowenstein would become something of a celebrity and everyone would have his story. He would call in the middle of the night and come over to sleep. He was always on the go, sleeping in his clothes, a kind of hobo of lost causes. Friends who were in South Africa, for instance, were not surprised when Lowenstein dropped in on them in their hotel, asking only if he could use the shower. He stayed for awhile and left. He was wearing dungarees and a New York Yankees baseball jacket.

But on election day in New Hampshire, Allard Lowenstein was not yet a celebrity. That day, he got into his white Mustang for the drive from Manchester to Concord. He sat in the back and talked with me while a student volunteer drove. It was beginning to snow, but Lowenstein wanted to make the trip anyway. He was going to see the student volunteers. He wanted to make sure they didn't flag on this last day. He was going to see a kid named Sam Brown.

We arrived in Concord as the snow was beginning to tell. Lowenstein flew into action. He cajoled the kids to work harder. He went from one to another, talking to them as they made their last minute get-out-the-vote calls from little pine stalls. He was a bundle of energy, a short man with hair combed forward, strong and kind and always distracted.

After exhorting the students to even greater efforts, Lowenstein returned to Manchester. In the evening, the results started to come in and pandemonium broke loose. McCarthy was winning. People cried and people laughed and finally, they called for Allard Lowenstein to say something.

Lowenstein stood in the glow of the television lights, a little man, strangely shy, and he said that McCarthy's victory proved that the system worked. He made it sound like it would all have happened without Allard K. Lowenstein but that is not the case. A couple of thousand people could tell you, but the whole nation ought to know.

He mattered.

ADDRESS TO
THE NEW YORK STATE
FEDERATION OF TEACHERS

Senator Edward M. Kennedy

March 15, 1980

I had looked forward to our meeting today. . . .

I had planned to come here today to speak of inflation and the economy, of education and the cities, and to state my opposition to the administration's policies.

But this is not the right day and that is not the right speech.

For yesterday in this city that he loved, in this state that he served, Allard Lowenstein was shot and killed. This peaceful, generous man became the latest victim of the senseless violence that stalks our generation, and of the arms race in our cities that threatens to make any citizen a casualty at anytime.

If no man is an island, then Allard Lowenstein was a continent, a universe, a vast expanse of compassion, conviction, and courage. These qualities drew out the best in all who knew him, but especially in the young, who heard his call and joined his ceaseless quest against injustice and indifference.

He was the irresistible force that made immovable objects move. Almost single-handedly, twelve years ago, he set out to stop the relentless escalation in Vietnam. When others thought nothing could be done to change an incumbent administration and its war policy, and that no one could make a difference, he insisted that we had to try, that it had to be done—and so he did it.

With his endless energy, with his papers, his clothes, his books, and seemingly his whole life jammed into briefcases, envelopes and satchels—all of it carried with him everywhere—he was a portable and powerful lobby for progressive principles. All by himself, he was more effective than an organization of thousands. He was a one-man demonstration for civil rights; even when he walked alone, he was a multitude marching for peace. He had a gentle passion for the truth.

As much as anyone I know, he proved that one person truly can make a difference.

The only public office he was ever elected to was Congress, for a single term. But his memory, his work in 1968, his record of commitment will live in the history on which he had such impact of his own.

Even as he lay dying, Al Lowenstein struggled as fiercely for his life as he had struggled all his life on behalf of others. The flame resisted the loss of its spark to the last; the fire that had burned so brightly was not easily quenched.

Al was always intense, but never selfish. He was a man who lived for the many he sought to help, and for the America he sought to make.

Whenever Al came to see me, at home or in the Senate, I knew that he brought with him a challenge to be met, a wrong to be righted, a dream to be fulfilled. He would show up unexpectedly; he would pace the floor; he would loose a shower of ideas; he was impatient with our country's failures; he was hopeful for its prospects. Standing in a living room, he would try to move the world.

So, when this campaign began, it was inevitable that he was everywhere. He would speak in Portland in the morning, practice law in the afternoon, and be off that evening for a forum in Des Moines.

For Al, no precinct was too remote, no reporter too resistant, no voter too insignificant. Let others have their legions of surrogates; give me Allard Lowenstein, who could outpersuade all of them combined.

There was electricity in his thought, and eloquence in his words. What this man, who was my friend, once said of my brother Robert Kennedy must be said of him: "He wanted everyone to see what seemed so obvious to him: that if people couldn't be roused to make a difference in the effort to reclaim their country, they would make a difference anyway by not trying . . . he managed to become a presence as well as a politician, an American resource."

Allard Lowenstein, who was also taken too soon, wrote his own epitaph when he wrote of Robert Kennedy: "If he were still around, he would be saying that we have dallied long enough, and that it is past time to do better."

Allard Lowenstein would say that we have a duty to protest when we know a policy is wrong—and that criticism of official error is not criticism of country. He was perhaps the greatest dissenter of his time, a patriot who understood that dissent is the essence of democracy.

In 1959, he left a Senate staff to travel across Southern Africa. And then he wrote a book warning us that we could not abide and abet the racism of that land—that once again we had to make "the word America sing out hope and generosity and compassion" to all the world.

His vision of justice recognized no national borders, no boundaries of race, or special concern, or political ideology. When Anatoly Shcharansky was sent to the Lubyanka prison, Allard Lowenstein stood in the United Nations and spoke the truth about the Soviet Union to the Soviet ambassador. He broke through the regular agenda: he cut through the diplomatic protocol—and he moved the Human Rights Commission, for the first time, to take up the individual cases of the human beings who were the victims of repression.

And if Allard Lowenstein were here, he would say that we must continue to speak for all those who have no voice in our own society. Minorities and the poor may be out of political fashion, but they were never far from his conscience. For him, inflation and unemployment were not statistics, but hard-working families who could not pay their bills. He thought not only of the deficit of dollars, but of the deficit of justice.

He was a gifted lawyer who could have made himself rich: instead he lived modestly, often it seemed from month to month, giving of himself to make this a better land.

If he were here, he would be speaking as he did last week, for economic justice, for energy that warms homes without bankrupting families, for taxes that treat both workers and the wealthy fairly, for schools with more teachers and less violence, for a public principle that puts the last and the least among us first in our priorities—and above all, for a government that cares about the people and their problems.

He would say the effort must be made; the promise must be kept; the work must go on. And if he were here, I would say to him: The work will go on.

We will not accept a society in which health is a function of wealth, where hospitals close in the inner city and millions worry that sickness will bring not only fear and pain, but financial ruin.

We will not accept a society in which houses are boarded up while hundreds of thousands of families wait in rat-infested tenements for decent shelter—and where other families lose the dream and the hope of owning a home.

We will not accept a society in which whole sections of our cities become a blighted wasteland—and where the urban crisis becomes a perpetual condition of decay and decline.

We will not accept a society in which prosperity rests on the backs of a permanent class of poor people—where young workers are made idle and children are told to go hungry for their country.

We will not accept a society in which students fail to learn because schools are understaffed and teachers are underpaid—and where half of an entire generation in New York City will never finish high school.

We will not accept a society in which discrimination still afflicts the minority who are not white and the majority who are women—and where crosses are still burned on suburban lawns and swastikas are still scrawled on synagogue walls.

We will not accept a society in which a handgun can be bought today and fired tomorrow to kill a man like Allard Lowenstein.

Two decades ago, Eleanor Roosevelt said of Allard Lowenstein in his youth: "I think he will always fight crusades because injustice fills him with a sense of rebellion."

He always fought crusades; he continually rebelled against injustice. And when he died at the age of 51, he was still young. He was a good man who could not stand by doing nothing. He sought to do everything, and he succeeded more than most people ever dream of. Sometimes he was called a gadfly; in fact he was a rare conscience for us all.

To me, he was a loyal friend who spoke with uncommon frankness.

To America, he was a loyal citizen who spoke the uncommon truth.

For him, the crusade is over.

For us, the cause continues—and in his spirit, with the memory to prod us though the man has passed away, let us resolve to seek justice, to search out the best in ourselves, to see and secure the bright possibilities of our country and of democracy itself.

Allard Lowenstein's life leaves us with the philosopher's question: "If not me, who; if not now, when?"

ALLARD LOWENSTEIN, R.I.P.

William F. Buckley, Jr.
Memorial Address, March 18, 1980

Possibly, as a dissenter, my own experience with him was unique, in that we conservatives did not generally endorse his political prescriptions. So that we were, presumptively, opponents of Al Lowenstein, in those straitened chambers in which we spend, and misspend, so much of our lives.

It was his genius that so many of those he touched—generally arriving a half hour late—discovered intuitively the underlying communion. He was, in our time, *the* original activist, such was his impatience with the sluggishness of justice; so that his rhythms were more often than not disharmonious with those that govern the practical, banausic councils of this world.

His habits were appropriately disarrayed. He was late to breakfast, to his appointments; late in announcing his sequential availability for public service. He was punctual only in registering (though often under age) for service in any army that conceived itself bound to righteousness.

How did he live such a life, so hectic with public concern, while preoccupying himself so fully with individual human beings: whose torments, never mind their singularity, he adopted as his own, with the passion that some give only to the universal? Eleanor Roosevelt, James Burnham once mused, looked on all the world as her personal slum project. Although he was at home with collectivist formulations one had the impression of Allard Lowenstein that he might be late in aborting a Third World War because of his absorption with the problems of one sophomore. Oh, they followed him everywhere; because we experienced in him the essence of an entirely personal dedication. Of all the partisans I have known from the furthest steppes of the spectrum, his was the most undistracted concern, not for humanity—though he was conversant with big-think idiom—but with human beings.

Those of us who dealt with him (often in those narrow passages constrained by time clocks and fire laws and deadlines) think back ruefully on the happy blend of purpose and carelessness with which he arranged his own career and his own schedule. A poet might be tempted to say, "If only the Lord had granted us that Allard should have also arrived late at his own assassination!"

But all his life he was felled by mysteries, dominant among them those most readily understood by more worldly men—namely, that his rhythms were not of this world. His days, foreshortened, lived out the secular dissonances. "Behold, Thou hast made my days as it were a span long: and mine age is even as nothing in respect of Thee; and verily every man living is altogether vanity."

The psalmist spoke of Al, on Friday last—"I became dumb, and opened not my mouth; for it was Thy doing." To those not yet dumb, the psalmist also spoke, saying, "The Lord is close to the brokenhearted; and those who are crushed in spirit. He saves."

Who was the wit who said that Nature abhors a vacuum? Let Nature then fill this vacuum. That is the challenge which, bereft, the friends of Allard Lowenstein hurl up to Nature, and to Nature's God, prayerfully, demandingly, because today, Lord, our loneliness is great.

RECOLLECTIONS FROM YOUTH

Gregory Craig

March 1980

Al Lowenstein was a name I grew up knowing. I only got to know him well as a person much later, when I was sixteen or seventeen, but then he became one of the most important persons in my life for almost a decade.

But when I was a child, Al was a mysterious character, someone who arrived late at night, stayed up late talking to my parents, and left sometime after I had gone off to school in the morning. He was someone who was loved and admired and laughed about and talked about by my parents, often with shakes of the head. He was someone who really was a "personage" with us even though the rest of the world certainly did not know who he was. Whatever it was that Al Lowenstein did, I had the impression that it was more exciting, more unusual, more daring, and much more significant than whatever it was that ordinary people did.

My first memory of Al was as a physical presence, a large lump under a blanket on our living-room couch in the morning. I was the first one downstairs that day and had not been warned that someone was asleep in the living room. I didn't notice him when I first entered the room, and I proceeded to do whatever it was that I had gone there to do, whatever it is that nine-year-olds do when left to their own devices. I was startled by a sound behind me and looked around to see this mountain of blankets moving and shifting in search of a more comfortable position. That was "Al," I was told in whispers later.

I remember that Al and I had our first sit-up contest during that visit. The rules of the contest were simple: who could do the most sit-ups in the space of one minute. He was the one who first proposed the contest. He asked if I knew how to do sit-ups. I was proud to be able to answer that I did. He described the contest. I agreed. He sat down on the floor, handed me his glasses, which were very thick and heavy, gave me his wristwatch, which also seemed heavy, and told me to tell him when a minute was up. He won then. In fact, he won that same contest many times against me. I challenged him while I was in prep school, during college, and even during my declining years in law school. He consistently whipped me. In fact, I remember that, at the height of my physical powers (the summer of 1965, when I was twenty), Al did sixty-three sit-ups to my fifty-nine in front of a cheering crowd of students and civil rights workers.

Al was really almost a fictional or mythical person to me while I was growing up. He came and went suddenly, unpredictably, without warning. He arrived late at night, and departed the next day, so when I was very young, it was rare for me actually to cross paths with him. Usually, I would find out the next evening over the dinner table that Al had breezed through the night before. That was when I would try to learn what he was doing and where he was living and why he was passing through town. I remember my parents talking about "South Africa" and "North Carolina" and "Eleanor Roosevelt" in the same breath as Al, but I couldn't figure out what Al had to do with these various, seemingly unrelated subjects. I knew that Al was involved in "exploits" and "adventures," but I could never really fathom what it was that he actually did. Whenever he touched our lives, either by telephone or by visit, my parents became excited and animated and the atmosphere was high with anticipation. Whatever it was that Al did, I wanted to do it too.

When I did manage to be around when Al arrived, Al paid a good deal of attention to me. I found out later that he was not being particularly attentive to me, but that he just loved to spend time with kids. I do remember wondering whether everyone knew Al, or whether other people had their own Al Lowensteins, or if maybe we were the only people who had an Al. I do know that I never tried to tell my friends about Al. I am not certain why I never told them: maybe it was because it would have taken a superhuman effort to really explain who he was and what he did and why he was so special; maybe it was because he was ours, and I simply didn't want to share him with anyone; maybe it was because I thought my friends might think me strange to be so enamored with such a peculiar character.

I had no memory of what Al looked like from those early days. As I said, he was more of a presence than a real person to me then. I was really too young, perhaps, to be conscious of the way people dressed or looked. I think I first really "saw" Al while I was a student at Phillips Exeter Academy in New Hampshire, age sixteen. I remember spotting the notice on the bulletin board announcing that William F. Buckley, Jr. would debate Allard K. Lowenstein, "a lawyer from New York City" about the House Un-American Activities Committee (HUAC) and "Operation Abolition," a film about the student demonstrations against HUAC in San Francisco. (Al Lowenstein was to "lawyer from New York City" as Clark Kent is to "mild-mannered reporter.") Again I faced the problem of telling my friends that I knew and, in fact, was friends with this man named Allard K. Lowenstein. We had discussions in the dining hall about the upcoming debate. Everyone had heard of William F. Buckley, Jr., but who was this New York lawyer, Allard K. Lowenstein, and why was he, of all people, the one who would be debating Buckley? I couldn't answer those questions to my own satisfaction, I didn't think I could possibly explain who Al Lowenstein was, so I kept my silence, hoping that Al, in the course of his appearance, would strip away the mystery once and for all.

I arrived very early to get a front-row seat in the Chapel in the Academy Building. I came by myself. The room filled to overflowing. There were many townspeople there as well as students, because the event was being co-sponsored by some local organization and, I think, the local Catholic church.

I remember seeing Al on the stage and being disappointed in what he looked like. It was, in fact, the first time in my life that I focused on Al's looks, and I was genuinely surprised at how unprepossessing he appeared. I began to tremble for him as I watched him hunched in his armchair up on the stage. Buckley would make mincemeat of him. Al would be humiliated. He would probably be too ashamed to stay around to say hello to his friends after the debate, and I prepared to make a rapid and invisible exit at the end of the program, to slink off into the night and return quietly to my dormitory.

First, the film was shown. It was a black-and-white documentary largely assembled from news film, a brutal, violent, carefully edited and slanted (by the Right) portrayal of the student demonstrations against HUAC in San Francisco. The theme of the movie was that the demonstrations were inspired, organized, and carried out by Communists, and although there were surely some well-meaning non-Communists who participated in the demonstrations, they were, at best, dupes. (I recall that the phrase "Communist dupe" was a particularly popular expression in those days.)

After the film, the house lights remained down, and the rostrum was lit with bright spotlights. Buckley walked to the podium, red rose in lapel, bathed in warm, welcoming applause. It is my recollection that the people in the audience did not share Buckley's politics but were really there to observe the performance of a master debater, much the way Spaniards would crowd into the bullring to watch El Cordobes dispatch the bull. Not so many people had heard of Buckley then (1961) but his reputation among those who knew him was not very different from what it is today. Then, however, he was younger, more aggressive, and still a phenomenon. But the audience—me included—had never seen Buckley perform before, and the Buckley style cut through that room like a rapier. He was arrogant, condescending, outrageous, witty, brilliant, biting, literary, arch, caustic, all of these and more. He curved his back and swept up onto his tiptoes, hands gripping the sides of the podium, nose and chin lifted high, patronizing, supremely confident. On his toes, he swayed slowly from side to side like a cobra, hypnotizing the audience, choosing his time to strike, to pierce, to paralyze. He was, in short, absolutely terrifying.

Al followed. He padded up to the microphone in a baggy suit, a complete and utter unknown to all of the people in the audience. He leaned on the rostrum, took off those heavy glasses and rubbed the bridge of his nose. The audience was deathly still. I was embarrassed for him. He was not the most elegant or dashing champion in the world. He was so homely, he was so rumpled, he seemed so terribly unorganized, he was the last person in the world one would actually choose to do battle with the Buckley dragon. He began to speak, and I held my breath. Maybe it was going to be all right. In fact, it was going to be terrific.

The ugly duckling took flight and began to soar like an eagle. He started slowly, circling upward almost lazily, gaining altitude, bringing the audience along almost effortlessly. He then picked up speed and started to cover ground. His speech developed a rhythm, gaining power and volume and force slowly, moving faster and faster, building, building,

building, and then crashing through to irrefutable conclusions. Then, a pause, a joke, a quip, and he would start over again.

Al's speech was always the essence of argument—one point connected to the next leading to a third, moving, always moving toward a conclusion. He stitched the case together right before your eyes. There was no hocus-pocus. He was never mean-spirited, never shrill (not then), never angry, never insulting, always reasoning, always logical. His words swept over the audience like an avalanche. They came so fast, you had little time to savor them. His speech was studded with historical and political references—to Eleanor Roosevelt, to Adlai Stevenson, to Frank Porter Graham—as if everyone in the room agreed with Al that, of course, these were America's greatest living public figures.

He met Buckley's satire with his own. His wit was just as quick. But Al was never arrogant, never pompous. He was, however, often hilariously funny. Al was everything you ever wanted a speaker to be without once losing his dignity or his composure or his control. And when people finally stood and applauded for him (and for Buckley), I could scarcely restrain the tears. I had an honest-to-God hero—and he was also my friend.

Ever since Al Lowenstein's death, people have written about Al's pied-piper quality, his ability, as a kind of modern-day Socrates, to lead America's young people. It is true that college students were fascinated by and attracted to Al Lowenstein, and it is also true that Al sought out young people to be his companions and to help him in his various projects. But it is also true that Al had a remarkable way with old people. He cared about old people and spent time with old people and devoted considerable energy to his friends who were old people. I suppose that Al cared about "the elderly" in the same way that most thinking, intelligent, and sensitive citizens care about the way our society treats its senior citizens, but he actually liked to be with old people. He had an unusual number of old people as very close friends, and he spent an unusual amount of time with these people simply because he enjoyed being with them.

There was, for example, Lucille Kohn, a New York woman who was well over eighty and lived to be well beyond ninety. Al would routinely visit Lucille in her apartment betwen midnight and two in the morning. He would call in advance, probably wake her up, and then dash over to her second-floor walk-up apartment overlooking Lexington Avenue. He would bring along his driver and whoever else he had in tow that night, and he would sit down next to Lucille (who would return to bed after opening the door), and he would take her by the hand and tell her about the day's events. He would ask, "What do you think about Mr. De Sapio?" or "Who are you going to vote for for mayor?" or "Why isn't Mayor Lindsay better at keeping the potholes repaired?" And then a long and rambling and high-spirited conversation would ensue, Lucille with her false teeth clacking away, Al interrupting with a running commentary, every now and then jumping up and darting to the refrigerator for a glass of milk and some pound cake, which Lucille kept on hand for him. Lucille wore a gold medallion around her neck with a profile of John Kennedy on it. President Kennedy was her one true political hero. "Even more than Eleanor Roosevelt?" Al asked one night in disbelief. "Even more than Eleanor Roosevelt," said Lucille. "After all," said Lucille, "Jack Kennedy did so much more for his people." Al would just break up laughing.

And then there was my New England aunt, Miss Effie Fletcher, a maiden lady who lived with us for many years, until she was well past ninety. (She actually lived to be one hundred and four.) Aunt Effie was as Republican a woman as one could possibly imagine, but she absolutely adored Al Lowenstein. Al would come by the house just to visit Aunt Effie, much to the surprise of Aunt Effie's various grand- and great-grandnephews. He would sit with her and hold her hand and chatter away with her as if they had known each other for decades. Once, when Al dropped by just prior to departure on a transcontinental trip in his Mustang filled with old newspapers and college students, Aunt Effie came tottering out to the driveway with her walking stick to say good-bye. Al leaned down to kiss her. Aunt Effie grabbed his face with both her hands and said, "Now drive carefully, Al. Remember, the life you save may vote Republican." Al collapsed.

Norman Thomas became one of Al's major heroes when Al got to know him well in 1965-1966. Al would go out of his way to spend time with Thomas during Thomas's final years, and Al loved to tell Norman Thomas stories. Once, when Al, my Harvard roommate, and I were driving Al's Mustang convertible out to Long Island, ostensibly to spend some time on a beach, Al decided mid-trip that we had to visit Norman Thomas, who didn't really live that far out of the way. We spent the afternoon drinking tea and eating cookies and talking politics and prying reminiscences out of Thomas. Thomas was extraordinarily feeble at the time, almost blind, barely mobile, scarcely audible, but as quick and witty and as opinionated as ever.

Al took great pleasure in introducing us to Thomas as "the leaders of the Harvard student movement." Thomas said, "Well, I went to Princeton, you know, and we didn't know very much about movements, student or otherwise." At the end of the visit, as Aunt Effie had done for Al before, Norman Thomas walked us to the driveway, cane in hand, and watched as we piled into the convertible. As we waved good-bye, he lifted his cane and pointed it to the sky, like a cavalry officer leading the charge with his saber upraised. "Long live the Harvard revolution," he shouted, with the most memorable broad grin creasing his face.

A CHANCE ENCOUNTER

Thomas Powers

Commonweal, April 11, 1980

The last time I saw Allard Lowenstein was in the changing room at the Yale Club. He was wine-dark with exertion and gleaming with sweat. The obituaries say he was 51 years old but he carried the years well. His body was short, chunky, heavy with muscle. I don't know what he did at the club; I never saw him on the squash courts. But he had obviously been doing something which required great effort—weight lifting, chin-ups, something strenuous and monotonous. I often saw him there in the last seven or eight years, always in the middle of the afternoon. A friend and I passed him once not long after he'd been defeated for the second or third time in a congressional race. "If he didn't spend so much time here," my friend said, "maybe he'd get elected." It was just a remark; we had no idea why he'd been beaten.

The first time I saw Lowenstein was in Jackson, Mississippi, in November, 1963. It was about 10 o'clock at night. A couple of friends and I had driven straight through from Yale. This was Lowenstein's doing but we didn't know it. I'm not sure what we thought we were doing there, but we had come anyway. On the outskirts of Jackson we'd filled up with gas and asked directions to Lynch Street. "What you wanta go there for?" asked the man at the pump. "Do you know what part of town that is?"

Lowenstein was wearing a white T-shirt. He looked about the way he looked when he died, perhaps not quite so chunky. Hair cut short, thinning wisps rising high on his crown, horn-rimmed glasses, lips pursed around prominent front teeth. His face had been designed for caricature. I heard him called the world's oldest living student leader; I didn't know any of the history behind the remark. Lowenstein made some phone calls, found us a place to stay, gave us directions. He had a brisk, liquid way of speaking; spittle caught the light. He gave an impression of force and directness; he stood erect, a bit squarish in shape, and looked right at you, eyes bulging behind his glasses. With him that night was a slight, soft-spoken black man named Robert Moses. Lowenstein and Moses seemed to be running the show.

Mississippi was having an election campaign for governor that fall. I've forgotten who was running, but the candidates certainly weren't courting the black community, which was almost totally disenfranchised through phony reading tests and sheer intimidation. The Student Non-Violent Coordination Committee (SNCC, pronounced snick) had been running a voter-registration program with limited success. Someone came up with an idea for a mock election campaign in the black community to dramatize how many people would vote if they could vote. Lowenstein suggested bringing in a crew of white student volunteers to help with canvassing and attract the attention of the national press. Large contingents came from Yale, where Lowenstein had gone to law school, and Stanford, where he had been an administrator for a time.

Mississippi was another country in 1963. There is no fear like the fear of men. Someone told me Lowenstein never slept more than a night or two in the same house, but I didn't understand why until I'd been there a couple of days. The second night, on our way up to the Delta, we were stopped by the local police. One of them grabbed me by the arm, swung me around, and pointed his pistol at me. In Cleveland we stayed with a young black organizer named Charlie McLaurin. He turned out his house lights before opening his front door at night so he wouldn't make a convenient silhouette for a sniper. The windshield on the car of a friend of his had been blown out with a shotgun blast. Shots had been fired through living room windows in Sunflower County, churches had been burned, people had been beaten. McLaurin told me he was about to give up on voting rights. What they needed was a revolution, a guerrilla war in the countryside.

Later, in Natchez with two black organizers early one morning, we got a phone call telling us to leave town immediately; another volunteer from Yale had been shot at the day before. When we left two or three rednecks in a pickup chased us for a while. We could see rifles hanging on a rack in the cab. I remember the pitching and bucking of the car as we tore down the long straight road, slowly pulling away from the pickup until it was lost in the distance behind us. I was plain terrified for a week straight. In Mississippi the very air was chemically one part fear.

One day in a small shack town on the edge of a big plantation a black man answered my knock. He was about my age, four inches taller, eighty pounds heavier. I was alone. "Have you heard that Aaron Henry is running for governor?" I asked.

"No suh, I don't have nothin to do with that."

"But he's trying to win the vote for Negroes in Mississippi."

"Yessuh."

"Have you voted in the election yet?"

"No suh, I don't do no votin."

"But this is important, he needs your support."

"Yessuh. What you want me to do?"

"I want you to vote for Aaron Henry."

"Yessuh, how I do it?"

I showed him where to sign his name. He was trembling, and his voice shook with fear.

I soon found I could get more votes if I cut the palaver and just told people what to do. They were quick to oblige. A black organizer joined me at one point while I was talking to a bent old man named John something. "Now, John," I said, thinking to be friendly, "it's important for you to help Aaron Henry by signing this card here." He did as he was told. When he had gone back inside the black organizer said, "Look, I'm going to tell you something. You call these people mister. White people have called them by their first names all their lives. *You call them mister.*" He was furious, and I was hurt, angry and ashamed in return. We'd spent a decade together in thirty-six hours.

The night before the regular election a rally was held in Jackson for Aaron Henry and his running mate, the Rev. Ed King. A meeting hall on Lynch Street was about a third full at the appointed hour. The hall was quiet but for the creaking of chairs. Two or three hundred black people in their Sunday best shifted nervously in their seats. Outside, Jackson city police slowly passed back and forth. Aaron Henry was late; one of the SNCC people said he was on "C.P.T."—colored peoples' time. An organizer went to the podium and said, Don't go away folks, Mister Henry is on his way. A long silence followed. Two or three couples got up and walked quietly to the rear, out the door. Others followed. Lowenstein appeared wearing a suit and tie. He told someone to *find* Henry and *get* him there and he went on stage to speak.

I can't remember his precise words, but I do remember his drift and tone. He talked about the Constitution and the Rights of Man. He recounted the history of Aaron Henry, the druggist from Clarksdale who had worked long and hard for the rights of Negro Americans. He talked about the thousands of voters who had cast their first ballots in the last week, he said the whole nation was watching, the day was fast coming when the vote would be theirs as a natural right. Then Lowenstein started to talk about the whites in Mississippi, the scared folks who crept around at night in white bed sheets and ganged up twenty to one before they dared beat up a Negro boy. They were quaking in their beds at night, all those plantation-owners, just plain terrified of the day when Negroes in Mississippi marched head-high to the polls. I wish I could remember how he did it, but Lowenstein got the audience to laugh, and then he got them to cheer, and then he got them laughing and cheering and whistling and he kept it up, never breaking stride, for the better part of an hour until Aaron Henry finally arrived, swept up onto the stage by a wave of cheers and yells and hallellujahs. Then Lowenstein disappeared and that was the last I saw of him in Mississippi.

Things moved quickly in those years. In 1965 Robert Moses dropped out of sight, saying he didn't think the Movement ought to have leaders. SNCC broke with Lowenstein on political grounds. Of course there had been a hundred sources of friction, but what SNCC *said* was that Lowenstein didn't belong, Lowenstein was a New Deal liberal recruiting black votes for the Democratic power structure. What this country needed was revolution. You had to understand that black people wanted no part of white imperialist capitalist America, fighting a racist war in Vietnam and murdering black people here at home. The white man was a beast. The Movement wasn't out there courting broken heads for the right to sit at a lunch counter; the struggle was for something else, something basic, something revolutionary. This wasn't no protest movement; this was a revolutionary movement. Lowenstein believed in the system, which made Lowenstein part of the system, which meant Lowenstein was the enemy—Whitey with a velvet glove.

The bitterness of the break is hard to exaggerate. Later, when Lowenstein won a measure of broader public fame for organizing the "dump Johnson" movement in 1968, he had two distinct reputations—as a kind of radical insurgent on the furthermost edges of mainstream American politics, and as a Red-baiting reactionary desperately trying to stem the leftward surge of the American student community. By that time the Movement—that is, the organizations like SNCC and SDS at the heart of the broader activist ferment—had firmly declared itself Marxist-Leninist, and had redefined its goal as revolution in the United States. By revolution they did not mean a kind of revitalization of American democratic ideals in the pursuit of populist reforms; they meant replacement of the government by a dictatorship of the proletariat. This sounds like a bad joke now. But the Movement was riding high in 1968; within a year or two it simply evaporated, paralyzed by a commitment to revolution, lightly given, which it could not make good. Lowenstein had opposed the leftist romance from the beginning; he feared nothing more than a return of the 1930s, when every legitimate grievance or aspiration was turned into an organizing tool of "the revolution." Naturally he was much resented by those who had exactly that in mind, but the real hate came from those who were the most innocent in their commitment, the "kids" who were not so much trying to change things, as to identify with the poor and oppressed. For them "their revolution" was a kind of spiritual earnest money. It meant they were serious, and worthy of trust by suspicious blacks, who gibed that the white kids hadn't put their lives on the line, and could always run back home to Mommy and Daddy and a station wagon in the suburbs.

But this is all ancient history. The Movement is as dead as the Popular Front. The passions are only cinders. The people who claimed Lowenstein was an agent of the CIA have forgotten all the details. "The revolution" seems like a dream. The burnt-out cases are raising organic vegetables or teaching crafts in community colleges or working on PhD. theses on Eugene V. Debs. Who can really say what went wrong? But the Movement was not without its effect.

In 1971 I went back to Mississippi to see how things had turned out. Charles Evers, the black mayor of the tiny town of Fayette, was running for governor. When his motorcade raced from one rally to another up through the Delta, State Police cars led the way with sirens screaming. I saw Charlie McLaurin at a rally in Sunflower County. He was running for the state legislature, had gained weight, gave a practiced, sensible speech supporting the Mayor.

The night of the election there was a party at the meeting hall on Lynch Street in Jackson where Lowenstein had spoken eight years earlier. The place was packed. City police directed traffic out front. Reporters were milling around. A local television crew was waiting to get the Mayor's concession speech. Evers was a good speaker too, a master of the Southern black antiphonal style who could build the "Yes, Lord!"'s into a roar from the audience. He spoke of the new day coming, white and black working together for a better life in Mississippi. Of course the Mayor was going home to Fayette, but they'd had those old white politicians running scared there for awhile ("Oh yeah!") and there wasn't no turning back now ("Yes, Lord!"). Evers admitted they'd whipped us, he'd bite no bones about that, but what he said sounded like a victory speech all the same.

For some reason I never spoke to Lowenstein. I couldn't find the words to begin, as we passed to and from the shower. What was I to say? Sorry you lost another race for Congress, better luck next time? I'd like to have said: Allard, you made a deeper impression on me than any other chance encounter of my life. But that's just not the sort of thing one can say to a stranger, out of the blue.

NOTES AND COMMENT
The New Yorker, March 31, 1980

When Allard K. Lowenstein died, last week, of gunshot wounds that are alleged to have been inflicted by a onetime colleague in the civil-rights movement of the nineteen-sixties, there was a deeper, more widespread, and more passionate sense of loss in the American political community than could be accounted for by the brief eminence he achieved as a congressman, or even by the considerable size of his accomplishment, which included probably indispensable contributions to the civil-rights movement and to the antiwar movement. It was not easy to define what he had been. Although he had clearly been a public man, devoted to the public good, he did not fit the customary mold of a politician. He had served for a term in Congress, but one did not tend to think of him primarily as a congressman—nor did he think of himself that way. In 1969, shortly after being elected, he confessed to a reporter, "I never think of myself as a congressman. I'm sometimes surprised when people remind me that I am one." He also said to the reporter, "There is nothing inherently immoral about trying to succeed, and in politics this society's idea of success is to get yourself elected. But once that has become the goal, all the other values and goals can be forgotten. The test of virtue becomes success, and people measure sucess by whether you get more votes. . . . So why shouldn't you think first about how to get more votes? So that becomes the 'first rule' of that kind of politics. It's also what makes the whole process so much less productive and honest. If you don't want to fall into that trap, you have to say no, you won't accept that view of things. My first rule in Congress is that if I don't do more by being there about the things I care about than I would if I weren't there, then I shouldn't be there." He was not there long, but that was because he lost his bid for reelection after his district had been gerrymandered to exclude many of his supporters; and he never did manage to win elective office again. Yet it would be impossible to class him among those who, while holding fast to their ideals, never manage to put them into practice: the barriers of segregation were breached and the politics of the South was transformed; the Vietnam War did finally come to an end. In their tributes to him, his friends from the political world acknowledged his peculiar effectiveness. Representative Andrew Jacobs, Jr., called him "a gentle tornado." Senator Edward Kennedy called him "a one-man demonstration for civil rights," and said, "With his endless energy, with his papers, his clothes, his books, and seemingly his whole life jammed into briefcases, envelopes, and satchels—all of it carried with him everywhere—he was a portable and powerful lobby for progressive principles." William F. Buckley, Jr., described him as being "in our time the original activist." Though Lowenstein, who was as scrupulous in his political means as he was selfless in his ends, did not survive long in office, few men were more profoundly devoted to the American political system than he. Allying himself with movements that were born on the street, he led them into electoral politics, thus both diverting them from possible violence and refreshing the mainstream with new thought and energy. But it was not with the aim of restraining angry activists that he led his supporters into electoral politics (that would have been nothing more than what radicals of the nineteen-sixties used to call co-optation); it was to bring their causes, in which he strongly believed, to fruition. It's often said that politics is the art of the possible. Lowenstein, ceaselessly busy in outlying regions of what is usually recognized as "politics," shifted the boundaries of the possible, so that other, more "political" men could bring it into being.

Chronology

1929   Born on January 16 in Newark, New Jersey.

1945–49   Attended University of North Carolina, where he met Dr.
                Frank Graham, its president; was active in student politics
                and worked against racial discrimination.

1950   Worked as legislative assistant to Senator Graham in
                Washington and in his election campaign.

1950–51   Served as third president of the U.S. National Student
                Association.

1952   Appointed national chairman, Students for Stevenson.

1954   Received law degree from Yale University.

1954–56   Served as an enlisted man in United States Army, sta-
                tioned primarily in Germany.

1956–57   Was educational consultant to the American Association
                for the United Nations, where he worked with Eleanor
                Roosevelt; worked in Stevenson presidential campaign;
                was active in Democratic reform politics in New York.

1958   Worked as foreign-policy assistant to Senator Hubert
                Humphrey.

1959   Traveled to South-West Africa (now Namibia) at the re-
                quest of native representatives to gather information on
                living conditions of black majority; testified on racial op-

pression in the territory before the Fourth Committee of the United Nations.

1960   Chaired William F. Ryan's campaign for Congress in Manhattan, the first congressional victory for the Democratic reform movement; practiced law in New York; worked in civil rights efforts; was alternate delegate to the Democratic National Convention.

1961–62   Appointed assistant dean and lecturer at Stanford University; publication of *Brutal Mandate* describing his African journey and calling for forceful U.S. action against apartheid.

1962–64   Taught at North Carolina State in Raleigh, where he was active in protest demonstrations; worked with civil rights movement in Mississippi; helped organize 1963 Freedom Vote and 1964 Freedom Summer.

1965   Helped organize Ryan for Mayor campaign in New York; directed 1965 Encampment for Citizenship; active in early teach-in and antiwar protests.

1966   Participated in reform congressional-selection procedure in Manhattan; observed Dominican Republic elections and criticized U.S. intervention in that country; married Jennifer Lyman of Boston, Massachusetts; continued antiwar activities.

1967   Taught at City College in New York; organized national "Dump Johnson" movement in opposition to President Johnson's renomination by Democratic Party, serving as co-chairman of the Conference of Concerned Democrats. Birth of first son, Frank Graham.

1968   Campaigned in New Hampshire and elsewhere for Senator Eugene McCarthy; chairman of Coalition for an Open Convention and delegate to the Democratic National Convention; elected to 91st Congress from 5th Congressional District, on Long Island.

1969-71   Served in the U.S. House of Representatives; helped lead congressional opposition to the Vietnam war and worked on House reforms, arms control and other issues; was defeated for reelection. Birth of second son, Thomas Kennedy (1969), and daughter, Katharine Eleanor (1970).

1971   Elected national chairman of Americans for Democratic Action; spearheaded nationwide "Dump Nixon" youth-vote campaign; taught at Yale and Harvard; was included on White House "enemies list."

1972   Was nominated by Brooklyn Reform Democratic Caucus to challenge veteran congressman John J. Rooney in primary election; overturned disputed Brooklyn primary in court, but failed to win official designation in court-ordered rerun; served as delegate to Democratic National Convention; was elected a Democratic national committeeman from New York.

1973-74   Attacked Nixon administration widely during Watergate-impeachment period; taught at New School in New York and elsewhere; ran for Congress in redrawn Long Beach district.

1975-76   Served as part-time adviser to newly elected California governor Jerry Brown; supported national efforts for review of Robert Kennedy and John Kennedy assassinations; helped manage 1976 Brown presidential bid; ran a second time from Long Beach district.

1977-78   Served as U.S. Representative to United Nations Commission on Human Rights and as UN ambassador for Special Political Affairs; separated from his wife and moved to Manhattan; made final congressional bid.

1979–80   Traveled several times to southern Africa, working with members of Congress and others on issues of transition of power in Zimbabwe; lectured widely and practiced law in New York.

1980   On March 14 was shot and killed in his office in New York.

References

Material by and about Allard K. Lowenstein is presently being gathered for the Lowenstein archives, deposited with the Southern Historical Collection at the University of North Carolina at Chapel Hill. The listings below suggest the range of relevant items.

BY ALLARD K. LOWENSTEIN

Brutal Mandate: A Journey to South West Africa. New York: Macmillan, 1962.

Statement on Aaron Henry for Governor Campaign. October 27, 1963.

Eulogy to Andrew Goodman. *Queens College Phoenix*, October 6, 1964.

With John A. Marcum. "Force: Its Thrust and Prognosis." In *Southern Africa in Transition*, edited by John A. Davis and James K. Baker. New York: Praeger, 1966.

Keynote Address. New York Coalition for a Democratic Alternative. January 6, 1968.

With Arnold S. Kaufman. "The Case for Opposing Johnson's Renomination." *War/Peace Report*, November 1967.

With Marcus Raskin. "Face the Nation," September 1, 1968.

With William F. Buckley, Jr. "Firing Line," September 10, 1968.

Remarks at Princeton Symposium: *The Endless Crisis: America in the '70s,* edited by Francois Duchene, New York: Simon and Schuster, 1969.

"College." *Glamour*, September 1969.

Speeches and Debate. *Congressional Record.* 1969–70. [References listed in *Index*.]

"Polarize or Persuade" (Interview). *Washington Monthly*, December 1969.

Closing Statement. University of Alabama Hearings, May 1970.

"Meet the Press," May 3, 1971.

With William F. Buckley, Jr., and Paul N. McCloskey, Jr. "Dump Nixon?" (Discussion). "Firing Line," May 26, 1971.

"To: ADA Members." *ADA World*, May–June 1971.

Nominating Speech for Sissy Farenthold. *Transcript of Proceedings: 1972 Democratic National Convention.*

Foreword to *Party and Opposition*, by Jeff Fishel. New York: McKay, 1973.

"Dissent." Taped address at Armed Forces Staff College, November 19, 1973.

With others. "Public Financing of Elections" (Debate). "The Advocates," February 7, 1974.

Campaign Statement. *Levittown Tribune*, October 23, 1974.

With Paul Schrade. Statement on the Assassination of Robert F. Kennedy. December 4, 1974.

"No Monopoly on Jewish Defense." *Newsday*, May 18, 1975.

"Reflections on a Third Force." *ADA World*, May–June 1975.

With Richard Kessel. "A Cynic's County Legislature." *Newsday*, June 5, 1975.

"Who Voted for the Concorde?" *Newsday*, February 2, 1976.

"The Kennedy Killings." *Argosy*, February 1976.

With Leo Pfeffer and William F. Buckley, Jr. "Church Schools and the First Amendment" (Discussion). "Firing Line," August 2, 1976.

Introduction of Governor Jerry Brown. *Andy Warhol's Interview*, July 1976.

Campaign Environmental Statement. *Long Island Conserver*, October 14, 1976.

With William F. Buckley, Jr. "Human Rights" (Discussion). "Firing Line," March 9, 1977.

Testimony on the Kranz Report. Los Angeles County Board of Supervisors, May 17, 1977.

Remarks. United Nations Holiday Service. December 14, 1977.

"South Africa Must Change or Stand Alone." (Interview) *Mercury*, April 24, 1978.

Testimony on Environmental Policy. New York State Transportation Plan Hearings. July 26, 1978.

With Steven Solarz and William F. Buckley, Jr. "Lifting the Trade Ban on Rhodesia" (Discussion). "Firing Line," June 15, 1979.

Testimony. Senate Committee on Governmental Affairs. *Congressional Anti-Gerrymandering Act of 1979*. June 21, 1979.

With others. "Kennedy vs. Carter in 1980" (Discussion). "David Susskind Show," November 3, 1979.

With William F. Buckley, Jr., and others. "Allard Lowenstein on Firing Line: A Retrospective." First broadcast April 22, 1980.

ABOUT ALLARD K. LOWENSTEIN

Astor, Gerald. "The Pied Piper of the New Children's Crusade." *Look*, August 25, 1970.

Breasted, Mary. "Lowenstein Ponders Challenge to Brooklyn's Rooney or Nassau's Wydler." *New York Times*, March 19, 1972.

Buckley, William F., Jr. "Democracy in Action?" *New York Post*, July 20, 1972.

Chester, Louis, Godfrey Hodgson, and Bruce Page. *An American Melodrama: The Presidential Campaign of 1968*. New York: Viking Press, 1969.

Cowan, Paul. "Free Lance Humanitarian Sets Sights on Congress." *Village Voice*, January 6, 1966.

Cowan, Paul. *The Making of an Un-American*. New York: Dell, 1969.

Crewdson, John. "Files from Hoover Said to Have Aided Backers at Capitol." *New York Times*, February 25, 1974.

English, David and others. *Divided They Stand*. Englewood Cliffs: Prentice-Hall, 1969.

References

Harrington, Michael. "Al Lowenstein: Our Triumph, Our Tragedy." *Village Voice*, March 24, 1980.

"Hurrah." *The New Yorker*, September 30, 1972.

Klein, Frederick C. "Liberal 'Shaker' Edges to Limelight." *Wall Street Journal*, November 1, 1967.

Knoll, Erwin. "Congressman on the Run." *The Progressive*, August 1969.

Kondracke, Morton. "Up from Shambles." *The New Republic*, May 19, 1979.

"Miracle Maker's Plight." *Newsweek*, June 10, 1968.

"Negro U.N. Delegate Barred from Two Raleigh Restaurants." *North Carolina State Technician*, May 1, 1963.

Newfield, Jack. *Robert Kennedy: A Memoir.* New York: E. P. Dutton, 1969.

"Rhodesia: A Way Out?" *Washington Post*, May 15, 1979.

Roberts, Steven B. "Lowenstein Asks Inquiry into Political 'Accidents.' " *New York Times*, July 16, 1973.

Schlesinger, Arthur. *Robert Kennedy and His Times.* Boston: Houghton Mifflin, 1978.

Side, Bob. "The Untold Story of the Lowenstein Campaign." *Brooklyn Heights Press*, August 17–September 14, 1972.

Torres, Jose. "Battle in Brooklyn." *New York Post*, July 1, 1972.

Tracy, Phil. "State Secrets." *Village Voice*, July 4, 1974.

Tyrrell, R. Emmett. "No Excuse Will Do." *Washington Post*, March 24, 1980.

Ungar, Sanford J. "Allard Lowenstein." *Harvard Crimson*, January 17, 1964.

Vecsey, George. "Another Leading Conservative is Backing Lowenstein in His Race for a Seat in the House." *New York Times*, October 5, 1976.

Viorst, Milton. *Fire in the Streets: America in the '60s.* New York: Simon and Schuster, 1979.

Wechsler, James. "The Leader?" *New York Post*, March 8, 1973.

Woolsey, R. James. "He Made a Difference." *Washington Post*, March 16, 1980.

INDEX

Index

F

E

G